D1339523

UPWARD
& ONWARD

UPWARD
& ONWARD

THE LIFE OF AIR VICE MARSHAL

JOHN HOWE
CB CBE AFC

BOB COSSEY

FOREWORD BY AIR VICE MARSHAL GEORGE BLACK CB OBE AFC* FRAeS FIMgT

Pen & Sword
AVIATION

First published in Great Britain in 2008 by
Pen & Sword Aviation
An imprint of
Pen & Sword Books Ltd
47 Church Street
Barnsley
South Yorkshire
S70 2AS

ISBN 978 1 84415 820 1

A CIP catalogue record for this book is
available from the British Library.

Printed and bound in England
by Biddles

Typeset by Sylvia Menzies-Earl

Pen & Sword Books Ltd incorporates the imprints of
Pen & Sword Aviation, Pen & Sword Maritime, Pen & Sword Military,
Wharncliffe Local History, Pen & Sword Select,
Pen & Sword Military Classics and Leo Cooper.

For a complete list of Pen & Sword titles please contact
PEN & SWORD BOOKS LIMITED
47 Church Street, Barnsley, South Yorkshire, S70 2AS, England
E-mail: enquiries@pen-and-sword.co.uk
Website: www.pen-and-sword.co.uk

Contents

Foreword

Air Vice Marshal John Howe had an outstandingly fulfilling career in the Royal Air Force following his decision to leave the South African Air Force soon after his return from operational service in the Korean War. As the chapters in this book clearly recall, he had the spirit of adventure from a very early age and the strong sense of purpose that his future was destined to be in military aviation. Until his retirement he was seldom to miss any opportunity of getting into the air and continue to widen his experience. Indeed, it was those very inspirational qualities from his early childhood days that were to remain with him throughout his service and would have been the envy and stirred the imagination of many less fortunate youngsters.

In his late teens, having completed elementary flying training and with few hours in his log book compared with today's standards, John was thrust into the harsh operational environment of another country as the Korean War was at its peak during the early 1950s. At an early stage the operational experience he gained quickly demonstrated many of his fine qualities of leadership and his outstanding ability in the air that were to typify his style and approach to the many and diverse roles and tasks that he was called upon to undertake, often at short notice. His strength of character and determination, always with an understanding for the important personal touches, were soon recognised by higher authority as exemplified by the wide range of key appointments he was selected to undertake. Not least of these was the introduction of both the Lightning and the Phantom into RAF service. Detailing the operational difficulties for the frontline squadrons and training units needed a Staff Officer with the right attributes and John was that man.

To be specially selected to command a frontline operational base in West Germany at the height of the Cold War clearly showed the confidence of higher authority in choosing the right man for the job in the highly sensitive areas close to the border between East and West Germany. Being a good fighter pilot and leading in the air is but one of the activities of a Station Commander but John was to prove conclusively that his thoroughly professional approach to all aspects of service life led to equally firm leadership in discharging his responsibilities with the many diverse aspects of commanding a large and very busy operational base. In summary, there is no greater challenge and finer reward than successfully completing a tour of duty as a Station Commander.

What appointments that were to follow in the latter part of his career recognised his lengthy and valuable operational experience combined with that ever-present strong sense of duty and purpose. John's career was to span almost forty years of active service. It was a career that was rightly to see him graduate to the upper echelons of his profession.

Upward and Onward is a fitting tribute to a friend and fellow fighter pilot who successfully gave loyal, dedicated and unstinting service to his career in the Royal Air Force. John Howe never once flinched when tough decisions had to be made and his impressive service record has been justly recognised by the many decorations awarded him.

Air Vice Marshal George Black (RAF retired)
Wendover
March 2008

* * * * *

Acknowledgements

I have to thank many people for their assistance in the writing of this biography, not least of course John Howe himself and his wife Annabelle who welcomed me into their lovely home on many occasions.

As the saying goes, there are far too many others to mention everyone individually and they will, I hope, forgive me if they are not included in the following list of those to whom I am especially grateful. In no particular order they are Peter Bowen, Eric Keevy, Mike Muller, Colonel Graham Barr SAAF, David P Frizell, Steven McLean (for comprehensive details of aircraft of the South African Air Force at the time of John's service and for great help in sourcing and providing photographs of that era), Kirk Kinnear, Ted Nance, Martin Bee, David Jones, Mike Cooke, John Langer, Peter Bairsto, Bruce Cousins, Jock Heron, Roy Cope-Lewis, Dr Simon Robbins, Rupert Birtles, Graham Clarke, John Spencer, Tim Miller, Andrew Gordon-Lennox and Paul Chandler, Alan Collinge, Richard Edkins, Dennis Caldwell, Kingsley Oliver, Martin Hooker, Min Larkin, David Barton, David Hastings, Peter Vangucci, John Rogers, David L Bragg and Peter Carr. And to George Black for writing the Foreword.

These days the 'World Wide Web' is a research tool of great value. There are too many sites to be mentioned individually but thank you to all of them and their creators. Then there are invaluable institutions such as the National Archive at Kew, Air Britain, the Suffolk Record Office and the University of East Anglia Library in Norwich whose staffs were always unfailingly helpful.

And finally a special thank you to my wife Angie for putting up with my frequent disappearing acts either to my study or to research elsewhere!

Bob Cossey
Norwich
March 2008

CHAPTER ONE

Young Dreams

The excellent body surfers were normally a good deal further out to sea than the 'rats and mice' waiting for that extra special wave to carry them back to shore. One day while I was on duty there was a shark sighting and I immediately swam out to the furthest group who happened to be John and two friends and told them to return to shore as soon as possible. With that the four of us caught the next suitable wave and John recalls that while surfing back he looked along the wave and there were three of them, plus me, plus the shark enjoying the ride! This idyllic existence came to an end when John went off to join the military college and the rest of us went our individual ways...

Peter Bowen

Air Vice Marshal John Howe, in his retirement years a farmer on the gentle grasslands of the East Anglian countryside, was raised in a far different environment, that of the South African bush. Brought up by caring and devout Church of England parents, his often rough and tough boyhood experiences mirrored those of all his young friends. These were experiences of the Cowboy and Indian variety, unrestrained childhood games exuberantly enacted with the bush as the playground, making for a free and wild childhood, full of the bumps and bruises that most youngsters then collected.

John's mother, Mary, was a Scot from Aberdeen whose family had emigrated to South Africa in the 1920s. His father, George, was an Englishman who, after he met and married Mary in Queenstown, went to live in the small east coast port of East London to work in the family printing works of F. Howe and Co. Theirs was a lovely house, which was the last in the road leading out to the bush. John Frederick George Howe (named after his father and grandfather) was born in March 1930. He would be presented with his brother Robert four years later. Mary was extremely keen on music, accompanying her husband on the piano as he sang and the pair would sometimes broadcast on the local radio. Mary was also involved in amateur dramatics, later turning professional, teaching drama and elocution and producing and directing plays locally. None of this rubbed off on John, although there is a distant memory of being pushed into a poetry reading competition (in Afrikaans), which he won.

For some reason that cannot be recalled the family moved from John's birthplace in Smuts Road to a series of hotels – one of which was the 'Athenaeum' – when John was seven. Having been living on the edge of the bush John and his brother could have found this move restrictive but John had a bike and he could go more or less where he wanted. However, this was at the time that war was brewing and there were increasingly other distractions, although when war was finally declared there appeared to be little effect on living standards. Petrol rationing was introduced, as was flour rationing, but otherwise there was little hardship. There was inevitably some impact in another sense. Coastal artillery guns were set up on Signal Hill by the harbour in East London. Guards were posted at strategic sites and more aircraft appeared in the skies above them. Some local families 'adopted' RAF crews who were training in South Africa. When John was at prep school, evacuees from the UK arrived. The stories they told of the Blitz were horrifying and when these young fellows heard the first air raid sirens sound in East London on practice days they were visibly shaken.

As for attitudes to war, those with British affiliations were of course whole heartedly in support of Britain and the Commonwealth. But those with nationalist leanings never forgot the Boer War, hated the British and backed the Germans. John's mother didn't like them. 'John,' she used to say, 'you must not believe what the Boers tell you. They don't tell the truth you know.' This was in response to his reporting that a group of them had announced that they all supported Hitler and they thought the English were cowardly. Mary's prejudice was largely as a result of what she read in the press for there were not many nationalists in the East London region and those that existed generally kept their opinions to themselves because they were in the minority. As for the black population, they had no particular attitude towards the war. John really didn't know anything about blacks at that time of his life other than the fact that his nanny was black and he thought she was wonderful. The Howe family also had black servants who were also well thought of. John's first recollection of blacks in uniform was seeing a company of black soldiers, their kit immaculate, in perfect step and singing a marching song. To the young John it was a stirring and exciting sight. At that stage he could have no idea that it would be issues concerning the nationalists and apartheid that would have such a profound effect on his life.

Whilst all this was going on John's education, which was a very good one thanks to the financial sacrifices made by his mother and father, was well underway. He was first sent to Queen's College (a boys' only government school) at Queenstown for a year in 1939, after which he went back to East London and the De La Salle Catholic School (1940–41) before two years at Preparatory School (1942–3) and the highly respected St Andrew's College in Grahamstown (1944–7). He did well at his academic studies at St Andrew's and proved himself to be a very good sportsman too, playing rugby and cricket at first team level, enjoying swimming and athletics and becoming captain of the school's shooting team. John didn't like boxing, however, despite enjoying fighting! St Andrew's still prospers very much. It is a school of great tradition, which traces its history back to its foundation in 1855, and John is proud to this day of being an Old Andrean.

The headmaster when he arrived was Ronald Curry, a strict disciplinarian but approachable and very supportive of his pupils. It is no exaggeration to claim that it was Mr Curry who opened the door that led to John's career in military aviation. Ever since the age of four or five he had wanted to fly. No other career ever appealed to him. He was an avid reader of Captain WE Johns' Biggles stories and coincidentally there would be a direct link between the Howe and Johns families later in life. John's future father-in-law, Cecil Gowing, served with Johns during the First World War and to this day a painting by him of aerial combat in France hangs in the Howes' house and proves him to have been a talented artist as well as successful author. John listened regularly to the news about the wartime air campaign in Europe, read about the Battle of Britain and watched aircraft fly wherever he was whenever he could. At first it was the sense of wonderment that aeroplanes *could* fly. He would watch them at East London airport and remembers in particular a passenger-carrying Ju52, which enthralled him when it flew in over the beach to land. Then came the war and the increase in aerial activity, which only served to fuel his determination to get into the air. Yet in those early years he had no opportunity to do so and thus the idea began to form in his mind that he should join the air force where flying would be unlimited. Mary and George didn't approve of their son's determination in this respect for they wanted him to take up a profession such as his brother Robert who became a very successful architect. But John was nothing but single minded in his ambition and when he later graduated from Military College and won his Wings they attended the ceremony, by this time having had no choice but to accept his chosen career path. As the years passed both were very proud of their son who had made such a success of his life.

Whilst at St Andrew's John and his friends used to regularly find themselves in trouble. During his matriculation year they were all caught drinking in a pub off campus. To say Mr Curry was upset would not be telling the whole truth. Suffice it to say that the escapade ended any chance of John becoming a school prefect, which was the goal of all who stayed on post matriculation. That presented John with the opportunity he was looking for and he decided there and then that he wouldn't go back to St Andrew's and faced up to telling his parents. Ronald Curry took a rather more pragmatic view of the decision than they did and set about helping him with his application for entry to Military College, even going so far as to get the necessary paperwork completed for him. It so happened that the Brigadier in charge of selection for that establishment was an Old Andrean himself so John's place was almost assured from the outset. Thus it was that at seventeen John went up to face the selection board. He sailed through the physical, completed aptitude tests with top marks, impressed at the interview and succeeded in the written exam.

A few weeks later he was told he had been selected.

CHAPTER TWO

Training

*Flying? I loved it, just loved it. It was freedom such as I had
never known and I never lost that feeling....*

John Howe

The air force that John Howe was so intent on joining was one that had been in the throes of re-equipment and reorganisation post war. When the South African Air Force (SAAF) was at its peak in September 1944 it consisted of thirty-five operational squadrons, 45,000 personnel and thirty-three types of aircraft. When peace came the service was rapidly reduced. Many squadrons were disbanded and aircraft were disposed of on a large scale as the SAAF was restored to peacetime operations once more. Many aircraft were returned to the US under lend lease arrangements and others were simply scrapped. In addition, its large volunteer force component returned to civilian life. The British government subsequently offered to donate aircraft to South Africa, including Spitfire Mk IXs, Beaufighter Mk Xs, Warwick Mk Vs and Sunderland Mk Vs. After some deliberation it was decided to accept eighty Spitfires as a gift and in addition buy a further fifty-six. It was also decided to retain twelve Sunderlands, which were already in South Africa, and buy three more. As important as the equipment to the capability of the immensely slimmed down air force were the reserve units of the Active Citizen Force, the equivalent to the RAF's Royal Auxiliary Air Force, and the Pupil Pilot Scheme, equivalent to the RAF's Reserve Flying Schools.

By June 1946 there were twelve air force stations in South Africa, which included a number of training schools, although the budget for training new pilots and ground crews was cut to the minimum. Flying training was performed using Tiger Moths, Harvards and Venturas at the Central Flying School at Dunnottar. Harvards were also used for training at squadron level and alongside Spitfires, Ansons, Venturas and Neptunes by the Operational Training Unit and the Bombing Gunnery and Air Navigation School at Langebaanweg. The new SAAF was to have a mobile attack force comprising Spitfire-equipped Nos 1 and 2 Squadrons at Waterkloof, for which the new Mk IXs were ordered and these became the first aircraft to wear South African serial numbers (during the war South Africa's Spitfires had worn British serials). 28 Squadron was the SAAF's transport squadron, flying Dakotas (which had been kept under lend lease arrangements) as well as Ansons, Venturas, Rapides and a single Avro York with a VIP interior. The maritime force comprised 35 Squadron equipped with Short Sunderlands supplemented by the PV-1s (the US Navy designation of the B-34 Ventura) of 17 and 22 Squadrons. Mosquitos of 60 Squadron were the standard bombers, once again backed up by the jack-of-all-trades Ventura. Photo reconnaissance was undertaken by Mosquitos and Ansons with tactical reconnaissance the remit of Harvards and Austers. Finally, during 1948 the first of three Sikorsky S-51 helicopters was purchased in the USA. Another new design to arrive in South Africa was the first jet aircraft, a Gloster Meteor F.3, one of a number sent to all Commonwealth countries for trials. Both the Meteor and the S-51 caught the imagination of the public and became star attractions at every air show at which they appeared. The Meteor was operated by the SAAF for two years before being returned to the UK.

This then was the state of military aviation in South Africa in 1948 when John presented himself at the Military College at Voortrekker Hoogte in Pretoria. Previously known as Robert's Heights it was renamed when the Nationalist government came to power. The other cadets in his intake of forty-two young men proved to be a very disparate group and as always happens those of a similar affinity banded together, becoming colleagues by virtue of shared interests, being from the same area, having the same home language (English or Afrikaans) and so forth. Throughout training this remained the case but it is also true that after two years of working and living in close proximity all the cadets who graduated knew each other very well indeed. Of the initial intake ten failed to make the grade and returned to civilian life. Of the remaining thirty-two, sixteen would go on to the air force and sixteen to various branches of the army. But for this first two years there was little distinction between those destined to serve on the ground or in the air and little if any reference was made to an individual's chosen option. All were treated exactly alike both in terms of physical effort and academic lecturing. Frustratingly for those who were air force bound, they learned all there was to know about the infantry, armour, artillery (John was sent to Robin Island for a coastal artillery course), engineering, signals and stores – everything except flying, the only concession being a study of the theory of flight and some tactics and history. But that was the system. It was a military college based on the British model of Sandhurst. There was no segregated air force college, although there was a navy college.

There are stories aplenty from the various establishments, units and squadrons that John was attached to as will become evident as we proceed (as indeed there are for any serviceman wherever he serves). Continuing the boyhood theme of cuts and bruises, one of John's colleagues at military college, Mike Muller, recalls:

...there was a planned 'attack' up a ridge and to make it more realistic cadets were given blank rounds of .303 ammunition. Cadet Barry Loxton, nicknamed Baby because he was the youngest on the course, decided to make it more realistic and dropped some pebbles down the barrel of his rifle. During a cat crawl John's backside must have presented a tempting target because he fired at it! Barry was as shocked as John to see the damage he did for he couldn't have realised the effect it would have. It could have been serious but although very painful John was back with his fellow cadets that evening having received attention to the wound at No. 1 Military Hospital.

John recalls a Corporal instructor with a particular sense of humour. One day he assembled his trainees before him. 'Gentlemen. This afternoon we are going to talk about the mortar. As you all know there are 180 degrees in a circle.'

John raised his hand. 'Corporal, there are 360 degrees in a circle.'

'Are you sure?'

'Corporal, I have just completed my matriculation, which included mathematics, and I can assure you there are 360 degrees in a circle.'

The Corporal paused and looked all around him and saw all the cadets nodding in agreement. He stood there for a while then suddenly said 'That is a bloody big circle!'

Then there was the RSM (Regimental Sergeant Major) who gave an opening address to the new recruits. 'During the course we are systematically going to break you down, then systematically we are going to build you up.' Discipline at Voortrekker Hoogte was indeed tough. A typical day started at 0600 with cavalry training followed by breakfast. Drill took place from 0830, usually at a high pace. Physical training was from 1130, followed by lunch. An afternoon could be devoted to bayonet charging with a competitive game of rugby at 1800. The programme varied from day to day but the effort required was the same. The college ethos was indeed 'we'll break you down then build you up'. They obviously built John back up very well for he graduated, after a gruelling two years, as a 2nd Lieutenant (see Appendix A) – the equivalent to a Pilot Officer in the RAF. But there was still no flying. In fact, the only time he had ever been in the air was when his father bought him a pleasure flight at East London airport when he was in his early teens. And whilst at military college there was an opportunity of a flight with fellow cadet Bob Crosby, who had a private pilot's licence, in a flying club Tiger Moth from the local SAAF airfield. (The SAAF had flying clubs on their airfields so that ground crew, if they wanted to fly, had the chance to do so.) This sticks firmly in John's mind because during the course of the flight Bob Crosby looped and went over the top a little bit too slowly. John came off his seat, but the quick stab of apprehension was quickly replaced by exhilaration, a feeling that would never leave him throughout his entire flying career.

Having graduated, John and his fifteen colleagues went to Swartkop on 1 April 1950 for a month to wait, doing very little, for places to become available on the next Permanent Force Officers' Flying Training Course at the Central Flying School (CFS). This was at Dunnottar, which lies thirty miles south-east of Johannesburg and was where Commandant Brian 'Piggy' Boyle was OC. Dunnottar had previously been known as Air Force Station Nigel and the CFS as 62 Air School. The latter had disbanded in February 1945, reforming as CFS in 1946 with Tiger Moths, Harvards and Oxfords. The School taught both pupil pilots and instructors. CFS was divided into various Flights and John's Flight Commander was Captain Stan Murray. The CFS Chief Instructor on the Tiger Moth was Major Barry Wiggett, the same Barry Wiggett who would briefly be John's CO on 2 Squadron in Korea. Dunnottar could be relied upon for its perfect training weather and it was rare indeed for flying to be suspended. On a late summer afternoon you could sometimes see thunderstorms brewing up but by then the day's flying was drawing to a close and there was time enough for the storm to clear before night flying began. The only drawback was that Dunnottar was 5,000 feet above sea level so engines weren't quite as powerful as they were at sea level itself.

There was a certain privilege in arriving at CFS as a commissioned officer as John would not be subject to the restrictions of a new entrant, non commissioned pupil pilot. The very fact John and his colleagues were housed in the Officers' Mess as opposed to barracks made a big difference but it did mean that the commissioned and non commissioned men went their separate ways. For John, friendships already formed at college tended to persist. There were Boers and British on the course but the relationship between the two was as if they had all been as one. These Boers were not of the same leanings as the civilians who vilified the British. They were true brother officers who had supported the war and the Commonwealth. It didn't take long for the air force way of life to cut in and to all these young students it was a revelation. There was a great camaraderie and *esprit de corps*, especially after the Korean War started. All were hoping to be sent out there and that resolve brought them ever closer. Hard work, if ever flying to John was hard work, was followed by some very good times. Friday night was party night if you could afford it. If you couldn't that was probably because you'd lost your week's wages at the races, although it cured John of betting for life after he lost all his pay (paid in cash in those days) in one afternoon!

During their early days at Dunnottar the students were introduced to the decompression chamber in which pressure is reduced to simulate gain in altitude and then increased to simulate the return to earth. Armed with pencil and paper, they were required to keep writing their names so that the deterioration in co-ordination due to anoxia (the deficient supply of oxygen to body tissues) could be monitored. There were many instances of surnames changing as the condition set in: Howe, for example, became Howard at some stage of John's decompression.

Once all the ground exercises had been completed John and his fellow students finally became airborne with their instructors. The aircraft was one of the school's DH82A Tiger Moths and the date for John was 9 May 1950. It soon became apparent that he was a natural pilot. He learned quickly because he loved being in the air. And because he loved it he worked hard at it. His first instructor was Jack Haskins, known to all as Ginger but who wasn't ginger at all. He was a nice guy who for John was the ideal instructor in that he wasn't one who thought the louder he shouted the quicker his pupil would learn. He was the opposite to Tommy Vanston who could be heard yelling at the unfortunate soul in the cockpit if you were downwind of him when aloft – not that Tommy didn't prove to be an excellent instructor as well. Indeed most, if not all, those at Dunnottar were good instructors in their own ways and of the sixteen who started at CFS, all sixteen completed the course.

The Tiger Moth introduced pupils to instruments and aerobatics, as well as cross-country and night flying – in fact to all the disciplines that make up a pure flying training course. There was more theory too, such as aerodynamics, navigation, meteorology and engines. This always came first, and only then flying with what had been discussed in the morning being practised in the air. John went solo after just eight and a half hours and he remembers it very well because it came unexpectedly after duals with no forewarning. But it was a truly magical moment for him. It was 19 May 1950 and Tommy Vanston had given him his solo check (not that John realised that this is what he had been doing, although it was generally the Flight Commander or an instructor other than a pupil's regular instructor who conducted such milestone checks). At 1145 he had sent him off by himself for a ten-minute solo. All John's dreams came true at that point. It had been just ten days since he had first climbed into a Tiger Moth cockpit. By the end of the month he had notched up three hours and five minutes solo.

It's a real paradox that John cannot stand heights unless he is in an aeroplane (he hates ladders for example). But to prove the point that the air is a natural element for him there was a totally unauthorised trick he very quickly taught himself. This was to climb to 7,000 feet, loosen the straps, turn upside down (a slow roll in which he stopped half way) and go into an inverted glide, wind in his face. This was freedom of the very best kind.

John stayed with the Tiger Moth until 25 August 1950: his course summary shows him as being of average ability as a pilot after eighteen hours' solo flying. On 30 August he stepped into a Harvard for the first time, still at Dunnottar but now with Captain Daphne as his Flight Commander and Major Baxter as the Chief Instructor. This again was pure flying, the honing of newly acquired flying skills. The Harvard was an aeroplane to enjoy, partly because by sitting so high in the spacious cockpit you could see so much of the world around you. After half a dozen dual flights John went solo on the Harvard on 1 September. Formation flying entered the syllabus, involving two, three and eventually four aircraft and other new skills were progressively learned. One such was instrument flying with take-off and general flying under a cockpit hood to prevent the pilot from seeing out, thereby forcing him to rely on his instruments. The hood would be removed for landing. There was always a safety pilot in the back seat for such sorties. At periodic intervals, as with the Tiger Moth, a pupil's Flight Commander would conduct tests. On 15 December 1950 and with sixty hours on Tiger Moths, 141 hours on Harvards and nine hours in a Link Trainer (to learn the rudiments of instrument flying) under his belt, John received his Wings from Brigadier HJ Bronkhorst who was acting Director General of the Air Force at the time. The report by the Chief Instructor shows him to have been 'a good pilot inclined to be overconfident' who was 'above average at navigation'. That surely was an overconfidence born of the sheer pleasure of being in the air.

After Christmas leave John returned to CFS for three months to convert to the Spitfire under Flight Commander Cliff Beech's instruction. John's first Spitfire flight was on 10 January and then on successive days thereafter, interspersed with solo flying in the Harvard as his skills continued to be practised. By the time the conversion had been completed on 5 March 1951, John had entered fifteen and a quarter hours on the Spitfire HF.IXe in his log book. He was in seventh heaven!

Langebaanweg, which lies sixty miles to the north of Cape Town on South Africa's west coast, was built towards the end of the Second World War as a training base, taking the name Bomber Gunnery and Air Navigation School (BG&ANS) in 1946. On 14 April 1947 it was renamed Air Force Station Langebaanweg with the BG&ANS as a resident unit. The first Harvards and Venturas arrived shortly afterwards with the first Spitfire HF.IXe in residence from 1948. It was used until 1953 to train the pilots who were bound for 2 Squadron in Korea. No. 4 Operational Training Unit (OTU), part of another Langebaanweg resident unit, the Air Operations School (AOS), was under the command of Colonel Danie du Toit. Given the role of 2 Squadron, the OTU course was principally designed around air to ground work, although air to air did feature to a degree as well. First of all though, pilots had to get used to the fact that Langebaanweg had paved runways. Hitherto the Tiger Moths, Harvards and Spitfires at Dunnottar had all been flown off a grass airfield so take-offs and landings could always be into wind. But there was no such luxury here. It was always more difficult to keep a Spitfire straight in a crosswind because there was no tail wheel steering. When the course first started there was such a spate of wing dips and clips that Colonel du Toit issued an edict, which essentially said that the next person to crash on his airfield would be sent back to Dunnottar to learn how to fly! The day came when du Toit himself flew down to Cape Town for a conference. When he returned and landed, as he taxied off the runway, instead of pulling up his flaps he pulled up his wheels. Unfortunately he had an audience of students who immediately burst into a round of ironic applause. That night in the bar he announced 'Drinks on me!' and quite a party ensued. That took a bit of courage on the part of the Boss after a considerable loss of face!

John had arrived at Langebaanweg on 8 March 1951 and his first flying there involved drogue towing in a Harvard. For air to air firing students towed drogues for each other with a corporal in the back seat as winch operator. The Harvard took off with the drogue laid out on the runway close to the aircraft but once airborne and in position it was wound out to the necessary safe distance before firing commenced. Once the sortie was over the Harvard would fly low over the airfield and the drogue would be jettisoned prior to landing. Bullets used in air to air firing exercises were dipped in paint so that entry points through the drogue could be easily counted afterwards.

By 2 April John was in a Spitfire IX cockpit and for the next six weeks or so the training was relentless – battle formation, fighter v fighter, dive bombing (learning the technique in a Harvard first), fighter v bomber, low-level bombing, high-level bombing, air to air, air to ground, bomber escort, bomber interception and rocket firing. Such training was not without its dangers. One of John's friends, Chris Venter, blacked out as he pulled out of a dive. It was thought that he had looked back to check his rear under g-force, thereby cutting the blood supply to his brain as he bent his neck. He carried on straight into the sea and was killed instantly. This was the course's first casualty. It was during his first sortie on 3 May that John encountered a problem of his own as he pulled out of a dive when his engine cut out at about 1,000 feet. He couldn't force land in the area he was in because of rolling sand dunes and so he had to head for the sea and bale out. He turned the Spitfire in a glide and went through all the drills, called 'Mayday, Mayday, Mayday' then went to slide the canopy back, only to find it wouldn't move. John tried everything until, almost too late, it released and he just had time to jump and pull the chord. He landed in Danger Bay (so called because it was shark infested) and was in his dinghy in seconds. He was quickly picked up by the crash boat *Impi Queen*, which patrolled there (see Appendix B). John was uninjured other than catching a cold – the waters of the Atlantic were icy and he was only wearing lightweight flying gear. The aircraft was lost and not recovered and so the definitive reason for the engine problem was not discovered but it was thought that there was a problem with the throttle linkage, which, when it came loose, caused the engine to throttle back and lose power. There had been several problems with Spitfire engines at Langebaanweg and there had been several exitings of the aircraft – five in total on previous courses, although John was the only one to do so on his. That was how he became a member of the Caterpillar Club, the criterion for membership of which is that a pilot must have saved his life by jumping with a parachute. The club was instigated in the 1920s by Leslie Irvin in the USA who developed a parachute that a pilot could deploy at will from a backpack using a rip-cord. It was called the Caterpillar Club because parachutes and lines in those days were woven from silk. Members of this exclusive club received a gold caterpillar-shaped badge with ruby eyes. Later other parachute manufacturers such as Pioneer and Switlik issued their own awards.

Within a day John was back in the air again on a tactical exercise. Within a week he had dropped his first live 500-pounder and by 18 May he had completed the necessary flying hours to pass out from the course. His OC had some interesting comments on his progress.

> Dive bombing below average: fixed gun cine – low average: air to ground firing – low average: low level bombing – low average: rocket firing – high average.

John can't specifically recall why he should have been better at rocket firing and less successful at the other disciplines. Probably using the aircraft's nose as the aiming reference was a factor. But that was common to all pilots. It was a combination of a fairly rudimentary ring and bead system and the sheer newness of such techniques coupled with the insufficient time, with fewer than thirty hours on the Spitfire by the time he left Langebaanweg, that accounted for such a mediocre assessment.

It was in Korea that all new 2 Squadron pilots very quickly learned – and spectacularly so.

CHAPTER THREE

The War in Korea

The role of 2 Squadron in Korea was close air support against enemy positions to soften them up for ground attacks, interdiction against the enemy's logistic and communication lines, providing protective cover for rescue operations, reconnaissance flights and to a lesser extent, interception of enemy aircraft
History of the SAAF – www.saairforce.co.za

The south-east Asian nation of Korea had been divided at the end of the Second World War with the infamous 38th Parallel becoming the border between the Russian-backed north and American-backed south of the country. However, military involvement by the US was initially limited as its people were tired of war and wanted peace to facilitate their pursuit of the American Dream. Politically therefore, Korea was not seen as a priority. By contrast, for the North Koreans under Kim II Sung the reunification of the north and south became an absolute priority and American indifference was seen as providing the opportunity for this to happen. With Moscow's backing North Korean forces invaded the Republic of South Korea on 25 June 1950 and 90,000 soldiers with hundreds of Russian-built T34 tanks crossed the border and overwhelmed the defending South Korean forces. This was the catalyst for a change from a passive to an active American attitude towards Korea. President Truman resolved to take immediate action and there were a number of reasons for this. Despite the desire to focus inwardly he was under domestic pressure for being too soft on communism. Hence the formulation of the Truman Doctrine, which advocated the opposition of communism everywhere as opposed to appeasement which, so it was believed, would only encourage further expansion. Truman therefore went to the United Nations for approval before declaring war on North Korea, approval that was given on 27 June in the temporary absence of the Russians who were boycotting the Security Council over the admission of Mongolia to the UN and who thereby were unable to use their veto. Although American opinion was solidly behind the venture, Truman would later take harsh criticism for not obtaining a declaration of war from Congress before sending troops to Korea.

The first act by the UN was to call for an immediate cease-fire but when this was ignored a resolution was passed authorising the sending in of troops. In South Africa, Prime Minister Daniel Malan felt it was his country's duty to side with anti-communist countries to combat 'aggressive communism' wherever necessary (as did fifteen other UN member countries) and a decision was taken on 4 August 1950 to:

> ...furnish such assistance to the Republic of Korea as may be necessary to repel the armed attack and to restore international peace and security in the area.

The statement continued:

> The government has decided that special efforts should be made to render military aid. This will be offered in the form of a fighter squadron with ground personnel. As members of the Permanent Force are liable for service only in South Africa, service in the Far East will be on a voluntary basis.

The fighter squadron was to be 2 Squadron. Formed at Waterkloof in January 1939 flying the Hawker Hartbee, 2 Squadron had spent a year in training as a fighter/bomber unit before renumbering as 12 Squadron in December of that year and then reforming again as 2 Squadron in Kenya. It was in East Africa that it established itself in the early months of the war, being one of the squadrons to take on the Italian Air Force, which was equipped with three hundred modern aircraft, with outdated Furies, Gladiators and only a few up-to-date Hurricanes. It was during the Abyssinian campaign that the squadron was nicknamed The Flying Cheetahs after two pet cheetahs that were kept as mascots. It moved to Egypt in April 1941, re-equipping with Curtiss Tomahawk IIBs in the process and being allotted the squadron code DB. Kittyhawks were received from May 1942. In North Africa 2 Squadron played a major part in enabling the Allied Desert Air Force to attain air superiority over the Axis air forces. It then supported the advance through Sicily and Italy in 1943. It was here that they re-equipped with Spitfire Vs and later IXs, which they flew until the end of the war when the squadron disbanded. The squadron reformed at Waterkloof once again with Spitfire IXs in 1948 before moving, without aircraft, to Korea in November 1950.

2 Squadron, whose motto is *Sursam Prorusque – Upward and Onward*, has been involved in every single combat action in which the SAAF has taken part. In its time it has operated the Hawker Hartbee, Hurricane and Fury, the Gloster Gladiator, Supermarine Spitfire, North American F-51 Mustang and F-86 Sabre in Korea, the de Havilland Vampire, Canadair Sabre, Dassault Mirage III and (appropriately given the squadron's nickname) the Cheetah, an upgraded Mirage III developed by South Africa's Atlas Aircraft Corporation. It is at the time of writing (in early 2008) about to take delivery of the JAS39 Gripen.

The call for volunteers for Korea was made by Brigadier JT Durrant, Director General of the Air Force. The response was overwhelming. Commandant Servaas van Breda Theron DSO, DFC, AFC, a veteran Second World War pilot known to his friends as SV, was given the task of preparing the squadron for overseas service against the backdrop of a war that was already going badly. The US Eighth Army had been pushed down the Korean peninsula by the North Koreans but still held the Pusan perimeter at the extreme southern end of the country. However, the UN retained command of the air and supplies and reinforcements poured in. Amongst these would be the South Africans. On 5 September 1950 forty-nine officers and 157 other ranks reported for duty at Waterkloof and a programme of medical examinations and injections began. Administration details were finalised and a small liaison staff left for Japan on 10 September. On 25 September the officers and men sailed for Yokohama in the MV *Tjisadane*, arriving on 4 November and transferring to Johnson AFB near Tokyo.

The Flying Cheetahs were slated to be attached to the 18th Fighter Bomber Wing (FBW) of the US Fifth Air Force (which acted as the tactical air force of the Far East Air Forces – FEAF) as one of its component squadrons, the others being the 12th, 39th (from May 1951) and 67th Fighter Bomber Squadrons (FBS). US Wings and Groups generally have convoluted histories and the 18th was no exception. It was established as the 18th Pursuit Group on Hawaii in January 1927 and comprised the 6th and 19th Pursuit Squadrons. Aircraft used to begin with were de Havilland DH4, Boeing PW-9 and Boeing P-12 biplanes, followed by Boeing P-26 'Peashooters' and then Curtiss P-36s. The Group insignia was a fighting cock with the motto *With Talon and Beak*. Restyled the 18th Fighter Group in 1939, it continued to operate from Hawaii through to December 1941 and Pearl Harbor, by which time it was flying the Curtiss P-40 Warhawk. The Group was destroyed in the attack whilst still on the ground (only two P-40s got airborne). It was two years before the Army Air Corps could rebuild it to operational fighting strength and the 18th reformed on Espiritu Santo Island in the Pacific in March 1943 with the 12th, 44th and 70th Squadrons as its components and as part of the Thirteenth Air Force. The following month it moved to Guadalcanal. It remained in the Philippines until the end of the war and then in November 1945 it converted to the P-51D Mustang. On 25 March 1947 it was deactivated but was not dormant for long. On 16 September it reformed at Clark Field in the Philippines on Republic P-47s then in June 1948 reverted to Mustangs. These began to arrive in July 1948, now styled as F-51Ds, P for Pursuit having been dropped in favour of F for Fighter in the new USAF vocabulary. A year later the 18th became a Fighter Bomber Wing flying the Lockheed P-80C. By now its component squadrons were the 12th, 44th and 67th. Lt Col Ira Wintermute became CO of the Group nine days before the invasion of Korea.

As soon as the North Koreans attacked, FEAF ordered the Thirteenth Air Force in the Philippines to form the Dallas Provisional Squadron from amongst the most experienced Mustang pilots in the 18th FBW squadrons. Captain Harry Moreland led this provisional squadron to K2 (Taegu) in Korea where they fell under the remit of the Fifth Air Force, as did all Mustang squadrons. (For a listing of Korean airfield identification codes see Appendix D.) Here they awaited the arrival of ten virtually unserviceable Mustangs, which had been donated by President Truman to the fledgling South Korean Air Force, and then flew combat missions from 14 July 1950. When the 18th FBW HQ moved to Taegu, Captain Moreland's squadron was renumbered as the 12th FBS which, after comments from South Korea's President Syngman Rhee about the courage of the volunteer pilots, painted its aircraft with a ferocious shark mouth, which they kept for the remainder of the war. Meanwhile, the 67th FBS had arrived without aircraft, having left its F-80s at Clark Field for the 44th FBS to fly as the sole air defence squadron in the area. (The 44th would also rotate pilots to the Korean-based squadrons during the conflict.) The shortage of aircraft for the 12th and 67th FBS was rectified by the arrival of the carrier USS *Boxer* and 145 Mustangs taken from National Guard units throughout the US. The two squadrons re-equipped with these well-maintained aircraft, having by now relocated to Japan together with the 18th FBW HQ as Taegu was about to be overrun by the North Koreans, or so it was thought, as they pushed southwards. In the event that did not happen and the 12th and 67th returned from Japan to K9 (Pusan East) in Korea. Inevitably K9 became 'canine' and the airfield was quickly, albeit unofficially, renamed Dogpatch after a popular comic strip village. The North Korean retreat towards the Yalu River following General MacArthur's Inchon invasion continued and in mid October Pyongyang fell, thus allowing the 18th FBW to move forward to K24 (Pyongyang East). Conditions here were primitive to say the least with the advance party living in tents in the bitter weather. No transport was available and all equipment had to be manhandled. The one short runway was soft and rough, which made operating from it very difficult.

By the time 2 Squadron arrived in Korea the UN's fortunes had been dramatically reversed. General MacArthur and the US X Corps had landed at Inchon on 15 September and the North Koreans withdrew. By 26 October UN forces had stormed through Korea and reached the Yalu River, which forms the border with Manchuria at several points. Such was the speed and success with which this all happened that 2 Squadron began to wonder whether or not they would be needed, thinking perhaps that the war could soon be over. But the situation was to change dramatically very quickly once again – indeed, it was already changing as UN forces reached the river. The day before, units of the Chinese Communist Army had begun crossing the Yalu in secret. When discovered it was initially thought to be a limited intervention by Chinese volunteers to help the North Koreans avoid total defeat: in fact it turned out to be China entering the war against the UN forces.

As soon as they arrived at Johnson AFB, 2 Squadron began conversion to the US-supplied F-51D Mustang, using aircraft that had been briefly held in storage since arriving on the *Boxer*. The decision had been taken that no aircraft or supporting technical equipment would be sent from South Africa but that they would be purchased from the US and made available when the squadron reached the Far East. The deal actually struck was that the South Africans would only pay for those aircraft written off and the rest would be returned once hostilities were over. The establishment was set at twenty-four (four Flights of six aircraft each), although it took a while for that number to be reached and then, once reached, it became a problem for that number to be maintained (see Appendix C).

Flying clothing was issued to pilots and they were lectured on air tactics, navigation and so forth, whilst ground crew got to grips with the technical problems of servicing and maintaining Mustangs. Unfortunately, initially at least, South Africa was seen as a country of little consequence and the pilots as youngsters with no experience, the Americans being completely unaware of the Second World War pedigrees of the combat-experienced pilots involved. Squadron Boss SV was not long in taking decisive action to correct their mistake and chose to do it by action, not words. As *South Africa's Flying Cheetahs in Korea* by Dermot Moore and Peter Bagshawe states, he put on an individual flying display:

> ...the likes of which the Americans had never seen before. On landing he found himself the centre of an admiring circle and a senior officer shook him by the hand. 'Commandant, we can't teach you anything about flying.' 'That's right,' said SV, 'and every pilot in my squadron is as good as I am, so give us the aircraft and we'll get on with the war.'

The first converted South African pilots had taken to the air on 8 November 1950 and so good was their progress that by 12 November it had been decided to send an advance party into Korea itself for further operational training 'in the field'. Five aircraft (flown by the CO and four Flight Commanders) and ground crew (who were flown in by C-47) arrived at an extremely cold and snowy K9 to join the 12th and 67th FBS. The remainder of the crews were left at Johnson pending the availability of more aircraft. From K9, SV and his charges very soon moved with their American allies to K24, recently captured from the communists, so that they would be closer to the front line. The benefit was that from K9 missions would have lasted as long as five hours but from K24 the time was reduced by at least two hours. The downside was that K24 gave the South Africans a very rude introduction to the realities of what was to be a cruel war often fought in cruel conditions as other elements of the 18th FBW had already found out. It had been bombed by UN forces when in North Korean hands and most of the buildings for men and machines were badly damaged. Tents were used as living and office accommodation, whilst an old wattle and daub, dirt-floored hangar of the North Korean Air Force, such as it had been, was used as an all ranks mess hall. There was little protection against the freezing wind. Water froze and keeping hot food hot was an almost impossible task. There was also the constant threat of attack by communist guerrillas, all of which combined to make for a somewhat miserable existence when it came to both rest and work. Ground crew in particular were badly affected, not only by the conditions but by the lack of proper equipment. The intensity of operations made severe demands on them, the arming and refuelling of aircraft being particularly difficult. For the pilots the condition of the single dirt runway was not improved by its constant use by transport aircraft delivering supplies to the base.

Commandant Theron and Captain 'Lippy' Lipawsky flew the first of 2 Squadron's 10,373 Mustang sorties on 19 November, taking off from K9 at 0700 and landing back at K24 as part of the move to that airfield. Similar close support missions by all the available South African pilots followed. On 24 November they were thrown into the major air effort to stop the Chinese. Meanwhile, the main body of the squadron at Johnson AFB was becoming increasingly restless at the delay in their departure for the front line and it was evident to SV that the ground crew with him at K24 were resentful because of their workload. Orders for those in Japan to join their hard pressed colleagues were issued but were then quickly rescinded when the 18th FBW was withdrawn to K13 (Suwon) from 1 December as enemy troops got closer and closer to Pyongyang. The ground crew were flown out by C-119. Conditions at K13 were no better than at K24 with tents pitched on snow-covered ground, which quickly turned to mud. The minus 30-degree temperatures delayed flying in the early mornings as snow that fell during the night froze on the aircraft and had to be removed by hand before take-off was possible. By now 2 Squadron had a slightly improved complement of six aircraft, eleven pilots and twenty ground crew in theatre but it was still an extremely demanding task not helped by the fact that within three days of arriving at K13 they were on the move again, this time to K10 (Chinhae). This was to be their final move and K10 remained their permanent base for the next two years together with a forward operating base near Seoul, which became K16. The squadron settled down to a long round of armed reconnaissance patrols, interdiction and close support, often operating two hundred miles beyond the bombline on sorties that lasted four hours or more as attention turned to the lengthening supply lines of the advancing enemy troops. In the short term K13 continued to be used as well as K16 with a small team based there for refuelling and rearming.

The Cheetahs lost their first aircraft on 5 December when John Davis was temporarily knocked unconscious when a railway truck he attacked turned out to be loaded with explosives and he was caught by the blast. He recovered in time to crash land. A Stinson L-5 Sentinel liaison aircraft landed near the crash site and rescued him, the L-5 observer giving up his seat for Captain Davis. The observer was later rescued by another L-5.

On 10 December five more pilots and eighteen other ranks finally reached the squadron from Japan and they were immediately put to work in support of the hard pressed air and ground crew already there who had thus far worked miracles under impossible conditions. The final tranche of manpower began to arrive from 17 December and with the squadron finally up to strength Colonel Low, the 18th FBW's CO, handed SV a letter that formally confirmed 2 Squadron as a component of his Wing. From 23 December the entire Wing was operational for the first time.

Although conditions at K10 were much better than at K24 and K13 in terms of less mud and less cold, the country over which they and the UN forces flew was unchanging. *South Africa's Flying Cheetahs in Korea* gives the following description.

> Weather and terrain have always influenced the success or failure of nations who have fought in Korea since time immemorial and that was certainly true during the war from 1950 to 1953. The terrain comprises a multitude of treacherous mountain ranges throughout the length and breadth of the country with heights from 200 m in the south to 3,000 m in the north. Precipitous slopes, deep valleys and ravines overlooked by jagged peaks and sharp ridges: mountains often cutting across one another making identification difficult or impossible. In these circumstances the roads and railways follow the course of rivers and are punctuated with tunnels. As far as weather was concerned Korea is a country of extremes. It is affected by two monsoons annually. The winter in the north is more severe than in the south, the average temperature in the mountains falling to a minimum of minus 17 degrees C. In the summer the temperature can rise to 40 degrees C in both the north and south of the country. The summer monsoon brings heavy rains in July and from time to time thick fog can result from the marriage of sea winds with humid inland air. During September typhoons sweep across the country from the south.

On New Year's Day 1951 the communists launched a nine division offensive across the Imjin River towards Inchon and Seoul and whilst fighter bomber support initially stemmed the flow of the Chinese and North Koreans, UN forces were forced to fall back. Two days later UN troops abandoned Seoul as air attacks intensified despite rain and snow storms. A new UN air offensive, Operation *Thunderbolt*, designed to slow the Chinese advance by disrupting their supply lines and making direct attacks on troops, transport, tanks and supply dumps, began on 25 January. Low flying Mustangs checked buildings, haystacks, ravines, woods, roads and railways with others flying top cover, looking for camouflaged enemy troops and equipment but in the process pilots were inevitably subjected to an increasing amount of ground fire and losses mounted. By the end of the month the Chinese had introduced increasing numbers of MiG-15s to the fray and were in control of north-west Korean airspace. The area between the Yalu and Ch'ongch'on Rivers known to UN forces as MiG Alley came into being.

Nevertheless Operation *Thunderbolt* succeeded and communist resistance crumbled. Ground forces advanced on Seoul and after two weeks they had established a new front line. Three 2 Squadron F-51s along with their pilots were lost during January, their first casualties of the war. On the 24th the first batch of replacement pilots arrived at K10 and on the 27th the first DFCs were awarded in recognition of what had been achieved thus far.

The South African Military History Society Journal, Vol 4, No. 3 tells of one new arrival.

New faces appeared on the squadron as replacements, one of whom was Lt Mickey Rorke who decided the squadron should have its own officer's club. So he set it up, initially in a tent, and later in a portion of the pilot's crew room. This appropriately became known as *Rorke's Inn*, becoming famous in Korea and perpetuating the memory of its founder after his untimely death in a flying accident at K16 [on 15 May when he crashed on take-off].

The Cheetahs opened March by establishing a new 18th FBW record of thirty-two sorties in one day and with Commandant Ray Armstrong taking over from SV as CO on 17 March. This also proved to be the month in which the highest number of combat sorties was flown by 2 Squadron – a total of 633. This was despite, or perhaps because of, temporarily moving to K9, in Allied hands once again, so that PSP (Pierced Steel Planking) could be laid at K10 thereby making it easier to operate from during the seasonal midsummer heavy rains. Living quarters and recreational facilities were much improved at the same time. In fact, what was put in place allowed for operations in any kind of weather and was almost equivalent to what was to be found on any permanent South African Air Force station.

An increased number of missions meant an increased incidence of loss (although the two do not necessarily go hand in hand) with a further three pilots failing to return. Nevertheless the broader picture was encouraging to the Allies with the 25th US Infantry Division crossing the Han River, the communists unexpectedly abandoning Seoul without a fight and the US Army driving into the central area of Korea. Captain Lipawsky became the first 2 Squadron pilot to complete a tour in Korea. For the South Africans this was seventy-five sorties. For the Americans it was a hundred. By 12 April the squadron had flown two thousand sorties. Lt General Stratemeyer, Commanding General FEAF, sent a letter to Ray Armstrong:

On 12th April 1951, just two months after flying its 1,000 sorties, No 2 Squadron SAAF completed 2,000 sorties in support of UN forces in Korea. This continuing high rate is most noteworthy. I wish to express my sincere appreciation to the personnel of No 2 Squadron who have contributed to this commendable effort.

General Partridge of the Fifth Air Force also commented:

> The compliments of the Commanding General FEAF carry the enthusiastic endorsement of this headquarters. The enviable combat record of the 2nd South African Air Force Squadron in the Korean War is a splendid tribute to the fighting spirit of the freedom loving people of your nation. My congratulations to you and the members of your command for the outstanding performance demonstrated. The aerial achievements of your organisation have reflected great credit upon yourself and the United Nations.

Shortly afterwards the communists launched another major offensive in this increasingly seesaw war and pushed seventy divisions into the fray. But by the end of the month this had petered out, largely due again to the efforts of the Allied air forces in disrupting enemy transport and supply dumps and by strafing and attacking any troops seen. Pilots on recce missions reported that the communists were repairing forward airstrips for possible use and so instructions were issued to disperse aircraft on UN bases. As the season changed increasing amounts of mud made operations (and living conditions) ever more difficult again. But nothing stopped for weather or conditions on the ground and the South Africans located and destroyed enemy troops, vehicles and supplies using napalm, rockets and machine-guns whilst 500-pound bombs were used against road and rail systems. Within 2 Squadron a system had been evolved whereby Flights were allocated certain specific areas so that they could become thoroughly acquainted with them. Pilots would therefore have a better idea as to where enemy vehicles or supply dumps could be concealed.

The North Koreans and Chinese were making supreme efforts to improve the transportation of supplies to the front line. With the availability of seemingly unlimited manpower, bombed roads were repaired in very short order and to provide the necessary protection for their vehicles the number of defensive gun emplacements had increased. However by 22 May the communist offensive had collapsed again. This was in no small part down to operations such as that of 9 May when three hundred UN aircraft struck the communist air base at Sinuiju in Operation *Buster*. The 39th FBS had by now been transferred to the 18th FBW and they participated in this. On the day sixteen aircraft of 2 Squadron acted as a rescue standby off the west coast over the Yellow Sea at a point where pilots had been briefed to head for if in distress. They were also briefed to act as close escort to surface vessels and flying boats detailed as rescue aircraft. As it happened there were no casualties during the attack.

The South African Military History Society Journal, Vol 4, No. 3, states that a couple of days later:

> Major [Jan] Blaauw was involved in an incident for which he was awarded the American Silver Star. While four aircraft were on an interdiction

mission 11 kms west of Singye the leader's aircraft was hit by ground fire and a wing of his aircraft collapsed. Lt. [Vernon] Kruger bailed out successfully but dislocated his shoulder and suffered 2nd degree burns when he landed. Two other members of the Flight, Major Blaauw and Lt. [Martin] Mentz, capped the downed pilot whilst Captain [Pat] Clulow tried without success to alert the rescue organisation. Shortage of fuel compelled Lt Mentz and Capt Clulow to return to K16 but Major Blaauw, in spite of fuel shortage, continued capping operations and when his aircraft ran out of fuel he crash landed it next to Lt. Kruger, sustaining abrasions and bruises to his nose and eyes. He immediately went to the assistance of Lt. Kruger until a helicopter arrived and rescued them both.

After the collapse of the communists' latest offensive UN forces launched a counterattack and by the end of May they had reached the 38th Parallel once again. By early June the US Eighth Army was in possession of virtually all South Korea.

This was the situation when John Howe arrived in Japan. His war was to be prosecuted in the air over the next four months and on the ground over the subsequent two.

CHAPTER FOUR

Learning the Operational Ropes

*The aim was to isolate the battlefield above what we called the bomb line,
which was a line drawn on the map a mile or so north of the United Nations
forces. There was therefore a gap between them and where you would
start attacking un-briefed as it were. Anything we saw moving we attacked
and so our missions would be recces of the main supply routes.
We attacked bridges, dockyards, marshalling yards, factories,
airfields, tanks, infantry, roads and mountain passes. If you could
thump a few five hundred pounders into the side of a mountain
pass then you'd close it. As for our sorties generally we did flak busting
and we did long range escort but the main role was attack and low level
recce. For instance your main target for the mission would be to go and
attack such and such a bridge and then when you'd done that with your
five hundred pounders you would then be given a route to recce and
anything you saw you'd then attack with rockets and guns.*

John Howe

A s we have seen, all those who fought with the South African Air Force in
Korea were volunteers, not because they had any particular aspirations
about defeating the communist foe but because they were young, newly
trained and entirely 'up for it'. The excitement of the possibility of getting into
action overrode all else and in John's case at least there were certainly no second
thoughts about personal safety. Of the sixteen who started with him on his Wings
course at Langebaanweg, all sixteen had volunteered to go before the course had
finished even though it was quite likely the majority probably couldn't find Korea
on a map! In the event only fourteen went. Bob Crosby got married and was
dismissed from the air force (in those days it simply wasn't allowed) and Eric
Venter had been killed. It's a sobering thought that at the end of their Korean tour
only seven returned to South Africa whilst two had been made prisoners of war.
Five had been killed.

The flight out to Korea took a week with groups of six at a time flying on commercial airlines. Accompanying John were 2nd Lieutenants Verster, Liebenberg, Sherwood and de Jongh with Captain Snyman in command. The route taken varied from group to group. For John's it was initially via South African Airways Constellation to Nairobi, Khartoum and Cairo before changing to BOAC for Basra, Delhi, Calcutta, Rangoon, Bangkok, Hong Kong, Okinawa and finally Tokyo where, whilst paperwork was being completed, the pilots stayed in an Australian-run hotel. Within a few days they were flown to K10 and war for them began in earnest. For Eric Keevy, he and his party were deposited in Rome for a few days before continuing on to Basra, then Karachi and on to Korea via Rangoon (where they night-stopped), Bangkok, Hong Kong (another night stop), Okinawa and Tokyo.

On arrival the first job was kitting out. However, because the equipment officer would only open the stores on a Monday and Wednesday, this was not as simple as it should have been. John wasn't on base on those days so he flew his first missions in civvies – a white shirt and fawn slacks in fact. (If he had been shot down over enemy territory wearing these he would in all probability have been executed as a spy.) John's Commanding Officer, Ray Armstrong, understandably insisted that he kitted up properly before he flew any more. John tried but because he wasn't on the ground at K10 on a Monday or Wednesday again he couldn't get the kit. Armstrong saw him climbing from his Mustang in casual gear once more, went and found the equipment officer and tore him off a strip. As a result in petty retribution he issued John with a flying suit that was torn with its pockets in shreds but shortly afterwards he was posted to Tokyo, was caught smuggling and received his just rewards. John was not unhappy!

Whilst he was trying to get himself kitted out John converted to the Mustang and that process was rudimentary at best. The first batch of pilots to arrive in 1950 had been trained by the Americans but those that followed were converted by 2 Squadron itself. There was a lecture or two, the pilot's notes were read and that, basically, was it before the first flight. There were no two-seat Mustangs. A big difference between the Spitfire on which John had trained and the Mustang was the steerable tailwheel on the latter, which was certainly beneficial when taxiing. But comparing rudders size for size, that of the Spitfire was bigger than the Mustang and consequently there was better control on take-off. On the Mustang if the tail came up too soon the torque and gyroscopic effect caused a tremendous swing. The trick was to keep the tail on the ground until airflow over it could be felt, otherwise there was a severe tendency to swing 90 degrees. One of John's friends, 2nd Lt Terry Liebenberg, failed to keep his tail down on his first combat mission and ploughed through several parked aircraft by the side of the runway. John sensed Terry had been nervous and concerned and had strapped him into the cockpit personally in an effort to reassure him. With two 500-pound bombs, six 120-pound rockets, guns fully armed and full fuel tanks the resultant explosion was ferocious. John was the first on the scene but it was hopeless. There was no chance that Terry Liebenberg had survived.

The F-51D was a very good aircraft for the job it had to do and whilst it didn't have the manoeuvrability of the Spitfire its strength lay in its tremendous range. It had earned its reputation as the long desired escort aircraft to American bomber streams during the Second World War. As a bomb truck itself the Mustang could carry virtually its own the weight in munitions and fuel and when fully laden, whilst it wasn't as well balanced on the controls as the Spitfire, it was very pleasant to fly. It was structurally strong and apart from the susceptibility of its glycol lines being hit (the biggest cause of loss in Korea) it could take a lot of punishment. Nonetheless loss rates were high. There were times when 2 Squadron couldn't put two Flights of four into the air. Interestingly, at one stage the Republic P-47N Thunderbolt had been considered as an alternative to the Mustang by the Americans and thus *de facto* by the South Africans because of the reduced vulnerability of its air-cooled engine to damage by ground fire. The idea was dropped because of the lack of sufficient airframes.

Ground crew integration with the Americans was a feature later in the war but initially 2 Squadron ground crews were virtually on their own as far as looking after the Mustangs in the field was concerned because the other component squadrons of the 18th FBW were at full stretch looking after their own aircraft. That didn't mean that personnel in off duty moments didn't get along and, indeed, close friendships were often formed. Messes were shared, for example, and the Americans were frequent visitors to the South Africans' 'Rorke's Inn' bar at K10. For the record, as the war progressed and particularly as the squadrons re-equipped with the F-86, co-operation at all levels entered a new phase and a new doctrine was implemented.

David P Frizell recalls:

I served in the 18th in Korea from October 1953 until October 1954. I remember fondly my association with the members of 2 Squadron. I was the Group Armament Officer both at K46 and K55. At K55 I was in charge of the consolidated fire control system maintenance shop and was responsible for the systems on all aircraft including those of the SAAF. My senior NCO was a SAAF Flight Sergeant and one of my line chiefs was also from South Africa. I supervised about fifty people about a third of whom were SAAF. I interfaced daily with officers and enlisted personnel from 2 Squadron and they did me the honour of making me an Honorary Member of their Officers' Club....The Flying Cheetah pin which they gave me is still one of my favourite mementoes of my military career.

John's relationship with the Americans was in the main good (in some cases very good) and he made some good friends amongst them – Ed Rackham of the 67th FBS for example. His and John's paths were to cross again in the early 1960s in England as we will see. As for other Allied troops, the South Africans used to see

Australians occasionally and the 8th King's Royal Irish Hussars, who were based not far from K16, were occasional visitors.

Once the newly arrived batch of pilots had converted to the Mustang they were flown in to K10 on a C-47 (each combat wing in Korea had is own C-47 assigned for the movement of personnel and equipment and the 18th FBW was no exception, the natural metal finish of theirs sporting a huge unit badge on the nose). Here there was a single PSP runway, the southern end of which dropped away to the sea and the northern end of which ran into paddy fields leading to 1,200 foot hills a couple of miles on. Fortunately there was a pass through which pilots could creep if there was cloud across the tops. Air Traffic Control was pretty good. Operations were directed from huts and recreation was undertaken in huts. All personnel, ground and aircrew alike, lived and slept in huts with beds in two long lines, each with a small cabinet for personal belongings. Showers were in a long line too in a separate building, as were the loos, which lay over a gutter that was flushed with water constantly. In hot weather it was all pretty foul and whilst John was at K10 it was very, very hot (in winter it could be very, very cold). It was the smell of the place that became John's most vivid memory for the surrounding fields were manured by animal and human waste. He remembers that when he flew from Japan to Korea for the first time he quickly became aware that he could smell Korea at 2,000 feet! It wasn't very pleasant to start with but as with all these things after a while everyone got used to it as they did the living and operating conditions.

The situation on the ground in Korea when John arrived in the increasingly fluid war was, as already described, that UN forces were once again in possession of all South Korean territory. The possibility of cease-fire talks was being aired (throughout the war such possibilities were constantly being aired) and indeed these began, but it was all rather short lived as the Chinese Air Force launched a new offensive. The UN response was to bomb North Korean airfields and make them unusable. This, however, became a costly business in terms of men and machines as airfield defences improved. The UN also struck at the North Korean transport infrastructure. Bridges, tunnels, railway lines and yards and roads under the code name Operation *Strangle* became the priority targets. Such attacks by both sides continued as the peace talks stalled and then ceased.

The operations in which 2 Squadron was involved were aimed at isolating the battlefield north of the bomb line. This was a line drawn on the map a mile or so beyond UN troops and beyond which UN forces could attack unbriefed. Missions were either reconnaissance of main supply routes or attacks on bridges, tunnels, dockyards, marshalling yards, factories, airfields, tanks, gun emplacements and infantry or roads and mountain passes (to block them). On a close support mission crews flew straight to the briefed area and reported to local controllers who transferred them to a Forward Air Controller (FAC) who in turn directed their strike onto enemy forces, be it troops, gun emplacement or bunkers. The Mustangs carried mixed weaponry so that in the case of bunkers, for example, the first two aircraft of a Flight would have 500-pounders with an eight- to ten-second delay fuse, which would be thumped into them and would hopefully blow the tops off. The next two aircraft would go in with drop tanks full of liquid napalm. Napalm was a particularly horrible weapon, which when it hit the ground burst into flames over a wide area killing and destroying men and equipment. Mustangs of all squadrons expended a huge number of tanks during the war, the preparing and filling of which was a messy and time-consuming process, which involved large numbers of civilian workers. Individual aircraft carried mixed weaponry with six .50 calibre guns, six 120-pound warhead rockets and either two napalm or two 500-pounders – or if it was a long-range sortie, drop tanks.

John recalls:

> Napalm is not very nice – but then again however you are killed it's not very nice. Looking back on it the whole bombing thing was horrendous. We would attack anything, absolutely anything, that moved beyond the bomb line – horses, oxen, cattle, farmers, tractors, individuals. It became so effective that nothing moved during the day, which meant we had established complete air superiority. What the North Koreans and Chinese did then was to travel at night. They would arrive at a village and conceal the trucks in and around that village. Sometimes they would knock the wall of a building out, drive vehicles in and hang camouflage netting down. When we found this out we would fly low – and I mean low, twenty feet or so – down the main road of a village looking into buildings. From the slightest glint you would know there was something there.

On John's first few sorties he was so busy concentrating on not losing formation that he fired where the leader fired, dropped bombs where he did and rocketed where he did. After half a dozen sorties he began to keep the big picture in mind, seeing where all the other aircraft were and picking out his own targets on the ground. He soon learned the different techniques for delivering his ordnance. Dive bombing, for example, could either be high-angle (sixty degrees) for 500-pounders with a barometric fuse or fifteen to twenty degrees with a delayed action fuse. The former would be used on flak-busting missions with the Mustang pushed into a steep dive, only pulling out as the bombs exploded a couple of hundred feet above ground, thereby ensuring a wider spread of destruction from the resultant blast. In the latter case pilots flew at the target until it seemed they were about to hit it with their aircraft, dropped their bombs and pulled away: in other words they virtually flew the weapon into the target. An eight- to ten-second delay doesn't sound a great deal but a Mustang travelling low and fast could be a long way away from the blast when the bombs went off. For steep-angle dive bombing and gunnery attack pilots used the fixed cross of the K-14B gyro-computing gunsight plus a bit of lay off, for rocket attack the six o' clock diamond at the bottom of the sight, for shallow dive bombing attack the nose of the aircraft. For napalm '… we used to say to the new guys coming in you don't drop the tanks, you scrape them off. In other words drop them at the lowest possible level.'

The enemy's air force was based in China, north of the Yalu River, and comprised Chinese, Soviet and North Korean equipment. Over the course of the conflict MiG-15s, Yak-9s, Yak-17s, Lavochkin La-9s, Ilyushin Il-10s, Yak-18s and ancient Polikarpov Po-2s were recorded. The MiG-15s were the commonest and most effective type at high altitude where they operated and where USAF (and towards the end of the war SAAF) F-86s engaged them. Every now and again a few would get through but generally there was not much opposition in the air as far as the fighter bombers were concerned and 2 Squadron rarely saw anything of them other than high above.

The main problems for the Mustang were the defending guns, which ranged from radar-controlled high-calibre flak to machine-guns. Many pilots were lost through flak and during the summer of 1951 whilst John was in Korea there were times when 2 Squadron was hard pressed to put eight aircraft up. The biggest problem with the Mustang was that it was liquid cooled and the radiator was underneath the aircraft behind the cockpit. Consequently there was a lot of vulnerable piping between the radiator and the engine. There were instances of pilots being blown out of the sky thanks to a direct hit by heavy flak but most came down through engine failure because the cooling system had been ruptured by smaller calibre weapons.

John recalls:

After a successful attack on a lovely day I remember a big white building on the side of a hill. I was leading and decided that the Flight should rocket it. I became so interested in it I got too close and flew through my explosion. The aircraft was peppered but fortunately the glycol lines weren't hit. This was the vulnerable part of the Mustang – the radiator was behind, the engine in front and in between were all vulnerable lines carrying coolant. A major cause of losses.

The cooling system had been the Mustang's Achilles' heel during the Second World War as well. And such were the losses sustained at low level in Korea that eventually the order went out that en route to targets medium level altitudes should be adopted.

Weather was a very real factor in Korea. It was certainly a country of extremes with bakingly hot summers and achingly cold winters. Cloud was a common limiting factor on operations. If there was a reasonable cloud base aircraft could fly up valleys under the cloud but if it became too bad they would have to pull up. Occasionally they would let down if there was a gap in the clouds to get to the target, otherwise it would be abandoned and ordnance taken to a known enemy area and dumped before returning to base.

Pilots new to Korea were on a very fast learning curve. For John, from his first flight in a DH82 to his first sortie in the theatre of war was thirteen months and from weapons training to attacking real targets barely two months. Low-level flying, delivery techniques, breaking away and rolling the aircraft to avoid ground fire were all learned in the heat of battle and John found that much of what he did was intuitive. He would of course be concentrating and thinking but that would generally be about the overall situation in which he found himself, not specifically about flying and operating his aircraft. He was reacting naturally to the Mustang. As an example, John recalls an occasion when his Flight was attacking troops, flying in a very tight circle so that as number one pulled out number two started firing and as number two pulled out number three started firing... and so on. Consequently there was a constant barrage of fire. John, however, was a little too far behind his colleagues so he cut corners, which meant that his speed going into the attack wasn't as high as it should have been. As he pulled out he stalled but instead of hitting the ground he disappeared into a quarry and was able to recover, an immediate and instinctive reaction to an unexpected situation. Riding one's luck in that way happened quite often.

CHAPTER FIVE

John's War

John was somebody who was always willing to take a risk without being reckless, coupled with the skill to carry it off. It is a fairly rare combination.

Eric Keevy

When John arrived in Korea in late May 1951 an intensive interdiction campaign had been launched against communist transport between the 38th Parallel and the front line. The western sector was allotted to the 18th FBW and aircraft of its component squadrons bombed roads and railway lines in areas where repairs would be difficult to carry out. For 2 Squadron this meant anywhere from two to six missions a day against routes between Kaesong and Sariwon. John's comprehensively kept log books (direct quotes from which are shown in italics) tell an intriguing story of a young man thrust into this war and through their pages we can see something of the excitement that he experienced. At other times it was all very routine.

1 June 1951 et seq.
John's first solo on the Mustang and subsequent familiarisation including aerobatics, spins, dummy attacks, napalm, rocket and gunnery.

5 June
A south of the bomb line tour, which was essential for orientation purposes.

6 June
0740 – K10 to K16 with recce and road cut south of Saigongni. Rocketed and strafed village.
1900 – road cut and recce. Rocketed and strafed village causing fair amount of damage.

These were John's first missions in anger and he recalls the surprise of meeting war head on for the first time.

> Can you imagine the damage done? But we quickly learned to be dispassionate and to remember that what we were doing was in part in

retribution for what the North Koreans were doing to UN troops and airmen. Generally it didn't bother me. If it had I wouldn't have been able to do my job. It was a cruel and bloody war.

He had quickly been introduced to the fact that he was going to be killing a lot of people.

Only once was I bothered by this. Intelligence knew there was a big convoy in this particular Korean village and to catch them we took off before it got light one morning. The village had one main road through it. Two of us napalmed one side of the road, two the other. We came round and then machine-gunned everybody who was in the street. I also remember we were napalming a bunch of Chinese in a depression on top of a hill. I was number three or four in the Flight. Those in front of me had dropped their napalm – as I was coming through this Chinese guy came running up over the top of the ridge straight into my napalm....

It was also John's first experience of how the airfields at K10 and K16 were most often used. You would take off fully armed from K10, attack the target then land at K16. You would then operate from there for three days or so then at the end of the last sortie return to K10 for aircraft maintenance and to give pilots a rest for a couple of days before deploying again.

At K16 if you were carrying a heavy load and it was hot with no wind, quite often you hit the ground again after you left the runway, so you made sure you didn't pull the wheels up too early! At one end you had to climb over a bridge and at the other you had to ease away from tall factory chimneys.

K16, incidentally, became Seoul City Airport after the war.

7 June
0645 – very low cloud. Found a village through a gap. Burnt it out with napalm and strafing then rocketed and strafed targets further north. Twelve houses destroyed.

At midday John returned to K10, diverting *en route* to drop napalm and give close support to ground troops. How were such targets selected?

At the briefing you would be told the weather, the situation as far as the war was concerned, where your targets were, the weapons you were going to deliver. For example, marshalling yards we bombed and rocketed. Tanks we napalmed. Convoys we rocketed, napalmed and machine-gunned. Having been told the target area our Flight Leader would decide the route to take. As the bomb line was crossed he checked in with a controller at an American HQ and told them our own call sign (*Dutch Boy* followed by a colour for the Flight and, if down to individual aircraft, a number), the

38

number of aircraft involved and where we had been briefed to go. We would then be given a specific target to attack and an area to recce, the latter usually along main supply routes. The fact we were the enemy side of the bomb line made anything a legitimate target.

John spent the next few days at K10 resting, air testing and continuing with familiarisation.

15 June
Rail interdiction Pyongyang area [the North Korean capital]. Cut railroad completely in two places. Rocketed buildings off a sideline. Weather hampered recce.

As *South Africa's Flying Cheetahs in Korea* states:

> The Flying Cheetahs experienced their first summer monsoon during June and July when south easterly winds blew in moist air and even when rain was not falling the overcast weather often made it difficult for leaders to locate their targets. On six days during these months the weather created impossible flying conditions. It also influenced the type of mission flown and when low cloud over North Korea made interdiction targets inaccessible fighter bombers were directed to close support targets identified by Mosquito controllers.

Mosquito controllers were Forward Air Controllers in Harvards and their story, so vital to the success of ground attack in Korea, is worth briefly recounting here, particularly as John would later be directly involved. Peter Smith, in his book *North American T6,* recalls how in the early stages of the war it became obvious that better use could be made of Allied tactical air power but there were three issues that needed to be resolved: first, the lack of accurate information about where troops, both friendly and enemy, were positioned; second, the length of time it took to organise air strikes once a target had been identified; and third, the poor utilisation of aircraft particularly in bad weather when targets could not be found. It was therefore suggested that the stable, slow-flying Harvard with its excellent visibility be used for tactical reconnaissance and tactical control for all friendly air forces, a role that had thus far been undertaken in a limited way by rather vulnerable Stinson L-5s. The first Harvard FAC mission was flown in July 1950.

> The first sorties were flown with no prior briefing as to the latest position of friendly or enemy units, no operational procedures and no defined mission requirements. Nevertheless the basic rationale of the force was there, to fly over the fluid front line, find the enemy, pinpoint his location and direct friendly fighter-bomber strikes against him to try and halt his advance.

Fifth Air Force HQ designated the T-6's missions for 15 July 1950 as *Mosquito Able* through to *Mosquito How* to cover different areas on the ground. The name

Mosquito stuck and very soon the T-6 squadron became unofficially known as the Mosquito Squadron and T-6 controllers and members of the 6147th Tactical Air Control Squadron under whose auspices the T-6s operated simply as Mosquitoes. Very soon the accuracy and precision with which T-6s pinpointed targets became their hallmark – the norm was within one hundred yards. And soon, too, the Mosquito Squadron became an international squadron with mainly American pilots but Canadian, Australian and South African observers.

On the night of 15/16 June K16 was attacked by a Polikarpov Po-2 biplane known to all as *Bedcheck Charlie*, which flew over the airfield with the crew of two tossing grenades over the cockpit sides. This happened on a fairly regular basis and was classed as a nuisance raid, which meant most residents of K16 kept their heads down whilst the Polikarpov was overhead. *Bedcheck Charlie* thereby caused some disruption. Very occasionally there was insurgency of another kind involving snipers. And rather more insidiously there were sometimes spies in the camp. John had returned to K16 on one occasion to find his Korean batman had gone, only to find out he had been been shot as a spy in his absence. It was summary justice.

16 June
0740 – helicopter escort to Sariwon. Attempted rescue of Scottie. Low cloud. One road cut.

Scottie was an American friend who was flying with the South Africans. A very high priority was placed on search and rescue (SAR). Each time a pilot took off on a mission he had a map on which the areas of operation of SAR helicopters were marked. If he was shot up over the frontline he would head, if he could, for one of those areas and he would be capped by his fellow Flight members, which meant they would circle overhead, if necessary keeping approaching enemy troops at bay with machine-gun fire. It didn't matter what the opposition on the ground might be, if he was seen to be alive the rescue helos would get the pilot out, or attempt to get him out, no matter what losses might be incurred in the process. This was of course a tremendous morale booster. On this particular day though Scottie sadly wasn't to be seen.

A further mission on the same day to Sinwonni resulted in a 'large building' being destroyed. A rocket attack damaged trucks. Light flak was encountered. After this John returned to K10 and on this occasion it wasn't until 23 June that he returned to the frontline.

23 June
Gus Marshall led the Flight, which was briefed to bomb a tunnel at Kumchon. With him were Larry Eager who cut the railroad and Jessie Verster and John who successfully hit the tunnel. John vividly recalls the almost surreal experience of his delayed action bomb disappearing into the mouth of the tunnel and then seeing

it emerge from the other end and exploding as he flew over! Once done the Flight recced the area to the west, which they rocketed and strafed when they found camouflaged buildings.

John recalls Gus Marshall as being a very religious man, so much so that he increasingly found what they were doing in Korea difficult to reconcile with his faith. At end of his tour he went back to South Africa to instruct but then left the air force, joined the church and went as a missionary into Central Africa. John's attitude to such matters was a rather more prosaic and common one.

> If ever you look down the muzzle of an enemy's loaded gun with him trying to kill you, you come to believe very quickly that there must be someone out there you can call on! My mother was very devout. At school I was a regular church attendee but after leaving school I stopped going. It was only when people started trying to kill me I thought about it a lot more.

2 Squadron had some very supportive and approachable padres with it in Korea and during John's time Major Cloete held the position.

> He was fantastic. He used to stand next to the runway to see the Mustangs off. A great help, a very visible presence, a great comforter of men in distress especially when friends had been lost.

24 June
The squadron's attention turned from tunnels to airfields. John's Flight had been pre-briefed to dive bomb the airfield at Anak but he had to abort as the temperature went off the clock in his Mustang immediately after take-off. Within a couple of hours he was airborne again, this time to attack the airfield at Haeju. Such targets were relatively rare but the enemy sometimes used them for the dispersal of tanks and equipment. The sortie was a success with eight direct hits on the runway thereby rendering it unserviceable and unusable. The adjacent railway siding was also rocketed and strafed and the line cut in two places.

The third sortie of the day was briefed as an interdiction north-east of Kaesong but the Flight, with Gus Marshall as leader, was diverted to Jefferson 6 (a controller's call sign) as soon as it became airborne. UN troops on the ground were facing a tremendous onslaught and there was a lot of fighting. Gus was told to attack enemy troop concentrations that were in a practically inaccessible location with the surrounding terrain defended by numerous enemy automatic weapons and heavy anti-aircraft guns. Without hesitation Gus, Jessie Verster, Larry Eager and John flew through this screen of intense and accurate enemy fire to deliver repeated attacks on the target. A 40-mm gun position was destroyed, another damaged and an unknown number of enemy troops killed, although later the South Africans heard it had been two hundred.

We found the enemy along a ridge and we had napalm. The first thing we did was to cover the ridge with it and that took care of the troops. We then went round and loosed off our rockets at the artillery. The flak was very intense.

Something of an understatement! In fact, the flak was so intense that a USAF Flight was placed on standby to cover a rescue operation in the expectation of casualties and both John and Jessie Verster actually voiced their surprise afterwards that they had survived. An American Marine subsequently wrote:

I'll forever recall with minute detail the most spectacular feat I've ever lived to witness and tell about. We had gained the ridgeline of our objective upon which we were catching all hell because of an overwhelming gook [American slang for the enemy] counter attack. The tide of battle was leaving casualties in its wake like seashells cast upon a beach. It was then we saw four silvery streaks plummet from the skies with guns blazing. It was so wondrous a sight we completely forgot our whereabouts and just stood up in our foxholes and cheered. The Hall of Fame does not possess any greater men than those who flew that day.

What the four South African airmen had achieved was recognised by the awarding of medals. Gus Marshall got the DFC and John, Larry and Jessie received Air Medals. Normally these were given after the completion of thirty sorties but the bravery shown by the young South Africans prompted an earlier award. John had completed just ten. He went on to win two further Air Medals and a DFC in Korea. The citation that went with this one read:

While flying as wingman to the Flight Leader in a Flight of four F-51 Mustangs north west of Kaesong, Lieut. Howe made successive hazardous attacks with relentless accuracy on a concentration of enemy troops in a most difficult terrain defended by numerous automatic weapons and anti-aircraft guns. By his intrepid aggressiveness and aeronautical skill he destroyed one 40 millimetre gun position, two automatic weapons positions, many enemy troops and damaged one 40 millimetre position.

25 June
0640 – bombed, rocketed and strafed the airfield at Onjongni. Six direct hits on the runway and damaged several surrounding buildings.
0930 – bombed runway at Haeju with good results. Eight direct hits. Recced area south of Sinwonni and damaged two boxcars.

After Haeju John returned to K10 and on the following day completed an air test. Such tests were usually done at K16 following maintenance (aircraft were sent there for attention as well as the pilots), although sometimes such tests would be at K10 if repairs had to be completed there.

27 June

2 Squadron was tasked to provide cover to the 24th Infantry Division as it thrust forward from the UN front line.

South Africa's Flying Cheetahs in Korea states:

> Continuous cover was given to the Division by Flights armed with napalm and rockets flying over the advancing columns in relays. Seven missions each lasting about two hours were flown, when pilots kept dislodging communist troops from commanding ridges and silencing hostile artillery batteries.

1830 – directed to Pistol Able for close support of 24 Division. Controller reported area well covered with eighty casualties. At least thirty enemy troops killed. Moderate flak.

On a close support mission controllers on the ground using binoculars could see and make assessments of damage done and numbers killed. Attacking pilots would be given this information when they returned to base. Occasionally it would be radioed to them whilst they were still airborne. Coverage of an area related to how much of an area a controller could see and had been hit during the attack by aircraft he had called in.

28 June

John was with an eight-ship mission that attacked a road and rail bridge north of Chinamro but on this occasion none of the aircraft hit the target. Bridges, because of where they were often positioned, over a river gorge for example, could be the most difficult of targets. John's second sortie of the day was aborted when his radio failed. A third mission was more successful as a road south of Hwangu was cut and the adjacent railway line was damaged in four places with rockets. The attack was not unopposed with flak from heavy and automatic weapons being thrown up as the Mustangs roared in.

29 June

The first sortie was a road interdiction mission between Hwangu and Sariwon. Two complete road cuts were made by the Flight. A flak gun was destroyed and four damaged and the crews killed.

John recalls:

> This was quite a fight. In other words they were shooting at us, we were shooting at them. I remember that afterwards we found and killed three pack animals and destroyed a cart, another instance of anything that moved being a legitimate target as far as we were concerned.

A second sortie resulted in another partial road cut and a complete cut on a double track railroad despite low cloud hampering bombing accuracy. Eric Keevy was hit but the Flight returned to K16 without getting the battery of four guns responsible. John's and Eric's careers paralleled each other during the early years through college, training and Korea. Eric, ever the modest man, plays down his involvement in the latter.

> I have my own recollections but to be honest I feel they are fairly routine if setting off in an aeroplane with the knowledge that at some stage a number of people will be trying to shoot you down can be categorised as routine! Good luck or good fortune plays its part and in many ways I remember what did not happen but could have as opposed to what actually did. When I look at what befell many of my friends I have to say I was extremely lucky.

1 July
1640 – attacked small caves on the side of a hill but could not observe any material results. Claimed unknown number of enemy troops killed.

Caves were used to store supplies and hide troops. On sorties to attack them 500-pounders with fifteen-second delayed action fuses were carried and the idea was to lob them into the mouth of the cave. The bombs were scraped off as close as possible to their intended target. The method of attack was chosen according to the cave's position. This dictated which dive bombing angle and what pull out height was adopted, the latter depending on the fuse setting.

On the same day that John and Eric Keevy *et al* were attacking the caves the recently decorated Jessie Verster was killed when ferrying a Mustang from K10 to K16. This was an instance where the belief that luck and circumstance play a big part in survival in theatres of war is substantiated. John recalls:

> A Mustang was scheduled for an air test and I was scheduled to be the pilot that did it. At the same time a Flight of four, including Jessie Verster and led by Larry Eager, was scheduled to take off from K10, do a sortie and land at K16. I wanted to get missions in whilst Jessie already had quite a few under his belt so I asked him whether I could do the mission and he do the air test. He agreed so we went to Larry to ask his permission and he also agreed. We duly set off on our sortie. Jessie left later. He never arrived. His body and the remains of the aircraft were found and the accident attributed to engine failure. An eyewitness stated that he had been thrown clear on impact. There was some talk that he had attempted to bail out but because of his height (he was a tall fellow) had become stuck in the cockpit. I don't know if this was true but what is certain is that but for my whim it would have been my engine failure. Whether I would have got out of the aircraft is anyone's guess.

Jessie was something of a gentle giant, very quiet and thoroughly pleasant. Ironically he was also a heavyweight boxing champion. He, Eric and John were all cadets together and in Korea they were often on the same Flight. The death of a colleague was always very hard to bear and looking back John feels that his having got away with so many things puts his own survival even more sharply into perspective.

2 July
0745 – interdiction of road in the Suan area. Obtained one road cut and one bridge damaged. During recce found two trucks and destroyed them. Encountered accurate automatic weapons fire. Destroyed two guns and killed the crews. I got my first hit.

On reflection it is quite remarkable that John had been on operations for almost a month and hitherto had not suffered aircraft damage from enemy fire. His F-51 having been patched up in the field – proper repairs would be completed back at K10 – John took off three hours later on his second sortie of the day as part of an eight-ship mission with an American Flight. This mission was to attack a rail bridge north-east of Pyongyang but it proved to be too narrow and curved for dive bombing and it escaped damage. If a bridge target proved to be difficult an attempt was often made to blow the ends off it instead of cutting it centrally – but even that failed in this instance.

3 July
Three close support sorties constituted a very busy day. On the first the South Africans napalmed, rocketed and strafed enemy positions on a hill and in the surrounding area. Seven troops were confirmed as killed but many more were expected to have been. The second sortie was a repeat with again an unknown number of troops killed. Flight Commander Larry Eager's radio failed so John took over as leader of the Flight, the first time he had done so. The third sortie of the day was again close support with three camouflaged positions and two artillery guns destroyed, three guns damaged and an unknown number of troops killed. This was the first mission assigned to John as Flight Leader from the outset. Once again one has to marvel at the steep learning curve he had climbed – a twenty-one-year-old with just a month's operations under his belt and he was entrusted with such a responsibility. But such are the exigencies of war. In this instance it came about because of the high loss rate amongst Flight Commanders and experienced replacements had yet to arrive. In some cases when they finally did arrive they proved not to have been fighter pilots at all or indeed if they had, they may not have flown for a while, finding themselves in Korea having volunteered when on a ground job.

At the conclusion of this third sortie John returned to K10 for a day's rest.

5 July

Back again at K16 John flew on an interdiction on the Suan to Koksan road, which led to two direct hits on a bridge and a partial road cut. He records that he found an ox cart and killed a North Korean and two oxen, damaging the cart in the process. Such things were legitimate targets because they could be used for carrying anything from human excrement for spreading on the fields to supplies for North Korean troops.

6 July

Attention turned to an enemy bunker containing an artillery field piece, which was hit with two 500-pounders. The bunker was destroyed, a gun damaged and an unknown number of troops killed. A second mission led to the napalming, rocketing and strafing of an enemy strong point, although the results were unobserved and unreported. John led a third mission on the day, in which an enemy position on a hill was attacked and once again an unknown number of troops were killed.

7 July

0555 – interdiction on an airfield at Ongjin. Obtained twelve direct hits on runway. Useless target.

John often referred to airfields as 'useless' targets. In other words they were routine and unopposed.

> Airfield attacks were so simple. You had an eight- to fifteen-second delay bomb, thumped them onto the runway and off you'd go. At this stage the Koreans had retreated northwards so the airfields were not defended but they were attacked to make sure they couldn't be used if the enemy took possession again.

The following day 2 Squadron first encountered the MiG-15. Ray Armstrong was leading a Flight of eight F-51s as part of a thirty-two-aircraft raid on the airfield at Kangdong. The South Africans went in last and after the attack an American voice called 'MiGs' over the radio. Ray saw them circling over the point where the Americans were reforming and they didn't seem to be paying any attention to the Flying Cheetahs until they set course for their secondary target. Then six Chinese dived to attack. The South Africans were prepared for them, however, and using tactics that they had discussed at length in the eventuality of meeting the jets they survived.

> As the first two jets closed in he [Ray Armstrong] turned his Flight towards them forcing the Chinese pilots to pull out of their dive without firing a shot. Further passes were thwarted as both Flights turned about continually crossing over each other so that one of them was always in a position to

meet an attack. As the Mustangs slowly lost height the communist pilots made five or six more unsuccessful passes, some so near the Flying Cheetahs pilots they could see their faces. The MiGs then broke away northwards. The entire engagement had lasted five minutes.

South Africa's Flying Cheetahs in Korea

Other than an occasional sighting of the Russian jets high above, John never encountered the MiG-15 himself. That was the preserve of the F-86 Sabre-equipped squadrons.

9 July
John flew on an interdiction mission to the airfield at Yongu, during which flak positions were attacked and destroyed to enable USAF Flights to go in and bomb. Today such an operation would be termed SEAD – the Suppression of Enemy Air Defences. The flak at Yongu was very intense and was only partially suppressed.

11 July
1840 – attacked the docks at Kyomipo. Low cloud hampered mission and the results couldn't be observed. Later informed that accuracy was not so hot.

12 July
1730 – low level bombing and destruction of a bridge. Recced and destroyed one building and damaged five. Flew through my rocket blast sustaining damage to wing and windscreen.

13 July
This was a three-sortie day, the first an interdiction of the Sonchon to Yangdok road and rail link, obtaining one cut of each in the face of automatic, 20-mm and 40-mm flak. The second sortie took John and his colleagues back to the same road, cutting it again and then strafing enemy troop positions. A third, late sortie at 2000 hours took the South Africans to the Pyongyang to Hwangu road, diverting *en route* to destroy three trucks. The road was completely cut. They also found a 20-mm gun, which was destroyed, and the crew killed with rockets and gunfire.

16 July
A twenty–four-ship mission to Kyomipo docks with the Americans. The attack caught the enemy by surprise and no flak was encountered.

17 July
John and his Flight successfully napalmed, strafed and rocketed enemy troops on a ridge. As they flew at low level from the target area grateful troops on British tanks of the Commonwealth Division waved at them. When he returned to base John was given a rollicking because he returned the waving instead of watching the tail of his

47

No. 1! On a second sortie they worked unsuccessfully with an FAC with only one ox cart destroyed, one road bridge damaged and supplies rocketed and strafed with negative results. John led the third sortie of the day, which was briefed as a further interdiction of the Sonchon to Yangdok road, although in the event low cloud prevented the attack. Secondary targets were found and trucks and camouflaged supplies rocketed, strafed and destroyed. Low cloud hampered the mission overall.

18 July
Napalmed, rocketed and strafed enemy troops on a ridge – good results obtained – ground controller gave the Flight 100% coverage. Sixty-seven enemy troops killed – have never seen so many dead people lying about.

Following this sortie John took five days' R&R at K10. If warm, there was a cove near Masan where crews would go and swim and relax. Pilots who had been fighting for longer periods were given a week's R&R in Japan and when this happened John and his friends would go up into the mountains where the Americans had a five-star equivalent hostelry. For a couple of dollars a day they could have a superb room in a lovely hotel in beautiful surroundings The pace at which life was led on the front line and the dangers pilots were readily subjected to was a physically and mentally draining experience. Adrenalin kept them going but they didn't realise how tired they were until they stopped.

23 July
John returned to K16 with practice gunnery at the Naktong range *en route* to check the harmonisation of recently realigned guns. Whilst he was doing this the Flying Cheetahs lost two more pilots.

The following description is given in *The South African Military History Society Journal*, Vol 4, No. 3:

> The weather was bad – solid overcast, with ceiling varying from 200 to 400 metres above ground level. After successfully attacking and destroying a bridge the Mustang piloted by Capt [Freddy] Bekker was hit by ground fire, burst into flames and crashed. A minute later 2nd Lt [Mike] Halley's aircraft was also hit and he bailed out successfully. While Lt [Roy] du Plooy remained over the area to provide cover for the downed pilot Lt Tony Green ascended to establish better contact with the rescue operation. Despite intensive ground fire Lt du Plooy prevented enemy troops from capturing 2nd Lt Halley until finally his ammunition was exhausted and the enemy closed in on the downed pilot. No further transmissions were heard from Lt du Plooy but Lt Green sighted the wreckage of another smouldering aircraft and subsequently he was presumed killed. He was posthumously awarded the American Silver Star for his bravery and

determination in attempting to protect a comrade from capture in the face of intensive and accurate enemy ground fire.

24 July

Jan Blaauw was promoted to Commandant and took over from Ray Armstrong as CO. John led an interdiction mission in the Yuli/ Suan area, which damaged a road bridge, cut the road, found and killed four troops, eight oxen and two horses, silenced a .50-cal gun position and damaged two revetments. An hour and a quarter later he led a second mission, working with Forward Air Controller Mosquito Pistol 6 who gave the Flight targets that were extremely difficult to get at on account of mountains. Nevertheless a supply dump was destroyed, five houses were damaged and another .50-cal gun was silenced.

26 July

1500 – I led this mission – USAF Major Deek took over after I had bailed out and he led the Flight on a successful mission – temperature off the clock – suspected gauge u/s [unserviceable] until coolant popped – was picked up by helicopter.

It was a support mission and one of those occasions when there weren't enough pilots and aircraft to put two Flights into the air, hence the presence of an American. As the eight aircraft were climbing away John noticed the temperature on his coolant gauge was giving a very high reading. He called in his No. 2 to have a look at his aircraft and see what the radiator flap position was. Mustang radiators had a flap, which, if open, meant the engine was hot. But it was closed on this occasion, which suggested all was as it should be and the gauge was unserviceable. But that wasn't so. At 10,000 feet John's engine blew and boiling glycol streamed into the cockpit, so he wisely jumped. His Mustang, serial 336, crashed into the side of a hill. Hearing explosions and the sound of gunfire John thought he was coming down over an infantry battle but he soon realised it was the ordnance of his aeroplane exploding in the fire. The rest of the Flight capped him until he was picked up after half an hour by a helicopter and taken back to K16.

On 1 August in East London, John's parents received a telegram.

IT IS CONFIRMED THAT THE FOLLOWING IS THE TEXT OF A MESSAGE RECEIVED FROM TOKYO STOP QUOTE WHILE LEADING A FOUR SHIP MISSION EN ROUTE TO AN ASSIGNED CLOSE SUPPORT TARGET ENGINE DEVELOPED APPARENT INTERNAL GLYCOL LEAK STOP GLYCOL STREAMED FROM ENGINE INTO COCKPIT FORCING 2/LT HOWE TO BAIL OUT STOP HE LANDED SUCCESSFULLY WAS PICKED UP BY HELICOPTER AND FLOWN TO K16 STOP UNQUOTE MESSAGE FURTHER STATES THAT 2/LT J F G HOWE IS NOT INJURED AND IS BACK WITH HIS UNIT.

Within an hour or so of returning to K16 John was in the cockpit again, this time to take another aircraft back to K10. At the end of the runway, whilst doing pre-take-off checks, he found the drop was very high on one magneto, which under normal circumstances meant that he should abort and get the problem checked out. On this occasion he was concerned that if he did that it would be thought that he was opting out. So, contrary to all the rules, he took off with an unserviceable aircraft. Talking about it now John simply puts that decision down to the idiocy of youth and a fear of losing face with colleagues. Fortunately he made it to K10 without incident.

29 July

After a few days' rest John was back at K16 on an interdiction of the Yuli to Singye road, which was partially cut with two bridges slightly damaged. The Flight then made a reconnaissance and found an automatic weapon position. They destroyed it together with an adjacent building. A second similar sortie led to the destruction of a bridge after low-level bombing followed by the destruction of a supply dump and damage to six vehicles and five buildings.

According to *South Africa's Flying Cheetahs in Korea*:

> The cumulative effect of the road interdiction programme was not satisfactory and pilots reported that the communists were losing no time in repairing damaged roads: in fact their ability to improvise with local materials and muster virtually unlimited labour both military and civilian enabled them to repair roads and bridges in a remarkable short time.

30 July

A new round of peace talks had started earlier in the month but as before combat continued whilst they were in progress. For South Korea and the UN the goal was to recapture all of what had previously been South Korea before any agreement was reached in order to avoid losing territory. Combat was also designed to persuade the North Koreans to be less intransigent at the negotiating table. A series of deep penetration raids had been launched to reinforce this objective and twelve 2 Squadron Mustangs under the leadership of Bob Rogers, alongside fifty-seven Americans of the 18th FBW, were involved in one such raid on 30 July when they napalmed an ammunition factory in central Pyongyang in the face of intense flak. John emerged with a hole in his propeller, which fortunately led to no problems on the way home. A second sortie to the same target under 8/8ths cloud prevented any aircraft from dropping ordnance and they all returned to K10 after jettisoning their loads.

It was now time for John, Bob Rogers and Dennis Earp to experience the fabled hospitality of the Americans in Japan. And experience it they did! When it came to returning to K10 they decided on a final drink or two before boarding their C-47 at

Tachikawa on 8 August. Too late they were told they wouldn't be travelling by transport aircraft but would be taking a Mustang apiece. Despite desperate attempts to sidestep this they were ordered to do so. So they did, with Bob Rogers leading but with little idea as to what course to set. They managed to hit the coast of Korea but it was a sobering lesson for all three. There was no more drinking and flying after that. John returned to collect a second 'new' aircraft for 2 Squadron three days later.

13 August
Prebriefed to bomb railway station at Hwangu – weather prevented us from getting through – one bridge partially destroyed and one damaged south of Sariwon.

The second sortie of the day involved a recce and interdiction in the Sibyonni area and a road bridge was damaged. Unusually, only one of the eight bombs dropped by the Flight went off.

14 August
This was a big day for the 18th FBW as they contributed towards a sixty-four-aircraft attack on strategic targets in Pyongyang. Seventeen of these aircraft were from 2 Squadron, led by Jan Blaauw. Because K16 was flooded (the Han River had burst its banks), the raids had to be flown from K10, which meant a flight of almost twice the distance and a total sortie duration in excess of three and a half hours. 2 Squadron's target was a cluster of warehouses, which they covered thoroughly with napalm. Anti-aircraft fire was not particularly heavy on this occasion. A second sortie a few hours later was another sixty-four aircraft affair. There were just eight this time from 2 Squadron, again led by Jan Blaauw, and the sortie was carried out under a certain apprehension because of the fear of repeat missions in a short space of time. No pilot was ever particularly keen on revisiting the same target in quick succession for if defences had not been ready for them the first time they were invariably on the alert for a second raid. The target for the South Africans was again a cluster of warehouses. The damage they did to these was not observed but not unexpectedly the flak was very intense. Two flak positions were strafed and a blockhouse building exploded when it was hit. Several fishing boats and their crews were destroyed on the river. A high price was paid in losses. The USAF had six F-51s shot down (as well as seven B-26s). The Flying Cheetahs lost Ian de Jongh, a talented athlete. The squadron flew a record thirty-five sorties on the day.

John recounts:

> I recall that the peace talks were about to start and the strategy was to bomb the enemy to the peace table and the decision was made to attack the North Korea capital Pyongyang. The Wing sent off sixty-four aeroplanes in formation in the morning – indeed I think every Wing in the FEAF did that.

51

We were briefed to fly this particular route and when we got near to Pyongyang we were to let down and fly in at low level. We were dropping napalm and as we flew over at telegraph pole level we could see the muzzle covers still on the anti-aircraft guns as we had caught them completely by surprise. In the afternoon it was a repeat exercise – the same route, same turning points, but different targets. This time they were waiting for us…A few days later a further identical mission was planned on which I didn't fly. Then the guys began to get *really* anxious. But in all the time I was in Korea and all the chaps I flew with, whilst I occasionally saw apprehension and anxiousness, I saw no cowardice.

The main attention turned from the roads to railways as the bulk of supplies was now coming from China by that means. By the end of the month the communists were for once struggling to keep the rail system working, despite attacks being compromised by a period of bad weather.

15 August

Once the flooding at K16 had subsided the squadron returned *en masse* from K10, which was itself now threatened by a typhoon. John with his Flight was prebriefed to napalm the marshalling yards at Chongju but the weather prevented them from reaching the target. As an alternative they bombed Yonan and destroyed ten houses.

16 August

The bad weather continued – it was very, very wet. The prebrief was to liaise with FACs on close support work but the weather put paid to that. Once again an alternative target was sought and a suspected supply dump was napalmed, albeit unsuccessfully.

17 August

Again the weather was too bad to get through to the prebriefed area so as an alternative a village south of Wonsan was napalmed and six houses destroyed. A camouflaged supply dump was rocketed, although the results of this were not clear despite seeing an explosion. A three hour ten minute sortie meant John and his colleagues had to land at Pohang to refuel before returning to K10.

19 August

An interdiction with bombs and rockets on the Chongju railway yards resulted in extensive damage. This was a forty-ship mission supported by high-level cover from F-86s, F-80s and Meteors, necessary because the target was well within the range of fighters in China. A second mission found and attacked with napalm, rockets and guns enemy troops who had dug themselves in. The South Africans' controller counted seven troops dead and two positions destroyed: John's aircraft was hit once. A third sortie targeted supplies found in a wood. These were heavily defended by flak but the attack went ahead using napalm. A bridge and four houses were also hit by rocket fire. One of John's Flight, John de Wet, was hit and escorted home whilst 'Horse' Sivertsen and John continued the attack and destroyed five of the surrounding gun positions with fifty-five troops killed. John's aircraft was hit four times but he made it back to K16 safely. He had in fact run out of ammunition during the attacks but had elected to stay in the vicinity and draw enemy fire so that Horse could see exactly where the guns were.

20 August

The rail system featured again when an interdiction on Kunuri resulted in three complete rail cuts despite heavy flak of medium accuracy. An attempted second sortie to the same target area was foiled by encroaching bad weather so the marshalling yards at Hwangu were attacked as an alternative. Once again the Flying Cheetahs succeeded with three rail cuts and five wagons destroyed or damaged.

21 August

Bad weather once more prevented the planned interdiction at Anju so the Flight was diverted to Chaeryong and a rail bridge was destroyed.

22 August

Further rail attacks at Sinanju (two complete cuts) and Chaeryong again (three rail cuts with rockets, four box cars damaged, one flak gun destroyed and a soldier killed) concluded a busy month for John who now had three weeks of air testing, training of newly arrived aircrew and some R&R back at K10.

The intensity and pace of operations is all too evident from the above. There were not just single daily sorties but often three, some of several hours' duration and all accompanied by the ever present dangers of flak and ground fire, bad weather and terrain. 2 Squadron operated at low level and crews developed an uncanny ability, a sixth sense almost, of recognising areas of particular danger and how to best avoid them. Screaming down village streets at house top height was in itself often a defence, although certainly not an infallible one, against guns that were unable to track them because of their speed and altitude. More dangerous in many ways were the heavily defended industrial sites and transport hubs such as marshalling yards, which the enemy knew would always be at risk of interdiction.

John returned to the fray toward the end of September with a total of fifty-nine operational sorties under his belt and just sixteen to go until the end of his tour, not that he was in any hurry to get away from Korea!

21 September

1620 – prebriefed strike at Haeju. Attacked underground locomotive shop. Bombs missed but obtained direct hits with rockets causing severe damage.

22 September

This was a four-mission day, the first (at 0955) being close support. Enemy positions were napalmed, rocketed and strafed and an unknown number of enemy troops killed and three tanks destroyed. On the second mission (1300) John attacked a further three tanks with napalm then hit eight rail wagons and a building with rockets. An FAC sent the squadron to attack two hundred troops on a ridge on the third sortie (1530). This was not easy to do as it necessitated, in effect, flying up a slope. Nevertheless their controller reported 60 per cent coverage, although he gave no numbers of troops killed. The final attack of the day (1720) was also on troops, again on a ridge.

Dog Flight joined in the attack and between us we clobbered the hill good and solid. Little flak encountered.

23 September

1005 – weather bad. Bombed railroad and then rocketed rolling stock but could not assess damage because of low cloud.

John returned to K10. Shortly afterwards the R&R detachment was moved to K46 at Hoengsong so that rebuilding works could be carried out at K10, but with John now being so close to the end of his tour he wouldn't be involved.

25 September

When John arrived back at K16 it proved to be on the day that 2 Squadron flew forty sorties, the highest number since its arrival in Korea. Greater demands than ever were made on air and ground crews. John's part in this was a rail cut at Hwangu and an armed reconnaissance of the main supply route from Yuli to Sibyonni when he rocketed a bridge and damaged it and then found a camouflaged vehicle and destroyed it with his guns. It wasn't all plain sailing though for there was intense 40-mm flak near Singye. He avoided being hit.

26 September

This day was the anniversary of 2 Squadron's departure for Korea from South Africa. In its first year it had flown 4,920 sorties, had lost thirty-six of its sixty-one aircraft and had destroyed over 2,000 buildings, 458 vehicles, fourteen tanks, thirteen bridges and killed over 1,600 enemy troops. It was also the day that Commandant Barry Wiggett, John's old CO at Langebaanweg, took command of 2 Squadron.

John flew three sorties.

0900 – napalmed, rocketed and strafed enemy troops on a ridge obtaining excellent results – 100% coverage and unknown numbers of enemy troops killed. I got hit twice by ground fire.

This was John's thirteenth from last sortie during which ground fire hit his windscreen, but because of the angle of trajectory the bullet had ricocheted off instead of coming though to the cockpit and possibly injuring, perhaps killing, him. It was also on this sortie that one of the napalm tanks didn't release. This caused John to roll suddenly and inadvertently. Because he was attacking a ridge John was relieved to find he had sufficient height in which to recover. If it had been an attack on flat ground he wouldn't have been so lucky.

1145 – napalmed, rocketed and strafed enemy bunkers and gun positions getting 95% coverage on targets – possibly destroyed three gun emplacements – destroyed two guns and destroyed seven bunkers.

1515 – napalmed, rocketed and strafed enemy in dug in positions on a ridge – 80% coverage and unknown number of troops killed. This controller was useless.

27 September

A further interdiction at Hwangu resulted in one complete rail cut before going on to recce the area where his colleague Dennis Earp had gone down on his sixty-sixth sortie after his cooling system had been damaged. There was flak at Dennis's co-ordinates and John destroyed a gun and killed a 'gook' but for his pains was hit by 40-mm fire and was forced to retire to K16. 2nd Lieutenant – later Lieutenant General and Chief of Staff of the South African Air Force – Earp had been forced to bail out behind enemy lines north-east of Kaesong. He had drawn small arms fire as he descended but was not hit.

South Africa's Flying Cheetahs in Korea gives the following description:

> His Flight began to circle the area and it was joined by a Flight from the 39th FBS. But these aircraft could not see communist soldiers closing in on Dennis who was very much aware of his predicament. He was in the path of a Chinese search party spread out in three lines searching the undergrowth. They had camouflaged themselves with branches and moved only when the aircraft were out of sight. Dennis hid in a ditch and avoided discovery by all three lines of searchers as they passed by. He decided that his best course of action would be to follow the search party and as he was on the point of leaving the shelter of the ditch to do so a single soldier stumbled upon him.

Dennis was captured and spent almost two years as a POW. *South Africa's Flying Cheetahs in Korea* continues:

> One of the worst experiences of the South African prisoners was the death march from Kangdong to Pyoktong on the Yalu River. Dennis Earp set out on this journey on 14th November with forty-one other prisoners. The relentless pace of the march, general weakness, dysentery and ill treatment

by the guards and passing civilians all took their toll. Some of the UN prisoners died on the twelve day march and some of the survivors arrived in Pyoktong in a serious condition...the support given by Dennis to his comrades on that terrible journey strengthened them both morally and physically and enabled them to withstand the harsh conditions.

John remembers the day of Dennis's capture vividly.

He was on a mission and I was waiting to go on one with my Flight. We were in the ops room and could listen to what was going on on the radio. We heard that he had been shot down and I could hear the RT transmissions. The rest of his Flight were losing sight of him. I was getting very anxious as he was a great friend. I asked a Captain whether we could take off and help with the CAP but my request was refused and I was told we had to stick to our time. An hour went by, by which time they had lost him and I really pushed for going. Permission was finally granted but we had to attack our main target first (which we did). We went to the area in which Dennis had been shot down to see if we could find him. It was a forested area and we couldn't see where his Mustang had gone in. The previous Flight had been forced to leave as fuel was getting low. I was hoping I could pick him up and I did a stupid thing. Wanting to look down through the trees I deployed my flaps so that I would slow down and was immediately sucked into a flak trap, which I was very lucky to escape from. I made it back to base and this again demonstrates how sometimes luck can work in your favour because we counted forty-eight holes large and small in my aeroplane and not one had punctured a glycol line, a tiniest hole in which would have meant me going down. The greatest damage had been done to the starboard wing root where metal had peeled back to leave a gaping void. This really demonstrated the strength of the airframe. I was lucky given my position in the cockpit in relation to the wing root that no shrapnel had hit me.

John's second mission of the day resulted in two rail cuts at Chungwha and a highway bridge damaged, a supply dump damaged, a flak gun silenced and two houses destroyed at Yonan.

28 September
John was back at Chungwha but all his Flight's bombs missed their target so he resorted to rockets to cut the railroad. He also silenced a flak gun and destroyed three camouflaged buildings. Whilst on a second sortie (to Chungwha again) he achieved three complete rail cuts and damaged a road bridge with rockets.

30 September
John came to the last two sorties of his tour in Korea, both of which were close

support. He first attacked enemy troops on a ridge then rocketed a .50-cal position and destroyed it. His final sortie unusually involved a take-off at dusk. He eventually found his target – troops on a ridge – which he napalmed before the Flight became separated into two components, which returned to K16 through increasingly bad weather and in complete darkness. To compound matters for John his instrument panel lighting had failed. He had to be able to see his speed at least if he was to make a safe landing. After some experimentation he found that if he clamped the stick between his knees it gave enough space for the fuel tank lights, which were on the floor, to cast sufficient glow to enable him to see what he needed.

1 October
0830 – K16 to K10 and end of tour.

It was John's mother's birthday. He had flown his allotted seventy-five sorties, spending 137 operational hours in the air in the process. Barry Wiggett's assessment of him was 'an above average fighter bomber pilot and Flight leader'.

CHAPTER SIX

On the Ground

We were under attack one day and from my hole in the ground I couldn't see where we should be directing the aircraft strikes. So I went and sat on a rise. I could see everything. I imagine the Chinese could see me too for they started firing artillery. Fortunately they weren't that accurate. I also remember the onset of winter when it was so cold you could hammer the ground with a pick, which would just bounce off and wouldn't even chip the soil. And I remember on Thanksgiving Day looking down into the valley and there were long lines of people coming up. They were South Koreans who would normally hump and dump the American's kit bringing hot meals to the troops in the front line.

John Howe

After the end of his flying tour John volunteered for another one. He was ready to continue the fight and whilst to suggest he was enjoying himself would be too simplistic a statement, he had adapted to life on the squadron, to the excitement of the flying, to the adrenalin rush of combat, to the camaraderie of fellow pilots and even to the loss of colleagues and friends. He was, in short, ready for more but the powers that be didn't agree and denied his request. He amended it to a further twenty-five missions but was refused again. John tried a different tack. How about joining the infantry, working as a ground controller? This met with a better response and the request was approved. The idea wasn't as preposterous as it might at first seem. John had, after all, been trained as a soldier at the military college.

He was posted to the 19th Infantry Regiment of the 24th Infantry Division, IX Corps, US Army, who were operating in central Korea. Before reporting to them he went to the 6150th Tactical Control Squadron near Seoul. The 6150th was the non-flying element of the 6147th Tactical Control Group, which handled all aspects of ground support, including the Tactical Air Control Parties, three-man teams with radio-equipped jeeps that co-ordinated the airborne Mosquitoes.

Peter Smith in *North American T6* tells us:

Their job was to go out and send back radio reports on enemy positions and likely targets. The team leader was always a combat-experienced Mosquito pilot assisted by a radio operator and radio mechanic. Travelling up close and sometimes mere yards away from the target area, these teams spotted targets for Allied artillery and radioed the information to the Mosquito which then came in to spot and dot the target with smoke rockets and directed the fighter bomber strikes that followed.

This was the job John would be doing after first being taken on two operational sorties in a Harvard to control fighter strikes in close support over the regiment he would be joining. This allowed him to see from the air the area he was going to be working in and to get some idea of what the opposition was like. The two trips served also to highlight one of the differences between the Mustang and the Harvard beyond the obvious ones. In the Harvard John could hear enemy gunfire from miles away. In the Mustang he hadn't been able to unless he had been too close for comfort!

Sorties completed, John caught up with the 19th Infantry Regiment on the ground. However, he was met with a less than enthusiastic welcome, the reason being it had recently been attacked twice by Allied aircraft as a result of his predecessor's inadequacies. John's operational flying had taught him that close air support should never be given unless the FAC could see both the target and the aircraft and was able to talk directly to the pilots. There were, however, some occasions where this golden rule had to be flouted in the interest of urgency and a target not in the sight of the FAC on the ground had to be attacked. In these circumstances the danger was that the wrong target could be hit, such as with the infamous incident when the Argyll and Sutherland Highlanders were napalmed by the Americans in September 1950. This happened on Hill 282 as the Argylls were repulsing wave after wave of North Koreans, were getting desperately short of ammunition and so called in air strikes. A US spotter aircraft arrived and reported that the Argylls were on a 'ridge-like feature'. Ground controllers launched an air strike and three Mustangs were soon over Hill 282, circling it before diving in to attack not the Koreans but the Argylls' position with napalm. B Company was virtually wiped out. Many were horrifically burned. Similar friendly fire incidents had happened with the 19th Infantry Regiment so their coolness towards John was in part understandable. They decided therefore to test his mettle but soon found they had chosen the wrong man to try this with for they hadn't reckoned on John's determination. The task was simple. He was allocated Gerald Haley as his radio mechanic and airman John Fitch, two jeeps, a trailer and radios and was sent up to the 19th's HQ, which, he was told, 'is on top of *that* hill'.

John recalls:

The Colonel wanted me on the top of a mountain by midday the following morning. We left camp in our jeep and drove over the top of a hill where there was an MP who directed us across a valley but warned us fighting was about to break out. The valley was full of tanks. We drove over to one of them to find out the best way to get up this particular mountain – the

Commander told us to go such and such a way but to get the hell out as they were about to go into battle. At which stage the firing started. So we turned away from the area, crossed a shallow river and went up and round the valley to another point at the bottom of the mountain. I carried the portable radio. It quickly became clear I was entering a battle zone for there were a lot of dead. The tank firing had stopped. By this time I was ahead of John Fitch who had had a flying accident, had broken almost every bone in his body and so wasn't as agile as me. I tried to traverse a narrow path and fell, landing in a huge hole on my back. As my eyes became accustomed to the dark I sat up and looked straight down into the headless chest of a Chinaman. I was in a dugout where everyone had been killed. I scrambled out of that pretty quickly. I continued up the mountain and as I got near the summit half a dozen or so Orientals came over the top. I pulled out my pistol and fortunately didn't fire as they turned out to be South Korean. I eventually reached our objective and found an American Major who told me the Colonel had just called to say he wanted me on the top of *that* mountain – not this one. I was pretty wound up by then and told the Major that I wasn't going unless I got help and he could tell the Colonel so. I got it and scrambled back down and climbed up to the next peak where the Regimental Commander was waiting for me. That, I think, had been my initial test, which I passed. That is when the Colonel accepted me. We got on very well after that.

John's job would be to support any advance by the regiment, calling in close support if it was being attacked. The increasingly bitter cold of winter was setting in and the valley beneath would frequently fill with fog, an occurrence that the Chinese used as cover to attack soldiers dug in on the lower slopes. When the fog cleared FACs in Harvards had an overview of the situation and would direct Mustangs to where they were needed most in close support. John and his fellow ground controllers would direct these aircraft to suppress specific threats. He described one such occasion to *The Johannesburg Sunday Times* when he returned to South Africa.

We were given orders to take up a position at a clump of trees facing a range of hills that were occupied by the enemy. We concealed the jeep and ourselves as effectively as possible and at dawn we were in position but unobserved by the enemy. The attack soon started and it was not long before our Commander decided to use air power to deal with an enemy stronghold only about two thousand yards away from us. Several Flights had already checked in with us and we immediately called the first Flight of four Mustangs, which happened to be four members of 2 Squadron. We advised them of the location of the target and gave the Flight Leader the all clear to attack in his own time with napalm and rockets. Because of the rugged structure of the stronghold the napalm and rockets could not silence the enemy fire and as soon as we realised this we called for a Flight with 250-lb high-explosive bombs to blast open the stronghold. This was successfully carried out and was followed by another Flight of four [US Marine] aircraft with napalm, which could now get to the enemy because the stronghold was blasted open. We three shook hands when the CO congratulated us over the radio for what he termed a very skilful, co-ordinated and successful attack.

Whilst John was with the 19th Infantry Regiment the fighting was virtually static and the war became one of attrition. He and his American colleagues were regularly under fire. On one occasion the enemy were attacking and dropping shells ahead of their approaching troops. John couldn't see exactly where to put in the air strikes unless he went to a forward slope where he could see the target and the attacking aircraft. This was an act of considerable bravery as shells were exploding on the mountainside all around him as he spotted. Conversely, there were occasions when John missed all the action. His barrack was basically a hole in the ground, his only concession to decency and hygiene being that every two weeks or so he would go back to the Regimental HQ for a shave, a shower and a decent meal. He awoke in this hole one morning to find Chinese and North Korean bodies lying all around after a night-time attack. It was 30 November, St Andrew's Day, and he had had a half bottle of spirits to share in commemoration of his old school's patron. He had invited an artillery controller to join him. The two had had a drink and because they were not used to it and it was the end of a long tiring day, they had both fallen into a heavy sleep during which the enemy attacked. They had heard absolutely nothing!

Many stories of the harsh conditions and deprivations endured by the troops on the ground in Korea have been told. American James Brady, who went as a rifle platoon leader in 1951, summed it up succinctly.

The dashing war of tanks and jets and stroke and counterstroke had bogged down into trench warfare. The fighting was as primitive as Flanders Field in 1917. The artillery on both sides was deadly by day so we fought by night, creeping out through the barbed wire and the mine fields with grenades and automatic rifles, with shotguns and knives, to lie shivering in the snow, waiting in ambush. And the Chinese and the North Koreans crept out to wait as silently for us. We lived in crude bunkers of sandbags and logs and when we coughed it came up black as soot. During shellings or thaws bunkers collapsed and buried men alive. And once in winter we went forty-six days without washing. When we came off the line that time they burned our clothes.

As a result of exposing himself to enemy fire as described above, the Americans recommended John for a Bronze Star. In the event he didn't receive it, probably because when there was a lull in the fighting he, by his own admission, became a nuisance, badgering his American superiors for a move to a more active environment or to be sent home. Which he was when his tour in Korea ended in December 1951 and as a consequence the medal recommendation was never followed through. He did, however, return to South Africa after two and a half months with the regiment with the American DFC and the three Air Medals already won. The Air Medals we have accounted for – the completion of the required number of sorties and the attack on 24 June. The DFC is harder to explain for John was never given any specific reason for its award, neither did he receive a written citation. He recalls mustering on parade, his name being called and the medal being pinned on his chest. There may be no further recollection than this on his part but the record of his time in Korea is citation enough.

John had been just twenty-one when he went to Korea. Many men in the South African Air Force that he had joined in 1948 had fought during the Second World War. They were John's heroes and as a young man who had been trained to fight he wanted to prove himself to them. His desire to go to Korea where he could do so was a genuine one. He gained much from his experience, although in retrospect he finds it very difficult to understand why that should be so. He does remember being very scared from time to time.

> I was never scared with the regiment because I had fellow soldiers around me, which was very different to being in the air, miles beyond the front line alone in an aircraft. For example, I had a huge fright one day when we were in cloud. We were being fired on when suddenly we flew through a very heavy downpour. My heart nearly stopped when the screen became almost opaque and I thought it was glycol. I also became anxious when we were bombing Pyongyang on 14 August (a big effort with lots of USAF Mustangs involved as well as our own). We went in low, caught them by surprise, dropped our napalm, flew back to K10 for a quick turnaround, grabbed lunch and flew back to Pyongyang in the afternoon on the same route on another maximum effort. I looked round and saw what I assumed was napalm being dropped by some of the aircraft in our strike package away from the target and thought 'you yellow buggers'. We dodged flak and got home but at debrief I found it wasn't napalm being dropped, it was aircraft being shot down. We went back for the third time on another day. I got anxious on that mission too. Everybody got a little nervous in those situations.
>
> People get older and far more sensible. As a youngster I looked for action, action, action. I remember that at one stage when they were talking about peace talks with the Chinese after we got to Korea, those of us who had just arrived were hoping they didn't negotiate peace before we'd done thirty sorties otherwise we wouldn't get our Air Medal.

In reflective mood John also says:

I look back at that time now and I can hardly believe the slaughter that went on. I've seen infantry come over a ridge as I was about to let my weapons go and I've turned round and seen them all taken out. I've seen people fall to pieces under my machine-gun fire. It's far worse on the ground as I later found out when I was with the infantry because you can hear and smell as well as see. It was just awful. It was a big war and little mercy was shown by either side. But I never had thoughts of not carrying on. Half of my friends had been killed. I knew nothing of communism: I didn't understand what all the implications of the invasion of Korea were. All I knew was that the north had invaded the south and we had gone to help the south. We weren't fighting any cause, we were simply fighting to make our squadron the best and to make the enemy pay for killing our friends.

Once back at the Central Flying School in South Africa John lost all direct contact with 2 Squadron and Korea, keeping up with the news as everyone else did via the newspapers and radio or by the occasional official briefing. After he had left the country the winter again proved to be a severe one with the ground so frozen that bombs bounced off it instead of penetrating. There are even records of damage to dropping aircraft as a consequence. 2 Squadron continued with its close support role. Interdiction attacks continued during April and May 1952 but such was the increasing concentration of enemy guns that there were now few, if any, flak-free targets. The North Koreans were more adept than ever at repairing rail cuts (in as little as six hours) and bridges (within a week). As the truce negotiations were making no progress it was decided to increase the pressure on the North Korean negotiators, this time by attacking hydro electric installations, the first such attack by 2 Squadron taking place on 23 June. In July they switched to industrial targets to further increase pressure on the negotiators and thirty such targets in Pyongyang were listed.

The increasing appearance of MiGs led to the squadron re-equipping with North American F-86 Sabres at the end of the year. As with the F-51, air and ground crews received their familiarisation training on the new type in Japan. The final Mustang mission was flown on 27 December and the squadron then moved to K55 at Osan, sixty-five kilometres south of Seoul, ready to receive its first three Sabres on 28 January 1953. Training on the type had been completed by March and the Flying Cheetahs' first operations were air-to-air missions to MiG Alley. They soon reverted to the ground attack role, however, as their new aircraft proved to be a stable platform for dive bombing, able to carry 2,000-pound bombs or napalm and rockets.

During June and July the communists launched a final major offensive but by 19 July any advances that they were making first faltered then halted and their delegates at the peace talks decided that the time had come to end the war. Accordingly, on 21 July 1953 the armistice was signed, effective at 2201 hours on that date. It had been agreed that the communists' airfields should be neutralised

63

to prevent a further build up of air power and 2 Squadron flew forty-one sorties doing so.

Statistics produced at the war's end make for interesting reading. 2 Squadron completed 10,373 sorties on Mustangs and 1,694 sorties on Sabres. Seventy-four out of ninety-five Mustangs were lost as were four Sabres (plus one after the armistice). Surviving Mustangs and Sabres were returned to the US Air Force: none were transferred to the SAAF. Thirty-four pilots and two ground crew had been killed whilst eight became prisoners of war. A Presidential Unit Citation was awarded to the squadron for extraordinary heroism in action against the armed enemy of the UN and those who served in Korea were subsequently entitled to wear the insignia of the citation on their right breast permanently. Next of kin of those who lost their lives or who disappeared during the campaign also received the emblem. 2 Squadron also received the Republic of Korea Presidential Unit Citation. Airmen and ground crew were awarded two Silver Stars, three Legions of Merit, fifty-five DFCs, one Soldier's Medal, forty-two Bronze Stars, 174 Air Medals and 152 Clusters to the Air Medal. Furthermore the 18th FBW decreed that:

> ...in memory of our gallant South Africa comrades at all retreat ceremonies held by this Wing the playing of our National Anthem shall be preceded by playing the introductory bars of the South African National Anthem. All personnel of the Wing will render the same honours to this anthem as to our own.

During the war the serviceability of aircraft on 2 Squadron was better than the American squadrons of the 18th FBW thanks to the indefatigable efforts of ground crew. When, for example, there was a serious shortage of aircraft three Mustangs that had been written off were cannibalised to make one. The work took a month. 2 Squadron actually meshed very well with its US counterparts without offering any unique capabilities other than highly trained and motivated personnel.

Incidentally, the 18th Wing, as it is now styled, is still (in 2008) based in the Far East at Kadena Air Base, Okinawa, the largest US military installation in the Asia-Pacific region and the largest Wing in the United States Air Force. The 39th is no longer a component squadron, but the 44th Fighter Squadron (which had been left in the Philippines during the Korean conflict) is, alongside the 12th and 67th.

The South Africans ceased operational flying in Korea on 1 October 1953 and on the 29th the last airmen left for home.

CHAPTER SEVEN

Instructing

*Gesertifiseer dat ekk, JFG Howe, instruksie ontvang het en dat ek
die Kajuit-dril, noodsaaklik handelinge, die werking van die brandstof,
olie, hidrouliese, verkoeling, elektriese, pneumatiek, suurstof en
noodsisteme, die handeling in geval van vuur en die metode van
verlaat in verband met bogemelde vliegtuig, volledig verstaan.*
Handtekening: JFG Howe Vlieer

After his long flight home from Korea John went straight on leave. His parents had no inkling that he was back and he was able to surprise them. Given it was Christmas, they regarded John's safe return as the best present they could have had. Leave over, he was posted at the end of January 1952 to 1 Squadron at Swartkop to fly the Vampire, the SAAF's first jet fighter. This was a temporary attachment, made so that he could convert to the aircraft to enable him to participate in a formation flypast at the end of March to honour the 300th Anniversary of the arrival on South African soil of Jan van Riebeeck, the founder of Cape Town.

The Vampires that John converted to at Swartkop were the FB.5 and FB.52 versions (the latter essentially an export version of the former). As there were no two-seaters in the air force at that time it was a case of some ground instruction and a sortie in a de Havilland Devon to experience take-off and landings with a tricycle undercarriaged aircraft first. Before he took off on his first Vampire solo John was required to sign a certificate which stated:

I, JFG Howe, have been instructed in and fully understand the cockpit drill, vital actions, the operation of the fuel, oil, hydraulic, electrical, pneumatic, oxygen and emergency systems, the action to be taken in event of fire and the method of abandoning in respect of the above aircraft.

JFG Howe

The certificate was in both English and Afrikaans (as reproduced at the head of the chapter) and was a consequence of the fact that it became compulsory for the student to be instructed in the language of his choice. In reality everyone was bilingual anyway. As for the jet itself, John characteristically took to it immediately. How did he find it compared with the radial engined aircraft he was used to? The noticeable thing was the absence of both torque and a whirling wind across the rudder. Otherwise it was not so very different, although it was of course much, much quieter. It gave a smoother ride than both the Harvard and Mustang and it was fast by comparison, which suited John admirably! Indeed, within three days of his first solo he was conducting a compressibility test, which took the aircraft to a maximum speed dictated by the build up of shock waves preventing it flying any faster.

The Cape Town flypast over, John, along with several of his erstwhile Korean colleagues, moved on to Instructor's Course 1/52 at the Central Flying School Dunnottar. Here, he found Tommy Vanston was to be his Flight Commander, Lt Keightley his instructor and Major Baxter the Chief Instructor, all familiar names from his time at Dunnottar a year or more before. Here he was also reunited with the Harvard as he prepared to learn how to instruct. The process was a relatively straightforward one as a QFI (Qualified Flying Instructors) ran through instructing practice in the form of individual exercises and then the pupil instructor would take a fellow pupil instructor aloft and instruct them. Each exercise was given a number and John's log book is full of cryptic entries as a result (6-12, 11, 21 for example) but they were simply numbered exercises such as circuits and bumps, stalls, spins and so forth conducted during a training sortie. There are also references to his role as safety pilot to a 'pupil' under a hood practising instrument flying. He himself would be similarly tested. There was no better aircraft than the Harvard at that time on which to instruct. They were the commonest aircraft in the air force inventory and continued as a trainer until 1994, retiring with a grand passing out parade at Langebaanweg. Many of the type are now enjoying a second life in private hands.

By the time student instructors had reached the end of their course and taken all the necessary tests, they were required to participate in a low-level aerobatic competition with a height restriction of two thousand feet. John won the cup for the best display of his course on 21 June 1952. That was the start of John's love of aerobatics and display flying. The routine he developed included a spin (six turns), recovery, loop, two flick rolls at the top, loop, one flick roll at the top, aileron turns and steep turns, by which stage he was near to the ground. At Dunnottar and in the Harvard he finished off by flying at ultra low level with the propeller tips actually below the sides of a drainage ditch by the aircraft parking area, being careful that a wing tip didn't come into contact with the ground. John was stopped from doing this, however, after one passing out parade when he decided to fly at the saluting dais instead of down the ditch!

There were one or two narrow escapes though. The Harvard was the workhorse of the South African Air Force and as a result it had been adapted for a variety of roles. One aircraft at Dunnottar was used to conduct the daily meteorological flights and had housings on the wing for related equipment, which altered its performance. It was also an aircraft that was a long server and was thus nearing the end of its service life so engine wise it was probably not the best. John was allocated this aeroplane to practise on on one occasion and coming out of a loop he realised that he wasn't going to make it so he quickly put the flaps down – which got him out of trouble only by a matter of feet. Low level takes on a different meaning in those circumstances! But such incidents didn't deter him. Having won the aerobatic trophy John participated in air displays from time to time (at Louis Trichardt and Senekal for example) and with his aerobatic skills as good as they were he was a popular performer. He was also involved in night air displays as well, an intriguing notion that involved a mass formation at night with all landing lights on the Harvards ablaze. It was quite spectacular when viewed from the ground!

With 105 hours of flying under his belt and with the necessary time in a Link Trainer (used as an adjunct to real flying much as a simulator is today), John completed Phase One of his Instructor's Course on 28 June 1952. He was rated as above average or high average and was qualified to instruct 'on probation' on the Harvard IIa. He completed this probationary period successfully by the end of August and was thenceforth a fully qualified Category C instructor (subsequently upgraded to Category B in January 1953). He had also by now been promoted to Lieutenant. He was allocated to A Flight with Henry Rose Martin as his Flight Commander.

Much to his surprise John found instructing to be rather enjoyable. But he was not a patient man if pupils didn't follow his instructions and in his view those that didn't probably shouldn't have been flying anyway. Cadet Wallace was one such. He would continually do irrational things on impulse. On take-off on 16 September 1952 and climbing out at the required 90 knots, John in the back seat followed his own usual procedure of putting one hand on the throttle mixture pitch lever so the pupil couldn't change that, his elbow on the trim wheel so that couldn't be adjusted and his other hand and feet just off the control column and the rudder pedals in case he needed to react quickly. As he climbed away on this occasion Wallace inexplicably allowed the speed to fall away despite John shouting frantically at him to 'get your bloody speed up!' At 300 feet the prop stopped and the aircraft fell out of the sky and smashed into the ground. John, still in his seat, went straight through the floor and ended up with the rudder pedals above his head. He was bruised but amazingly otherwise uninjured. Wallace hadn't strapped himself in properly and his face smashed into the instrument panel. Thankfully there was no fire. John extricated himself and helped a dazed and bloodied Wallace out of the cockpit. Both had had a remarkable escape. At the subsequent Board of Inquiry it emerged that the sun had shone on the fuel low pressure warning light and Wallace had stretched down and switched the tanks but in the process only moved the switch to an interim position, which meant that neither tank was feeding fuel. On his return from sick leave Wallace was for the moment allowed to continue flying before being scrubbed from the course after John and other instructors had tried to mend his ways. But for each cadet who failed there were many more who succeeded and several who were outstanding.

As a team, instructors from the Central Flying School toured SAAF airfields around the country to check instructors based there. A typical itinerary over a week started with Dunnottar to Durban and on to Grahamstown. Despite being on his home patch here there was rarely a chance for John to get to see his parents and in fact he only managed to see his family a couple of times a year. From Grahamstown the team would carry on to George, to Ysterplaat (Cape Town), to Langebaanweg, to Bloemfontein and back to Dunnottar. Within the space of a few days John had two narrow escapes on one such tour. On 22 June he was taking off with Captain John Bolitho (who by now had taken over from Major Baxter as Chief Instructor at CFS) as second pilot when his No. 2 collided with him as they were climbing away, hitting the elevator so hard it nearly dislocated John's thumb as he held the control column. There was a bit of *déjà vu* here as the same thing had happened on 12 June when John's No. 2, Vincent Kuhn, collided with him and bent the wing tip over the aileron so that the Harvard could only be turned one way, enough to get him back to Dunnottar to land.

Not content with instructing military pilots John would go to nearby Germiston Flying Club at weekends and instruct on three private Piper Cubs as he continued to quench his insatiable desire for flying. He also instructed on Aeroncas and Tiger Moths that were used by the Defence Flying Club. This is one of the oldest flying clubs in South Africa, having been inaugurated as the Training Defence Flying Club at Swartkop in March 1931 at the instigation of SAAF ground crew who wanted specifically to found a club for other ranks. Their first aircraft were a rebuilt Tiger Moth and an Aeronca C3. The Defence Gliding Club was formed six years later. The war stopped the activities of both until 1947 when the powered and gliding arms reformed, initially as the SAAF Aero Club then as the Defence Flying Club again, still based at Swartkop but soon with outstations at Dunnottar, Langebaanweg, Durban and Ysterplaat. Tiger Moths from the Joint Air Training Scheme became available in large numbers, the club acquiring thirty-one between 1947 and 1956. Leading lights of the Club post war included several of John's Korean War colleagues such as Jan Blaauw and Dennis Earp and from his days as a pupil pilot, Tommy Vanston.

His time at CFS wasn't all about instructing. On the sports field he represented the CFS at rugby and cricket. He also played a bit of squash but not competitively. In the air he volunteered to take civilians flying in the Harvard to show them what the air force was all about (shown as 'flips' in the log book). They were only twenty-minute trips but it was very good PR. And on occasion he acted as a ferry pilot, such as the time he took Warrant Officer Lewis to M'Tubatuba in northern Natal. This was an isolated base that flew anti-malarial spraying sorties with Ansons first thing in the morning and just before dark.

In the South African spring of 1953 John undertook a Ground Controlled

Approach course at Langebaanweg, which involved his controlling by radar as well as flying GCAs. This was designed to facilitate his understanding of the procedure from both sides. John was invariably rated as very good with voice control and presentation excellent.

From 7 January 1954 John moved on to the Air Operations School (AOS) at Langebaanweg for the official Vampire conversion course using the FB.5 and two-seat T.55 (with which the SAAF had by now been equipped). Once completed, he instructed from 11 March he began instructing the regime including battle formation, dive bombing, simulated attacks and air-to-air work as well as aerobatics. Whilst the Vampire was very different from the Harvard it was nonetheless a straightforward aircraft to fly and teach on. The side by side seating allowed an instructor to feel much more in control of a training sortie and also made checking aiming and firing guns, rockets and bombs that much easier as the instructor and pupil had similar sighting systems. Those whom John was instructing weren't *ab initio* pilots of course, they were converting to the type.

Here again John sought the opportunity to instruct on other aircraft as well. Langebaanweg boasted one of the flying clubs established so that ground crew and other non-flying personnel could be taught to fly. Here he instructed on Aeroncas. A Spitfire became available on one occasion and John didn't miss the chance to take that aloft either. He also flew a Harvard from time to time on drogue-towing sorties for air-to-air firing.

The AOS at Langebaanweg was to be the last posting for John within the SAAF. On 26 May 1954, having resigned, he made his final flight after 1,391 hours and 35 minutes in the air. He was grounded pending his leaving despite an acute shortage of instructors.

But what was it that led to what appears to be an extraordinary decision on John's part? The answer lies in the world of South African politics.

CHAPTER EIGHT

Resignation

The SAAF had to a large extent stagnated after the war. Somehow
the people in charge had seemed to have lost their way. This can be
blamed on the extent to which politics played a significant part in
promotions and appointments and in decision making in general.
Some senior English speaking chaps were retired early, many
resigned and others seemed to be marking time until they could
claim early retirement. It was like a rudderless ship trying to make
its way across the ocean with the captain fast asleep in his cabin and
the navigator washed overboard. While one could do a certain amount
at junior level it required proper control and command from the top.
Like I am sure many others did I swore that if ever I had the opportunity
I would do something to bring about drastic improvements.

Bob Rogers. His Personal Story as told to Roger Williams

Two aspects of life in South Africa that were becoming increasingly abhorrent to John after the Nationalist government came to power in 1948 were those of apartheid and the infiltration of the ranks of the SAAF by government-appointed Nationalist staff. Both filled him with dismay and they in equal measure led to his resignation and leaving his country of birth to join the Royal Air Force. John was by no means alone in his action and there was an increasingly steady stream of emigration to the UK in the 1950s. Others with similar feelings and concerns elected to stay in the hope that they could progress, often against the odds and by dint of sheer hard work and determination, to a position from which they could help determine the future of the SAAF along rational lines.

Looking briefly at the apartheid issue first of all, John had never had any problem with sharing the country with the black population whom he remembers being told were 'descendants of the biblical Dan, hewers of wood and carriers of water'. He was brought up with a black nanny, Nobi, who became a close family friend. The family also had a black cook, Grace. The Howes certainly didn't like the way the Africans were sometimes treated and they did their best to ensure that blacks within their circle could lead as fulfilled a life as possible. Apartheid was therefore something of which John was unaware in his early life and not just because of family attitudes. There were black soldiers, sailors and airmen serving alongside white for instance. And whilst the antipathy of Boers towards blacks was well known, when John was young he remembers it as a time of peaceful coexistence. In fact, there seemed to be more tension between the Boers and the British, with each distrustful of the other, but this didn't become clear until the Second World War started and John realised there was a lot of support on their part for Germany. In the Howe household that distrust was very evident. 'Don't ever believe anything the Boer tells you,' John's mother used to regularly say. In truth, it would be more accurate to turn that statement round and explain that the Boer was always very eager to say things he thought you wanted to hear. He would rarely tell a deliberate lie.

A year after John's birth, the Statute of Westminster of 1931 reduced South Africa's dependency on Britain. In 1933 a coalition government was formed by JBM Hertzog and Jan Smuts under the auspices of a new United Party with a policy of promoting the interests of the 'superior' white population at the expense of the 'inferior' non-whites. The Hertzog-Smuts alliance didn't survive the outbreak of the Second World War with the former advocating a policy of strict neutrality and the latter one of alliance with the British. The coalition broke up and Smuts became Prime Minister. Hertzog's downfall created a split in the United Party with many conservative Boers continuing to resent the British and regarding neutrality as the better policy but with radical Boers supporting Nazi Germany. Daniel Malan's new National Party capitalised on this by picking up support from those who were disappointed with Hertzog's downfall and it was when they came to power in 1948 that the horrors of apartheid began to become apparent to John, Malan's campaigning having been based on that issue.

Increasingly, Afrikaner nationalists had been speaking of themselves as a chosen people, ordained by God to rule South Africa. They had for a long time been establishing their own cultural organisations and secret societies and arguing vociferously that South Africa should be ruled in the interests of Afrikaners, rather than English businessmen or African workers. The system of apartheid (an Afrikaans word meaning 'apartness') was intended both to bolster nationalist pride and to compensate the Boers for the suffering they had endured in the previous century at the hands of the British. Its purpose was the segregation of the races – not simply blacks from whites or indeed coloureds (Asians or Malays) from whites as is often perceived, but of non-whites from each other as well. Urban areas were the first targets of segregation and large segments of black and coloured populations were forced to settle in new townships well away from the cities. By law all races were to have separate living areas and separate amenities. Non whites were not allowed out at night without a pass. There was to be no mixing. Education was to be provided according to the roles that people were expected to play in society. The vast black majority was excluded from any role in national politics and from any job other than that of unskilled labourer. Even the Dutch Reform Church preached from the pulpit that a black was an inferior being

71

who had to be treated as such. And the Suppression of Communism Act was passed and police powers were greatly increased in anticipation of resistance to the new policies.

As this process gathered momentum the government began the steady transfer of the military to Afrikaner management, a process that caused many divisions within the SAAF. A programme was introduced that eliminated advancement for women, blacks or coloureds. Great efforts were made to eradicate the Britishness of the armed forces and many senior British officers were forced into early retirement, whilst the requirement for bilingualism for all officers, NCOs and new recruits discouraged British recruitment, the force increasingly being filled with Afrikaners with little or no combat experience. The bulk of promotions to senior rank was politically inspired, leading to many English speakers feeling unwelcome. The air force was particularly affected. RAF contracts were not renewed and the financial budget was reduced, which effectively prevented, or at the very least limited, the purchase of new British equipment. A home-grown air force culture was developed with blue-grey uniforms and new rank insignia being introduced. Equally visibly, in November 1950, when 2 Squadron began operations in Korea, the SAAF adopted the springbok for the centre of the roundel displayed on all its aircraft, finally giving the air force its own identity.

John lived and worked with Boers when he went to military college as he did in the air force itself. These were mainly honest men, many of whom John befriended and who had joined up for similar reasons to him. But they tended to be the exceptions. One of his best friends in Korea had a brother who was a major in the SAAF '...and who praised the Nationalist government to the heavens. Six years later he arrived as a defence attaché in London as a brigadier. Six years from major to brigadier – if you toed the line you were very quickly promoted.'

Bob Rogers, who eventually became Chief of the Air Staff (CAS), was one who resisted the nationalist influence in the SAAF as far as he was able to at a time when English-speaking officers were not well thought of. Unlike John and many of his colleagues, when he returned from Korea Bob decided to stay on and to try and do something about the iniquitous new attitude at government level towards the air force. He had held the rank of Lieutenant Colonel (equivalent to Wing Commander) during the Second World War (indeed at twenty-two he had become the youngest Lieutenant Colonel in the SAAF) when he commanded 225 Squadron RAF and then 40 Squadron SAAF but at the end of hostilities he accepted a permanent commission in the SAAF at the rank of Captain (Flight Lieutenant). He was determined to get to Korea with 2 Squadron and had been promised command of that squadron by the then CAS, Brigadier Jimmy Durrant, but when Durrant was replaced in the top job by Stephen Melville the arrangement was changed and Bob went out to Korea as a Flight Commander instead of Squadron Commander. After his return to South Africa the government, despite their policy of promoting nationalists, had begun to realise that they needed the right men in the top jobs if the air force was to survive and Bob Rogers, as a great leader of men and an astute administrator, had been an obvious choice. Meanwhile, Jimmy Durrant, South Africa's most experienced air officer, resigned in 1952 because despite ministerial assurances that there were no politics in the air force it soon became apparent that along with the army and navy it was becoming a political toy. Furthermore, its personnel were becoming increasingly discontented and frustrated. Men without war service were being appointed to command whilst those who played prominent and distinguished roles as leaders in the field were suppressed, dismissed and degraded.

It was at this time, that one of the great wartime Spitfire Aces was creating headlines in South African newspapers. Sailor Malan, whose 74 Squadron John was to lead in England ten years later, led demonstrations in South Africa against apartheid. Sailor had left the RAF to return to South Africa in 1946. In the 1950s he formed a protest group of ex-servicemen called the Torch Commando to fight the ruling National Party's plans to disenfranchise Cape coloured voters and fought the franchise battle for more than five years. At its height it had 250,000 members, making it one of the largest protest movements in South African history. Daniel Malan's government (he was no relation to Sailor) was so alarmed by the number of judges, public servants and military officers joining it that those in public or military service were prohibited from enlisting. Slowly it was suppressed. Sailor Malan himself succumbed to Parkinson's disease in 1963.

When John joined the air force and went through the training process he initially gave little thought to political considerations. He was, after all, finally fulfilling his young life's dream and taking the first steps towards flying. It was only when he was in Korea and saw at first hand what happened there that the full impact of what was happening at home began to dawn on him. Hitherto, he simply hadn't realised how the blacks were now being treated. For example, he remembers a rescue in Korea, the corollary of which angers him to this day. A South African was shot down and he bailed out, coming down in a heavy enemy troop concentration. His colleagues in the capping Flight were using their guns to keep the enemy at bay. When they started running out of fuel another Flight came in, a helicopter having been called in the meantime. Then another Mustang and the helicopter were shot down. Capping continued, Flight replacing Flight, until a second US Navy helicopter appeared and lifted the downed South African out. By this time the radio transmissions had drawn attention to what was going on and the UN press and photographers were alerted. When the rescue helicopter got back to base, as the cameras clicked the Mustang pilot and the chopper pilot emerged and hugged each other – they had after all been through quite an experience together and the helicopter crew in particular had shown tremendous courage. The hug was a case of sheer gratitude on the Mustang pilot's part, sheer relief on the chopper pilot's part. But that picture was never published in South Africa because the helicopter pilot was black. It was this incident in particular that started John thinking. There were a significant number of blacks in both the SAAF and USAF. Here were people who flew as well as whites, were as brave as whites and after the action partied just as well as whites. What was the difference other than skin colour?

When John later went to the American infantry, as he moved towards the battle lines he passed through what had been a killing ground a few hours previously.

> The place was littered with bodies – blacks, yellows, whites, browns – but they all had red blood, red flesh, white teeth and white bones and they all smelled of death in exactly the same way. Those are the things that began to make me wonder. That particular day I will never forget.

A couple of weeks later John was coming down the hill on which his post was situated for his fortnightly shower when he met a young black American soldier struggling up. As they passed John commented 'this is heavy going soldier.' 'Yeh!' was the response. 'If they ironed out Korea it would be bigger than Russia.'

> They had the same humour as us! It really came home to me that what was happening at home was not acceptable. I learned one of the greatest lessons of my life when I was in Korea. Having been born and raised in South Africa in the days before real apartheid, the new attitude which I had never come across before was completely alien to me. When I got to the Far East I saw black fighter pilots and they laughed and cried and fought and died and drank just like the whites. So why should they be shunned?

As far as nationalist infiltration of the SAAF was concerned, by the time John resigned his commission in 1954 things had for him become intolerable. The government was bringing into the air force as administrators men from trades not allied with the military in any way. These men were paid more and given a rank above that of serving members who had been through the full training programme and who had fought in the Korean War, simply on the basis of their commitment to the National Party. Promotion seemed to depend entirely on the manner of an individual's praise of the government. This of course led to a situation where men in the higher echelons of air force hierarchy were not at all competent. Their ignorance, and ignorant approach, could not be endured.

When John was at the Air Operations School at Langebaanweg these growing problems with the SAAF led to his decision to resign. Local Boer railway workers were brought in and commissioned as Lieutenants in what can only be described as yet another blatant move to get as many nationalists into the air force as possible. It was very apparent that having a name like Howe did not fit the air force profile any longer. Incidental to that was the fact that pay and pensions in South Africa lagged behind the rest of the Commonwealth air forces. Resignation really became the only option if he was to put these issues behind him.

John's initial letter of resignation was short and to the point. In it he simply said that he wished to join the RAF to broaden his experience. It was returned and he was told that he would have to be more explicit. In other words his reasons in full were required. John now produced five pages in foolscap based on pension, pay, promotion, policy and politics and he pulled no punches. His letter went all the way up the tree from the Brigadier in Cape Town to whom he had sent it. Both were summoned to see the Chief of Staff, Brigadier Steve Melville, at the South African Defence HQ in Pretoria, a thousand miles away. John reported on the Monday morning having flown down with his CO to be faced by General Melville (whose son John had taught to fly). Melville threatened him, tried to blackmail him and ultimately told him that if he didn't withdraw all that he had written he would be given a stinking record of service so that 'no one in the world would touch you'. John was also threatened with a Board of Inquiry. But he wasn't daunted and angrily refused to withdraw his statement. He was shown into a small, sparsely furnished room and left by himself for a while. Eventually the ADC to the CAS came in and put a piece of paper on the table. He was told 'If you sign this you can go.' It had been the political content of John's tirade that had caused all the problems, for Brigadier Melville was an Afrikaner sympathiser: but he gave way when he saw that John's mind wouldn't, indeed couldn't, be changed. For his part John is still slightly incredulous after all these years at the way in which he addressed his superior.

He was certainly not alone with his resignation for many of his colleagues did the same. Phil Lageson was one. As AOC RAF Germany and by then *Sir* Philip Lageson he was to be John's boss in Germany. He had been the adjutant from whom John and his colleagues had collected their airline tickets prior to flying out to Korea. John's mother had insisted on looking at them and when she did she was appalled to see that they were single tickets only! She was far happier with the impending move to Britain. 'John,' she said. 'You're going home.' At a farewell party at Langebaanweg, in response to some leg pulling, John said: 'Never mind. You'll get to hear of Air Marshal Sir John Frederick George Howe soon enough.' He came pretty close to that prediction! Mike Muller recalls the party and the years afterwards.

> I followed John's career in the RAF with great pride. By that time I had shared six years of my life with him. They stand out in my memory as very special years and John as a very good friend. I always envied his easy, flowing, beautiful handwriting and in his letters from England I experienced his story telling writing style. For my part correspondence came that much harder, especially in a foreign language like English!

After John had moved to England Mike, Bob Rogers and Dennis Earp came over on various courses and then ultimately they came over to convert to the Buccaneer when the SAAF ordered that aircraft. Whenever they were in London every opportunity was taken to meet and for John to hear all the news from home.

CHAPTER NINE

The Royal Air Force

*I had no family contacts in England to get in touch with so it was
very much a case of going it alone although when I arrived I realised
how little I knew of the country. When I got on the train at Southampton
I couldn't get over the number of houses packed tightly together. They
were all so small. I had never seen so many chimneys either. And the
countryside was very different. Its greenness after the drought
we had been experiencing back home was a revelation.*

John Howe

John's final decision to join the RAF came as a result of a visit to South Africa
by the Central Flying Establishment (CFE). It would be the RAF for him and
the main reason was the impending arrival of the Hawker Hunter, which John
had decided was the aircraft he most wanted to fly. Amongst the CFE team was
Ken Cooke. The next time John was to see him was as his boss on his first RAF
squadron flying Hunters!

Along with a couple, of other former SAAF officers John sailed to
Southampton in the UK on the *Windsor Castle*. One of these was Tony Green. The
other (rather ironically given the reasons for John's resignation) was an Afrikaner
who didn't get into the RAF because of his lack of English but who eventually
joined the Canadians. Much to their relief Tony and John were accepted, for
although they had decided it was to be the RAF for them there was no certainty
that the RAF would want them. Indeed, the RAF had answered none of John's
letters prior to his leaving South Africa. It was only when he walked into the Air
Ministry building in London and a file was opened and John saw his letters that
it was explained to him that the reason they hadn't been answered was that there
was no protocol between the British and South African governments for the
former to take on personnel from the latter. For all the other Commonwealth
countries there was such an arrangement. Thus if the RAF had responded they
could have been accused of poaching. It was therefore only when John and Tony
arrived in London, to all intents and purposes jobless, that they could apply to
join, fill in the necessary paperwork, undergo medicals and interviews and be
accepted. That hadn't happened immediately. For a few weeks after
disembarkation they worked in Watney's Victoria brewery, rolling barrels and

loading drays to earn enough to feed and shelter themselves at the Malcolm Club. Soon though, RAF kit was drawn (the trunk issued to hold it is still in the Howe household, now full of horse tack in the Home Farm stables) and the pair sent to No. 4 Squadron of the Central Flying School (CFS) at Little Rissington in Gloucestershire. A familiar aircraft, the Vampire, awaited them and John's first flight as an RAF Flying Officer was on 12 October 1954.

John had strongly stated his preference for a Hunter squadron during his interviews but had been told that there was a long waiting list of potential Hunter pilots and that that particular queue couldn't be jumped. As there indeed was for the Canberra. No, if John wanted to fly it would have to be the Vampire, teaching others how to fly, initially at least. 'Instruct for a year,' he was told, 'and then we'll get you on to the Hunter.' Regular reminders to those that mattered that there was one very eager and willing South African here who was tailor made for the fighter became part of John's strategy during that year and as the months passed by his reminders increased in frequency.

All this was happening at a time when the RAF were re-equipping for the Cold War and thus they were very happy that two experienced jet QFIs had applied to join. It had only been nine years since the end of the Second World War but those nine years had seen a profound change in the RAF as they contracted from a wartime to a peacetime force. But at best it turned out to be an edgy peace. The Soviet occupation of East Germany and the closing of road and rail entry to Berlin led to the Berlin Airlift of 1948 and 1949 and demonstrated only too clearly that because of post-war disestablishment the RAF had already contracted too far and was hard pressed to meet its commitments. Then on the other side of the world the Korean War erupted and in Malaya communist insurgents kept the RAF very occupied under Operation *Firedog*.

In the light of the new communist threat that had emerged a programme to recruit and train new ground and aircrew for the RAF was put in place. It also became a time of re-equipment as obsolescence and a profound shortage of aircraft was remedied. The British aerospace industry of the time designed and built new aircraft and invested in new technologies, both of which were also imported from the USA. At the time of the formation of NATO in August 1949, Bomber Command had been reduced to just 150 Avro Lincolns and de Havilland Mosquitoes but the following year B29D Washingtons came into the inventory. Canberras arrived in 1951 but it was 1955 before the first of the V bombers, capable of carrying an atomic bomb, arrived. Fighter Command had similarly wound down to 200 Meteors, Vampires, Hornets and ubiquitous Mosquitoes but again in the wake of Berlin had doubled in size and also had 160 aircraft in the Royal Auxiliary Air Force. However, the jets of the RAF were no match for MiGs so North American F-86 Sabres were bought to fill the gap until the indigenous Hunter arrived. Javelins entered service in 1956 and at that year's end there were 600 Fighter Command aircraft and thirty-five squadrons in place.

Those who served in the RAF at the time when John and Tony Green arrived in the UK will tell you it was a good time, an exciting time.

The mid 1950s and the years immediately thereafter were good ones to serve through. New aircraft, radar and all manner of equipment was pouring from the factories or being imported. Recruits joining then could look forward to serving at locations all over the world for despite the gradual withdrawal from Empire the Commonwealth still provided many attractive stations and the oil interests in the Middle East ensured that a fair proportion of serving personnel, both Regular and National Service, got their knees brown.

The Modern Royal Air Force

It would be true to say that to begin with John didn't know a great deal of the detail of the RAF's transition to an air force ready to fight the Cold War.

I knew a lot of the history of the Royal Air Force, especially as regards the Second World War. But in the relative isolation of South Africa we knew the Cold War was building up but didn't, in truth, take much notice of it at our level. When I joined the RAF though I soon realised what the score was. And I realised why I couldn't fly Hunters to start with. They wanted guys trained to go to war. I was told I would be promoted to Flight Lieutenant as soon as I passed my promotion exams so I started to do a lot of reading and studying and it was then that the big picture became very clear to me.

Little Rissington in Gloucestershire is regarded as the home of the CFS and from 1946 (when it first moved there) until it was vacated by the RAF in the mid 1980s it was responsible for maintaining high standards of flying instruction and the training of QFIs. It was the place where John and Tony Green were introduced to flying with the RAF. Built in 1936, Rissy as it is affectionately known, is on top of a 750-foot hill, making it one of the highest airfields in regular use in the UK (it remains active for Elementary Flying Training conducted by a civilian company). This fact also produces some interesting weather conditions, one of the immediate things John had to come to terms with after the clear blue skies and unlimited visibility of the African veldt. To not see the ground for long periods of time was certainly a novelty for him. Familiarisation under the watchful eye of his instructor Keith Mossman proceeded quickly and by the end of the course in December close to forty hours had been spent in the air learning again how to instruct on a Vampire but more importantly learning about RAF procedures. In truth there were few differences, the main ones relating to instrument flying, which in South Africa used to be practised but in the UK was done for real. Let down procedures were different as well but again that was because of the weather factor. The Vampire T.11 was used almost exclusively with the exception of one forty-minute Meteor T.7 flight, John's first on the type. The T.11 had only come into service a couple of years earlier. Having been successful in selling the single-seat version to fourteen air forces around the world by June 1950, the need for a dedicated training version of the aircraft was essential and so de Havilland decided to go ahead with the design and construction of a prototype. Just four months later this prototype took to the air. The RAF wanted the aircraft as an advanced trainer, which would be used on the second half of the standard Wings course, and a specification was drawn up and issued in September 1951. A fortnight later production began. Three examples were sent to the A&AEE (Aeroplane and Armament Experimental Establishment) at Boscombe Down for evaluation. Its report concluded that the T.11 would be an excellent intermediate trainer for the more advanced aircraft expected in the near future. There were two criticisms of the aircraft however – its unpleasant behaviour in a spin (more of a tumble than a spin is a good way of describing it) and the lack of ejection seats.

When it was introduced the T.11 marked the end of the Advanced Flying School (AFS) stage of a student pilot's course. This had provided the stepping stone between a Flying Training School (FTS) and an Operational Conversion Unit (OCU) and aircraft used had been the Tiger Moth or Percival Prentice then Harvard, Balliol or Oxford before jet conversion on the powerful Meteor T.7. When the Vampire T.11 arrived in 1953 the Percival Provost T.1 arrived as well and henceforth these two aircraft would form a training partnership. The Vampire, being less powerful than the Meteor T.7, would be better for initial transition to jet flying. A consequence of the advent of the new aircraft was a shake up of Advanced Flying Schools, which were absorbed by Flying Training Schools. At the time of John's arrival the CFS at Little Rissington was changing to support the Provost/Vampire syllabus. Nearby South Cerney became CFS (Basic) and Rissy was CFS (Advanced). It received its first T.11s in the autumn of 1953. Air Cdr GJC Paul was Commandant and Gp Capt PWD Heal Station Commander. The Chief Flying Instructor was Wg Cdr FL Dodd and OC 4 Squadron, to which John was assigned, was Major Emmons, on exchange from the USAF. The Meteor T.7 and Vampire T.11 were present in considerable numbers and there were a few Ansons and Harvards for communications duties too. Something that suited John down to the ground was the fact that lots of sport was played or participated in on the station – rugby, football, hockey, netball, basketball, badminton, table tennis and shooting included. Sport of one kind or another has always played a large part in John's recreational life.

Hardly surprisingly, given all his South African experience on the Vampire, John emerged from the course on 10 December with another 'above average' endorsement and a Green (as opposed to the lesser White) Instrument Rating, awarded according to the number of hours flown under actual and simulated instrument conditions. There was then plenty of time to enjoy Christmas in London along with other ex-pat South Africans, Kiwis and Aussies before reporting to 4 FTS with whom he was to instruct for the next year.

The restructuring of the RAF's training regime meant that Advanced Flying Schools were themselves renumbered as Flying Training Schools. 205 AFS, which had until January 1954 been based in Rhodesia where it was known as the Rhodesian Air Training Group, renumbered as No. 4 FTS in July 1954. With its home at the old wartime bomber base of RAF Middleton St George in County Durham (the most northerly bomber base in the country during the war) it operated Meteor F.4s and T.7s and from October 1954 Vampire FB.5s and T.11s, a combined total of over sixty of which would eventually be on strength. Now pupils who had completed 130 hours' basic flying training on the piston-engined Provost T.1 went directly to 4 FTS for 110 hours of jet aircraft training without any intermediary instruction. John was assigned to A Flight of 1 Squadron of the FTS. The Squadron Commander was Sqn Ldr RJ Colston.

Pilot Officer Roy Cope-Lewis was a student who came to Middleton from 2 FTS Hullavington and the Piston Provost and by his own admission was not a particularly proficient pilot. He considers it to be his great good fortune that John was his instructor for the eight months he was there.

When you are a student pilot all you want is your Wings on your chest and to help you on your way you take inspiration from those who instruct you. Indeed a student will tend to put instructors on pedestals because in most cases they have already done what they, the student, aspires to do. Knowing John's background, particularly as far as Korea was concerned, I knew that this was somebody who could most certainly inspire. That, coupled with his recognition of my abilities, meant that I got the maximum benefit from my time at Middleton. He knew intuitively how to mould the skills he drew out of me. He was a perfectionist as I was. I wanted to be the very best and he wanted me to be. Because of this he was not slow to criticise and on one particular Instrument Flying sortie, when I was under the hood flying purely on instruments, throwing the Vampire around the sky a little as John kept his eyes peeled for conflicting traffic, that criticism nearly cost me my place on the course. I was not having a particularly good day and things weren't going right however hard I tried. John made an increasing number of helpful comments whilst we were airborne but they didn't help either and so, when we landed and as we taxied in, he tried to make light of the sortie and cheer me up a bit. But in my frustration I bit back by telling him that perhaps if he had kept his bloody mouth shut and just let me get on with it I might have done rather better. The atmosphere in the cockpit changed immediately and we continued our taxi in complete silence.

I hadn't been out of the aircraft long before I was summoned by the Flight Commander and torn off a strip. I regretted what I had said of course and acknowledged that I had probably justified being thrown off the course. In fact I had already started to pack my things. I was told not to be so hasty. Perhaps a change of instructor might be the answer to which I immediately responded by saying that if that were to happen I was definitely leaving the course. I have never been one to shrink from speaking my mind! As it happened things calmed down and John and I stayed together. I apologised, he accepted the apology, we carried on and I passed out well at the end of the course.

My subsequent RAF career was largely modelled on the precepts that John taught me. I instructed and I flew displays, always remembering the things John had both told me and advised me on. Without this I am convinced that I wouldn't have been half as successful. He also taught me humility, not to be afraid to admit when a mistake had been made. Such as an imperfect aerobatic manoeuvre which he used to demonstrate and just occasionally get slightly wrong. When that happened he simply said 'I cocked that up' and then asked me for a critique of what he had just done.

To be a successful instructor you have to be good. John was damned good. He set a high standard and told me to aim for it – which I did.

At Middleton, as at Rissy, weather caused problems from time to time. On one occasion John was airborne in a T.11 with Tony Green (having collected him after a ferry flight) when they encountered 8/8ths cloud cover. They decided to transmit for a fix to give them some idea as to where they were. This they duly did and were told 'you are eight miles south of Doncaster' – which was very helpful other than the fact they had no idea where Doncaster might be! However, they recognised the name as a place they had gone through on a train down to London so the South African pair, still strangers in a foreign land, knew they were heading roughly in the right direction. Incidentally, Tony and John were at Middleton for about the same duration but after that their paths diverged and other than an occasional meeting at a London 'reunion' they gradually lost touch.

The Wing Commander Flying at Middleton, Roy Edge, was liable to send instructors and pupils off in the most appalling weather on the understanding that they were expected to land elsewhere! John took off one day with snow falling from grey leaden skies. As he accelerated he hit a bank of snow across the runway. This caused a momentary loss of power as it was ingested but the engine wound up again and John got airborne. Let downs in poor conditions could be equally interesting but there were well established procedures to help. For example, if there were several aircraft airborne they would form line astern above cloud and follow each other down until they flew into cloud. Timing and positioning was then of the essence with the leader being controlled by direction finding rather than radar. The following aircraft, at a separation of around 800 yards, maintained their speed, direction and rate of descent until they successively broke through to find the runway dead ahead. Pairs of aircraft, and indeed a succession of pairs, could be brought down this way when Air Traffic Control was working at full efficiency.

Those were the days when aircraft at training establishments, and indeed in the

Royal Auxiliary Air Force, were available as personal taxis for weekend visiting. Instructors would fly down to Biggin Hill or North Weald from Middleton, hangar their T.11 and take a train into London. But such jaunts could be eventful for reasons other than social ones. On one occasion John took off with a colleague in reasonable weather with the expectation that Biggin Hill would, as advised, have a cloud base of 250 feet and visibility of half a mile, which as far as they were concerned was within limits. But near to London their radio packed in and by that stage of the flight they didn't have the fuel to get back to Middleton. Because they couldn't transmit they could get no help as regards position so had no option but to seek out a hole in the cloud cover to look for themselves. Normally flying into such holes was not permitted but this one was big enough to allow John to circle, gradually losing height until he came out at the bottom only to find the surrounding hills were all shrouded in cloud. Landing at Biggin Hill was out of the question so North Weald it had to be as the alternative. As John's colleague was local to the area he elected to navigate and came up with a succession of headings that eventually brought them over an airfield – a rather large one – followed in short order by the very familiar sights of London. The airfield had been Heathrow, which they had flown over at 200 feet!

Shortly afterwards they found North Weald, whose transmissions they had been able to just make out on their faulty radio as they got closer. John landed and found a Land Rover waiting to take him straight to Wing Commander Flying who, it transpired, was not best pleased for he had been tracking them across London by means of all the complaints he had been getting on the telephone! However, the Wingco's displeasure didn't prevent John from enjoying their weekend in the capital before returning to Middleton and another interview, this time with their own Wing Commander Flying to whom John was ordered to report in No. 1 uniform. Needless to say, a full report of their aerial exploits had preceded him and John was left in no doubt that he had broken every ATC rule in the book! Punishment was then meted out – no aeroplane for the next weekend! But that was it and the availability of an aeroplane was quickly restored thereafter.

It was around this time that John spent a weekend of reminiscence when Tommy Vanston, now promoted to Captain, who arrived from South Africa on a course. John flew over to Strubby in Lincolnshire to collect him and bring him back to base before returning him safe and sound, but with perhaps a hint of a hangover, on the following Monday. It's a safe bet that there was much to talk about, not least the SAAF compared with the RAF, as well as recounting stories of flying training South African style. RAF Strubby, incidentally, was under the control of the nearby RAF Flying College at Manby, airfields and establishments that have since long gone and have now been returned to agricultural use or converted to industrial use.

On 24 May 1955 John bailed out of an aeroplane for the third time in four years. On a day with a cloud base of around 300 feet, poor visibility and a student named Ollis at the controls, they climbed to 30,000 feet where they started a speed run when the fire warning light came on. The laid down procedure was to throttle back and if the light didn't go out to cut the engine. John was faced therefore with a bailing out situation for he couldn't take a risk and undertake a flame-out landing under such poor weather conditions. An emergency call was transmitted and John briefed his pupil that he was going to invert to allow him to exit the aircraft. First though, Ollis had to connect his emergency oxygen, necessary as they were still at 25,000 feet, but instead of doing so he managed to inflate his Mae West. Notwithstanding this inconvenience, John got him out and quickly followed. They came down together and as they descended they heard the steady chuff of a train immediately below them. Fortunately they landed beside rather than on the track with the train disappearing, its passengers oblivious to what had been going on above them.

The Board of Inquiry that was subsequently convened to look into the causes of the accident concluded that instructor and pupil should have stayed with their aircraft but both the Station Commander and Wing Commander Flying overruled this, saying that there had been absolutely no option but to jump. The Board maintained that the engine should have been used and a forced landing made with the chance of saving the aircraft, despite the fact an engine wasn't to be used with a fire warning showing. What is more a forced landing with a 300-foot cloud base was in itself virtually impossible in those days.

John's latest escape made the news back home with the *Daily Dispatch* in East London reporting:

> A Royal Air Force Vampire jet fighter crashed in Northumberland, England, on Tuesday and floating down out of the sky by parachute came Flying Officer JFG Howe of East London. It was the third time that the twenty five year old airman had taken to a parachute to save his life....

John's father, George, was interviewed and he rather dramatically recalled the previous two occasions when John had jumped. As for John, he was by now rather hoping that three was enough and there would be no further need to exit an aircraft he was flying!

As a brief aside it is worth wondering why there was, initially at least, no ejection seat in a Vampire. Whilst the original design had omitted it, when it came to drawing up the specifications for the FB.5 single seat fighter-bomber version of the aircraft the RAF insisted that one be incorporated. But as David Watkins recalls in his book *De Havilland Vampire. The Complete History*:

> The requirement for an ejector seat was soon to cause many problems for the design team at de Havilland. A preliminary examination into the fitting of either a Martin-Baker or Malcolm seat had been undertaken in August 1946 but as the cockpit was only 22 inches wide an ejector seat could not be installed without considerable alterations to the cockpit and airframe

structure. Between April and October 1947 a mock-up of a redesigned metal fuselage was assessed on a standard Vampire Mk 1. A memo from de Havilland to the Air Ministry in April 1947 suggested that if the aircraft was eventually fitted with an ejector seat pilots would have to be trained to keep their elbows in!

Ejection seats were later fitted to Swiss Vampire FB.6s under a modification programme in 1960 and RAF Venoms, designed to take advantage of the new powerful de Havilland Ghost 103 turbojet engine thus making the type faster and more manoeuvrable than its cousin the Vampire, had them from 1954. As for the T.11, the lack of such seats in a training variant was, as we have seen, criticised from the outset. In April 1953 a modified design incorporated two manual release ejection seats but these were not well received by the A&AEE at Boscombe Down as David Watkins explains.

> The unit's report was highly critical of the ejector seats which restricted the rearward stick and control movements in an already cramped cockpit. The rearward view from the cockpit, made worse by the seats' headrests, was also disliked as was the lengthy strapping in procedure in the confined space available. The report recommended that the Martin-Baker seats be modified or replaced by another type of ejector seat.

The result was that from the 144th T.11 built the Martin-Baker Mk3B seat was fitted and a modification programme, which ran between March 1954 and December 1957, installed them in all the earlier aircraft.

After the bailing out instruction carried on without further incident and all the routines and regimes of an FTS became second nature to John. He enjoyed a spell when he took on the mantle of Red Leader, taking off in an FB.5 with varying numbers of students following and teaching them the rudiments of formation flying. There were also diversions outside the training regime. For example, in August the station played host to a Hastings and four C-119s in a joint services exercise as the 16th Air Division and the Parachute Battalion used the airfield as a dropping zone for men and heavy equipment: then in September forty-five 4 FTS aircraft participated in Exercise *Beware*. On a personal note, John successfully completed his promotions examinations and was awarded the rank of Flight Lieutenant. These exams covered air force law, Queen's Regulations, the structure of the RAF, history, roles of the various commands and so forth. It was fairly intensive study interspersed with operations and social activities and was done individually as there was no course to attend. But if he wanted to get on John knew he had to buckle down and do it. And wanting very much to get on, it was no chore. He buckled down and did it.

John left Middleton on 31 December, having escaped the attention of an Air Commodore who for a reason that John cannot recall decided that he was ADC material. For a newly arrived South African who only wanted to fly this was not good news, not only because it would restrict his ability to do so but because he had no wish to be anybody's servant. A few well judged letters to the right people secured John's release and the threat of being grounded was lifted! Instead, he was posted to Chivenor in north Devon for a three-month conversion course with 229 Operational Conversion Unit (OCU) before moving on to 222 (Natal) Squadron at Leuchars. He had been instructing for exactly a year. Now his much anticipated Hunter beckoned.

CHAPTER TEN

The Hunter

I loved it. The controls were extremely well balanced. I'd never flown anything hydraulically powered and therefore quite so light, which meant that the wings were kind of shaky to begin with, for the tiniest movement of the stick had an immediate effect. I quickly got the hang of it though. You sat there looking over the short nose and therefore enjoyed wonderful visibility with a powerful engine behind you, which I hadn't experienced before. It certainly didn't disappoint.

John Howe

RAF Chivenor, on the banks of the estuary of the River Taw in north Devon, was a busy place in 1956. When John arrived there were thirty-six Hunter F.1s, twenty-five Vampire FB.5s, seven Vampire T.11s, nine Meteor F.8s, a lone Meteor T.7, six Mosquito TT.35s (for target towing), one Mosquito T.3, two Chipmunk T.10s and a single Balliol T.2 on strength. These days Chivenor is a very different place, being a barracks for the Royal Marines. The only RAF presence is a pair of 22 Squadron SAR Sea Kings.

The Hunters had arrived in 1954 and were now being progressively modified to operational standards by teams at Horsham St Faith in Norfolk with a view to allowing air firing practice to be commenced in the near future. Green Salad homing equipment, DME (Distance Measuring Equipment), improved demisting and other modifications were being made at the same time, all part of the upgrade programme designed to iron out early problems with the type.

In early 1948 the Ministry of Supply had issued Specification F.3/48 to Hawker Aircraft Ltd for a single-seat fighter capable of Mach 0.94, to be armed with either four 20-mm Hispano or two 30-mm Aden guns, to have an endurance of sixty minutes, to be equipped with an ejection seat, to have a radar ranging gunsight and to be powered by either a Rolls-Royce Avon or Armstrong Siddeley Sapphire engine. Sidney Camm and his team took up the challenge and produced a design numbered P1067. Initial calculations suggested that the performance would be at least equivalent to the North American F-86 Sabre, which had just flown in prototype form. Thus encouraged the Air Ministry ordered three prototypes and the Hunter was born.

The first to fly was WB188 in the hands of Neville Duke in July 1951. This was four months after the Air Ministry had ordered its first batch of aircraft (at a cost of £172,000 each). Two years later the first of 139 production Hunter F.1s rolled off the Kingston production line but it would be another twelve months or more before the RAF received its first example. The problem was that three prototypes proved to be totally inadequate and the first twenty production models had to be used as development aircraft to help iron out problems that had become evident during early testing. Endurance had been found to be lacking, severe misting of the canopy occurred when descending from high altitude and there were instances of engines flaming out during gun firing. Nonetheless, experienced pilots of the Central Fighter Establishment at West Raynham in Norfolk were given the opportunity to fly the new aircraft under a limited Certificate of Airworthiness release from July 1954 and the same month 43 Squadron at RAF Leuchars became the first operational Hunter unit. Chivenor and 229 OCU received its aircraft shortly afterwards as did 233 OCU at Pembrey in South Wales. Hunter F.2s (of which forty-five were built) equipped with Sapphire engines, and which were unlike Avons immune to surging, went to RAF Wattisham and 257 and 263 Squadrons whilst the remainder of the F.1s equipped 222, 54 and 247 Squadrons by mid 1955.

> It was the knowledge that remedies were being found and introduced into the Hunter production lines that prompted the decision to go ahead with further deliveries of the Mark 1s and Mark 2s with their known deficiencies. In matters so politically delicate as national defence capabilities it was not possible to disclose to the public just how serious Fighter Command's problems were at this time....
>
> *Hawker Hunter – Biography of a Thoroughbred*

Such matters are outside the scope of this book. Suffice it to say that the problems were ultimately solved and the Hunter became probably the RAF's best-loved aircraft from a pilot's perspective at the time and indeed since. From John's point of view, problems notwithstanding, it was an aircraft he and so many of his contemporaries just couldn't wait to get their hands on. In their eyes this was the RAF of the future with an aircraft capable of matching any in other air forces around the world.

Under the circumstances it was slightly galling, although necessary, that the first six weeks of John's time with the OCU were in fact spent on Vampire T.11s and FB.5s. As was often the case with single-seat fighters of that era, trainer versions were slow to materialise and so surrogate trainers had to be used. In the case of the Hunter it was the Vampire T.11 and Meteor T.7: a little later in John's career in the case of the Lightning it would be the Hunter T.7. The first Hunter two-seater was delivered to 229 OCU as late as August 1958. Simulators were available though and it was in these that converting pilots got to know the cockpit layout, drills and emergencies. Prior to the first solo sortie the simulator was used to test a pilot in various emergency situations.

John was posted to 2 Squadron of the OCU. Vampires were used to teach and practise gun firing, which John hadn't previously done on the type. A dual sortie on the T.11 was followed by several on the FB.5. Cine work dominated to begin with – ranging and tracking, battle formation and so forth – then actual firing on the flag followed. John soon found that he was pretty adept at it, scoring an above average 17.1 per cent over the duration of his conversion. It's not as easy as it might sound for the pilot had to get the range, angle and deflection right before he could hope to actually hit the flag. As with flag flying in South Africa counting the number of hits once the flag was dropped was made easy, for ammunition was dipped in coloured paint before take-off, which left its mark as it passed through.

The first time John climbed into and took off in a Hunter F.1 was on Valentine's Day 1956. This was after thirty sorties in Vampires and an indeterminate number of visits to the simulator since 4 January. His subsequent pleasure at flying the type was reflected in the consistently above average endorsements he received for all aspects of his flying and it was with these ringing in his ears that he moved north in early April to RAF Leuchars in Fife and 222 Squadron.

It is a little ironic that the first operational squadron that John should be posted to in the RAF should have South African links, for its official title was 222 (Natal) Squadron, a throwback to the wartime years when money was raised in that country, or in the city of Durban to be precise, to buy aircraft that were subsequently assigned to 222. Its Zulu motto was *Pambili Bo* (Go Straight Ahead), and its badge, depicting a wildebeest in full flight, symbolising speed, came from the armorial bearings of Natal. The Squadron actually had its genesis in the Royal Naval Air Service in the Aegean at a time when naval flying units were being allocated RAF squadron numbers. 222 came into being in June 1918 when A Flight of No. 2 Wing at Thasos was renumbered. Initial aircraft on strength were Sopwith Camels and de Havilland DH4s and DH9s. With a primary function of attacking Turkish targets in the Balkans, 222 was short lived for by the end of February 1919 it had been disbanded. It was to be over twenty years before it reformed on Blenheims at RAF Duxford in October 1939. Blenheims were soon exchanged for Spitfires and in May 1940 it helped cover the Dunkirk evacuation and amongst its pilots at this time was Douglas Bader. It participated in the Battle of Britain when based at Hornchurch and then was engaged in offensive fighter sweeps from southern bases, as well as defensive duties in the north of the country. In mid 1943 222 was transferred to the 2nd Tactical Air Force and carried out sweeps in preparation for the D Day landings over the invasion convoys for which it provided air cover. Moving onto the Continent it supported Allied troops advancing through France and Belgium, re-equipping with Tempests in the process. Immediately after the war it became a jet-equipped unit with the Gloster

Meteor, moving around several bases before settling at Leuchars in 1950. Its initial complement of Hunter F.1s, delivered in December 1954, had been replaced by F.4s a year later and it was to these that John was to be introduced at Leuchars.

John has often wondered whether or not his posting to 222 was in fact in recognition of the fact he had recently arrived from South Africa but concedes that it is unlikely. Another direct link with his homeland was the fact that the squadron's CO was Ken Cooke, whose arrival in South Africa with the Central Fighter Establishment team and whose subsequent exchanges with John had helped persuade the latter that the RAF was the service he wanted to join on his resignation from the SAAF.

> I couldn't believe it. He knew I was coming of course but I didn't know who my CO was to be!

John was airborne from Leuchars on 10 April 1956 for the usual sector recce in a Vampire T.11 with Flt Lt Sumner. This was mandatory for all newly arrived pilots so that they could see the lie of the land. Leuchars, situated just to the north of the home of golf, St Andrews in the ancient Kingdom of Fife, is currently (2008) the most northerly air defence base in the UK in the same way that it was the most northerly Fighter Command base. 222 Squadron shared its ramps with 43 Squadron (Hunters), 151 Squadron (Venoms, re-equipping with Javelins in May 1957) and a Search and Rescue squadron, 275, equipped with Sycamores. When 222 disbanded its place was taken (although not until a year later) by 29 Squadron on Javelins. Leuchars was also home to a Mountain Rescue team, which was naturally at its busiest during the winter months. As one Station Commander ruefully recorded after a busy weekend for the team:

> They were called out to assist mountaineers and hikers in trouble. In both cases rescue was impossible as one had died from exposure and one from a fall. This brings out the need for mountaineers and hikers to pay careful heed to weather conditions and local advice. Unfortunately it is those amateurs who are too overconfident to pay careful heed to advice that break their necks and die of exposure. These people appear to belong to clubs and it would seem their organisations do not exercise sufficient supervision over their members.

Leuchars is one of the few front-line airfields that have endured, the majority of famous bases having closed in the wake of the drawdown after the collapse of communism in Eastern Europe. From the beginning Leuchars was intended as a training unit, taking aircrew of the First World War from initial flying training through to fleet co-operation work. Building of the airfield and its infrastructure was still underway when the Armistice was signed in 1918, in the aftermath of which much was made of Leuchars' seaside location when it was designated a Naval Fleet Training School. It became RAF Leuchars in 1920 but retained its strong naval links with Navy aircraft in regular attendance, particularly as a shore base for carrier aircraft as the service worked up with the new aircraft carriers.

In 1935 Leuchars became home to 1 Flying Training School but as the war clouds gathered this moved out to Netheravon and the station came under the control of Coastal Command and enjoyed an operational rather than training role for the first time. It remained an active station to the end of the War, concentrating on anti-submarine and anti-shipping strikes. Life returned to a gentler pace in peacetime with a school for general reconnaissance and the St Andrews University Air Squadron complete with Tiger Moths. Then in May 1950 Leuchars entered the jet age as it passed from Coastal to Fighter Command and the Meteors and the Hunters of 222 Squadron made the station their new home.

After familiarisation with Leuchars and the surrounding countryside from the air came a familiarisation sortie in a Hunter F.4. For John, from a handling perspective, the F.4 was not so very different from the F.1s that he had been flying at Chivenor. However, this new mark of Hunter was otherwise a somewhat different beast from the early production model. In *Hawker Hunter – Biography of a Thoroughbred* Francis K Mason states:

> With the evolution and introduction by Rolls Royce of the surge free Avon RA21, the Hunter was transformed as at a stroke the gun firing limitations were removed.... To meet the chronic endurance criticism the internal fuel capacity was increased from 337 to 414 gallons and provision was made to carry two 100 gallon drop tanks on inboard wing pylons.... Also introduced in the Hunter 4 was a full flying tail.

In total, 368 Hunter F.4s were built. Squadrons were still testing the aircraft's capabilities as John soon found out when all 222's aircraft were fitted with a full load of ammunition and stores for the first time, the extra weight having a marked effect on climb over 40,000 feet and indeed on manoeuvrability overall.

Amongst the things that firmly remain in John's memory about those first few months at Leuchars was the exhilaration of the high altitude interception of Canberras, cine work and flag firing at Acklington. 222 was the first Hunter-equipped Fighter Command squadron to attend an Armament Practice Camp, scoring an average 10.2 per cent in the process. John also recalls moving to Acklington for two months whilst the Leuchars runway was resurfaced (43 and 151 Squadrons went to Turnhouse) and the many exercises, such as the Ciano series. In the 1950s and 1960s there were a great number of exercises, large and small. So big was the service in those days and so numerous the squadrons that many serving officers and airmen were unable to keep track of all the different units that visited RAF bases when these were underway! Also memorable was the first Fighter Command interception of a U-2, the USAF's (and CIA's) new high altitude surveillance aircraft, by a pair of 222's Hunters. They were vectored onto a target two miles ahead and above at pretty much the Hunter's operational ceiling of 51,000 feet but could only watch the distinctive shape way above them against a dark blue sky. They reported what they had seen and when they landed back at Leuchars were taken straight into the debrief and warned to tell nobody. Other squadron members, including John, who were airborne at the time could hear what was going on and so were similarly warned not to talk about it.

U-2s apart, there was much that was routine about 222's programme. On exercise John got a Boeing B-47 into his sights on 11 May and a Valiant four days later. There was a reasonable amount of Vampire T.11 flying – IF (Instrument Flying), dual checks, familiarisation on type and so forth – and lots on the Hunter. He was introduced to the discomforts of Battle Flight, an early form of QRA (Quick Reaction Alert) with pilots on standby and strapped in the cockpit ready to scramble to interrogate any target that appeared. These could include anything from Valiants to Canberras to B-47s, Thunderstreaks and Sabres. These may have been Allied aircraft but Battle Flight was for real. Ground training also formed a part of a pilot's day. Shortly after John arrived at Leuchars he was introduced to SARAH – a Search and Rescue and Homing beacon that had recently been fitted to all life jackets. Aircrew kitted out with such jackets were stationed at various points around Leuchars and after switching on SARAH a helicopter homed in on them and picked them up. As the 540 – the daily diary of events kept by every RAF squadron – records: 'Pilots were impressed'.

It was whilst with 222 that John's Fighter Command Hunter display flying started. His first appearance was on 21 July 1956 at Anthorn, home at the time to a then busy naval air station, 'HMS *Nuthatch*'. John was responsible for displaying in area north of Newcastle whilst he was based at Leuchars. His opening manoeuvre was copied from Neville Duke and the first thing spectators would know was a sonic boom, followed by the Hunter a couple of seconds later at low level! Then he throttled right back, put the dive brakes out, did a very tight 270 degree turn to slow down and came before the crowd to begin the routine proper, which lasted for eight minutes or so.

As it turned out there wasn't a great deal of opportunity to display fly that summer for on 28 August 1956 John flew his last sortie with 222 until the beginning of 1957. The reason? He went to participate in the Suez crisis, not as an airman flying Hunters but on the ground as an invading Royal Marine.

CHAPTER ELEVEN

Suez

*When Nasser closed the Suez Canal I remember Anthony Eden on
TV talking and saying that the British Government might well
be taking military action alongside her allies France and Israel.
It came through the RAF network that Forward Air Controllers
were required so, given my Korean experience, I immediately
volunteered. My assignment came through pretty quickly and I was
posted to 40 Commando Royal Marines at St Andrew's Barracks in Malta.*

John Howe

On July 26 1956, six weeks after the last British troops had withdrawn from Egypt, that country, then under the leadership of President Nasser, announced the nationalisation of the Suez Canal, a vital link in the trade route to the east and in which British banks and business held a large stake. Nasser's motive was to raise revenue for the construction of the Aswan High Dam. The US and Britain had initially agreed to help pay for this project but they changed their minds after Egypt bought tanks from the then communist Czechoslovakia and extended diplomatic recognition to communist China. Convinced that Nasser posed another expansionist military threat the British Prime Minister of the time, Sir Anthony Eden, tried to persuade the British public of the need for war by comparing Nasser with Mussolini and Hitler. Eden had been a vigorous opponent of Neville Chamberlain's policy of appeasement twenty years earlier and it seems he had convinced himself that a display of force was needed now.

In the months that followed the canal's nationalisation it was agreed at a secret meeting between Israel, France and Britain that Israel should invade Egypt. Britain and France could then intervene, instructing the Israelis and Egyptians to pull their troops back to a distance of ten miles either side of the canal and then placing an Anglo-French intervention force in the Canal Zone around Port Said. Thus it was that Operation *Musketeer* was conceived. Israel's willingness to be involved in this subterfuge stemmed from 1952 when the Egyptian King Farouk had been overthrown, a republic declared and Egypt under Nasser began to assert Arab nationalist identity and his country's independence after years of what he saw as British subjugation. Egypt and Israel were at odds over the Straits of Tiran, the only gateway to the new Israeli port of Eilat. They were also at odds over Egypt's interference with shipping bound for and leaving Israel. Israeli Defence Forces had launched a series of retaliatory strikes against Egypt and the Suez Crisis gave them another opportunity to do so. Meanwhile, France had become involved because it was the French Compagnie Universelle du Canal Maritime de Suez that operated the canal: it was thanks to the vision of the French diplomat Ferdinand de Lesseps that the canal was built in the first place.

On 29 October 1956 Israel invaded the Gaza Strip and the Sinai Peninsula and made rapid progress towards the Canal Zone. According to plan, Britain and France offered to mediate. Predictably, Nasser refused the offer and this gave the pretext for a joint invasion to regain control of the canal and topple the Nasser regime. An astonishing air, sea and land force had already been deployed to Cyprus and Malta by the UK and France in anticipation of this. Britain alone committed 45,000 personnel, seventy warships including five carriers, (including *Albion, Eagle* and *Bulwark*) 300 aircraft and 12,000 vehicles. The French ultimately had 34,000 men in theatre, as well as 9,000 vehicles, 200 aircraft and thirty warships (including the carriers *Arromanchers* and *Lafayette*). The overall Operation Commander was General Sir Charles Keightley and General Sir Hugh Stockwell commanded the landing force. Vice Admiral Robin Dunford-Slater was the Royal Navy commander and Air Marshal Dennis Barnett commanded 205 Group Middle East Air Force. The Fleet Air Arm deployed twelve squadrons flying Sea Hawks, Sea Venoms, Wyverns, Whirlwinds and Skyraiders and the RAF deployed thirty-one squadrons flying Canberras, Shackletons, Hunters, Venoms, Meteors, Valiants, Valettas and Hastings. There was one joint RAF/Army unit, the Joint Helicopter Unit, flying Whirlwinds and Sycamores.

The initial plan was to attack Alexandria but this was subsequently amended to Port Said. Situated on a narrow peninsula between Lake Manzala and the Mediterranean Sea, Port Said lies at the mouth of the 200-kilometre long Suez Canal that traverses the Sinai Peninsula to connect the Mediterranean and the Red Sea. Its long history as a duty-free port had made it one of the most prosperous cities in Egypt.

Operation *Musketeer* would proceed in three phases:

i. The neutralisation of the Egyptian Air Force.

ii. An air offensive against selected targets combined with a psychological campaign aimed at destroying the Egyptian will to resist.

iii. A landing at Port Said to seize the harbour and airfield at El Gamil and use them as a base for subsequent operations designed to secure the canal itself.

This would also be achieved in three phases:

i. An assault on Port Said by air and sea.

ii. The reinforcement of the Port Said bridgehead.

iii. An advance southwards to Abu Sueir to capture the operational airfield prior to occupation of the remainder of the Canal Zone.

When the call went out for volunteer Forward Air Controllers to work with the seaborne invasion force John had no hesitation in responding. From 28 August until he returned to 222 Squadron shortly after the New Year in January 1957, apart from the flight out to Malta and his return to the UK when it was all over, his feet remained firmly on the ground. When he arrived at Luqa he was met by Lieutenant Mike Wilkins of 40 Commando, Royal Marines (Wilkins would later become Commandant General). 40, 42 and 45 Commandos were the constituent parts of the 3rd Commando Brigade. Two signallers were assigned to John to keep the radio serviceable and a French Navy pilot, Jean Gautier (who retired from military service as an admiral), completed the four-man Air Control Team, designated No. 1 ACT. The Frenchman was there because Suez was to be a joint operation and each team needed to be bilingual. However, there was a problem. The French F-84Fs that would have been called in were fitted with UHF radios: the ACTs were equipped with VHF sets. In fact, their equipment was inappropriate in all respects. For instance, they did not have any small portable radios. Instead, John was given a dismantled vehicle radio, which weighed about eighty pounds. And there was no transport so everything had to be carried. They were due to receive a Land Rover but this unhelpfully arrived after they left Malta *en route* for Suez.

> When I was carrying the radio I couldn't stand upright but had to lean forward to counter the weight, which was trying to pull me over backwards. I had been on Malta a little while when a parade was held at which General Keightley was the inspecting officer. All troops on parade were in full battle kit and were standing smartly to attention. Except me, who was leaning forward under the weight of my pack. The General said to me 'Good heavens man! How much does that weigh?' And somewhat miffed at what I was expected to carry around, I came straight back with 'A f—g ton sir,' which of course startled everybody, especially the General and his entourage! After a few moments silence they had the good grace to laugh and the conversation continued with me explaining that I had done FAC work in Korea where I had a proper radio, which could be easily carried.

According to the handbook, if carried as opposed to being fitted in a vehicle, the radio constituted a four-man load! In the end it was reduced to two. John carried the set itself, the power supply unit and the aerial whilst one of the signallers had a 12-volt portable battery. A report compiled after Suez laconically stated 'although it worked it was most unsatisfactory'. A little later we will look at the issue of Forward Air Control and the singular failure of the British to have any properly equipped units to undertake the task.

Work in preparation for the landing continued in Malta. Exercises undertaken involved embarking during an afternoon, sailing around the island and disembarking on the beach at Mellieha Bay at dawn (to simulate a Port Said landing) or the docks at Marsaxlokk (to simulate Alexandria). Nobody relished the thought of the latter if it were to become reality for it involved climbing up the side of a concrete jetty and sticking one's unprotected head over the parapet. There were joint exercises with the Fleet Air Arm operating from Royal Navy carriers too, John controlling simulated strikes so that FACs and aircrew got used to each other. Another very important aspect of the training concentrated on ensuring that all officers of all units down to troop commanders knew how to obtain air support.

The people of Malta were of course quite intrigued by all this and as is so often the way of things they often got to know what was going on in advance of any of the serving men. John's first inkling of the invasion came when he decided to have a suit tailored in Valetta. A short while afterwards he received a message to say that work on his new suit had been suspended in view of his impending move! The tailor proved to be right.

> 40 Commando's CO, Lieutenant Colonel David Tweed, summoned me and as I would be landing and fighting with the men of his command asked whether I would like to wear the Green Beret. I of course considered this to be a tremendous honour but an honour which I felt I had to decline, explaining that if I wore my RAF blue people around me would quickly identify who I was and if speedy access to aircraft was required would be able to more easily make contact. Years later a friend on 40 Commando did actually give me my long promised beret, which I still have.

On 30 October the order was given for 40 and 42 Commandos to embark on the .LST (Landing Ship, Tank) HMS *Striker* and sail east with her sister ships of the Amphibious Warfare Squadron, HMS *Bastion*, HMS *Redoubt* and HMS *Reggio*, to join up with the French and Royal Navy fleets from Cyprus before heading south towards Egypt. 45 Commando were ordered aboard the light fleet carriers HMS *Ocean* and *Theseus*. The LCT (Landing Craft, Tank) HMS *Lofoten*, laden with their stores and vehicles, had already sailed for Port Said. *Theseus* was carrying 845 Squadron's Whirlwinds and support units such as engineers and administration staff whilst HMS *Ocean* had the Joint Helicopter Unit (JHU) aboard with its Sycamore and Whirlwind helicopters as well as 600 men of 215 Wing of the RAF Regiment. The initially named Joint Experimental Helicopter Unit was an interesting one. It had been formed in 1955 at RAF Middle Wallop as a joint RAF/Army unit to examine the use of helicopters in an operational role, little thinking that it would be used in an operational situation itself a year later. Its initial tasking was to study the feasibility of delivering heliborne troops from an aircraft carrier. By the time of L Day at Port Said JEHU had evolved to JHU, the E for Experimental having been dropped for purposes of morale.

The bombing of Egypt by Britain and France began on 31 October 1956, the first flights over Egyptian territory being by photo reconnaissance Canberras. Shortly afterwards bomber versions of the same aircraft attacked Egyptian military airfields and, inadvertently, Cairo International Airport. Nasser's immediate response to this show of force was the sinking of all forty ships caught in the canal and closing it to further shipping. Valiants joined the Canberras and the following day Fleet Air Arm Sea Hawks and Sea Venoms attacked more military installations. Further photo reconnaissance showed that the larger part of Egypt's Air Force (mainly MiG-15s and Il-28s) had been destroyed on the ground so communications were then targeted and the railway system disrupted and military barracks destroyed. On 4 November the Fleet Air Arm flew 350 sorties whilst Shackletons and Meteors patrolled the sea between Egypt and Malta. Their presence didn't prevent the US, which was opposed to the action the British and French were taking, from provocatively sending elements of the Sixth Fleet to sail through the rendezvous point of the fleets from Malta and Cyprus. Cold War politics were at work and the UK and France found their relationship with the US becoming strained. There were two issues here. The first was that the USSR was seeking to extend its influence in Africa and in the Suez Crisis they saw an ideal opportunity to support Egypt against the West. The US was determined that such influence should be minimised. The second was simply that the Americans had been kept in the dark about what Britain and France were going to do and this displeased them greatly.

Meanwhile, the decision had been made that the seaborne assault, the first since the Second World War, was to be a beach landing at Port Said. Having avoided any collision with the Americans the fleet continued on its way, sailing at just five or six knots whilst destroyers ran defending circles around it, HMS *Diamond* shepherding the Amphibious Warfare Squadron with whom John had embarked. Early on 5 November those on board watched as RAF Hastings transports flew overhead. On board were the soldiers of the 16th Independent Parachute Brigade Group who were dropped to secure El Gamil airfield. This they successfully did with the airfield ready to receive allied aircraft by 0845 hours. The French, meanwhile, had dropped paratroops at Port Fouad to the east of Port Said and captured two bridges intact over the Junction Canal. This was enough to intimidate the Governor and the Garrison Commander of Port Said who indicated that they were ready to discuss surrender terms. A cease-fire was ordered with the soldiers already on the ground remaining in position but ready to open fire if fired upon. By 1930 hours terms had been agreed and enemy forces were reported as laying down their arms. A curfew was imposed in Port Said and Port Fouad and the instruction was sent out that Operation *Musketeer* would proceed the next day as planned – but without fire support. In other words it would be a peaceful landing. Hardly surprisingly, doubt was expressed that Nasser would allow the Port Said Commander to accept the surrender terms imposed by the Allies and indeed by 2030 hours they had been refused. The assault would go ahead as originally planned.

On board *Striker* (and other ships of the fleet) this led to a seesaw of emotions. Supper was served and before going to bed a church service held. Shortly before turning in for the night it was announced over the Tannoy that the Garrison Commander at Port Said had surrendered. The next day's landing would therefore be unopposed and the whole thing could be treated like a normal exercise. Back home, Anthony Eden also said in the House of Commons that a cease-fire had taken place (albeit *after* Nasser had rejected it). The pressure appeared to be off and on board ship troops slept more comfortably, unaware that an about face had taken place. Everyone was up early and ready to go on the morning of 6 November. It was still dark and as the troops mustered by their landing craft *Striker*'s Tannoy came to life again. 'Nasser has instructed the Garrison Commander to fight to the last man so, gentlemen, the beaches are mined and they are waiting for you.' So much for an unopposed landing!

Men and vessels were lowered from *Striker* into the water in LCMs (Landing Craft, Mechanised). These were designed for troops to sit in three long, tightly packed rows, the middle row facing forward and the other two facing inwards. By sitting, those on board could take advantage of the cover afforded by the sides of the vessel. But the marines wouldn't sit. So fired up were they that they stood on the benches, willing the LCMs on. The destroyers HMS *Diamond* and *Duchess* fired salvos towards the beach until they peeled away to allow the assault craft to run in to the shore and at 0445 hours (H Hour) the Royal Marines of 40 Commando poured out onto a dark beach code-named Sierra Red from seven LCMs. There was no light from the buildings beyond and smoke from burning oil tanks hung in the air. There were no mines. Five minutes later John and his ACT hit the beach in the second wave of five LCMs and ran with everybody else. But because of the weight on his back John stumbled and dropped his Sten gun, which, thanks to the sand, was immediately rendered useless. At H + 15 eight LCAs (Landing Craft, Assault) disgorged the final wave of troops. Navy guns from warships moored offshore were providing the covering fire, causing considerable damage to Egyptian gun emplacements whilst Port Said itself was being badly hit as well.

The first objective was to clear the area between the beach and the first main lateral road, a wide boulevard. Three enemy soldiers fired at LCMs crossing the beach but two were quickly killed. All the initial objectives, including the Western Breakwater and Liberation Barracks, were quickly taken by Y Troop. There was no resistance. Indeed, it appeared that the majority of the Egyptians had fled. Centurion tanks of the 6th Royal Tank Regiment disgorged from LCTs and came ashore to 40 Commando's left whilst HMS *Lofoten* later landed the rest of the marines' transport. By 0535 the tanks were ready to move off and lead the advance down the waterfront road, closely followed by P Troop. This effectively bypassed all enemy opposition in the town. The advance was watched by Egyptian civilians on the balconies of their houses (who were left unharmed by the marines). At the same time the marines were coming under fire from Egyptian soldiers in side streets (whose fire was returned by the marines). Commercial Basin was reached by Y Troop in fifteen minutes. Still supported by tanks they advanced around its perimeter and cleared the Canal Company building. Accurate small arms fire hindered them and a marine was killed. All the time the Egyptians were seen withdrawing south but not without loss for a Centurion tank destroyed two enemy vehicles full of soldiers. B Troop, which cleared the Fishing Harbour area, subsequently came under heavy fire from the customs warehouse but this was suppressed and the building cleared by X Troop, although two marines were wounded as they advanced towards it. On the ground floor there was stiff opposition and one of 40 Commando's officers was killed. Another officer led an assault that cleared the rest of the building but he too was killed. Three marines were wounded. Seventeen Egyptians were killed during this part of the operation and two taken prisoner.

John was involved in the clearing of the customs buildings.

X troop was led by Major Pat Willasey-Wilsey [another future Commandant General of the Royal Marines]. Nine Egyptians were found inside and one of these shot at two of Willasey-Wilsey's men, injuring them. So angry was he that he went in alone and wiped the nine out. We went through the rest of building room by room. Each was empty until the last where there was a wounded Egyptian officer, terrified because he had been told the allies didn't take prisoners. The Marines tended to him, tried to calm him, tried to reassure him. A vehicle arrived to take him to hospital but because it had been carrying casualties all day the inside of the vehicle was spattered with blood. Willasey-Wilsey ordered that it be washed and scrubbed before the Egyptian was taken in. Such is the apparent contradiction of a Royal Marine – ruthless fighters on the one hand and men of extreme compassion on the other.

As 40 Commando advanced John inevitably made comparisons with the Americans he had fought alongside in Korea. Whilst it was a very different conflict against a very different enemy (indeed a large proportion of the Allied force found it difficult to perceive the Egyptians as the enemy in the true sense of the word), he quickly came to appreciate the true worth of the Royal Marines.

They could hardly wait to get ashore – they were fantastic. I think they cleared what opposition there was on the beach in minutes. Then we went through the town and started down the side of the canal. The Royal Marines fought like tigers but if they came across a wounded enemy soldier they would give him a cigarette or some chocolate then carry on with the advance. In Korea they would have been killed. How different this was to that operation! Civilians not involved in the actual fighting were left alone. In Port Said some civilians sat and watched on balconies and no harm came to them. In Korea if you found a supply depot in a village you flattened the supply depot and it didn't matter if it was surrounded by civilians. Nothing like that happened in Suez to my knowledge. Nothing that wasn't capable of threatening us was attacked. I can honestly say that I never felt a moment's fear or apprehension with the Royal Marines despite the heavy fighting because they were there around me and I felt totally fire proof.

At 0700 hours 40 Commando's mortar officer inspected the High Lighthouse to assess its possibilities as an observation post. To his and his men's surprise twenty Egyptian soldiers emerged from the cellar and surrendered to him and amongst them was the Garrison Commander. For the second time in twenty-four hours he wished to stop the fighting and was taken to Brigade HQ but once again it became clear that the Egyptian did not possess any authority to do so.

X Troop continued the advance and cleared the warehouses on the waterfront one by one. In the process eight Egyptians lost their lives and two more were taken prisoner. The waterfront buildings were relatively isolated, open spaces providing good killing grounds and there was no means of escape for the defenders. Within the customs complex, the Navy House, formerly a British Admiralty building, was proving to be a problem and at 1605 hours John called in eight Sea Hawks equipped with 56-lb rockets. Most of the building was destroyed and set alight. Fierce fighting followed, the fiercest in fact the marines had encountered thus far. Thirty Egyptians were killed and twenty taken prisoner. This had been a tricky and precise operation because elements of 40 Commando were only eighty yards from their target. It was in fact the only close air support carried out for 40 Commando on the day (two others were called by 42 Commando), largely because the marines were moving forward so quickly and the situation on the ground was consequently very fluid.

The attack fully bore out John's insistence that he would only call in an attack if he could see the troops and the attacking aircraft, something that he had learned to be essential in Korea and that became a personal mantra when working in the FAC role. Incidentally there was no coloured smoke available for target marking for the attacking aircraft. Three-inch mortar Sky Trail coloured smoke arrived, like John's Land Rover, too late.

Meanwhile, orders had been received elsewhere instructing A Troop to secure the British Consulate where the Consul was under house arrest. Consulate Square proved to be well defended but the strong points were quickly neutralised by the twenty-pounders of Centurion tanks and the Commandos' own 3.5-inch rocket launchers. Twenty enemy were killed and fourteen prisoners of war taken. A large cache of weapons and ammunition was recovered. Eventually darkness halted any further advance. Navy House Quay was sealed off, all positions were consolidated and battle was suspended for the night, although intermittent sniping continued. On the following day, 7 November, the remaining four Egyptian naval officers and six ratings in Navy House finally surrendered and at midday what was left of the building was occupied without incident.

Meanwhile, 42 Commando had landed on the beach code-named Sierra Green to the west of 40 Commando in three waves. The assault went almost according to plan, although it was fortunate that the first wave came ashore at H Hour + 3 as the final air strikes on the beaches were late and arrived at H + 2 instead of H minus 5.... 'an exciting moment through the smoke and haze' as the war diary records. The troops came ashore and immediately started house clearing, the first blocks of buildings being taken against light opposition. When the tanks came ashore 42 Commando formed up with them as 40 Commando had done, ready for their first sortie into town. Their objective was the power station and cold storage depot. After a short ride along the Shari Mohamed Ali under intense small arms fire both were taken and contact made with the French who had parachuted onto the golf course. An air strike was called on a concentration of enemy troops east of the interior basin and close to the prison and succeeded in dispersing them. This marked the beginning of the end of organised resistance to 42 Commando who were then ordered to take the Italian Consulate. This was peacefully achieved using a tank to force a conventional entry through the front door! It was H + 8 hours.

It was to 45 Commando, which had been kept as a flexible mobile reserve, that the honour of conducting the world's first ever helicopter landing and assault fell. To prepare for this possibility they had carried out a heliborne exercise on the island of Comino on 1 November. Initially the assault had been planned for the north of the interior basin at Port Said. However, the task of seizing the bridges there had been allotted to the French parachute brigade so the assault was instead directed to two other vital bridges across a water gap in a built up and well defended area, which could not be outflanked by land. John didn't see much of the helicopters (although he heard them) as 40 Commando were preoccupied with their own advance at the time and there wasn't much opportunity to look back.

The first helicopter, an 845 Squadron Westland Whirlwind HAS 22, carrying Lt Col Norman Tailyour, 45 Commando's OC, had taken off at 0545 and headed towards Port Said to confirm which of three pre-selected landing zones should be used. The first was close to the site of the recently established 3 Commando Brigade HQ but this was obstructed by overhead wires. (The HQ was eventually re-established in two blocks of flats on the sea front.) The second was the sports stadium where the five marines the Whirlwind was carrying were offloaded. Egyptian defenders at the stadium had been caught unawares by the sudden arrival of the aircraft and it was not until it took off again that they opened fire and caught the marines unawares in turn. The pilot hurriedly landed and the marines scrambled back on board to be finally landed near the waterfront on a piece of waste ground close to the statue of Ferdinand de Lesseps, the Suez Canal's builder, at 0630. The signal was given then for the rest of the airborne assault force to start ferrying troops ashore from *Ocean* and *Theseus* eight miles offshore. Incredibly there were no maps on board the carriers and nobody knew precisely where de Lesseps Square was until the Commanding Officer of the Sycamore Flight produced a postcard of Port Said that showed the statue of de Lesseps, sent to him by his mother who had been there recently. The first heliborne assault in history was, so legend has it, initiated on the strength of a picture postcard!

By 0800 hours 425 men and 23 tons of stores had been landed in the area secured by 40 and 42 Commandos. This was achieved by the eight Whirlwind HAS 22s and two Whirlwind Mk 3s of 845 Squadron and the six Whirlwind Mk 2s and six diminutive Sycamore Mk 14s of the JHU. They flew a total of eighty sorties, which, given the limited capacity of the aircraft involved, was quite a remarkable achievement. Carrying a hundred miles' worth of fuel the Whirlwind Mk 2 could carry just five troops who, in the absence of seating, sat on the floor. There was no radio communication between pilot and passengers, the only means of communicating being by tugging at the pilot's legs to attract his attention and then shouting. An HAS 22 could carry seven men and a Mk 3 six. The Sycamore carried only three men, two with their legs hanging out either side of the fuselage and the third between them. He was not only responsible for hanging on to his colleagues but had six mortar bombs balanced across his knees: each of the others had a three-foot anti-tank shell to contend with. There were of course considerations associated with such a lift that are not immediately obvious. Refuelling for instance. Only six Whirlwinds could be refuelled simultaneously and because the remaining aircraft were forced to orbit until deck space became available, speed in refuelling was vital. The amount of fuel each helicopter could carry was dependent on a compromise between reduced fuel and a bigger payload. Full tanks meant a reduced payload but less refuelling meant delays. After the operation, 45 Commando's analysis of the heliborne assault concluded that *Musketeer* proved that the helicopter was a highly suitable vehicle for landing troops across water or other obstacles, was less vulnerable than commonly perceived and in sufficient numbers provided an extremely flexible and rapid means of building up and maintaining a force in an assault area. At the time of Suez though the potential of helicopter operations was limited by unsuitable aircraft and thus troops lifted in became comparatively immobile until vehicles could be landed by other means. The advent of the Wessex, capable of lifting a quarter-ton vehicle, was looked forward to, but the first flight of the type was still two years away. Nevertheless, Operation *Musketeer* proved that the possibilities for employing a helicopter-borne striking force, whenever local air superiority could be obtained, was far reaching.

Once the assault was completed the helicopters were fully involved in casualty evacuation (casevac) and flying in the men of the RAF Regiment, although several helicopters were hit by fire from shore batteries in the process. On the ground 45 Commando's vehicles began coming ashore from LSTs and LCTs in the fishing harbour prior to fighting their way through to secure the Shari Mohamed Ali north of the Shari Eugenie and securing the Brigade's right flank. Then suddenly a blue on blue situation erupted. 3 Commando Brigade's HQ and two of 45 Commando's Troops were hit by a Fleet Air Arm Westland Wyvern of 830 Squadron. The Joint Fire Support Committee (JFSC) on HMS *Meon* had ordered that an enemy gun that was firing on destroyers supporting the landing should be engaged by three aircraft patrolling the skies above Suez. They were directed onto a map reference that was one square too far to the east. Sixteen marines of A and B Troops were wounded, including 45 Commando's CO, Lt Col Tailyour, and the Intelligence Officer. All wireless sets were damaged and for a short period contact was lost. 40 Commando's ambulances assisted in the ensuing casevac by taking the wounded to helicopters that took them out to *Ocean* and *Theseus*.

Some marines were trying to lay out fluorescent identification panels at the very time the attack started. As with so much other equipment, despite the relatively long lead time, these panels had not been delivered to 3 Commando Brigade until just before embarkation and thus could not be used on any of the Malta exercises. There was much speculation therefore that one of the reasons the Wyverns pressed home their attack was that they were not familiar with the panels and didn't understand their significance. Another opinion was that Navy pilots were not able to obtain maps in a scale larger than 1/100,000, which reduced Port Said to the size of a penny, unacceptably small for close air support purposes. Whatever the reason or extenuating circumstances may or may not have been, the same aircraft went on to attack 42 Commando a short distance away. This was not a strike of which Forward Air Controllers on the ground had control and John and his team, despite trying to call off the aircraft on the common ground frequency (as indeed did the ACTs with 42 and 45 Commando), could only watch as the reality of what was happening dawned on them.

The Wyvern attack was later the subject of much investigation. Lt Col Tailyour was very critical of the JFSC on HMS *Meon*.

> The shortcomings of HMS *Meon* were obvious...the ACTs never reached the stage where they had any confidence in the JFSC. Events unfortunately confirmed our misgivings. There appears to be no excuse for the omission of adequate military briefing being given to the pilots of the close support aircraft. This is the one salient factor which would have avoided 30% of the total casualties suffered by our own side being inflicted by our own aircraft.

The close air support at Port Said was provided from a cabrank (a holding pattern used by the fighter bombers enabling them to be called down by radio to give immediate support to ground troops), which was controlled either by the JFSC or the Offensive Support Annexe ashore. Aircraft on the cabrank, the JFSC and the

ACTs all listened on a common frequency and when aircraft were allotted to an ACT the JFSC told the mission leader which frequency he was to use for the strike. Having contacted the ACT, the mission leader told them to change to the allotted frequency and the strike could begin.

The Wyvern attack didn't stop 45 Commando's advance. At 0840 opposition was met in the grounds of Government House but this was soon cleared and the building occupied. By 0915 B Troop were moving forward to assist in clearing snipers. The houses and seven-storey blocks of flats lining Shari Mohamed Ali were cleared by 1100. 45 Commando was now ordered west to clear all houses north of the Shari Eugenie and to make contact with the 3rd Parachute Battalion coming from El Gamil. At 1320 C Squadron of the Royal Tank Regiment joined them and they became invaluable in speeding up the house clearing, which carried on for much of the rest of the day. The opposition varied considerably with much of the fighting being spirited if not well coordinated and directed.

Once Port Said was taken, the British Royal Marines and the French Foreign Legion advanced a short way down both sides of the canal south of Port Said at rather uneven speeds because of the slower British heavy tanks on the west bank and the lighter French on the east. By 1730 gathering darkness meant a cessation in the advance at El Cap where the tired troops prepared for the night. Road blocks and patrols were set up and organised. Then to everyone's amazement a cease-fire was called – could it really be over so quickly? Most surprisingly of all and much to the disbelief of senior officers, they didn't learn of it through official channels. As one afterwards commented:

> I realise how bedevilled the Superior Commanders were by the politicians but it is incredible in retrospect – and was indeed at the time – that the first news of the cease fire that I received was at 1815Z from the BBC, later repeated on the 1900Z BBC News. My orders for the cease fire arrived from HQ at 2314Z.

The cease-fire became effective at 2359 hours.

CHAPTER TWELVE

Debrief

*The servicemen did all that was asked of them, reacting swiftly to
changes of plan resulting from indecision in high places but
committed to battle with obsolete equipment, the result of
indifference and parsimony by ministers.*

Royal Marines. From Sea Soldiers to Special Force

T he operation to take Port Said and open the way for the advance down the
canal towards Suez itself had been planned for three months and was over
in a matter of hours. It was certainly successful from a military point of
view, although the troops were disappointed that they weren't allowed to finish the
job they had started. Politically, however, Operation *Musketeer* was a disaster for
France and Britain. The US was incensed that two of her Allies should have acted
as they did and was particularly concerned about the prospects of a wider war after
the Soviet Union had threatened to intervene on the Egyptian side and launch
attacks by 'all types of modern weapons of destruction' on London and Paris. The
Eisenhower administration forced the cease-fire, largely by threatening financial
sanctions against Britain, threats that included selling the US reserves of the
British pound, which, if it were to happen, would cause a collapse of British
currency. Anthony Eden had no choice but to resign. The last of the invading
forces withdrew in March 1957.

When the cease-fire was called the 19th and 39th Infantry Brigades of the 3rd
Infantry Division landed at Port Said and remained there until replaced by UN
forces. Within a few days the first of the Royal Marines sailed back to Malta. The
FACs stayed on a little longer in case they were needed if the cease-fire came
under threat. John was garrisoned for a few days with the 1st Royal Scots
Battalion, the Black Watch, but then he too, along with the other controllers,
returned to Malta on board the troopship *Empire Fowey* with more of the Royal
Marines, arriving on 17 November. From Malta John flew back to the UK, had a
week in London, then rejoined 222 Squadron at Leuchars in the New Year. He had
been away for four months and for a while he was the centre of attention as
interested RAF colleagues wanted to find out exactly what he had been up to. For

John, Suez represented another significant step in his career and the opportunity to have participated in the way he did and to have experienced the fighting qualities of the Royal Marines at first hand was something that he has never forgotten.

Whilst he was busy briefing his squadron colleagues, military assessments of the Suez operation were well underway. It had been successful but there were elements of it that needed urgent attention. The lack of up-to-date equipment was certainly a restrictive factor.

In *Royal Marines. From Sea Soldiers to a Special Force* Julian Thompson states:

> Although 3rd Commando Brigade had been brought back to Malta from Cyprus and 42 Commando sent out to join it from England one of the main problems was the lack of sufficient amphibious shipping immediately available and in commission for the Brigade and all the necessary follow up units....Such LSTs and LCTs that remained from the Second World War, eleven years earlier, had been mothballed, sold or scrapped. Time had to be spent gathering together and commissioning mothballed ships and finding crews.

Another very real problem the Allies had had to contend with during the crisis was the absence of properly trained, properly equipped FACs. Steps were taken to rectify this immediately after Suez. These steps were prompted in part by a report entitled 'Close Air Support of 3 Commando Brigade and the 3rd Infantry Division' by a Major TW Whittaker of the Royal Welch Fusiliers who had been responsible for the training of the Air Control Teams that were deployed to Suez. He describes how the Royal Air Force, Fleet Air Arm and French Air Force and Navy were tasked with supporting British and French troops on the ground. It was decided that strikes in support of troops should be directed onto the target in the initial assault by a FAC and furthermore by a FAC of the same nationality as the pilot. ACTs were thus formed to match the forces available, most of which consisted of both British and French personnel. Three were formed in Malta at the end of August 1956 and were joined by others from the British Army of the Rhine and Cyprus. They were completed by the addition of a GLO (Ground Liaison Officer) from the UK.

During the assault on 6 November, ACTs placed under the command of the 3rd Commando Brigade engaged three targets at the request of the Commandos and controlled three visual reconnaissance missions. The fact that the Egyptians used no artillery, mortars or tanks in the battle meant there was little need for close air support. Nonetheless, given that it was impossible to use naval gunfire support in the town and given that the Commando Brigade had no artillery of its own, ground support aircraft were all that was available. But there were no Mosquitoes – those aircraft acting as eyes in the sky for reconnaissance purposes, which had been so successful in Korea and not to be confused with the de Havilland Wooden Wonder. As Major Whittaker stated:

> The indication of targets in built up areas is very difficult due to the restricted field of view. Similar difficulty is found in heavily wooded or hilly country. The provision of Mosquitoes to supplement the ACTs in Port Said would have been most useful. Mosquitoes can only be used when the air situation is favourable but they can make a big contribution to the efficiency of close air support. Their role is similar to that of the Air Observation Post.

In the light of his Korean experience John was asked by Major Whittaker to contribute directly to his report on the matter of Mosquitoes. Their role, said John, was:

- to identify targets that are in dead ground and so are not visible from the ACT.
- to mark targets as ordered by the ACT. This is much more efficient than using coloured artillery or mortar smoke.
- to relay messages between JOC (Joint Operations Centre) and the ACTs in the event of communication failure.
- in carrying out these duties the Mosquitoes can provide much information about enemy dispositions in the forward area.
- the aircraft chosen to act as a Mosquito should have a pilot and observer, should have two to three hours' endurance and should work with a number of ACTs concurrently. Mosquitoes can also be laid on for special ops or at the request of an ACT to cover a specific situation. They are not required to be on station all the time.

John and two other RAF officers who had also had experience with the SAAF in Korea (one as an FAC and one operating as a Mosquito), were assigned to the Royal Marines. In addition, there were also ACTs formed to support the 3rd Infantry Division (a substantial part of which had been deployed from the UK to Malta) but these were without GLOs, were untrained and short of even unsuitable equipment. The three ACTs formed on Malta had been able to carry out a large number of exercises with aircraft from carrier squadrons and consequently an acceptable standard was reached. Similar opportunities were not available for the controllers with the 3rd Infantry Division and they thus arrived in Port Said unprepared.

FACs were required not only to work with the ground forces but with the paras as well. The problem was that the RAF were unable to provide suitable officers who were also trained parachutists. This fact had been overlooked, it being thought that the only qualifications necessary for an FAC were the ability to 'fly an aeroplane and to talk on the wireless'. To fill the gap army officers from the 16th Parachute Brigade were selected, four of whom underwent special training.

Two were assigned to 16 Para itself and two to the French 10th Para Division. Two French pilots were also found to drop with 16 Para, thereby satisfying the requirement for an ability to talk to British and French pilots. In addition, two REME officers were trained by the RAF to drop with the 3rd Parachute Battalion at El Gamil. They were particularly successful, controlling strikes to within a hundred yards of their own troops.

Another major problem had been the equipment for the ACTs. To start with much of it was not immediately available and when it arrived it was found to be categorically not man portable. It had to be obtained on special War Office authority and took up to six weeks to come through and when it did it was in dribs and drabs.

Other recommendations made by John were that:

- ACTs should be established as part of the Air Support Signals Unit.
- FACs should be trained before being sent to ACTs.
- A man portable VHF and UHF ground to air set was essential.

As a result of this and other reports and the discussion they prompted, the Joint Forward Air Control Training and Standards Unit was formed at RAF Brawdy. Two Jet Provost trainers were assigned to the unit, which moved to RAF Finningley in 1993 where it operated two Hawk fast jet trainers. In 1995 it relocated again, this time to RAF Leeming where it still resides.

Apart from the specifics of Forward Air Controlling, there were of course reams of more generalised analytical reports produced after Suez. It is interesting to briefly consider what the Commanding Officers of the three Marine Commandos contributed. 40 Commando's David Tweed felt that more time should have been spent in the joint planning of the exercises in Malta. As it was, the planners operated from London and were thus unable to apply lessons learned to subsequent exercises. When it came to the landing itself he said:

> We should guard against the belief that there was sufficient fire support at Port Said. If the enemy had fought, which he was perfectly able to do, we should not have got a firm footing on the beaches without considerable casualties. The fact that the enemy did not fight on the beaches should not lead us away from the fact that this is the most vulnerable point of an amphibious operation which if done in daylight needs enough fire support to neutralise the opposition.

On air support he said: 'When correctly used the air arm is the outstanding support weapon.'

Lt Col Norcock, OC 42 Commando, agreed:

> The controlled air strikes were first class thanks to the amount of practice the ACTs had during the training period in Malta. The fear caused by these strikes to the enemy was instrumental in saving many lives on both sides.

On training in general, no amphibious training had been carried out at any level by 3 Commando Brigade prior to arriving in Malta. Two major exercises followed individual and unit training – *Septex I* on 5 and 6 September was an assault landing on the beach at Mellieha Bay and *Septex 2* on 13 and 14 September involved the docks at Marsaxlokk. After these two exercises a completely new invasion plan was ordered and no further large-scale exercises were held until 6 October when Exercise *Fridex* took place and 9 and 10 October when Exercise *Wedex* was planned, both taking place in Mellieha Bay. The exercises were undoubtedly useful but once the men had landed there was nowhere for them to operate with any degree of achieving realism. If an 'energetic enemy' had been made available for each landing it would have been better.

As for 45 Commando's heliborne assault, Lt Col Norman Tailyour acknowledged its success but qualified it by saying: 'It must be clearly understood...that a helicopter force on landing suffers from a total lack of transport.'

As for the use of helicopters for casevac, Lt Col Norcock had this to say:

> The evacuation of wounded by helicopter when part of my unit was isolated on the Golf Course area was instrumental in saving life and was carried out with great skill under difficult and dangerous conditions.

It is perhaps appropriate to let Major General Julian Thompson, a Royal Marine himself for thirty-four years, provide a concluding summary of Suez. The following is from *Royal Marines. From Sea Soldiers to Special Force.*

> To this day the Suez operation is frequently tagged a military fiasco. It was nothing of the kind. It was a political fiasco. The servicemen did all that was asked of them, reacting swiftly to changes of plan resulting from indecision in high places but committed to battle with obsolete equipment, the result of indifference and parsimony by ministers....Eden, having decide to topple Nasser against the advice of his Chiefs of Staff, did not have the will to see it through. Britain's standing in the world and with the Arabs in particular plummeted. British casualties were twenty two killed and ninety seven wounded. Of these the Commando Brigade had nine dead and sixty wounded. Some of the latter would have died had they not been casevaced to the ships by helicopter. The French lost ten dead and thirty wounded.

CHAPTER THIRTEEN

The Sandys Era

Flt Lt Howe was welcomed back to the squadron after his detachment to the Middle East where he had taken part in the occupation of Port Said.
222 Squadron Form 540

It was good to get back to Leuchars and the squadron. If I wasn't on the ground fighting I wanted to be flying and I was very happy to be flying again.
John Howe

The above sentiment is reflected in the first entries in John's log book on his return to Scotland. On 8 January 1957 he had a refamiliarisation sortie in a Vampire T.11. And then on 9 January an exuberant 'height climb, Mach run and aeros'. There had been a change of command whilst he was away. Ken Cooke had gone to be replaced by the rather less outgoing but well liked Jed Gray who gave John command of C Flight and thereby responsibility for ground ops. This included writing operations orders for deployments and there was soon one required for Armament Practice Camp (APC) at Acklington. This John duly did and, once the deployment was completed, he completed a further order for the return to Leuchars. By this time he and Jed Gray were getting on well enough for this to be written thus: 'Amend original order, replace from with to and the date to 20th March.' The CO didn't quite know how to react until John passed over the real, properly written, order!

The disciplines of an air defence squadron soon fell back into place. Cine exercises were at the top of the list in preparation for an air firing programme at the end of January. High-velocity ammunition was being used for the first time with all firing done between 20,000 and 25,000 feet. But with no air firing having been possible since the previous year's APC this proved to be a difficult exercise, for there had been a turnover of pilots since then to the extent that only six of the fourteen taking part had any previous experience of air-to-air firing in a Hunter. At the end of the programme John came out as top scorer with an average of 16.7 per cent, which was a good way in which to re-establish himself on the squadron.

Whilst John had been away the runway repair and resurfacing work that had started at Leuchars before he left for Suez had progressed significantly. The main runway had been completed but now the contractors were disrupting operations on the ground as they turned their attention to taxiways and pans. Not all of the squadron's aircraft were at Leuchars, however, for 222 maintained a detachment at RAF Ta'Kali in Malta and in February John and Jed Gray flew out via Tangmere and Istres to exchange aircraft. Their return was delayed both by poor weather and the unserviceability of the Hunters they were bringing back so they took the opportunity to visit 40 Commando and for John there was the chance to reacquaint himself with his former colleagues in arms. Back home, Suez and the consequent fuel shortage was temporarily having an effect on squadrons' flying hours' targets with pilots restricted to just twelve hours a month each. By this time Leuchars' main runway was closed again to allow the construction of an extension, which meant the secondary 1,650 yard strip was in use (and would be until November when the main runway reopened permanently). Some of John's twelve hours were taken up with a series of night checks on a Vampire T.11, the pilots being checked including Flying Officers Alcock and Brown! Then came the first of numerous fly-past rehearsals leading up to the presentation of a new Standard to 43 Squadron on 4 June by the Queen. This was a complex affair flying wise with the three Leuchars squadrons picking out a difficult 'ER' in the sky with their Hunters and Vampires. It took a lot of practice but by the time the actual day arrived four months later it was perfect. Of interest on the ground on that day was the small display of static aircraft that included a Fireflash-armed Supermarine Swift, the prototype English Electric P1A and the Fairey FD2.

It wouldn't be long before John would be inheriting the traditions of 43 Squadron himself. In the meantime he was part of a detachment to RAF Horsham St Faith for Exercise *Fabulous*. It is interesting to note what mounting such detachments entailed. The majority of the ground party made the long journey to Norfolk by train. Six Hunters and a Meteor T.7 were flown down, with reserve pilots making the journey in rather slower time in a Valetta. Support equipment was loaded onto a couple of three-ton lorries and a Land Rover. What was deemed necessary to support seven aircraft away from base for a week's detachment in 1957? Amongst the items were:

- Six main and two nose wheels complete with six spare covers and tubes
- Six wheel chocks
- Wheel jacks
- One tow arm
- One steering arm
- One hydraulic dispenser
- One engine oil dispenser (full) and four gallons spare
- Six aircraft ladders
- Six full sets picketing equipment, covers and blanks

- Electrical spares pack up
- Instrument spares pack up
- One large tool box, special tools and equipment
- One large tool box for airframe spares
- Individual tool kits
- Spare ammunition
- Armament tool kits
- Two gun pack cradles and trolleys
- Two gun packs
- Meteor 7 control locks and cover

Back at Leuchars Raymond Davidson was lost on 25 March when he crashed into the sea at night. John was fifteen seconds ahead of him on the QGH (the radio direction finding let-down procedure) in poor weather. It is thought that Davidson misread his altimeter, which was possible in those days because of the way it was displayed. For instance, 10,000 feet could be easily mistaken for 1,000 feet if glanced at quickly in a heavy workload situation. April was a month of intense training and preparation for the AOC's inspection in the first week in May. Then John started his conversion to the Meteor F.8 by going solo on the Station Flight T.7 after asymmetric training. One of the great problems with the Meteor, which had an engine on each wing, was the fact that if one engine failed the aircraft would slew because of the sudden transfer of power to the other wing and this was the cause of a considerable number of accidents. So it was that asymmetrics (as it was known) was writ large in any conversion to the type. It took seven sorties on the T.7 before John first took the F.8 aloft. But the Meteor did not feature for long in John's log books for it was disappearing fast from the front line by this time. It was used at Leuchars for target towing.

Exercise *Vigilant* was held over two days at the end of May. This was a United Kingdom Air Defence Exercise sponsored by Fighter Command, which tested the country's air defences with three major attacks by NATO aircraft (two by day and one by night) on each day. 222 Squadron was heavily involved alongside 43 and 151. They moved temporarily to RAF Turnhouse where excellent weather helped ensure a high interception rate. On their return to Leuchars almost all training flying ceased with the main thrust being in preparation for the visit of Her Majesty. The fly-past was on 4 June as already recounted and 222 contributed seven Hunters. From the next day the squadron stood down for twelve days, although John was involved in a ceremony on 7 June to commemorate the Norwegians who had flown from Leuchars during the war, a newly erected memorial being dedicated on that day. John's contribution to that and to the fly-past itself had evidently been recognised for two weeks later he received a letter from the Station Commander, Group Captain Beardon.

Dear Howe,

Just a short note to thank you for:

(a) Acting as a 'guide' on the VIP coaches on 3rd and 4th June.
(b) Holding the 'R' together on 4th June [in the formation].
(c) Acting as a host to the Norwegians.
(d) Standing at attention for a very long period without moving on 7th June.

All these tasks you performed very ably and very smartly: well done.

July saw total squadron flying hours climb to 400 for the first time in a year. However, this was halved in August and Wing Commander Flying was increasingly putting 222 Squadron's CO under pressure to maintain higher totals despite the fact that they had been on detachment to Horsham St Faith again as well as Middleton St George, thereby reducing the opportunities for the concentrated flying programme necessary. In addition, for John at least, August 1957 was a month largely given over to aerobatics in preparation for the September Battle of Britain airshows at Leuchars itself and Kinloss. Such shows were numerous throughout the UK at this time and involved dozens if not hundreds of RAF aircraft. It was a sad fact that in those days the RAF regularly lost more aircraft to practice and rehearsal for them than on any other operational deployments throughout the year.

Commemoration of the summer of 1940 over, September finished with the week-long Exercise *Strikeback*. This involved 150 warships from six NATO nations in large-scale combined fleet manoeuvres that ranged over the whole of the North Atlantic and into the Norwegian and North Seas. It was the largest peacetime naval exercise ever held up to that time and the RAF was quick to seize the opportunity to participate. But the exercise also sadly marked the demise of 222 Squadron for immediately afterwards it disbanded, a victim of Duncan Sandys' infamous White Paper, which predicted the end of fixed wing aircraft in favour of the missile.

The following is from the 222 Squadron Form 540:

A sad day for the squadron was the 28th September when it flew its last sorties as an operational squadron. With effect from October 1st the squadron becomes non operational and it is to disband on November 1st. Unfortunately spirit, morale, determination and efficiency cannot always be taken into consideration when disbanding squadrons otherwise No 222 (Natal) Squadron would continue. We are one of the squadrons which has been chosen for disbandment under the new future defence policy....Needless to say morale at the moment is extremely low but this is unavoidable. All ranks are to be commended on the final months' flying effort in which 387 hours were flown. Fl Lt Ewan will take over command of the squadron on 11th October until final disbandment on 1st November.

The squadron's silver was handed over to the Officers' Mess at Leuchars for safekeeping. 222 Squadron did reclaim it in 1960 when it reformed at Woodhall Spa as a Bloodhound missile unit (which was a little ironic given the cause of its demise in 1957) but by 1964 it had gone for good.

As a postscript to these events, an ex-222 Squadron pilot who moved into civil aviation enjoys relating the following story.

> As pilot of a British Airways flight I was informed Lord Sandys was on board. I put on my hat and went down to the rear of the aircraft. Greeting Lord and Lady Sandys the conversation went as follows.
>
> 'Lord Sandys, I have wanted a word with you for a number of years.'
>
> 'Good Lord, Captain. You weren't in the RAF in 1957 were you?'
>
> 'I was and that is the point I wished to raise.'
>
> 'Ah yes. I really made a total cock up of that, indeed I did. Got it completely wrong!'
>
> He didn't say 'we' did as a government but 'I' did as an individual. What does one say to such an honest confession? It quite took the wind from my sails and he went up in my estimation as a politician after that.

Much has been written over the past fifty years about Sandys' White Paper and the impact it had. However, not all that has been postulated has been accurate and this seems like a useful point at which to attempt a balanced picture of what led to the Paper, its ramifications and its longer term impact.

By 1956 the austerities of the war and the early post-war period had been replaced by the increasing demands of a consumer society. The longer term effect this change had on social, economic and political life ultimately affected Britain's ability as well as political will to maintain a world position, and accordingly the need for a reappraisal of defence and foreign policies would not go unrecognised. However, that reappraisal would come a few years hence. In 1956, the emphasis militarily as far as forward planning was concerned was a move towards smaller conventional forces and a greater reliance on the nuclear deterrent, which would enable a reduction in the costs of defence without abandoning any major commitment. In 1956 Fighter Command contained fifty-five squadrons of 578 aircraft with an additional 143 in the day fighter squadrons of the Royal Auxiliary Air Force. Plans to introduce Surface to Air Guided Weapons (SAGWs), developed in close co-operation with the USA, into the air defence of Britain with more and better weapons to follow would, it was argued, diminish the size of Fighter Command considerably – and so it did, so much so that within ten years it would disappear as a separate Command, but not because of SAGWs.

The 1957 White Paper set out the government's view of the future of the country's defence and underscored the new technology that would effect that defence. Much of the Paper's content had been discussed and formulated in the era prior to the arrival of Duncan Sandys as Defence Minister but, having been persuaded of its relevance, it fell to him to present it to the nation. What primarily moved the government to the key decisions it contained was a belief that economic performance had to be improved if an important world role was to be sustained and that, in 1957, was what government of the day still foresaw as being desirable. So the nuclear dimension of defence was seen as providing the opportunity for economies that would make a major contribution to economic progress without any sacrifices in national security or international influence. Key to this was the balance that could be struck between nuclear deterrence and conventional forces given that there were limits to the extent to which security could be achieved by nuclear capability alone.

In 1957 it was considered that as part of these proposed economies a substantial reduction in the allocation of manpower to all three Services was necessary and this focused attention on National Service, which, it was projected, would be phased out over the ensuing few years. The significance of this decision, taken incidentally against the advice of the Chiefs of Staff, was a failure to appreciate the cost to future defence budgets of recruiting and maintaining volunteer forces as opposed to conscripted forces. Also underestimated was the ability to recruit the necessary numbers to maintain the Services. In addition, with the move towards greater reliance on nuclear deterrence the government reduced the resources devoted to research and the development of conventional weaponry. Thus the period from 1956 was notable for projects abandoned or replaced by others less worthy, although to be fair there were also some projects successfully brought into service during the same time.

Rumours about the radical nature of the White Paper had been circulating for a while before Duncan Sandys delivered it to the House and it was therefore awaited with an expectancy that marked no other similar post-war document up to that time. And if only by the controversy it inspired those expectations were justified. To take just one point, the perceived threat from thermonuclear weapons as expressed in the Paper led to much parliamentary and public debate about the morality as well as the effectiveness of the new government policy. For the Services themselves the impact of the Paper differed. The Royal Navy would be the least affected by the decision on National Service but there was uncertainty about its future role. The Army faced major reductions in total strength and the consequent task of disbanding or amalgamating large numbers of units was not a particularly palatable one. Its commitments within and outside Europe would remain: it would simply have less with which to meet them.

As for the RAF, the logic of nuclear deterrence coupled with the foreseeable developments of offensive and defensive guided missiles was widely interpreted as the beginning of the end of manned aircraft, although what some commentators missed was the fact that the Paper recognised the impossibility of providing adequate protection for the whole of the UK were that to happen. That being the case the overriding consideration in all military planning would henceforth have to be to prevent war rather than prepare for it and the only realistic safeguard against major aggression was the power to threaten retaliation with nuclear weapons. The primacy of the US as a protective power was acknowledged. Nevertheless it was imperative, the Paper said, that Britain possessed an appreciable element of nuclear deterrent power of her own and the means of delivery of her kiloton and megaton weapons would be the V bomber force, supplemented by ballistic missiles such as the Thor Intermediate Range Ballistic Missile (IRBM). Duncan Sandys accordingly announced the cancellation of the development of a supersonic bomber in favour of such IRBMs for they would ultimately replace the manned bomber in the way that SAGWs would replace the manned fighter. In the meantime Fighter Command, which would no longer be required to provide an effective defence for the whole country, would concentrate on the defence of the V bomber airfields as an essential part of the deterrent. There was unlikely to be a need therefore for a fighter more advanced than the Lightning. Thus it was announced that work on future fighter projects would stop as well. So the decision to cancel an all-weather supersonic twin-seat interceptor fighter with a seventy-five-minute sortie duration was added to that of the supersonic bomber.

The government actually found it necessary to put out a memorandum after the White Paper's publication, which was at pains to stop intense speculation about the future of manned fighters, stating that they would continue in service in the United Kingdom 'for a considerable time'. But all in all the message had been clear: the fighter was a declining feature of defence against the weapons and the means of delivery that would threaten Britain in the relatively near future. Interestingly the Paper gave no indication of what that threat would be nor its timescale. Looking back we can see that the state of Russian ballistic missile development in 1957 meant that they would have a missile capable of use against Britain from launching sites in Russia by 1961. By mid 1957 the first missile-firing Russian submarines were already at sea and the first Russian Intercontinental Ballistic Missiles (ICBMs) were expected to be deployed by 1962. Neither was anything said in the Paper about those tasks for which a fighter would still be needed (even if the utmost reliance could be placed on SAGWs), such as the interception of unidentified aircraft approaching British airspace in peacetime or the support and reinforcement of fighter forces stationed overseas, fighters on a very different tasking to those under NATO's aegis.

The 1957 White Paper with its radical proposals and controversial actions was viewed with incredulity by serving members of the Service, most of whom could only reflect on the implications for them as individuals. The proposed reduction in squadrons, squadron sizes and thus aircrew would make that point obvious. The Chiefs of the Air Staff and the Air Council fought long and hard with the Defence Ministry to minimise the impact in the years subsequent to the Paper. However, shifts in defence policy, modified NATO policies and in the longer term a realisation that Britain would no longer be able to afford to continue to police the world and more specifically the by now shrinking Commonwealth as she had hitherto done whatever adjustments were made to defence spending, meant that come 1963 much of the 1957 White Paper's premise had changed. The most significant factor was the failure of the projected missile defence of the country to replace defence by manned fighters. From 1957 there was a constant round of discussion and debate of this issue involving the MoD, the Air Ministry, the Chiefs of Staff, the Defence Council and government and whilst debate raged little progressed, with the consequence that by 1960 the actual deployment of SAGWs had been very significantly reduced. Bloodhound Mk 1 survived because the money had already been spent or committed and Bloodhound Mk 2 was introduced from 1964. The White Paper had planned for twenty squadrons supported by at least twenty SAGW squadrons. But despite the demise of SAGWs, by 1963 there were just three squadrons of Javelins and five of Lightnings. And after the planned disbandment of the Javelin force by 1965 the latter were seen as the total interceptor force for the rest of the 1960s and beyond. The ten squadrons of Bloodhound Mk 1s were expected to disappear by 1965, leaving half a dozen squadrons with the Mk 2.

To complete the bigger picture, the future Bomber Command had been envisaged as consisting of twenty-three V bomber squadrons, five Canberra squadrons, four recce squadrons and a small tanker force. It was not expected to retain this strength indefinitely because of the advent of ICBMs, but Phase 2 would nonetheless consist of one hundred upgraded V bombers with updated British air-to-surface weapons and sixty Blue Streak ballistic missiles. By 1963 the force was expected to comprise no more than eighty-six aircraft for the rest of the decade for which Blue Steel would be available. But Blue Streak and Skybolt were scrapped and Thor was close to being withdrawn. Canberra bombers had gone and the recce asset had been reduced to two squadrons. The position of the tanker force had been improved with three squadrons of Victor Mk 1s due in service but this was because of the needs of overseas reinforcement rather than the bomber role in Europe. RAF strategic forces were thus very much smaller in capability as well as numbers than had been planned in 1957.

The reductions in Fighter and Bomber Commands were offset in part by two additional Coastal Command squadrons. RAF Germany was also stronger than anticipated, with no reductions in strike and recce forces and two fighter squadrons unexpectedly retained. A start had also been made in creating a helicopter force. Transport Command had increased from eight squadrons of Britannias, Comets, Beverleys and helicopters to three Britannia/Comet squadrons, six tactical transport squadrons and three of helicopters. Finally, outside the sphere of NATO there had actually been significant improvements with thirty-two squadrons in three overseas Commands, although this would be reversed within ten years.

CHAPTER FOURTEEN

Fighting Cocks

*I was a Flying Officer on 43 and had only recently moved up from
being the junior pilot when John arrived. Unfortunately his move
also meant my move within the month to a not brief enough ground
job and premature release. I had known John in the mess whilst he
was on 222 and was fascinated by his having flown Mustangs in
Korea. Quite a few years later I was Captain of a British Airways
flight and after making the usual cabin address a hostess came up
front to tell me that a passenger knew me from my RAF days
and presented his card. It was John, looking much the same
as he had all those years before.*

Bruce Cousins

After 222 Squadron's demise John, together with a few of his colleagues, didn't have far to go for his next posting – just across the pan in fact to Sqn Ldr John Langer's 43 Squadron, which he joined on 2 October 1957 as B Flight Commander with Peter Bairsto on A Flight. 43 hadn't totally escaped the Sandys axe. Fewer squadrons meant fewer men and that resulted in many aircrew on Short Service Commissions throughout the RAF being grounded. Flt Lt Powell, whom John replaced on B Flight, was one such.

43 Squadron, motto *Gloria Finis* (Glory is the End), was formed at Stirling on 15 April 1916 as a unit of the Royal Flying Corps. It took a year for 43 Squadron to reach the Western Front in France with its Sopwith 1½-Strutters, which were used on reconnaissance. Following re-equipment with Sopwith Camels the men of 43 Squadron forged an excellent fighting reputation for themselves. After the war, the squadron briefly moved to Germany, returning to the UK in August 1919 prior to disbandment at the end of the year. It lay dormant until July 1925 when it reformed at Hendon tasked with fighter defence, equipped with Snipes and then Gamecocks. It was taking the latter aircraft on charge that inspired the squadron's badge and the nickname The Fighting Cocks. Siskins and Furies followed, both used for formation aerobatics at the annual Hendon displays. By September 1939 43 Squadron was flying Hurricanes. It covered the Dunkirk retreat and during the Battle of Britain formed part of 11 Group and was credited with sixty kills. In

1942 the squadron flew fighter sweeps over France before departing for North Africa. Spitfires replaced the Hurricanes and the unit played a leading role in the air battles over Sicily and Italy before moving on to Austria as the war ended. The squadron was disbanded again in Italy in May 1947. Two years later the Meteor-equipped 266 Squadron at Tangmere was renumbered as 43 and moved to Leuchars. In 1954 the first Hunters to enter RAF service were received and by the time John arrived the early F.1s had all been replaced by F.4s and John Langer had just taken over from Major Roberts USAF as CO.

Just prior to her presentation of the new Standard to 43 Squadron in June 1957 the Queen had sent a message:

> In two World Wars No 43 Squadron has earned our country's gratitude. The Standard is emblazoned with battle honours, the names of which are enshrined in the hearts of my people, for they are names which speak of dauntless courage and endurance, of freedom saved and victory won. I am sure that you who have inherited this great tradition will be true to it and that the spirit of service and devotion to duty upon which it was built will always be your inspiration. I am confident that it will be your guide in peace and that if the need to fight arose you would be worthy of the great deeds done by your predecessors. It is in this belief that I commit this Standard to your charge.

John Langer recalls very well the sequence of events that led to John Howe joining his squadron. Apart from the Short Service Commission officers leaving 43 Squadron and the consequent reduction in squadron establishments, other pilots had left of their own volition, being worried about the implications of Duncan Sandys' edict for the future of the RAF and opting for a life in civil aviation instead. So, ironically, vacancies were created at the same time as pilots were being forced out.

> I was offered the opportunity to select three pilots from 222 Squadron. Amongst those chosen was a brash young South African whom I believed would make a good Flight Commander, not least because of his operational experience in Korea. I hate to think what might have happened to him if I hadn't picked him but I accept fully the blame for enabling his subsequent career to blossom! John Howe fully lived up to my expectations. He proved to be a first class pilot and an excellent leader. He demanded high standards from his pilots but, whilst firm, his sense of humour made him popular.

This is a sentiment echoed by Peter Bairsto who recalls that:

> ...he was a very professional aviator who, as a Flight Commander, could be tough when necessary but was at heart a kindly chap with a strong sense of humour. At the same time the John of the mid 1950s was very much the bachelor boy who lived a bachelor life to the full.

John Langer concurs:

> In the air he was peerless but back on the ground he had little difficulty in
> going astray. His pilots would follow him anywhere if only out of curiosity
> to see what sort of trouble he could lead them into. He displayed a great
> propensity for quaffing vast quantities of ale. However I never knew him
> to be late for met briefings or to appear any the worse for wear. And
> although essentially a man's man John always had an eye for the ladies and
> could charm their socks off. He was seldom without a girl on his arm –
> until he met his future wife Annabelle I hasten to add!

43 was a busy squadron, regularly exceeding the proscribed number of flight
hours each month, 480 at that time, and John in his new role of Flight Commander
threw himself wholeheartedly into the fray by working long days, planning,
supervising, flying and debriefing. This was the period of his RAF career that laid
the foundations for all that was to come. During his time with The Fighting Cocks
he was to clock up 500 hours' flying a year, the majority of them on Hunters but
including Meteor T.7 instruction and F.8 flag towing as well as checks on a two-
seat Vampire interspersed with the air defence work. Because of the heavy
workload that fell on everybody's shoulders and because of the great opportunities
to get into the air, there was a great camaraderie on the squadron amongst aircrew,
amongst ground crew (who saw it as a matter of pride to have the maximum
number of aircraft available each day to allow the target to be reached) and
between aircrew and ground crew. Morale was sky high. Flying included all the
disciplines one would expect to find: everything from snake climbs (after a stream
take-off at fifteen-second intervals, levelling off at say 10,000 feet and then
turning on to a new heading, still at fifteen-second intervals) to cine on flag; from
PIs (practice interceptions) to doggers (dog fighting); and from battle formations
to squadron balbos. (Balbo is a term used to describe a large formation of aircraft
and named after the Italian fascist Italo Balbo who in the 1930s led a series of
record-breaking attempts that used large aircraft formations to promote Italian
aviation.) There was also periodic work concentrating on the winning of the
annually presented Dacre Trophy (given by his mother in memory of Flt Lt
Kenneth Fraser-Dacre who had been killed in 1943) to the squadron with the best
air-to-air firing record of the preceding twelve months. In later years, once air
firing took less of a priority, the Dacre changed to become the trophy awarded for
the best assessed squadron in *all* disciplines on the ground, including
administration, and in the air as John recalls:

> When I was at Bentley Priory in 1962 I recall that one of my tasks was to
> write a paper to recommend a winner for the Dacre Trophy. I had to
> investigate all aspects of participating squadrons' tasking for the year. At
> the end of that quite lengthy process I had to collate the results and the
> squadron that came out top was a Javelin squadron which happened to be

commanded by a navigator. So my recommendation to my seniors was that such and such a squadron should be awarded the Dacre Trophy and that a policy of awarding all Fighter Command squadrons to navigators should be adopted in future!

John's log books clearly show the pace of operational life on 43 Squadron with entries frequently demonstrating that he was in the air up to four times a day. On 18 November 1957 his 2,000th hour was celebrated in a Hunter on a flag-firing sortie. As we have seen, Leuchars' long runway had been closed for resurfacing and then extension work and this had restricted what the squadron could do, how much they could carry and in what weather conditions they could fly. When it reopened, to celebrate the release from this restriction the squadron flew a formation of eleven Hunters and three Meteors before getting down to cross-country exercises to gain navigational and diversion experience. They also embarked on two weeks of air-to-air gunnery above 20,000 feet and with the majority of pilots averaging over 15 per cent on the flag they were well satisfied. In December for the fourth month running they topped the squadron flying hour target of the time with 503 hours. In fact, during 1957 43 Squadron flew more hours than any other Hunter squadron of Fighter Command. They also came top of the Flight Safety ladder for that year. John reached a personal milestone – the granting of a General List Permanent Commission. Everybody celebrated in style with a barrel of beer donated by the Courage Brewery! This leads neatly on to the fact that, overall, life on 43 Squadron was very good in a social sense too as John Langer has already hinted. Too good sometimes! John and his colleagues got into the habit of calling on the Station Commander, Geoffrey Millington, at the end of each Friday night's partying. The response was usually to summon transport to dump them at the farthest end of the airfield and make them walk back to the mess.

This was a time in the RAF when strict dress codes still applied. For instance, on the stroke of 7.00 pm in the mess no flying suits or other unsuitable dress such as shorts were to be seen. In July the squadron was deployed to Cyprus. If on morning standby at Nicosia, crews would regularly go to the beach at Kyrenia in the afternoons, visiting a few pubs *en route* to the blue Mediterranean waters. On one particular occasion John and his colleagues arrived back at the mess slightly the worse for wear, dressed in tee shirts and gaudy shorts. Afternoon turned to evening and nobody noticed the time until the President of the Mess Committee (PMC), an RAF Regiment Squadron Leader, came in and was horrified at the sight that met him. Did they not know that shorts were not to be worn after seven o'clock? Sadly (given their inebriated state) but predictably perhaps, their response was to take them off there and then. The PMC furiously retreated. But it was such incidents that helped make the RAF tick and they have been repeated many, many times over the years.

Sport is another factor that plays a prominent part in air force life and John had always been a great participator, both in South Africa and in his early years with the RAF. But he was at a stage in his career now where he had to think about his involvement given the injuries he was picking up. He continued to play squash every evening but gave up rugby (he had played wing forward for the CFS) and then cricket. When 43 Squadron deployed to the Mediterranean John took up windsurfing. Later in life he continued his affinity with water-based sports by taking up sailing from Plymouth having already discovered the excitement of skiing in the States.

The year 1958 literally started with a bang for John when he got airborne for Big Thunder aeros on 2 January. These were aerobatics during which sonic booms could legitimately be laid as the Hunter was pushed into a shallow dive, the only way in which it could be induced to become transonic. At the other end of the spectrum there was innovative use of a Vampire T.11 as it was found to excel in a snow-clearing role.

> Because the Vampire was low on the ground and the jet pipe was angled downwards, we'd take off and with flaps down would fly up and down the runway at zero feet with the hot efflux burning off the snow of the uncleared portion. It was also very good for clearing runway ice as we taxied out from the pan. Those were very harsh winters. You often couldn't walk across the sports fields because they were under three feet or more of accumulated snow.

John's first experience of the new Hunter F.6 came in mid January 1958 with the squadron fully converting to the new mark by the end of February. John made his last Hunter F.4 flight on the 21st of that month when he delivered 'F' to North Weald. The F.6 was the big-engined Hunter with a 200 series Avon of 10,000 lb thrust. It also incorporated other modifications such as wing store hardpoints, link collector tanks and wing leading edge extensions. Such were the differences between it and the Hunter F.4 that the F.6 came to be viewed as virtually a new aircraft. But it would never be a supersonic aeroplane in level flight and most development flying henceforth concentrated on the aircraft's role as a ground attack aircraft as opposed to an interceptor. From the time that 43 Squadron took the Hunter F.6 on board, Hawker was extending its capabilities in respect of ground attack work, employing combinations of bombs, rockets, napalm and drop tanks. This was a period of deteriorating political conditions in the Middle East and with the prospect of this being the new theatre of operations for the Hunter there was some urgency to the process.

John recalls:

> I liked the Hunter in all its versions. I suppose if I had to choose the Hunter 6 would probably be my preferred mark but in truth each had its attributes and don't forget that as it developed it may have increased its operational capabilities but its flying qualities wouldn't necessarily be changed as a consequence. It was always a lovely aeroplane to fly.

Exercise *Buckboard* in January 1958 entailed the interception of USAF B-47s flying into Scottish airspace from the west at 35,000 to 45,000 feet. Tactical exercises of this kind were becoming more interesting overall with targets becoming more varied. Apart from the American input and the familiar Canberra continuing to play an important role, Valiants, Victors and Vulcans were now also being intercepted as well. Exercise *Grabhook* followed shortly after *Buckboard*, with the B-47s this time flying in from the north over Shetland and Orkney. As the year progressed, other than the regular Fighter Command *Ciano*, *Kingpin/Adex* and *Bomex* exercises, *Rough Game*, *Snow Flurry*, *Argus*, *Full Play*, *Fresh Wind* and *Sunbeam* would occupy RAF squadrons alongside their NATO counterparts and aircraft of other Commands.

Monthly hours totals climbed inexorably – 528 in January, 548 in February and then 571 in April. The Hunter F.6s onto which all pilots had now converted were loaded with four drop tanks to enable the completion of 900-mile cross-country exercises and deployments to Europe. John saw a photo opportunity here for he tried very hard to get a box of four aircraft all carrying four tanks inverted over the Forth Bridge with a photographer in a chase plane in attendance. Unfortunately the shot never materialised. On 11 March John and the Boss flew to Aalborg in Denmark to make final arrangements for Exercise *Fawn Echo*, an exchange with a Danish Air Force Hunter squadron. The deployment proper began on the 24 March with four of 43 Squadron's Hunters led by John flying across for a busy period of activity including defence exercises and participation in a formation fly-past to honour the Queen of Denmark. The Danes' 724 Squadron had flown in the opposite direction to Leuchars but weather during their stay in Scotland meant that they could complete only a half day's operations. However, both the Danes and the British were found to be excellent social hosts in their respective countries so lack of flying opportunities wasn't always regretted!

As pleased as the RAF was with the Hunter F.6 there were soon problems with it. By the end of March sixteen were on strength with 43 Squadron but two of these were in ASF (Aircraft Servicing Flight), one with skin wrinkling and the other with defective pylon bolts. More seriously the spares situation was not good and numbers on the line were only maintained by robbing the hangared aircraft for parts. Two F.4s were retained to maintain the establishment of aircraft. The arrival of Captain Wegman as a USAF exchange engineering officer meant that he would be tested from the very beginning, although his task was perhaps lightened a little by the reallocation of all Leuchars' squadrons training aircraft – the Meteors and Vampires – to the Station Flight. In April Peter Bairsto was promoted to Squadron Leader and given command of 66 Squadron at Acklington. John stepped into his A Flight shoes and this encouraged him and sixteen fellow pilots to make the long trek to London for the Twelfth Annual Reunion of the Fighting Cocks Association at the Faviours Arms. To boost morale even further a new mascot was adopted by the squadron, a shelduck that was found wandering along the flight line and on which was conferred full squadron membership! A new Fighter Command record was also captured by 43 Squadron, that of firing their Hunters' guns at 51,000 feet.

John 'Jock' Heron recalls his two years in A Flight, to which he was posted at this time.

When I joined 43 Sqn John was the A Flight commander and deputy Boss to John Langer with 'Bodger' Edwards as OC B. I joined B for a brief period before moving to A where I received very firm guidance from John on how to conduct myself as a Junior Pilot. He carried authority easily, unlike the younger Bodger who was very much in John's shadow. Both enjoyed a few beers with Bodger's powers of recovery truly remarkable whereas John's were slower but better judged! John, as a QFI, taught me to fly the Meteor and I recall being forced to fly the old lady at around 135 knots merely to demonstrate asymmetric difficulties at very slow airspeeds, the inevitable result being a dose of 'Meteor knee' when it was difficult to prevent the appropriate leg shaking some time after the sortie.

John had been the squadron aeros pilot and I was asked if I was interested in taking over the commitment when he was due to leave the squadron in the Summer of 1959, so just before his departure he taught me to perform low level aeros in the Hunter T.7 and his demands on accuracy and practice kept me alive for the four years or so in the low level aeros role, despite a number of incidents.

I admired his ability and style both of which were to influence me in the pursuit of a modest career in the cockpit.

Nobody who knew 'Bodger' Edwards, OC B Flight, will ever forget him. This is borne out by the almost legendary status he achieved, certainly as far as partying was concerned, not forgetting the fact that he was a highly competent aviator too. John and he became firm friends but there certainly was an element of competition between them as far as leading their respective Flights was concerned.

When Jock Heron joined 43 Squadron there were only two QFIs on the squadron, John Howe and John Langer. This became a problem as they found it almost impossible to carry out the necessary number of dual and night checks on the Meteor and Vampire two-seaters without prejudicing their main roles. This was thrown into sharp relief on 17 June when the squadron was brought to forty-eight hours' readiness in preparation for duty in the Middle East where growing unrest was centred around Jordan. After Suez the US had replaced Britain as that country's principal source of aid but did so without any formal treaty or agreement. Instead, the so-called Eisenhower Doctrine was quoted whereby support was pledged to any country asking for help in resisting the communist influence. This, in those nervous times, was enough for the US to act. At the same time as requesting economic assistance from the west, Jordan's King Hussein, also concerned about the nationalistic fervour that was seeping through many Arab countries at the time, approached his cousin King Faisal in Iraq seeking and agreeing an alliance, the Arab Union. This alliance would counter the United Arab Republic, formed by Egypt and Syria on 1 February 1958. However, it was short lived. King Faisal was overthrown by elements of the Iraqi army on 14 July 1958 and he and members of his family were murdered. Jordan was suddenly completely isolated and appealed to Britain and the US for military assistance. The RAF flew 2,200 troops of 16 Para into Amman and deployed aircraft and equipment to Jordan and the eastern Mediterranean, including 43 Squadron. 208 Squadron was based in Amman itself for a while. The US airlifted in petroleum to keep the vehicles on the ground moving. For some weeks the atmosphere in Jordan was extremely tense but the Army remained loyal to King Hussein and at the beginning of November the British troops went home. Meanwhile, the US was landing troops in Lebanon to support the regime there and the Sixth Fleet was very much in evidence off the Lebanese coast. It was critical time in the Middle East.

At Leuchars, all leave for 43 Squadron's personnel was cancelled as were weekend passes. Operational practicalities had to be addressed. The adoption of four underwing tanks meant that the squadron were unable to practise dogfighting, which was undoubtedly the most important aspect of training they should have been carrying out in the light of what they might be expected to do when they reached the Mediterranean. However, the initial order was modified in July to seventy-two-hour readiness. Leave recommenced and personnel were again sent on courses. Just four days later 43 Squadron was informed it would be flying to Cyprus the following day! Twenty-three men were recalled from leave and the aircraft frantically made ready for the transit to the Mediterranean. A pair of aircraft was flown in from 74 Squadron, the Tigers, to make up a serviceable complement of twelve. But then departure was delayed because the mistral was blowing a storm in the south of France. A night stop had been planned at Orange to the north of Marseilles but the crosswinds on the single runway there were well outside Hunter limits. John, however, had cause to be grateful for the delay.

> A few days beforehand I had contracted flu and was laid low. I was confined to bed and out of my window could see them tanking up the Hunters on the ASP (Aircraft Servicing Pan). I was desperate to go of course so I called the station doctor and asked him to give me something to help. An hour later my batman stuck his head round the door and said 'the doc says drink this' – and he produced a case of lager! Which I did – all of it – and the next day I was fit enough to fly! So thank goodness for the thunderstorms – and Carlsberg!

The delay also precipitated the implementation of a bold plan on John Langer's and John Howe's part as the former recalls:

I discussed with John the idea of making up the lost time by flying to Cyprus in one day, which we agreed could be done with a full fuel load and 200 gallon drop tanks on each aircraft. Convinced of the urgency, HQ Fighter Command agreed, albeit reluctantly, and so at dawn on 17th July I led a formation of Hunters on what was to be an epic flight. Just over six flying hours later we landed at dusk at RAF Nicosia, somewhat bushed but happy to have arrived without incident.

They were met by Peter Bairsto and 66 Squadron who dished out very welcome cans of cold beer. 66 Squadron's ground crew dropped 43 Squadron's tanks and refuelled their aircraft in the absence of their own ground crew who arrived the following morning. The lot of ground crew in Cyprus turned out in the main not to be a happy one. They were billeted in overcrowded conditions and the experience of having to work long hours in temperatures often in excess of one hundred degrees Fahrenheit was not pleasant. Nonetheless, they managed to maintain a high aircraft availability rate, which was often at the maximum.

There were administrative 'discomforts' to be borne too as John Langer explains:

As John and I walked towards the station buildings the Station Commander drove up, not to congratulate us on our flight but who to our astonishment launched into a 'I have had you fighter boys up to here and if I have any trouble with you lot you'll be on the next aircraft back to the UK' routine! Needless to say this got right up our noses and was really asking for trouble especially when the pilots found that they were to spend the first night sleeping on camp beds in a squash court because Admin Wing had assumed that we would be arriving the next day despite HQFC having signalled our intent to fly out in one day.

By 1000 hours on the first morning six aircraft were 'on state'. At this stage the requirement was for the dawn to dusk availability of two pairs of Hunters at ten minutes' readiness and two at thirty minutes – a state of readiness known as Battle Flight with the aircraft and pilots on the ORP (Operational Readiness Platform), plugged in and ready to go when alerted. Scrambles were shared by 43 and 66 Squadrons with the squadron not on standby undertaking flying training, the emphasis for the moment on air-to-ground work. John quickly took the top dog position in this (with John Langer not far behind) firing on ten feet square targets. Conducted at the Larnaca range this was the first time any 43 Squadron pilot had flown air-to-ground sorties on a Hunter. Meanwhile, Nicosia sector patrols were taking off every hour and the squadron soon found there was a high interception rate, averaging twenty a day. Most were friendly aircraft but there were also United Arab Republic Il-14 Crates and Viscounts. In the early days there were three attempted interceptions of unidentified high-flying aircraft at around 65,000 feet. They were assumed to be American U-2s but when the planforms were seen

– they were never reached – they didn't seem to fit the Lockheed high flier. John recalls his interception of an Egyptian Viscount.

I remember thinking 'he's bit far north' so I flew close formation with him, watched by all these people looking out of the windows at the back of the aircraft. Then I flew round in front of them and they of course flew into my slipstream and tumbled all over the place. A couple of days later I met the AOC and was told I mustn't do that sort of thing because those in the Viscount had experienced a quite terrifying few minutes. This was by no means an official rocket however, just a friendly suggestion confirmed by a pint in the bar afterwards.

By the end of July the method of operating changed from alternating between the two squadrons – 43 and 66 – to a structured programme involving three (initially 208 and then 54 being the third), which ran:

Day One – Battle Flight
Day Two – air to ground training
Day Three – operational training or day off.

Nicosia Station Flight provided the aircraft for instrument, dual and asymmetric training and for keeping the necessary checks up to date. On 11 August, however, training was momentarily forgotten when the Middle East Air Force brought 43, 66 and the newly arrived 54 Squadrons to a two-hour readiness in response to the heightened tensions in Jordan to enable them to react to the possibility of a coup. This state of readiness lasted until 23 August when the political situation appeared to have settled down somewhat. Within a few days 43 Squadron were told they could expect to be home by the end of September. Meanwhile, training days began to encompass additional disciplines such as Air Control Team work with paratroop Ground Liaison Officers. Then there was Exercise *Royal Sovereign* with the 3rd Infantry Division and the Guards Brigade operating the ACTs and Exercise *Grapevine* with one of 43 Squadron's pilots – Flt Lt Hay – joining the Guards as a Forward Air Controller.

So as to ensure the squadrons couldn't get too used to routine, the flying programme changed again, this time to:

Four days Battle Flight followed by a day off
Four days training followed by two days off.

In addition, after each sortie on patrol, time was usually found to slot in additional training such as practice forced landings and battle formations at high and low level. Little wonder that 43 Squadron continued to consistently exceed the monthly flying target. But after the initial excellent availability rate the Hunters started to become less reliable, probably as a result of intensive flying in hostile conditions. Cracked ailerons were becoming a major problem and by the end of the tour six aircraft were categorised AOG – aircraft on ground. Replacements arrived in the nick of time from the UK and the squadron was able to fly a farewell balbo over Cyprus before returning to Scotland via El Adem for refuelling, Luqa for a night stop then Orange and Leuchars on 1 October. The ground crew returned by Comet and Beverley.

The Fighting Cocks had been in Cyprus for two and a half months. It had been valuable experience, the opportunity to train in the air-to-ground role had been relished and the day-to-day possibility of action lent an edge of excitement to everything. John's reward for the work he did there was the award on 14 June 1959 of a Queen's Commendation for Valuable Service in the Air.

John Langer sums up the deployment:

> Despite the provocation implicit in the Station Commander's less than friendly welcome, the squadron behaved impeccably for the time we were in Cyprus. In fact we had little opportunity to do otherwise as we were invariably on standby from dawn to dusk. Largely due to the enthusiasm and drive of my two Flight Commanders the squadron met every standby and patrol commitment and flew more hours than the other two squadrons put together. On 29th September we held a farewell party in the Ladies Room of the mess (to which the Station Commander was *not* invited). After the guests had left one of the boys dreamt up a game which involved throwing empty beer cans up into the fan. The Flight getting the greatest number through without hitting the blades won. Needless to say most cans hit the blades and were sent flying round the room and needless to say as well there was a little damage, mainly cracked glass and stains on the wall. Next morning I was accosted by an angry PMC who demanded we should pay a rather stiff sum for redecoration. As we were due to take off for the return to the UK within an hour I had no option but to write out a cheque. On hearing this John carried out such an effective whip round of the squadron pilots that I actually ended up in profit!

On their return to Scotland the first job as far as the aircraft were concerned was their reconversion to burn AVTAG (Aviation Turbine Gasoline) as opposed to the AVTUR (Aviation Turbine Fuel) that had been used in Cyprus. The two have slightly different properties as regards volatility, freezing point, specific gravity and so forth, which become meaningful when operating for any length of time under significantly different conditions as 43 Squadron had just been doing. It then became a matter of urgency to get aircrew up to date with their checks, particularly bad weather and instrument flying, which had piled up in Cyprus. The Meteor T.7 and the Vampire T.11 were consequently busy for a while. Incidentally, a newcomer to the squadron at this time was Fl Off Sulaiman. His full name was Sulaiman bin Sujak and he was the first Malaysian to serve in the RAF. He was later to become the Malaysian Air Force CAS.

This catch-up period was followed by a fortnight's block leave for the entire squadron. John's schedule on their return was as full as everyone else's. A demonstration of formation aerobatics was flown for a TV news channel on 16 October. More exercises and training occupied much of November – battle formations, PIs, doggers, dusk landings, dual checks, GCAs, manual landings, night navigation exercises, close formations, cine work (quarter attacks) and flag firing. From 20 November to 11 December the squadron worked out of Wattisham. This was for their *Halyard* commitment, later known as QRA (Quick Reaction Alert), taking over from 111 Squadron and for the duration of which they had two Hunters at two-minute readiness and two at ten minutes. There was just one operational scramble and the target turned out to be a Valiant. 54 Squadron, also recently returned from Cyprus, took over from 43 Squadron from 12 December with Valettas arriving to take the latter's ground crew back to Leuchars.

Much the same routine occupied John in the New Year with a considerable amount of instruction and dual checking on the Meteor and Vampire two-seaters respectively, although this was often restricted by heavy snowfall, which meant there were days when no flying at all could be undertaken. A significant moment, however, was the first entry in his log book for a two-seat Hunter T.7 on 12 January 1959, whilst over the next few months the Vampire T.11 disappears. John was sent down to Chivenor to familiarise himself with it. The two-seat Hunter had long been waited for by the squadrons.

The following is from *Hawker Hunter – Biography of a Thoroughbred.*

It is strange that in neither of the RAF's second generation of interceptors, the Hunter and Swift, was any potential two seat requirement foreshadowed in the original specifications. As it was, production of the Hunter F.1 was underway before any thoughts turned towards the evolution of a two seater. Indeed the Meteor T.7 was considered wholly adequate for conversion training. Although the transonic performance of the Hunter did not itself pose complications in the RAF's training syllabus it was recognised that in due course the range, endurance and weapon delivery characteristics of the Hunter could only be realistically experienced by young trainee pilots in a two seat equivalent.

The first production Hunter T.7 was flown on 11 October 1957. 229 OCU took the first deliveries in August 1958 and single examples were issued to the fighter squadrons over the ensuing months. 43 Squadron took XL611 on 10 March 1959 but it stayed on the ground until the beginning of April for servicing, modifications and bringing up to operational readiness, at which time squadron pilots began their conversion. John had already converted at Chivenor and was qualified to fly it as captain from the right-hand seat day and night. XL611 and later XL613 feature regularly in his log book with a succession of second pilots in the left-hand seat that included senior officers such as Wing Commander Paddy Harbison and the Station Commander, Geoffrey Millington.

Another significant moment for the squadron alongside other Fighter Command squadrons was the reduction of its complement of Hunters to twelve on 31 January with a concurrent reduction in the pilot establishment to fifteen. The monthly flying target was reduced to 320 hours and a minimum of 200 hours a year for each pilot was set. The impact was profound. The need for pilots to continue with their non-flying duties and to focus on such things as promotion examinations meant that at times the flying programme almost ground to a halt, a far cry from the situation a few months before. This didn't, however, stop the inception of an intensive air firing programme using radar ranging on the flag for the first time, a concept explained and demonstrated by three pilots who flew up from the Day Fighter Combat School (DFCS) at West Raynham. They imparted other snippets of tactical advice too whilst at Leuchars. The weather was fine for the fortnight they were in residence and the scoring was high. Given the CO was at Durham University on an International Affairs symposium, one pilot was in hospital, one was sick, one found himself at DFCS and two were ferrying Hunters to India for the Indian Air Force, all leave had to be stopped to enable enough pilots to be found to complete the programme. (The Indian Air Force had ordered 160 Mk 56s, essentially equivalent to the RAF's F.6. Seventeen T.66 two-seaters were also later delivered.)

At the end of April John Howe and John Langer flew down to Odiham to prepare for an impending detachment there of the squadron, which was to provide an escort for the Shah of Persia on a State visit. This commenced on 5 May and two sections of three Hunters flew in line astern either side of the Shah's Viscount from the French coast. At the end of May, 43 Squadron were back in Denmark for a ten-day detachment. This time they were at Skrydstrup exchanging with 724 Squadron. During the week a NATO exercise brought the Danish and British Hunters up against F-84Fs and F-84Gs of the Belgian Air Force.

Back in the UK John was coming towards the end of his time with 43 Squadron with solo displays at RNAS Arbroath and Abbotsinch. The latter, on 20 June, was his last sortie for the squadron for he was then posted to the DFCS. Then John's career would take a major step forward, for from being a Fighting Cock he found himself to be a Tiger and a Tiger with a brand-new aeroplane to boot.

CHAPTER FIFTEEN

Tigers!

The ages of the pilots on 74 Squadron in 1960 ranged from 22 to about
30 years old with John Howe being the oldest. Many pilots had less
than one thousand hours total flying experience. So the squadron's
transition to the Lightning was a major task for John, a task he
achieved without accident or major incident and for which he deserves
much recognition. On top of that John had a big task setting up a
'heavy metal' formation aerobatic team that was inevitably always in
the public eye and closely scrutinised by the Air Marshals. It was
both a challenge, a world first and a success which he achieved
with care and attention to detail while incorporating that flamboyance
so necessary to show off the RAF's latest weapon system.
Martin Bee

RAF West Raynham, close to the market town of Fakenham in Norfolk, had a proud wartime record and later an equally proud record as home to the Central Fighter Establishment, most famously perhaps when the Tripartite Squadron was based there to evaluate the innovative new Kestrel, soon to become the Harrier. However, in 1975 West Raynham was closed for flying and Bloodhound missiles were sited on the station to defend East Anglian military installations. These were removed in 1991 and West Raynham went the way of so many surplus RAF facilities, being closed in July 1994. These days it stands forlornly waiting for a new use, infrastructure decaying badly.

The purpose of the Day Fighter Combat School at West Raynham was to teach experienced pilots how to instruct on battle formations, cine, gunnery, fighter recce, air to ground, rocket firing and so forth – indeed all the things a fighter pilot needed to know. As a Flight Commander John had already done such instruction from time to time in a supporting capacity at Leuchars, helping the often over-stretched Fighter Weapons Instructors (FWIs) assigned to the squadron. Now came the opportunity to formalise that arrangement. John joined No. 5 DFCS Course at West Raynham on 22 June 1959 and three months later he was an accredited Fighter Combat Leader with his by now usual above average assessment as a day fighter pilot and an exceptional rating in air gunnery. During those three months John flew over fifty hours on the Hunter F.6 (and occasionally the Hunter T.7) honing his instructional skills. Coincidentally, DFCS was commanded at the time by Tony Carver, a fellow South African who had been Head Boy at John's old school, St Andrew's, in Grahamstown.

Towards the end of the course Group Captain Pitt-Brown from Fighter Command came to visit and to talk about the process of experienced pilots becoming FWIs and the practicalities of assuming this position in addition to Flight Commander duties. John recalls:

> When it came to my turn to comment, I forthrightly told him that a Flight Commander simply didn't have the time to be an FWI – this from my recent experience on 43 Squadron. A Flight Commander's day finished with him writing the following day's flying programme and then during the day running it, making sure all aspects of it were in place and adhered to, leaving no time for anything else. Conversely it would be really useful for a Flight Commander to *have been* an FWI. The Group Captain didn't argue the point but was obviously considering my opinion.

John was always one to say precisely what he thought and although at times during his career it got him into hot water it always earned the respect of those with whom he was working and this was undoubtedly a factor in his progress. He feels to this day that his discussions with Pitt-Brown helped as far as his next promotion and posting were concerned.

Flying apart, the most important thing to happen in John's life occurred whilst he was at West Raynham. He met his future wife. She was one of two Community Relations Officers at nearby RAF Sculthorpe, which was an American base hosting the 47th Bombardment Wing flying B-66 Destroyers. A civilian employed by the Air Ministry, her job was to meet all the families coming over from the States, brief them, help organise accommodation and generally help them fit into the English way of life. A group of pilots, including John, regularly went across to Sculthorpe to party, play blackjack and otherwise enjoy themselves. On one such night he was introduced to Annabelle Gowing. For John the impact was immediate and by the end of the evening he was telling his colleague Black Fergie that she was the girl he was going to marry. And marry her he later did as we shall see.

After DFCS John returned to Devon, for he was posted to 2 Squadron of 229 OCU at Chivenor. This time he was not on the receiving end, rather he was putting into practice what he had just learned at West Raynham. Chivenor was still flying the Hunter F.4 (and also had Hunter T.7s, Meteor F.8s and a single Meteor T.7 and Anson on strength – the Meteors were used for flag-towing sorties). As with John a few years before, pilots were coming through, having gained their Wings, to be prepared for their first operational squadron. Some ground instruction came first then the pre-flight briefing before taking off in a two-seat Hunter or as a pair in single-seaters so that the instructor could monitor his pupil's progress. If it was a straight forward handling sortie the pupil would go off solo.

It was whilst at Chivenor that John applied for the Junior Command and Staff School (JC&SS) course at RAF Bircham Newton. Formerly known as the Officers' Advanced Training School (OATS), it was first formed in 1944 at Cranwell to provide training for officers destined for Flight and Squadron Commander posts. After an interim period at Hornchurch it moved to Bircham Newton in 1948 at the same time as becoming a component of 22 Group Technical Training Command and was soon joined by the schools for Secretarial and Equipment Officers to form the RAF School of Administration. A further change in 1956 saw the arrival of the Administrative Training School from Hereford and a name change to JC&SS. John was granted a place and in the New Year of 1960 he drove up to north-west Norfolk to attend. The timing had been deliberate. To progress further in the RAF the course was a necessity but John reasoned that he would lose flying time if he applied at the wrong time of year. So he timed his application so that he arrived at Bircham Newton in January with the greater likelihood of bad weather, which, if he had been flying, would certainly have grounded him!

The Bircham Newton course was not a particularly popular one. There was no flying involved and was almost totally based on administration. So the pupil learned how to write hand-written letters RAF style – *don't start with your request but state your case clearly and lucidly which, if well written, will mean that when you conclude with what you want it will drop into your hand like a ripe plum*. He learned about the organisation of the RAF; he participated in role-play on both sides of a court martial, defence and prosecution; he learned how to plan and conduct a ceremonial parade; he was instructed in accounting procedures; and he became steeped in the history of the RAF. It was the first such course an aspiring career officer had to attend.

As it happened John never got to finish OATS. He was called to the telephone one day towards the end of February to find a very polite and refined English voice on the other end telling him that he was to be promoted to the acting rank of Squadron Leader and was to make his way to RAF Coltishall where he was to take command of 74 Squadron. John immediately thought he was being subjected to one of his friends' practical jokes and he told the voice on the other end of the phone to stop 'buggering about'. History records that an irate senior officer was fortunately content with tearing John off a strip for his insubordination and taking it no further. Very contritely he packed his bags and on 22 February drove across Norfolk to Coltishall. There he found willing WRAFs to sew the additional ring onto his uniform so that he could at least present himself to his new squadron properly dressed, but it would be some weeks before he got the rest of his belongings and his log books from Chivenor. John recalls:

I had never consciously chartered my career path in the RAF. Every promotion came as a complete, although not unwelcome, surprise. I didn't think along the lines that I had to be a Squadron Leader by such and such a date. Flying was what I wanted to do. So I worked hard to ensure that I got the maximum amount of flying possible and it was almost as though promotion came as an ancillary to that. But having gained promotion I worked damned hard to justify people's faith in my ability. It was only later when I was promoted to Air Commodore that I realised that I wouldn't be able to fly forever.

This was John's first encounter with RAF Coltishall, a Battle of Britain station that closed in 2006 with the final ceremony on 30 November of that year. Over 6,000 people from the local community and those who had served there (John included) attended. It was a very emotional occasion and marked the end of almost seventy years of military flying from that part of Norfolk. Planned initially as a bomber station, it was pressed into use by fighters in May 1940 while still incomplete when 66 Squadron (which recorded the first kill of the Battle of Britain) with their Spitfires moved in. They were joined three days later by 242 Squadron under the command of Douglas Bader. As the Battle progressed Coltishall was used as a base for resting squadrons from No. 11 Group, which was in the forefront of the air fighting, including the squadron John was now taking command of, 74, who were there in September and October 1940. Throughout the war the station's own squadrons played a prominent part in the defence of the country. In August 1945 Coltishall was handed over to the Polish Air Force and became RAF Coltishall (Polish) before returning to Fighter Command in February 1946. Mosquitoes, which had flown from Coltishall throughout the war, stayed on with 141 Squadron until September 1951. Early in 1957 a contract was given to extend and strengthen the runway and strengthen the taxiways, during which time its aircraft were moved to nearby Horsham St Faith. Other extensive alterations to the station were made in preparation for the arrival of the Air Fighting Development Squadron (AFDS) of the Central Fighter Establishment (CFE) and the very first English Electric Lightnings into RAF service (pre-production P.1Bs) arrived on 23 December 1959. Around the same time Coltishall's resident Hunter unit, 74 Squadron, which had recently moved across from Horsham St Faith, were informed that they were to be the first front-line operational squadron in the RAF to be equipped with the Lightning, and on 29 June 1960 it indeed became so. Which is where John came in.

The first squadron any officer takes command of has a special place in his heart and this is no exception as far as John is concerned. For a start he was inheriting one of the RAF's most famous units, thanks largely to its Second World War exploits under such COs as Sailor Malan. John read up on the history and quickly realised that its reputation as the RAF's Tiger Squadron had been well earned. He would have much to live up to.

74 Squadron was formed at Northolt on 1 July 1917 as a training squadron of the Royal Flying Corps and on 20 March 1918 it was sent to France equipped with SE5s. It was in France that it earned its nickname of Tigers as a result of the

133

aggressive spirit shown by its pilots, amongst whose ranks were to be found the likes of Mick Mannock, Ira Jones and Keith Caldwell. Within seventy days of 74 Squadron's arrival on the Continent, 100 enemy aircraft had been shot down with the loss of just one of its own. By the war's end and after just seven months in theatre, this total had risen to 224 (a total that included 'probables' and balloons). However, its wartime exploits did not prevent 74 Squadron's disbandment in July 1919. It would be September 1935 before the squadron was re-established, an event that actually happened whilst on board ship *en route* to Malta with Hawker Demons as part of the British government's response to the Abyssinian crisis. Returning to the UK in August 1936, 74 Squadron's new home was Hornchurch and it was whilst here that the squadron's tiger head badge and famous *I Fear No Man* motto was authorised. In April 1937 the Demons were exchanged for Gloster Gauntlets and then in February 1939 the Tigers received their first Spitfires.

The outbreak of the Second World War found 74 Squadron still at Hornchurch but often operating from the satellite aerodrome at Rochford. By this time Sailor Malan had joined the squadron and during the months ahead he and his colleagues, including HM Stephen, John Freeborn and John Mungo Park, were to be involved in extensive operations against the *Luftwaffe*. In the Phoney War there was little operational activity but when the Low Countries were invaded in May 1940, 74 Squadron flew on offensive operations. Soon afterwards, when Fighter Command was engaged in establishing air supremacy over the beaches of Dunkirk, the squadron was fully employed on convoy protection and patrols over the French coast. During the Battle of Britain and with Sailor now its Commanding Officer, 74 Squadron flew against German raiders over London and the Thames estuary and they met with considerable success. On 11 August, for example, they flew into battle four times and at the end of the day claimed twenty-four enemy aircraft destroyed and fourteen damaged. But the hectic pace of operations took its toll and on 14 August the squadron was retired to Wittering for a short rest before moving to Kirton-in-Lindsay, Coltishall and then in October back to the front line at Biggin Hill. The RAF had now gone on to the offensive and during November 1940 74 Squadron destroyed twenty-six enemy aircraft. In February 1941 it moved to Manston but was then sent up to Acklington before moving across to Llanbedr and Long Kesh where, after the hectic pace of operations, they found themselves in a backwater by comparison.

In 1942 74 Squadron set sail for the Middle East, reaching Palestine in July. However, it was a squadron without aircraft, as the ship carrying the aircraft it was due to have flown was sunk. For a while, in an unprecedented move, the squadron was used to provide maintenance facilities for a USAAC Liberator unit before moving to Teheran where it started to receive second-hand Hurricanes. Under the command of 'Spud' Hayter, it transferred to the Western Desert and undertook convoy escort duties in the eastern Mediterranean as part of 219 Group. The squadron exchanged its Hurricanes for Spitfire Vbs and Vcs and transferred to Cyprus from where it was sent to the Aegean islands of Cos and Simi, only to be caught up almost immediately in the German invasion. Air and ground crew were drafted in to help in the islands' defence, during the course of which seventeen ground crew were captured and imprisoned.

Returning to England and flying new Spitfire IXs, 74 Squadron flew patrols over the D-Day invasion fleet and after the landings attacked German positions. Then the Tigers moved to France as a component of the 2nd TAF (Tactical Air Force) with 145 Wing, advancing as the Allies advanced. In March 1945 it received Spitfire XVIs, which it flew alongside LFIXs. By April it was at Droppe in Germany and that is where, on 2 May, it received news of the German surrender. Its last wartime operation was an armed reconnaissance in the Wilhelmshaven area. Back in the UK, 74 Squadron was one of the early squadrons to equip with the Meteor F.3. Based initially at Colerne, it then took up a long residency at Horsham St Faith where it became a component of Fighter Command's first post-war jet fighter Wing. In December 1947 the Meteor F.3 gave way to the F.4 and then in October 1950 the F.8. 74 Squadron became the first winner of the Duncan Trophy, awarded to the day fighter squadron making the greatest contribution to day flying in all weathers, which it won again in 1952. In 1953 this was followed by the Dacre Trophy for weapons firing at the Acklington gunnery school. In March 1957 the Hawker Hunter F.4 was introduced, followed a few months later by the F.6. Then came the Lightning!

Squadron Leader Peter Carr, from whom John took over as OC 74 Squadron, explains how the change in command came about.

> During my time at Nellis between 1954 and 1956, when I was on an exchange tour with the USAF Fighter Weapons School, I was asked to provide what assistance I could to Donald Campbell who was making an attempt on the world water speed record at Lake Mead, an attempt which was initially unsuccessful because after the first run, whilst *Bluebird* was being refuelled, wash from the dozens of spectator boats flooded the engine jet pipes and it started to sink. It was stopped from doing so and dragged towards dry land but was so badly damaged underneath that the attempt had to be abandoned. *Bluebird* was repaired at Nellis by kind permission of General Roberts, the base commander, and a further attempt a fortnight later raised the record to 216.20 mph. In the process I became quite friendly with Campbell and later he offered me the post of Project Director and reserve driver on his land speed record attempts in the early sixties. The offer came not long after Duncan Sandys' infamous White Paper so I took what at the time seemed like the more exciting offer. Donald Campbell pulled a few strings and I got early retirement in March 1960. As

it happened I only drove *Bluebird* once (and that at low speed) before Don crashed at Bonneville and his attempt on the world land speed record came to an end. Of course the White Paper was hopelessly wrong and I lost out on commanding the first Lightning squadron which 74 became within six months of my leaving them. Duncan Sandys doesn't feature on my list of most popular characters!

John arrived at Coltishall by no means as an unknown to his men for his reputation as a Flight Commander on 43 Squadron had come before him as had the fact that he had been a Mustang pilot in Korea. This was enhanced to a degree by the fact that he had not been Cranwell-trained and thus his appointment must have been truly on merit, which is not to minimise the value of a Cranwell background at all. Once at Coltishall, Wing Commander David Evans (OC Flying Wing) and Group Captain Harold Bird-Wilson (the Station Commander) taught John the difference between being a leader, as he had been hitherto as a Flight Commander with 43 Squadron, and a Commanding Officer. John recalls:

As a Flight Commander you are doing what the Squadron Commander says. As a Squadron Commander you are responsible for a 150 men and their families and you have to be able to relate to every one of them. You must have their interests at heart. Your sole responsibility should be their ability, welfare and happiness. By doing that you get the best from them. If you don't understand that you can be the finest leader in the world but as a commander you aren't going to be followed, a fact I didn't fully appreciate until Birdie and David Evans taught me.

Group Captain Bird-Wilson, known to all as Birdie, was a Battle of Britain pilot of some renown.

David Jones recalls:

He was small in stature but huge in presence and was a man who made it his job to know his station and all who were on it very well. He was totally supportive. For example at the Paris Air Show in 1961 spares were urgently required and Birdie flew back to the UK in the Hunter T.7 himself to collect them, running the gauntlet of HM Customs en route! As an example of the sort of man he was, I had only been at Coltishall for about ten days along with the other newly arrived 74 Squadron pilots and we were in the mess bar one evening when the Group Captain walked in with a guest. He marched up to us and said to his guest 'I'd like to introduce you to some of 74's pilots' and he proceeded to do so, calling us all by name and including snippets of autobiographical detail too! All done from our photographs which he had obviously been familiarising himself with.

Birdie was awarded the CBE in 1961 for establishing the first ever base for RAF supersonic fighters.

John's promotion to Squadron Leader and his assumption of the command of 74 Squadron led him into a world very different to that to which he had hitherto been used. But it was a world that led to John developing a very personal style of leadership and management and one in which he had to become accustomed to the scourge of many operationally minded men in the RAF – paperwork. But with a career progression ahead of him that would include staff positions that took him away from the front line he had no choice but to come to terms with and accept that this is what he would have to contend with.

George Black was posted to 74 Squadron as QFI in January 1961 from Linton-on-Ouse and has the following observations to make.

My career paralleled John's in many respects. We were both later at 11 Group, both became Commandants of the ROC and both were Station Commanders in Germany. Our approach to such postings was very often similar. As I saw it, when John arrived at Coltishall it was at a time in the RAF when everyone needed to move on, when re-equipment with exciting new aircraft was beginning, where the threat was ever changing. We all had to become a part of a much more professional air force and John was in the vanguard of those who would make it so. He was a strong and determined leader out to do the best he could with a squadron that was in the limelight and he quickly demonstrated a capacity for good ideas, ideas which he pushed hard for his seniors to accept. For example, on 74 it had been decreed that only experienced pilots should be posted in. But John wasn't going to have that because that would only lead to a squadron top heavy with 'prima donnas'. As a result junior pilots had a role to play also and it consequently became a very well balanced squadron. When the formation aeros started some of the younger guys missed out on the Lightning of course, but John was at pains to keep them current and they went across to West Raynham and the Hunter to do so. He was a damned good squadron commander and as a result 74 did so well in the early days.

Such was John's ongoing commitment to his squadron and its success operationally that he often found difficulty in relaxing.

George Black continues:

If for whatever reason the squadron was working late, John would stay late as well. He felt he needed to be there whilst his men were there and in the early Lightning days that usually meant the ground crew working against all odds to have aircraft on the line the next morning. It became a source of amusement that although this would have been the ideal time to catch up with the paperwork, he rarely did. And if he did have to be elsewhere than with the Tigers, we knew where his mind really was.

One thing that anyone serving under John could be sure of was the fact that he never had any favourites. John's character would never allow for that so consequently everyone knew exactly where they stood with him. As they did if ever they crossed him (which rarely happened) for when John's ire was up everyone ducked for cover!

George Black again:

When John had been angered there was a lot of bluster and real, earthy South African language! Later at Bentley Priory for example you could often hear John tearing somebody on his staff off a strip from the other end of the corridor! He was intolerant of any misdemeanours amongst his officers and perhaps could have been a little more understanding of some situations. His was undeniably an unequivocal, no nonsense approach, something which particularly came to the fore later in his career when he was at Gutersloh as Station Commander. But the other side of the coin was that if you supported him you got full marks. There was no in-between stage, no grey areas. He was a straight talker and wanted, indeed expected, you to be as well. The truth was that everyone grew to be very careful with him but you respected him all the more for that.

Ted Nance remembers his then CO's great sense of humour.

John Howe, a lively character on and off duty, had a wealth of funny stories and anecdotes to tell in his pronounced South African accent. On more than one occasion he recalled to us a day in his recruit training in the South African Air Force when he was lectured by a tough South African sergeant who said: 'Yentilmen, today we are going to talk about the 4.2-inch Mortar. The 4.2-inch Mortar, if it 'it a tank at a 'undred yard…which it will, the crew will be concussed, if they live…which they won't!' Such was the humour of our Boss that as Squadron pilots we tried to capture and preserve the moments. We had a skiffle group, ably led by Vaughan Radford. Our abilities were limited mainly to making up our own topical verses and adapting them to Lonnie Donegan's 'Putting on the Style'. Our verse for John Howe went like this:

> The new boss of our squadron, his name we'll not give now
> We'll give you one small clue though; he came to show us how(e)
> His tales from deepest Africa have taught us how to say…
> If they live which they won't…they will be concussed. Aye

John was also a man who liked to confuse his adjectives from time to time – whether deliberately or by accident nobody was quite sure. Two of the expressions I remember were 'I want that done as fast as quickly' and 'the trouble with houses in this country is that they are too close apart'. He also had particular Afrikaner phrases he'd regularly use such as 'now then jong' when he first started talking to you, 'jong' meaning 'young man'. [Peter Bairsto clearly recalls this as well.

Life under John on 74 was very good indeed. He was a first class leader. He brought the first RAF Lightning squadron into service without losing a single aircraft, a pretty rare achievement in those early years. I cannot speak for others but for me Squadron Leader John Howe was the best Boss I had throughout my RAF career.

There was a world of difference between the Hunter and the Lightning. The latter evolved from an idea promoted in 1946, which was transcribed into Experimental Requirement 103 the following year. This called for a research aircraft to explore transonic and low supersonic speeds up to Mach 1.5. Teddy Petter of English Electric took up the challenge (before he moved to Folland, his place being taken by Freddie Page) and the result was the P.1A powered by Hawker Siddeley Sapphire engines. It was taken into the air for the first time by test pilot Roly Beamont in August 1954. Three P.1B prototypes were subsequently ordered (these had Rolls-Royce Avons and provision for airborne intercept radar and two Blue Jay missiles). The P.1B was thus a much redesigned aircraft. It fortunately survived Duncan Sandys' edict that missiles were the future of the RAF because the P.1 was needed to defend the emerging V bomber force. The Lightning (as it had by now been christened) first flew in its F.1 version on 30 October 1959, powered by a pair of Rolls-Royce Avon RA24R engines (each giving a mighty 14,430 lb of thrust in reheat). It was also equipped with two Aden cannon in the upper front fuselage, the AI23 Airpass radar and a Firestreak infra-red missile each side of the forward fuselage.

Alan Merriman was the project pilot for the Lightning on the Fighter Test Squadron (FTS) at Boscombe Down. He recalls that as 74 Squadron had been nominated as the first squadron to receive the aircraft a period of pilot indoctrination at Boscombe was arranged and some spent a week there going over the aircraft itself and discussing its various characteristics. This was when Alan first got to know John.

Considering the responsibility he was exposed to – the aircraft had attained a very high political profile – he remained completely relaxed and at ease. We described him as a typical Yarpie (South African) in the mould of Sailor Malan and other famous South African wartime pilots. John was clearly a fighter pilot with considerable knowledge and experience of the role.

In July 1960 the first tiger-headed aircraft arrived at Coltishall. John clearly remembers his conversion to type.

There were no two-seat Lightnings early in its career so it was a matter of ten sorties in a simulator and then away we went by ourselves. I thought the leap from the Vampire to the Hunter was pretty big but this leap to the Lightning was huge! I was confident enough on that first occasion until I actually started down the runway – then I began to have doubts! But we were of course ready for it. In modern parlance the adrenalin rush we had was quite something. Everyone inadvertently went supersonic (without reheat) at 18,000 to 20,000 feet on their first sortie for we simply weren't used to that sort of power! From brakes off to 35,000 feet took three and a half minutes in cold power. No wonder it was considered the most desirable aircraft in the inventory to fly and that competition to get on to a Lightning squadron was fierce.

John's first Lightning sortie was in XM165/F on 14 July 1960 and it lasted fifty minutes. For the rest of July and throughout August Lightning and Hunter flying was integrated but from September it was all Lightnings as 74 Squadron attained its full complement. 74 had stopped posting new men in some months prior to the Lightnings' arrival so those already on the squadron were known quantities. Experience was needed, not least because of the demanding display schedule the squadron was given. Nevertheless, there were also those junior Flying Officers who blessed Lady Luck for giving them the opportunity to be involved in such an exciting project so early in their careers. David Jones was one such. He had joined the RAF in 1956, trained in Canada for two years and then returned to fly Hunter F.4s at Chivenor before becoming a Tiger in 1958.

The Lightning was an exceptionally pleasant aeroplane to fly. It had no vices unless you count its prodigious fuel consumption. And there were various suspect systems on the aircraft in those early days too but as a pilot you were aware of them and could cope with them if anything failed when airborne. If they became a major problem the aircraft was grounded anyway. The relative ease of transition from Hunter to Lightning was a testimony to its characteristics and to the training procedures that had been created by the AFDS. For a start there was a good simulator which had a representative cockpit with good presentation and instruments that all behaved correctly. It was of course bolted firmly to the floor – there was no motion in those days. Another very important factor was the quality of the pilots on the AFDS who not only instructed in the classroom but accompanied you on your first flight or flights. In my case it was Ken Goodwin who took off in his Hunter before I did in the Lightning and then formated with me at the top of the climb out and proceeded to follow me around as best he could, cutting many a corner to keep up, and then taking up a position from which he could monitor my speed on the approach. It was good to have him there. Once you had completed your first few solo flights you were on your own but once again you always flew predetermined sorties and only a mechanical emergency could change its parameters. However, I have to say that flying overall in those early days was pretty infrequent for the likes of me. Aircraft availability meant that more senior pilots were given preference and I still spent a lot of time in Hunters. Nevertheless I was a qualified Lightning pilot and that couldn't be taken away from me. And of course I knew it wouldn't be too long before the squadron was up to strength and the Hunters would finally go.

With no Lightning OCU as yet and no twin-seat Lightning anyway, it fell to the Air Fighting Development Squadron to devise a conversion programme. This started with a five-day aviation medicine course on which pilots tried out their new flying clothes and Taylor pressure helmets (already used by Canberra PR.9 crews) and on which they also underwent physiological tests. The helmet wasn't popular because it was big and cumbersome and restricted head movement. A fighter pilot has to be able to scan the skies all around him and with the Taylor helmet that wasn't possible. The clothing included g-suits and pressure jerkins, both of which inflated. There was also the option of an air conditioned suit, which could be hot or cold depending on conditions, but the cockpit environment was actually very good in the Lightning F.1 with no demisting problems and no excesses of heat or cold (in the UK at least – it was to be a different story abroad). The cockpit was also very snug. John is a man of average height but some of the big guys must have had problems when the canopy came down!

The aviation medicine course was held at RAF Upwood. On the pilots' return to Coltishall there followed seven days of lectures from the AFDS team, covering everything from aircraft systems to emergency drills, and then ten sorties on the very good for its time General Precision Systems Mk 1 simulator. The first Lightning solo followed and this took the form of flying away from the airfield circuit, experiencing the aircraft's amazing acceleration and rate of climb, then rejoining the circuit for a couple of ground controlled approaches then a GCA or visual landing. As David Jones has just described, on this first sortie each pilot was escorted by an instructor in a Hunter but for the pair to be able to formate at operational height the chase aircraft had to be given a head start of 28,000 feet! Once familiar with performance and handling, Donaldson Davidson, a navigator on the AFDS, taught the fledgling Lightning pilots radar and interception techniques.

Ken Goodwin was a member of the AFDS team.

I had all of thirty hours on the type! The CO, John Robertson, had one or two at the most and the remainder almost nil. However we did have a set of multi coloured display boards, pilots' notes from English Electric and the confidence of the blind leading the blind. After the lectures the first solo was preceded by a good briefing before the instructor got airborne in a Hunter chase aircraft, the main objectives of which were firstly to tell the convertee if his nosewheel was still down after selecting gear-up. This became a fairly commonplace occurrence with new pilots being a little behind the rapid acceleration take-off, thus allowing aerodynamic pressure to out-do the hydraulics. The second objective was to advise generally from close proximity on the unexpected or unfamiliar, which was better psychologically from an accompanying aircraft than from a remote ground station. The third was to offer an opinion on various spurious and real fire warnings.

Each pilot approached his first sortie in different ways. Mike Cooke had flown his many times in his room, sitting in his chair with his eyes closed and imagining the flight from walking out to the aircraft to climbing down from the cockpit and debriefing. As for pre-flight checks he called into play the mnemonic TAFIO – Trim and Tailplane: Air Frame: Fuel and Flaps: Instruments: Oxygen. Only then was it was time to taxi out to the threshold. Mike's had been planned as the fifth solo but Jerry Cohu who had been detailed to go before him had developed a cold so Mike was called upon a day earlier than he expected. He walked out to the big, shiny, impressive beast and on his cockpit check found a problem with one of the instruments so he walked back to the crew room to wait whilst the problem was fixed, which did absolutely nothing for his nerves. This was mercifully done quickly so he was soon on his way back to the aircraft, adrenalin flowing again. There was perhaps a hint of showmanship in his take-off. It went contrary to the briefing, which had stipulated a climb straight ahead and then a turn away from the centreline initiated at a set height. Mike, in fact, started to turn as he climbed almost immediately his wheels had left the runway. Perhaps it was a statement born of confidence as to how easy this aircraft was to fly? Whilst he was aloft on this first sortie the wind direction at Coltishall changed, which meant, for approach, changing runway ends. He came in on a visual, concentrating hard every inch of the way and made one of the best landings of his life. Mike had just become the first supersonic RAF Flying Officer.

Martin Bee remembers his first airborne sortie vividly too.

Climbing aboard a Lightning F.1 for one's first flight was both exhilarating and daunting. The cockpit was twice as high off the ground as that of the Hunter. It had two engines, not one. The usual round instruments were replaced by 'tape' speeds, digital instruments and a zero reader. It had a rudimentary autopilot and an autothrottle plus a Head Up Display, all far ahead of other aircraft of the 1960s and 1970s (and often the '80s and '90s). And it had two big afterburners that gobbled fuel. Navigation was pretty basic. Look out of the window, use your TACAN and use help from the ground radar controller!

It was undoubtedly a very exciting time for all concerned as John Howe recalls:

Here we were, a famous squadron with a great tradition and a great bunch of people, air and ground crew alike, who were committed to this new era in the RAF as epitomised by this hugely impressive aeroplane. And whilst for we pilots it was a challenge, in many ways for the ground crews it was a bigger one. There were lots of problems with the jet and they never stopped working. It was quite incredible how much they had to put into it over a period of many months – long, long hours over the week and weekends too. It wasn't just that as a new jet there were gremlins to be sorted. It was new technology that hadn't been tried before, which threw up lots of unforeseen problems that had to be solved either in terms of fixing it if it broke or implementing modifications, some of them major ones, which regularly arrived from English Electric by signal for immediate action. Lots of pressure was put on the engineers to have the jets on the line each morning, particularly as our task was not just to prove the aircraft on operations. We were also regularly flying demonstrations to show the aircraft off to the British public whose taxes had paid for it and to prospective customers overseas who English Electric and the British government wanted to sell the aircraft to. In many ways these two objectives were incompatible and operational training suffered badly as a result. Whilst the fact that we had a brand new aeroplane and the fact that we were committed to showing it off at Farnborough and Paris and at RAF stations around the country made for an exciting time for the Tigers, for me what I really remember above *all* else was the unwavering commitment by the ground crew with great support from Coltishall itself to keep the aircraft serviceable. Everyone realised that this was a special challenge that had to be met and won. And win it we did, albeit sometimes by the skin of our teeth.

John played his part in keeping his Lightnings in the air by creating his own acquisition of spares system, necessary because the RAF was unable to get those that were urgently required down to Coltishall in anything less than a few days. He would ring Warton directly and speak to test pilots Roly Beamont, Jimmy Dell or John Squier, tell them what was wanted and then send the Meteor T.7 or Hunter T.7 up to collect the items. Paperwork would catch up later! This of course bypassed Fighter Command and their slow and cumbersome system completely and John got the expected rocket from those whose sensibilities he had offended in the process. But realising the urgency of the situation, they then changed their procedures so that spares could be ordered one day and be delivered the next, a system known as Early Bird. It has to be said that both English Electric and Rolls-Royce were extremely supportive and did all they could to ease the Lightning into service.

John had some great engineers working for him in all trades from the outset and they were led by exceptional men such as Chief Technician 'Red' Kyte who were in turn supported by very understanding wives. A party held at a Norwich pub gave John the ideal opportunity to weigh everyone up and he is still highly amused by Mrs Kyte who, having been introduced to John, was asked by him if he could buy her a drink. She promptly responded with 'No thanks. I'd rather have the money!'

John's promise that he would marry Annabelle Gowing came true when he moved to Coltishall. Annabelle's family lived a few miles down the road from Coltishall. She had been born at White Hall Farm in Sprowston on the outskirts of Norwich where the Gowing family had farmed for over three generations. Her father Cecil bought Home Farm, Rackheath (where John and Annabelle now live), in 1950 when the estate of Sir Edward Stracey, the owner of Rackheath Hall, was disposed of after his death. The western boundary of Home Farm abutted White Hall Farm, so it was that Cecil came to farm a very large area to the east of Norwich. The land was mainly arable but with a few cattle as well. (A brief overview of the Rackheath estate can be found in Appendix E.)

Annabelle's intention after her time at RAF Sculthorpe came to an end was to join Pan Am as a stewardess. John had proposed to her in July 1960 (and been accepted) but he had already said to everyone on 74 Squadron that nobody could expect leave until the squadron was declared operational. This of course meant that he couldn't very well have any leave either, so Annabelle spent six months with Pan Am as planned. The squadron was declared operational in February 1961 and John and Annabelle were married at the church of St Mary and St Margaret in Sprowston on 25 March. John delights in telling the story of the wedding day to which Arthur Read, one of his best chums on 43 Squadron, had been invited, as had John's brother Robert who arrived from South Africa with his newborn baby son. As John and Annabelle were about to leave the churchyard for the reception at the Horsham St Faith officers' mess Arthur picked up the carrycot and shouted 'you've forgotten him!' This of course led to a stunned silence, understandable perhaps in 1961, but quickly explained away by Arthur! The honeymoon was in the south of France and when they returned the couple moved into quarters at RAF Coltishall.

Ted Nance recalls:

> Annabelle was a delightful squadron commander's wife who, amongst many other achievements, led the 74 Squadron wives' fan club at the end of the Coltishall runway during display rehearsals and further afield, such as Leconfield, where the squadron performed before HM The Queen Mother.

It is worth pausing to consider the family into which John had married for he found that Annabelle's father Cecil had strong aviation links. He was a veteran of the First World War having served with 98 Squadron. Post war, Cecil was very involved with the Norfolk and Norwich Aero Club, which was founded at Mousehold Aerodrome just outside Norwich (now the site of a sprawling council estate) on 25 February 1927. Cecil Gowing was elected to the Committee that raised funds through public subscription and its first aircraft was a de Havilland Moth. Within a few years Mousehold had become the first Norwich Airport. Unfortunately one of the first bombs to fall on Norwich during the Second World War landed on the clubhouse. During the war Cecil was involved in a little known 'underground army'. 202 Battalion of the Home Guard was part of a British resistance movement, which would fight on if the Germans invaded. In Norfolk there were around thirty-five units of the battalion, involving two hundred men. There were forty operational bases, which in the main were no more than underground lairs concealed in woodland. The men were trained in guerrilla warfare tactics and would have emerged from their secretive hideouts to attack German positions. But Cecil could be a secretive man and he rarely talked about such things. On the other hand he was a jovial, entertaining and very interesting individual and became a popular figure when he attended Mess Nights at Coltishall once John was installed there. (Cecil Gowing's career in military and civil aviation is discussed in Appendix F.)

Another aviation link was one of place. White Hall Farm lay on the edge of the site of Rackheath airfield, home during the war to the B-24 Liberator-equipped 467th Bomb Group of the Second Air Division USAAF – the Rackheath Aggies (see Appendix E). It was inevitable therefore that the farm should become a meeting point for Americans and the legacy of those links remains to this day with contact being maintained with a few of the airmen who served at Rackheath, although sadly with every passing year these are inevitably decreasing in numbers. Rackheath Hall was home to a few USAAF officers (mainly Newfoundlanders) who were billeted with the Stracey family during the war. Although most of the airfield has now been returned to farmland and the technical site turned into an industrial estate, a memorial plaque and a bench, dedicated to the memory of the men and women of 467th Bomb Group, is located near the Rackheath village sign as a permanent reminder of all those who served there.

John and Annabelle moved into Home Farm in 1976 after Cecil Gowing died. By the terms of the lease, in the event of the death of the leaseholder the rented White Hall Farm and its land reverted to the landlord. Some of Home Farm had to be sold too and as a consequence those who were employed had to be laid off. What was left was 150 acres of farmland with Annabelle's mother Pauline (known to everyone at Paul) isolated in the house and with nobody to work the land. So it was that when John later returned from his tour in Germany he and Annabelle moved into Home Farm and John, when he was not being an RAF officer, was a farmer. During the rest of his RAF career he worked Home Farm when he was able to. When he wasn't, a contractor was hired. When John retired from the RAF in 1985 he became a full-time farmer, known by many of the locals as Airfield Marshal Howe, which given his frequent assertion that trimming a plough was just like trimming an aeroplane in pitch, roll and yaw might have some relevance! By this time bureaucracy, both European and home grown, was creeping ever more into agriculture and officialdom was beginning to dictate what could and couldn't be done. John was not prepared to be dictated to so the decision was made to put the whole 150 acres down to grass and sheep were bought. It was sheep that Home Farm became known for until 2003 when John finally retired. All the animals were sold off and these days the fields are grazed by horses, which are stabled there as part of a livery business that has been handed over to John and Annabelle's daughters.

CHAPTER SIXTEEN

Display or Ops

John Howe, a man who always did every job to the best of his ability, with a great sense of humour and without any thoughts of self aggrandisement.

Ken Goodwin

Formation aerobatics in a 60 degree wing sweep aircraft brought home the meaning of induced drag since the aircraft slowed quickly as it reached high angles of attack and then when aerodynamically unloaded accelerated fiercely. Compared with the Hunter there was a considerable increase in inertia and the wingtips on which we were wont to position ourselves were now swept back well past the normal cockpit view. What should we look at to maintain formation position? Then add in the variable of afterburners, which were far less reliable than they are today.

Martin Bee

John's first ever sortie in a 74 Squadron aircraft was in Hunter F.6 XE559 on 3 March 1960, a sortie that consisted of half a dozen GCAs to Coltishall. It was followed during the rest of the month by ten more, which comprised familiarisation, PIs, GCAs to nearby Horsham St Faith and so on. The real thrust of this first month though was to establish himself as Boss of the squadron and by all accounts he did this with a minimum of fuss but a maximum of determination to carry on the famous Tiger tradition.

Ted Nance recalls:

1960 was a very difficult time for John Howe because MoD decided to make 74 a 'show case' squadron to demonstrate the RAF's new Mach 2 fighter. Unfortunately the pilots on the squadron had to be divided into the 'haves', who were chosen to fly in what ultimately became a nine ship aerobatic team and the 'have nots', who had to wait some time before converting onto the Lightning. For the lucky ones like me the Boss proved from the outset to be very operational, very decisive and an excellent leader. In one of his less rational moments he said that he would take me as his No. 2 if we ever went into combat. This was surprising because as

No. 4 in the team I flew line astern and he rarely saw me. Perhaps it was because I never actually hit him in formation!

During his first couple of weeks John had to cope with an AOC's inspection during which 74 Squadron was called upon to demonstrate a typical PI sortie ending with some simulated emergencies as well as an OTR – an operational turn round. All went well, although John would be the first to admit that this was largely down to his predecessors and the discipline of the squadron.

April, May and June saw the consolidation of John's position in the air (where, using the Hunter T.7, he conducted dual checks by day and night on his pilots) and on the ground (where he got to know all his engineers and took a keen interest in all they were doing and were expected to do). The squadron made ready to move back to Horsham St Faith – these days grandly titled Norwich International Airport – from which it had only recently moved after a tenure of thirteen years. This was to allow the resurfacing of Coltishall's runways and make other facilities ready for the advent of the Lightning. The runways were like a skating rink in the wet. Contractors attempted to solve the problem by cutting grooves to help the water drain away and thereby stop a tendency to aquaplane, but that didn't work so a full resurfacing became necessary. Once the work was complete, 74 Squadron operated Hunters from Horsham St Faith and Lightnings from Coltishall for a short while.

Lightning F.1s started to arrive at Leconfield during April 1960 for the AFDS, which had relocated there while the contractors were at Coltishall. The F.1s supplanted the P.1Bs, which had been delivered to AFDS at Coltishall at the very end of 1959 for service handling trials. John (later Sir John) Nicholls had delivered the first of these, seasonally dressed in a Father Christmas outfit! But this Christmas present for AFDS nearly came to grief. Tiger Mike Cooke recalls sitting in his Hunter on the alert pan when he saw a car jump the stop lights on the perimeter track at the runway's end as the P.1B was a few seconds from touch down. He tried in vain to alert the tower but then realised he was connected to the GCI station by umbilical and couldn't speak to ATC anyway – so he could only hold his breath and then feel an immense surge of relief as the Lightning passed safely over the car.

74 Squadron's early complement of Lightnings was delivered to Leconfield too, the first on 29 June by Jimmy Dell. They were entrusted to the care of the AFDS until the squadron's return to Coltishall when virtually the whole of the camp turned out to watch the arrival of all the aircraft. Meanwhile, the squadron's engineers were assigned to English Electric to start to get to know and understand their new charge. In May pilots were sent on pre-Lightning conversion courses to Rolls-Royce and Ferranti.

While all this was going on 74 Squadron was still fully involved in its front-line duties with the Hunter and this included exercises, such as *Yeoman*, in mid May. In those days newspaper correspondents were sometimes allowed to fly in two-seaters and participate! In the squadron records this account of the exercise survives and it gives a taste of what they were all about.

At Horsham St Faith, where we correspondents had waited since lunchtime Thursday for a chance to fly on a Fighter Command interception, the weather was dull and overcast but conditions were not sufficiently bad to stop flying if a raid came. After an early breakfast we were driven to the ops room of 74. There we found the Hunter pilots, fully briefed for the missions to come. For some hours we shared their feelings of lassitude mingled with anticipation for the order to scramble, although in the case of the press party it must be admitted that slight apprehension about our reactions to flying around the speed of sound added to the air of suppressed excitement. Gradually the weather cleared over the bomber stations and the readiness states were reduced from one hour (when playing cards, rolling dice, reading or brewing cups of tea or coffee in the crew room were the norm) to all pilots sitting in their cockpits ready to scramble at a moment's notice. A direct line to the Master Controller is plugged into the rear of each fuselage and the pilot receives orders to take off over the earphones. Eventually the long awaited blips appeared on the distant radar screens, the order to scramble was given and the jet engines roared into sudden life. Two by two the interceptors taxied out to the runway and in our aircraft we adjusted our oxygen masks and waited our turn. Soon we were at the start of the runway. As we roared down the tarmac the absence of engine noise in the cockpit was most noticeable. There was only the rasp of our breathing carried through the microphone of the mask and the clicking from the battery of instruments on the dashboard.

The transition from ground to air had hardly registered before we banked steeply to port and the fields and houses slipped sideways under our nose. Then we received our permission to climb and we broke through the cloud into a sunlit fairy world. At 40,000 feet the sun shone dazzlingly on a snow white carpet of cloud. We seemed to have the sky to ourselves but as we headed out over the North Sea to look for the battle the vapour trails of the fighter squadrons appeared in the distance. Soon we were in the thick of it and had a grandstand view of Hunters and Javelins moving in for the kill against bombers of the RAF, USAF and NATO....

John flew a single sixty-minute *Yeoman* sortie on 20 May and thereafter he registered a further couple of dozen Hunter flights until 14 July when his first long-anticipated Lightning sortie (in XM165) took place. And it wasn't long after that that the reality began to dawn on 74 Squadron of not only bringing this potent and brand-new jet into service but of showing it off to the world as well. John still remembers that when he got the signal telling him that he was to put four aircraft over Farnborough every day, he didn't have four aircraft! Nevertheless, despite

149

having a very limited complement to choose from, by 10 August they were flying formations and on the 14th were at Duxford displaying for the Royal Observer Corps. Mike Cooke made his first solo Lightning displays at Gaydon near Leamington Spa and Bassingbourn near Royston in September. His brief? Keep it low and make plenty of noise! So the routine at both venues was a high speed run on arrival followed by tight 360-degree turns in afterburner in front of the crowd (which supplied the noise) and then a power climb away. By the time he had completed his Bassingbourn routine Mike's fuel state was pretty low so at 20,000 feet he set course directly for his return to Coltishall, lost height and went straight in.

A portent of things to come is registered in the 540s. *The ground equipment so far supplied to 74 Squadron for Lightnings was inadequate to operate even one aircraft.* But that was the thick – not the thin – edge of the wedge. August was bedevilled by lack of aircraft. There were only five Hunters left on strength in anticipation of the arrival of a full complement of Lightnings but with delivery delays only five of these were available, four of which spent much of the time on the ground with unserviceabilities. To keep themselves suitably qualified in terms of hours the station Meteors were used as much as possible by the pilots and a few even flew with the ATC in Provosts and Chipmunks, as well as in the simulator. John spent eleven hours in it in July.

The first half of September was almost wholly dedicated to continuing practice for Farnborough. The new fighter was certainly presenting a challenge but with the help of pilots from AFDS the squadron worked up to an efficiency level that enabled it to fly four aircraft at the prestigious show, operating from Boscombe Down each day. Training for this had started in July as John recalls, training that wasn't without its mishaps.

We started flying high-speed, low-level runs (just subsonic at about 200 feet) in formation but this put the aircraft's airframe under more than normal aerodynamic pressures. One day during that summer Alan 'Lefty' Wright was leading a box formation when the fin came off Jim Burns' aircraft. I watched from the tower as bits fluttered to the ground. Jim now had no fin and no radio either so I told Alan to close in and try to tell Jim of the problem. The weather was perfect and the wind straight down the runway so he was cleared to land, which he did by making a long straight in approach and using aileron control. Thereafter he was known as Finless Jim. As a result the C in C ruled out high-speed low-level runs in formation so we flew high speed at low level spread out in battle formation instead. [As a direct result of the incident all aircraft's tailfins were strengthened.]

At Farnborough John led the formation with Ted Nance, Jerry Cohu and Alan Wright filling the other slots. Mike Cooke was reserve. Briefings from John before each four-ship display went something like this:

- Taxi at one hundred yard intervals and line up on the runway in echelon.
- We'll use 80% rpm holding on the brakes and roll at three-second intervals for maximum reheat take-off.
- Aim to use the same pull up point for an 80-degree climb.
- I'll call cancelling reheat and use 82% rpm to give us 300 knots at 6,000 feet. Join up in box.
- The display will start with the flypast in Swan with wheels and flaps down. We'll clean up the aircraft in front of the crowd to move into the rest of the display.
- No. 4 – remember to call 'clear' for the change into line astern and Nos 2 and 3 guard against dropping low in the very steep turn.
- Rejoin in box for the run in and two-way break.
- We'll fly synchronised circuits leading to the ten-second stream landing.
- Any questions?

At the end of each day's flying a party was thrown at Farnborough following the drive back to Boscombe (Alan Wright was teetotal so was happy to oblige). Boscombe was interesting because of some of the other aircraft the Tigers found there, including the Short SB.5, which had been built for low-speed trials of the swept wing configuration proposed for English Electric's P.1. First flown in 1952, it was modified to accommodate different angles of sweep and different tailplane positions. After completing trial flights *vis a vis* the P.1 and Lightning it went on to conduct further tests. In its final configuration its angle of sweep was at 69 degrees, it had a Bristol Orpheus turbojet, instrumentation was revised and a zero-level Martin-Baker ejection seat was installed, which, if necessary, enabled a pilot to eject whilst still on the runway. Furthermore, the SB.5 was painted a fetching glossy light blue to distinguish it from the similar-looking Lightning, which was very dissimilar in performance. It was this aircraft that the Tigers saw a month before its first flight in its new configuration.

A few days after Farnborough the four ships were in the air again for Battle of Britain At Home days. Solo displays at various venues were entrusted to Mike Cooke as we have seen. For the Coltishall display the formation was increased to five aircraft and the printed programme proclaimed the base as the station of firsts....

> ...being the station with the first squadron to equip with the Lightning making 74 the fastest and most effective in Fighter Command: the station with the first Wing capable of carrying the de Havilland Firestreak [23 Squadron's Javelins could carry them as well as 74's Lightings]: and the station with the first squadron in Fighter Command equipped for air to air refuelling allowing 23 to fly anywhere in the world non-stop.

John took two weeks' leave at the end of September. He returned in October when the conversion to type programme faltered because of poor serviceability. He recalls:

> That month was one of intense technical slogging as is usual with the introduction of a new aircraft into service. A lot of time is spent diagnosing faults and this coupled with the poor spares backing resulted in few flying hours.

We have already seen how John dealt with the spares situation by circumventing the conventional supply chain and going straight to Warton. It was also the time when John's great admiration for the work of the ground crew was forming, an admiration that has always remained with him. The engineering crews could tell many a story about their commitment and the many, many hours of work they put into getting aircraft into the air only to see them come down again with another catalogue of unserviceabilities that would ensure their further grounding. Red Kyte was one of those in the front line, a Chief Technician of what we would probably now call the 'old school'.

> At times the going was extremely tough. Modifications apart, the squadron was going flat out to become an operational unit again and the demand was for six of the twelve aircraft to be on the line at one time. That meant the working of a day and night shift system. With the added responsibilities of a sustained programme of aerobatics and demonstrations during the first couple of years, this led to an increased requirement for nine out of the twelve to be on the line. Inevitably this meant working all hours. The edges of the shift system became blurred at times with crews overlapping 'to enhance manpower: the complexity of the Lightning as opposed to the Hunter meant that our complement of servicing personnel had already doubled. Weekends would often disappear completely, particularly if there were shows on. And leave? Everyone seemed by necessity to be saving that for Christmas. All the effort paid off though. We usually managed to achieve our target and the only things that beat us were grounding orders brought about by the need for emergency modifications. Morale remained pretty good throughout although there were times when we all wondered whether the aeroplane would ever work properly.

For the rest of the year technical issues continued to dog progress and it was impossible to give a firm date on which the squadron would reach operational capability. By the middle of November nine of the twelve aircraft were grounded because of the failure of a component in the aircraft's electrical system. December saw some improvement (although the AI23 radar was still proving to be very unreliable) but then foul weather stopped flying. It would perhaps be best therefore to put 1960 behind them and look forward to 1961 and hope for improvement, but then to do that would deny the success of

Farnborough and the very fact that the Lightning F.1 was flying with an operational squadron at all.

One very significant event occurred on 25 November when five members of the 79th Tactical Fighter Squadron of the USAF were guests of honour in the Officers' Mess at Coltishall. John was fully aware of the USAF's Tiger Squadron an hour's drive down the road at RAF Woodbridge: indeed, first contacts had been made a few years before John's arrival as CO. What made him pick up the phone one day and make a call to his counterpart on the 79th can be put down to serendipity. But the discovery that the man he was talking to at the other end of the line was Ed Rackham, an old friend of his from Korean War days and by now a Lieutenant Colonel, led directly to the foundation of the NATO Tiger Association. It was immediately agreed that the two commanders should get together socially: then it was agreed that there needed to be operational contact as well, particularly as John wanted to show off his squadron's shiny new aeroplane. Legend has it that at the (very late) end of a (very successful) party at Woodbridge in which 74 Squadron and the 79th participated, Lieutenants Mike Dugan and Merril McPeak (each of whom incidentally went on to become USAF Chiefs of Staff) were instructed to find a French Air Force Tiger Squadron to join them in the future. A directive had just gone out from C in C United States European Command that every opportunity should be taken to further professional and social relationships between the two countries and here was an ideal opportunity to do so and with the Brits participating as well. At Cambrai such a French squadron was found (EC1/12) and as a result on 19 July 1961 the first ever Tiger Meet was held. Lightnings flew beside F-100 Super Sabres and Dassault Mysteres. John is rightly proud of the part he played in creating such a long lasting and meaningful example of co-operation between NATO countries and beyond, for the Tiger Meet family has grown beyond recognition since the first humble gathering. The NATO Tiger Association thrives today.

In 1961 the squadron returned after Christmas and New Year leave ready to face the challenges of the next twelve months. It started well enough with over one hundred hours being flown despite poor weather. (Snow lay heavily on the runway but just as once John and his colleagues used Vampires' jet efflux to clear runways, now 23 Squadron used their Javelins with their pronounced nose-up attitude.) A positive note was struck by the fact that the AI23 radar was at last beginning to function more reliably and pilots' confidence in it consequently rose. That is not to say all engineering problems on the aircraft had been solved by any means: for example, a requirement for all jet pipes and reheat systems to be removed for an x-ray inspection was soon in progress. A contractor's working party was *in situ* at the same time and their work involved removing both engines on each aircraft. February was consequently an unproductive month with flying time being virtually halved compared with January. On 28 January the whole squadron was grounded because of the discovery of a serious fire hazard in the area between the ventral tank and the No. 1 engine and jet pipe. A temporary solution was quickly found – the removal of the ventral tanks.

The squadron continued to be diverted from its task when three days were given over to a huge gathering of the local, national and international press, BBC and ITV News and news film companies. Many of the contemporary Lightning photographs and paintings illustrating the raw power of the aircraft were of, or based on, a take-off John made from a wet runway. A *Daily Mirror* photographer was standing on the side of the runway at the time and such was the noise and the concussive effects of full reheat that it disorientated him and he fell over. Of course, the standard of reporting was sometimes questionable or simply sensational. 'Dressed in a spaceman's outfit of four pressure and survival suits one on top of the other [one paper suggested five] the pilots are fed with all the information they need for a sure kill by a computer', trumpeted one report. 'The Lightning is the first robot fighter. Amazing eyes and brains built into its eighteen ton fuselage tell the pilot where to go and what to do from the moment he starts his engines to the time he lands back at base...all without having to bother to look outside his cockpit', cried another. All essentially true. And John was extensively quoted too.

> We know we can catch the bombers and going on past experience we know we can outfight any known fighter in service today. The performance of the aircraft coupled with the ease with which it is flown gives the pilots confidence and the fact that it is felt to be the best fighter in operational service gives our Lightning pilots the highest possible morale.

March saw an improvement in hours flown again. The RAF had recently declared that the role of 74 Squadron had changed from that of a short-range day fighter squadron to that of a night all-weather squadron and by the month's end fourteen pilots had been cleared in that role. What is more, the squadron was about to be declared fully operational and John's embargo on leave was lifted. There continued to be problems with the aircraft and its systems but the fact that 74 Squadron was again in the front line gave everyone a feeling that real progress was being made. Problems weren't confined to the engineering side of things for inevitably there were airborne incidents as well, such as when Tim Nelson's drag chute failed to deploy on landing and he applied full power intending to do a go-around. As he rotated the chute extended and was incinerated by the reheat. Braking without a chute often led to brakes burning out so when he touched down again he was closely monitored by an attendant fire truck. He stopped very close to the airfield boundary fence. However, such incidents were infrequent and the fact remains that 74 Squadron suffered no fatal mishap during this induction period, which by the standards of the time and considering the ground-breaking technology was a testimony to good discipline, good training and sheer hard work. The noisy silver aircraft with their tiger's head on the fin were becoming an increasingly common sight in Norfolk's skies.

The lifting of the embargo on leave meant that John could at last allow himself some time off to marry Annabelle as recounted earlier. He was not back from his honeymoon in time to participate in Exercise *Matador* in April, the first in which Lightnings took part, missing it by a day. But he was there when it mattered as May was given over to practice for and participation at the Paris Air Show at Le Bourget. Formation aerobatics were practised from 2 April and Paris Air Show routines were rehearsed from the 10th. It was an intense schedule because this year the Tigers were to be flying a nine-ship formation with John as No. 1, Jerry Cohu No. 2, Alan Wright No. 3, Ted Nance No. 4, Mike Dodd No. 5, Tim Nelson No. 6, George Black No. 7, Martin Bee No. 8 and Maurice Williams No. 9.

John recalls:

> As far as the air displays were concerned I worked out that for training I only needed three aeroplanes for a diamond nine – nobody within such a formation is more than two away from the leader. So with three aeroplanes I could train them all, which made it easier for the engineers to get through the servicing apart from anything else.

The display sequence that evolved started with the nine-ship formation coming over low in an arrowhead, approaching and flying past the crowd, then doing a 360, changing to a diamond and flying past the crowd in that formation. Then came a wing over and while doing that Ken Goodwin would come in for the first of his solos. And so the sequence continued with Ken filling in the gaps whilst the remainder of the team was out of view changing formation. Ken wasn't a Tiger but still an AFDS pilot, loaned to 74 Squadron for displays. (Ken was to command 74 Squadron when it was based at Tengah, Singapore, ten years later.) He was a natural solo display pilot on the Lightning. John would have undoubtedly been able to demonstrate that he too would have been a natural if he had been able to fulfil that part of the display as well as lead the formation. Formation flying with the Lightning was an exact science, be it with the four aircraft of 1960 or this progression to nine, as John explains:

> The Lightning was a very difficult aeroplane to display as you had to be absolutely spot on with your positioning. I found out that if you didn't get your nose position absolutely right in a descending turn for example, you were going to have to roll out before you got to the heading you wanted otherwise you were going to fly into the deck. You had to be exact and very careful and be ahead of the game all the time.

The secret to successful formation flying was the ability to relax. Different pilots had different ways of doing this. Mike Cooke's method was to sing if ever he felt himself tensing up. Imagine if all in the formation adopted the same solution?

Ted Nance recalls:

> The Boss worked extremely hard for 74 and produced a creditable nine-

ship display team using the Lightning, which had very different and perhaps more difficult control characteristics to the Hunter. The latter had already set the highest standards for multi aircraft aerobatic formations. John Howe's flying as leader was smooth and accurate. His steep turns with the diamond nine were breathtakingly low but neither Mike Dodd (No. 5) nor Tim Nelson (No. 6) ever felt threatened although they were the ones invariably nearest the ground. The Boss had the confidence of his team.

On 31 May the squadron deployed to Creil, which was to be their operating base in France for the duration of the Paris Air Show. This was designed to give them plenty of time to check out the facilities at Creil and at Le Bourget where they would be displaying as well as time for additional practice. However, they waited for three days with no sign of an opportunity for a practice session. In the end John phoned Le Bourget to say that if he were not given an opportunity to practise he would take the squadron home. Needless to say a slot was quickly found. On the day of the first display on 3 June John's compass toppled.

Ted Nance recalls:

As a formation we heard the display controller call in the Tigers to commence the routine. I and one or two others in the team were a bit uneasy to see Le Bourget looming into sight but too far to port. The Boss replied to the controller that he would call airfield in sight once he had contact. At this point, eight other voices within the formation shouted in unison 'Turn hard left Boss!'. This he promptly did and calmly announced 'Airfield in sight pulling up for roll'. The subsequent manoeuvre was led to perfection as though nothing unusual had happened! At which point John reset his compass.

The Parisians enjoyed the display as a crewman on a 99 Squadron Britannia testified afterwards.

One manoeuvre at the end had the Parisian spectators on their feet applauding. As the main formation of Lightnings wheeled away with spectators turning to watch them, a singleton came screaming from behind and over their heads at near sonic speed with afterburners at full blast and at very low level. The sudden shock of noise hit like a thunderclap and startled everyone but when it was realised that it was part of the display and the spectators had recovered from the shock, they were on their feet and cheering and clapping, something I'd never experienced before.

Ken Goodwin thoroughly enjoyed his contribution to the formation and as a singleton.

It was an exciting display venue, manoeuvring between blocks of flats and looking up at residents on their balconies…well, it seemed like it at least!

But as far as formations were concerned, as No. 10 I sometimes came perilously close to the ground as we roared past the crowd!

C in C Fighter Command, Sir Douglas MacGregor, was appreciative too. He sent a signal that read:

> My congratulations on the fine part your squadron played at the Paris Air Show. Your performance was up to the highest traditions of the Royal Air Force. I appreciate that this achievement would not have been possible without the AFDS Lightnings and the support given by HQ 12 Group and Coltishall. Well Done!

English Electric were understandably very pleased with the Tigers and in appreciation they organised a night out in Paris for the nine participating pilots. John wasn't happy with this and insisted that reserves Mike Cooke and Peter Philips were included too for whilst they hadn't flown they were very much part of the team. English Electric demurred and changed their plans to allow Mike and Pete to join in.

When 74 Squadron left Creil at the end of the deployment nobody could have missed their departure for all nine aircraft took off in reheat and it was a mass take-off! Allegedly the Lightnings' reheat roar loosened the reception tent's pegs, a first hand demonstration of the aircraft's power and a very good advert for English Electric. These were indeed exciting times. The world of military aviation was racing forward at breakneck speed by necessity with the Cold War demanding constant evolution, increased capability and ever more sophisticated weaponry. At Paris that year it was the new B-58 Hustler that epitomised that way of thinking. Whilst *en route* to the show the Hustler set a New York to Paris speed record, covering the 3,626 miles in three hours, nineteen minutes and fifty-eight seconds. Sadly the return flight crew were killed when the aircraft crashed following departure from Le Bourget Field.

Ken Goodwin recounts:

> On the day of B-58 Hustler crash, a brilliant blue skied day, as the formation approached the airfield we could see a pall of black smoke rising from an area close to it. I called John and asked whether he could see what I could see. He could. There was lots of excited chatter on the radio, mainly in French, but amongst it came the message to the effect that we Tigers should go away. John made an immediate decision, based on the fact that the squadron had been rehearsing for two months and the ground crew had made superhuman efforts to make aircraft available, that we weren't going to go away. John ignored the French instruction, the formation changed radio frequency and we pressed on with the display. I should add that there was no conflict as only a few helicopters were in the air over the crash site and not interfering with our air space.

Alongside the aerial exhibition of the RAF's new aircraft John was still trying to build on the operational quality of his squadron. As far as possible normal training carried on after their return from Creil until the end of June and on to the middle of July. However, this was interspersed with formations flown for a NATO press day and then six aircraft flew at American Armed Forces Days at Sculthorpe and Mildenhall. Added to this there was a stream of visitors who wanted to see the Lightning at Coltishall – the Netherlands Chief of Defence Staff, the Inspector General of the RAF and an Italian delegation amongst them. Then the BBC arrived for two days' filming. The squadron stood down from 20 July until 8 August, a well-earned rest for all concerned. On their return all pretence at normal operational training was abandoned as the Tigers worked up for Farnborough at which they would again fly a Diamond Nine, but this time end their sequence with a Diamond Roll. How that came about is recalled by John.

> I went down to Fighter Command to discuss the Farnborough display. The C in C chaired the meeting. Much was discussed, so much in fact that I forgot to ask whether we could do some formation aerobatics with the squadron instead of simply flying formations, rolling the Diamond Nine formation for example. The following day I therefore phoned through to Fighter Command and asked to speak to the C in C – the temerity of it – but I was told that as he was unavailable I would have to speak to the Senior Air Staff Officer (SASO) to whom I explained the purpose of my call and was given permission. There was one condition though. 'One touch and you're fired!'

So John found himself in a situation where his Wing Commander Flying, his Station Commander and his AOC didn't know that he'd spoken directly to Fighter Command and bypassed them all in the process. John prudently decided he ought to tell Bird-Wilson. But such was the evident regard in which he was held by his seniors that he was only given a pleasant talking to, reminding him that he must not do things other than through the proper channels. And John did roll the Diamond Nine, the first time this had been done by a Mach 2 aeroplane anywhere in the world.

Post Farnborough there were Battle of Britain displays at Coltishall (where Douglas Bader was a guest) and Biggin Hill to undertake. Finally, during the last week of the month the Tigers reverted to full operational training and completed night dual checks of all pilots, many of which John undertook himself on one of the two Hunter T.7s the squadron now had on strength. This continued for a couple of weeks into October but was interrupted by a deployment to Leconfield to display for the Queen Mother on 23 October, something of an honour as the crews would be presented to her beforehand. The Blue Diamonds were in Cyprus at the time so the Tigers were asked to do it in their place. When it came to the display itself (which Her Majesty observed from the roof of the annexe to No. 2 hangar)

Vaughan Radford had the responsibility of standing with her and talking her through the manoeuvres with her ADC standing beside them. The ADC had to continually remind Vaughan that he mustn't nudge the Queen Mother in his excitement at watching and briefing her on the Tigers!

John comments on the Leconfield deployment by saying:

> ...the squadron had had a break after the Farnborough show. In such circumstances I would recommence practice by building up the numbers in formation from four to the nine. On this particular Saturday morning the squadron and I had been practising and on our return to Coltishall I decided to make a low-level pass over Group Captain Bird-Wilson's house. Birdy happened to be looking out of his window at the time and he got a hell of a fright as the sudden appearance of the Lightning and its associated noise (and the shadow over his lawn) came from nowhere. He leapt into his car and sped off to the tower and got on to the R/T telling me to 'stop this bloody nonsense straight away'. What amazed the tower staff as much as anything was the normally impeccably dressed Group Captain appearing in slippers and casual wear! At the next Station Officer's meeting (held every Monday morning) I was told to stay behind and then simply told 'not to do that again'. The gods continued to be kind to me!

Once again there was tremendous pressure on the ground crew as the squadron was still recovering from the intense period of flying for Farnborough and the Battle of Britain displays. The ground crew was trying to prepare for the deployment to Leconfield and at the same time carry out engine removals on eight aircraft as a result of another manufacturer's instruction. But as ever they pulled through and all the necessary aircraft were available on the day.

Leconfield was the last display that John flew with 74 Squadron for his time as a Tiger was drawing to a close after twenty-one months as their Boss – twenty-one months that had been the most fulfilling thus far in his career. The aircrew were able to show their feelings for him as they flew back from Leconfield. John as usual positioned the formation in echelon starboard as they approached Coltishall from which the aircraft would break off individually to come in and land. On this occasion he led the formation in as usual, or so he thought, but nobody followed him. He couldn't understand why for there was nothing wrong but as he taxied in he heard the formation call up to say they were overflying the airfield. When they appeared John could see 'JH' picked out in the sky as a salute and a farewell to their Boss – a special but emotional moment. Group Captain Bird-Wilson was leaving at around the same time, but before doing so he endorsed John's log book with the words 'Best of Luck John'. A few months earlier he had signed Form 41A (the summary of flying and assessments of individual officers) with remarks such as 'exceptional' and 'above the average' and with the comment 'Commander of an excellent fighter squadron, No 74 Sqn'. John had certainly made the right impression as he proved that he was up to the job and for the work he did with the Tigers he was awarded the Air Force Cross.

That wasn't quite the end though for he still had all of November to go and after all the presentations and display flying of the previous months the squadron finally settled down to four weeks of uninterrupted operational training. Then on 29 November 1961 John left Coltishall three months short of the normal two-year tour. This was earlier than he might have expected but was simply down to timing. His successor, Peter Botterill, needed to settle in before the 1963 season of formation aerobatics got under way again. Needless to say, John wasn't allowed to leave without a huge party being thrown. The squadron's tiger skin was hung in the 'snarling position' from the window behind his seat at the top table in the Officers' Mess, hidden by a remotely controlled curtain. David Jones was entrusted with some pyrotechnic arrangements and as John stood to make his farewell speech the dimly lit mess burst into light and through clouds of white smoke there appeared the tiger in the very best of pantomime traditions.

When John departed 74 Squadron knew they had lost a fine commander and their send off reflected their feelings towards him. Making their way to their quarters in the early hours after the party was it the throb of Zulu war drums the Tigers could hear? And was that John doing his amazing war dance one last time?

What is John's abiding memory of 74 Squadron and his first command?

I don't have an abiding memory. There are too many. It all started with that telephone call I thought was a hoax and it became a brilliantly enjoyable tour during which of course I got married. There were the valiant efforts of the ground crew. Then the air displays. The local public were very interested to see what this noisy new high performance aeroplane was all about. Whenever we were operating there were crowds of people at the runways' ends or at the crash gates watching us. But with all the emphasis on showing off the RAF's new aircraft we weren't able to progress operationally. It was the other squadrons that were taking on the Lightning that were doing the bulk of operational readiness work in the first two years.

John had met the challenge of bringing a very significant new aeroplane into RAF service with his by now customary enthusiasm and commitment. There were times when it took its toll. Trying to juggle operations, displays, spares, pilot training and morale was demanding in the extreme. Many men under such situations would help themselves through the trying times with a good drinking session. John certainly wasn't averse to that for he was as sociable as the next man and enjoyed every party he could attend to the hilt. But when the pressure was really on he would contrarily go on the wagon, his reasoning being that to get through pressure you need a clear head not a muddled head.

Because I was only thirty years of age I felt there was nothing I couldn't do and with that confidence I could cope with all the pressures. It's only when

The first uniform? John pictured after kitting-out at the South African Military College at Voortrekker Hoogte in Pretoria, known as Robert's Heights before the Nationalist Government came to power. (*The John Howe Collection*)

At the Passing Out Parade for Course 57G at the College on 31 March 1950. (*The John Howe Collection*)

Of the six identifiable DH82s seen here at CFS Dunnottar. John flew 509, 592, 2303 and 4709 between May 1950 and December 1953. (*Steven McLean Collection*)

John proudly wearing his Wings, conferred at Central Flying School Dunnottar on 15 December 1950. (*The John Howe Collection*)

Spitfire HFIXe 5555 was one of the aircraft John flew during his OTU course at Langebaanweg although he was not responsible for this landing accident in August 1951. (*Steven McLean Collection*).

Monty Montanari imparting something of obvious interest in this posed shot taken at Langebaanweg on the OTU course with close attention being paid (left to right) by Mike Muller, John, Jan de Wet, Howard 'Horse' Sivertsen and Dennis Earp with Eric Keevy looking down from above. (*The John Howe Collection*)

When the 2 Squadron pilots arrived in Japan after their multi-staged flight from South Africa they had to convert to the F-51D Mustang before going to Korea. This they began immediately they arrived at Johnson AFB near Tokyo. Here Bill Sykes is seen briefing Captain H. Snyman and Ian de Gough, Terry Liebenberg, John Howe, Jess Verster and Ray Sherwood. (*The John Howe Collection at the Imperial War Museum London.*)

Taken in August 1951, John on the left and 2nd Lieutenant Lewis F. Creed Jnr on the right flank K10's padre. John always found the help and guidance of the padres assigned to the 18th FBW essential, particularly when coping with the loss of friends. (*The John Howe Collection*)

Believed to be taken at K10 Chinhae, this fascinating shot shows aircraft from two wars. An aircraft which John flew, F-51D 303 receives attention alongside a Japanese suicide MXY7 OHKA Model 11 'Baka'. 303 was lost on 7 October (after John's tour ended) when Lt Lombard baled out following electrical failure. He was made a PoW. (*Bob Rogers Collection via Brian Stockland*)

Another of the many Mustangs John flew in Korea was 302. This again was later lost when Lieutenant Biden failed to pull out of a dive and was killed during a napalm attack on communist positions on 5 September 1951. (*Bob Rogers Collection via Brian Stockland*)

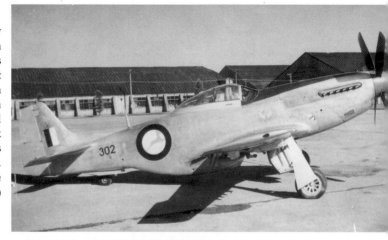

An evocative image of a 2 Squadron Mustang being run up at night at K10. (*Bob Rogers Collection via Brian Stockland*)

Deep in conversation by a radio jeep are Major Jiminez of the USAF (left) and Jan de Wet and John. (*The John Howe Collection*)

After his flying tour in Korea ended John joined the 19th Infantry Division of the US Army as a Forward Air Controller and had to quickly get used to a very different life on the ground and under enemy fire. (*The John Howe Collection*)

The two men assigned to John in his FAC role with the 19th Infantry Division were Gerald Haley, his radio mechanic, and airman John Fitch seen here. (*The John Howe Collection*)

John on standby, waiting to call in air support if needed. The photographs of John and his crew were taken on Hill 690 in the Kumsong area. (*The John Howe Collection*)

When 222 Squadron disbanded at Leuchars, John moved across to 43 Squadron on the same station. He had already been involved in the formation flown at the presentation of 43's new standard on 4 June 1957 by Her Majesty the Queen when the resident squadrons flew an impeccable 'E R' across the airfield (*The John Howe Collection*)

Accompanied by Prince Philip, the Queen reviews Leuchars' squadrons. Prominent are 151 Squadron and its Venoms. (*The John Howe Collection*)

Personnel of No. 5 Course at the Day Fighter Combat School at RAF West Raynham in June 1959. John is on the back row on the right. Next to him is 'Black Fergie'. It was to him that John confided he would marry Annabelle immediately after meeting her at nearby RAF Sculthorpe on a social evening! (*The John Howe Collection at the Imperial War Museum London.*)

74 being the first Squadron to have the Lightning on charge brought with it many additional pressures, not least the attention from the media and the need to constantly be available for publicity photographs. John stands before one of 'his' Lightnings at the International Press Day held at Coltishall in February 1961. (*The John Howe Collection*)

To be given command of 74 Squadron was one of the high points of John's long and successful career, particularly as he and his fellow Tigers were entrusted with the job of bringing the Lightning into RAF service. Photographs of all twelve aircraft of the Squadron on the line at Coltishall at the same time were rare in the Lightning F1's early days as serviceability problems manifested themselves. (*74 Squadron Association*)

Climbing aboard .... (*The John Howe Collection*)

John settled in what he always calls 'his favourite seat'. The first truly supersonic aircraft in level flight that the RAF possessed, the Lightning's phenomenal power accelerated it to twice the speed of sound but the penalty was low endurance thanks to the quick consumption of available fuel. The Lightning carried a de Havilland Firestreak air-to-air missile either side of the forward fuselage. (*The John Howe Collection*)

Emerging from 74's hangar at Coltishall, unmistakeable with the Squadron's famous markings over the entrance. Pilots also had a tiger's head on their flying helmets. (*The John Howe Collection*)

A dramatically posed shot which demonstrates the revolutionary design of the Lightning, optimised for speed with its thin, swept wings and which also gives a good impression of the scale of the aircraft. (*The John Howe Collection*)

Another duty which fell to the Tigers was participation in the Paris and Farnborough air shows. Here a quintet from the nine-ship which flew at Le Bourget in June 1961 make their way across to France. (*The John Howe Collection*)

ater the same year the team were at Farnborough. In 1960 they had flown a four-ship, in 1961 they lew a nine and included in the routine was a Diamond Nine roll. John stands in front of his team at rain soaked Coltishall. To the left of John as we look at them are Tim Nelson, Jerry Cohu and Martin Bee. Immediately behind John is Ted Nance and behind him Maurice Williams. To John's ight are George Black, 'Lefty' Wright and Mike Dodd. (*The John Howe Collection*)

The occasion (and the names) have been forgotten, but the Tiger Squadron fraternity is a world-wide one and whilst in the States John never missed an opportunity to promote 74 – as evidently he was doing in this photo by exchanging shields, scarves and ties! (*The John Howe Collection*)

Having brought the Lightning into RAF service and having experienced the mighty F-4 Phantom in the States whilst with Air Defense Command, John sought an opportunity to introduce the aircraft to the RAF's inventory as well. His wish was granted when he was given command of 228 OCU at RAF Coningsby. The officers selected to run the courses at Coningsby first had to convert to the F-4 themselves and this they did at Davis Monthan AFB in Arizona. Here the first pilots to do so pose in front of a well worn F-4C. John is by the aircraft's steps. (*The John Howe Collection*)

McDonnell Douglas Phantom F-4C 637566 at Davis Monthan with John at the controls. (*The John Howe Collection*)

The version of the Phantom that the RAF received was designated F-4M in the McDonnell sequence but was the FGR.2 to the RAF. It was a unique version in that it had a high content of British avionics and components, not least Rolls Royce Spey engines. XT891 was the first to arrive at Coningsby, flown in by John on 23 August 1968 with Squadron Leader Freeman in the back seat. (*The John Howe Collection*)

Having landed safely before a crowd of enthusiastic onlookers, pilot and navigator were greeted by Coningsby's Commander, Group Captain (later Air Chief Marshal Sir) John Rogers. (*The John Howe Collection*)

The absolute highlight of John' career was for him his time as Station Commander at RAF Gutersloh from 1973 to 1975. Amongst the many things he particularly remembers with pride are the forging of new links with the local German populace and the greeting of many VIPs at this most easterl' of the RAF's front-line European bases very close to the Iron Curtain. Something has certainly caught the attention of the Duke of Edinburgh! (*The John Howe Collection*)

Princess Anne visited just one week after an abduction attempt in The Mall and consequently security was at the highest of levels at Gutersloh with nobody except essential personnel allowed within two hundred yards. There was a huge turnout on the station as people reacted to what had happened by showing their support. (*The John Howe Collection*)

I look back now that I realise the absolute importance to the RAF of introducing that aeroplane. At the time it was getting the job done that was important. Although you were aware of the bigger picture you had your head down doing what you had to do. Other people worried about the other things.

The final words on John Howe as a Tiger come from Martin Bee, his Adjutant at the time.

As the Boss he looked after his men, aircrew and ground crew alike. I remember so well sitting in my tiny office next to his big office as it got darker and darker in the evenings. John stayed at his desk. He could not yet go home to the mess as the maintenance staff were still working on the many defects that the Lightning could produce so John Howe had to wait too. He was indeed a leader of men. His tasks were big yet he handled them with an all over practical approach, which yielded results without undue drama. Can you ask for more?

CHAPTER SEVENTEEN

Grounded

*John, the first staff officer at Fighter Command who was also a
qualified Lightning aviator, directed his energies towards the operations
and training of the Lightning and its aircrew. His experience was invaluable.
All the things that he and the Tigers had initiated were carried on and
expanded to encompass the growing Lightning force.*

When John walked through the doors of Bentley Priory, home to Headquarters Fighter Command at RAF Stanmore, to which he had now been posted as part of the Operations and Training Branch (Air), he had mixed feelings. He could foresee no chance of other than occasional flying over the next two years and that he would miss greatly. But he also recognised that he was going to be working in probably the most evocative of all RAF buildings, the mansion transformed into the operations centre from which the Battle of Britain was directed in 1940 (see Appendix G). Walking through the corridors lined with portraits of the most famous of RAF leaders and the most famous of RAF aircraft, standing at the bottom of the great staircase of Portland stone, seeing Air Chief Marshal Dowding's office, John couldn't help but know that here was inspiration, if inspiration were needed, to see him through two years of administering the newly forming Lightning squadrons. He felt a real sense of occasion underlined by the fact that the huge Battle of Britain operations room was still in use, albeit having been extensively updated and upgraded, where exercises were regularly held to test Fighter Command's proficiency. These ranged from in-house short-term affairs over in a few hours to full-scale exercises (such as *Matador*), which involved working with other Commands. These lasted for days at a time and meant twenty-four hour alerts designed to really test the RAF in preparation for going to war again. A further very real link with the past was the fact that John got to know some of the Battle of Britain veterans who would turn up at Bentley Priory from time to time, Douglas Bader for instance and Bob Stanford Tuck who in the early sixties was helping to set up the RAF Museum at Hendon and had an office at the Priory.

When John arrived in December 1961 at the height of the Cold War, Fighter Command was in transition. By the end of 1956 it had numbered almost six hundred aircraft in fifty-five front-line squadrons. Now those numbers were declining rapidly until in 1966 they would number just sixty new Lightnings and older Javelins, all armed with the Red Top missile, successor to Firestreak. Duncan Sandys' idea that the UK's best form of defence was the surface-to-air missile together with the supersonic Lightning with its air-to-air missiles has already been discussed in Chapter Thirteen. The fact that it was thought in some quarters that there could be no defence against the destructive power of Russian surface-to-surface missiles and consequently fighters were becoming increasingly irrelevant in the scheme of things, meant that John's job with the Lightning and its missile power was all the more important if its detractors were to be persuaded otherwise.

A secret report was commissioned by Fighter Command during 1962 in response to concerns that Britain's air defences and the means of detecting incoming Russian manned bomber raids or missiles were inadequate. Entitled 'Soviet Nuclear Offensive Tactics and United Kingdom Detection and Alerting Requirements', it considered a surprise global attack by the Soviets. Its conclusion was that Britain and often her allies too were not best equipped to deal with such a scenario. Even though intelligence warning may have been available this would not be sufficient to bring Western forces to advanced states of alert at the optimum time for scrambling intercepting aircraft. The report recommended a 'Tactical Intelligence Ready Reckoner', which involved a detailed written assessment of the time scale of events in the pre-launch phase of Soviet attack. Any information gained through intelligence channels could then be related to the 'ready reckoner' in a systematic manner and thus a (hopefully) accurate calculation of the likelihood and timing of the attack could be arrived at. Another recommendation was the deployment of over the horizon (OTH) radar, which would be able to detect Soviet bombers shortly after take-off thus giving positive warning of a threat. Such OTH radar should be forward deployed thus facilitating advance warning of sufficient duration that would allow defensive forces to react. Such deployments would rather obviously be 'especially advantageous in periods of international tension'. There was also an undoubted requirement for a new Bomb Alarm System. The current system was considered to be slow, vulnerable and provided incomplete cover. It consisted of special sensors, which were installed near military facilities and cities so that the locations of nuclear bursts would be transmitted before the expected communication failure. They were set up to display a red signal at command posts the instant that the flash of a nuclear detonation reached it and before the blast put it out of action. Normally the display would show a green signal or a yellow if the sensor was not operating or was out of communication for any other reason. It was recommended that any new system should be linked to the US to provide collateral information to the Ballistic Missile Early Warning System (BMEWS). This consisted of three radar stations, each with a range of three thousand miles, built to give early warning of Soviet trans-polar nuclear missile attack. One of these radars was in Alaska, another was at Thule in Greenland and the third on Fylingdales Moor in Yorkshire. Such a system would, it was estimated, give up to eighteen minutes of advance information on nuclear bursts in Europe, particularly useful to the US of course if it was also to be a target.

A comprehensive UK ground-based system consisting of three detection stations had been discussed by Fighter Command for some time. An airborne detection system would only be valid if a continuous patrol could be maintained or if it could be guaranteed that the aircraft with the sensors could be scrambled in very short order. Associated with this, the Broadcast Alarm and Signalling System would fulfil an urgent need for the rapid transmission to flying stations and SAM units of BMEWS alarms, Bomb Alarms and indeed instructions to come immediately to higher states of alert. There was also a need for a Fighter Command blind scramble facility. However, the essential problem with this was the accurate determination of the time of arrival of a Soviet bomber raid against the UK, although this would be solved by the deployment of the OTH radar. But the current breed of reconnaissance aircraft was outdated and would need to be superseded by Airborne Early Warning (AEW) aircraft – Canberras with Airborne Interception radar and Ultra High Frequency radios perhaps or by NATO fighters operating under joint procedures. Other means of obtaining raid information that were being actively considered included the use of radar-equipped trawlers but whilst it was conceded these would be of value their vulnerability was a factor for concern, not to mention the cost to buy and maintain such a fleet of vessels.

John's log books show just fifteen entries for 1962 and 1963. Predominant amongst the types recorded is the Anson, which John converted to, the reason being that this was invariably the aircraft flown (from RAF Bovingdon, close to Bentley Priory) when visiting Lightning bases. He was reasonably content to be flown but when he could he preferred of course to fly himself, although this only happened on three occasions. Far more excitingly, over a couple of days in August 1962 John enjoyed three familiarisation flights in the new Lightning two-seater, the T.4, recently introduced to fill the gap in Lightning conversion training and which allowed first tourists to be appointed to Lightning squadrons. Ken Goodwin was the first to take him up and John duly qualified to fly solo on the type. A year later John made another couple of trips in the T.4 during Exercise *Ciano* prior to a couple of Hunter T.7 sorties as second pilot. But that was the sum total.

At Bentley Priory John had no staff under him but was responsible to Group Captain Ops, Group Captain DH 'Tom' Seaton (whom he had first met at West Raynham). Air Officer Commanding in Chief at Fighter Command during John's early days was Air Marshal Hector Macgregor: he later handed over to Air Marshal Sir Douglas Morris. When John arrived the Lightning force was still a small one but, as squadrons were added, by the time his tour ended he had become responsible for his old squadron, 74, as well as 19 Squadron, which began conversion to the Lightning F.2 in October 1962; 56 Squadron, which began conversion to the F.1 shortly after the Tigers and was the first to receive the F.1A version; 92 Squadron, which began equipping with the F.2 in late 1962; and 111 Squadron, which received its first F.1A in March 1961. After John's departure, 5, 11, 23 and 29 Squadrons would be added to the list. The AFDS continued to operate from Coltishall until September 1962 when it moved to Binbrook, its brief being to carry out tactical and operational trials and to investigate all equipment and aircraft systems. Its work also now came under John's aegis. Very importantly – and this too came under John's brief – the Lightning Operational Conversion Unit came into being. 226 OCU's first incarnation was within the AFDS at Coltishall, responsible for the training of 74 Squadron using their own aircraft. From August 1961 such training centred on Middleton St George where the Lightning Conversion Squadron formed, using 56 and 111 Squadron's aircraft, usually on a daily use and return basis as with 74 Squadron earlier. The first two-seat T.4 arrived on 27 June, followed by nine more, and 226 OCU was officially constituted in June 1963 when it took 74 Squadron's F.1s when the Tigers converted to the F.3.

Establishing the OCU necessitated the writing of a training syllabus and this was one of the first projects John became involved with at Fighter Command. In doing so he and those who worked with him bore in mind the fact that the experience level within a Lightning fighter squadron varied from pilot to pilot, from those with just six months' fighter experience to those on their second or third tour, for there was no longer a block on the posting in of inexperienced pilots. For conversion purposes thirty-five hours' dual and solo flying was allocated to each one but there was no provision for night flying on the course, which would be left entirely to the pilot's Squadron Commander. Each course would have a compliment of five pilots and last for a minimum of six weeks. The syllabus would run along the following lines:

- An introductory sortie in a Lightning T.4.
- Ground instruction – systems and controls. Lectures on handling including pilot's checks and emergencies. This would give a pilot a sound knowledge of the aircraft.
- Simulator instruction. Nine exercises designed to enable a pilot to simulate all the operating techniques that he would cover when flying the Lightning during conversion, to familiarise him with cockpit checks and to train him to act swiftly in the event of an emergency. The simulator syllabus would be integrated with dual Lightning conversion and ground school.
- Dual conversion flying. The first three T.4 exercises would be flown dual after which an average pilot would be expected to have reached solo standard.
- Solo conversion standard. With comprehensive briefing and debriefing

before and after each sortie. It would be a requirement that radar surveillance be available for all Lightning conversion sorties flown from Middleton St George.

• Weapons training. A full programme of ground instruction would be given on the Lightning's fire control system during the flying phase of the course. There would be lectures on theoretical aspects of weapons training as well as instruction and applied practices in the simulator. The aim of this part of the programme would be to prepare pilots for operational training when they returned to their squadrons. Dual weapons' sorties would be flown on the T.4 to consolidate what had been covered.

• Operational training. All to be done at a pilot's home base on squadron aircraft.

Another aspect of Lightning operations with which John became directly concerned was the writing of its Standard Operating Procedures (SOPs). On 5 June 1962 he, together with three others from HQ Fighter Command staff, representatives from 11 and 12 Groups, Ken Goodwin from the Lightning Conversion Squadron and a pilot each from 56, 74 and 111 Squadrons gathered at Bentley Priory under the chairmanship of Wg Cdr J Leggett (Wing Commander Ops). They met to discuss the way forward, influenced in part by changing threat scenarios and also with an eye to the changes being postulated as far as Fighter Command itself was concerned (and consequently the way in which aircraft under its control were utilised). It was, for instance, being proposed that 11 and 12 Groups disband as components of Fighter Command and their role be taken on directly by Bentley Priory itself. It's hard to say whether any in the room discussing Lightning SOPs on that June day in 1962 could foresee the total disbandment of Fighter Command itself six years later. It was generally realised, however, that as the RAF continued to shrink as the 1960s progressed it was becoming too small to justify the continued existence, as separate entities, of Fighter Command, Bomber Command and Coastal Command. Accordingly, in April 1968 Fighter Command and Bomber Command joined forces to form Strike Command. Coastal Command was absorbed in November of the same year and Signals Command in January 1969. Air Support Command (previously Transport Command) was absorbed in September 1972. Thus was the new shape of the RAF created. There is now (in 2008) just one Command – Air Command.

But that was in the future as far as those now closeted at Bentley Priory were concerned. Their deliberations were far more immediate and some ground rules were laid down as far as the Lightning SOPs were concerned. In future the emphasis would be on:

• Close control training for both pilots and GCI controllers.
• Training for the visual identification pass by night as well as day.
• Overseas reinforcement with the capacity for in-flight refuelling. 56 Squadron were the first to be converted to allow this.

A Fighter Command order was subsequently issued stating that:

> ...during periods of political tension it may be necessary to deploy limited numbers of Lightning aircraft to RAF Germany to indicate our ability to reinforce this theatre at short notice. These will normally be deployed at RAF Geilenkirchen and will be flown directly there from their UK base. Servicing personnel and freight will follow. On receipt of a warning order the squadron will have six hours to arrive in Germany. The aircraft will carry two Adens with ammunition and two Firestreaks.

The type of pilot henceforth being sought for the Lightning must be capable of intercepting supersonic recce aircraft or at the other end of the spectrum a subsonic intruder who might hide himself amongst civilian traffic in upper airspace. A successful interception would require a great deal of skill not only on the part of the pilot but the ground controller as well. Lightning SOPs would henceforth be presented in two parts. The first would relate to the handling of the aircraft, briefing and debriefing, ground signals, R/T procedures and control, close formation flying, navigation and ATC, in-flight refuelling, night flying, landing techniques and recovery, GCA and ILS including dive circle procedures, TACAN, free let down and diversion action. All of this should be written by the squadrons themselves. The second part would detail operational tactics and would incorporate the basic procedures taught by the LCS (later the OCU) and include practice interceptions, weapons and cine handling, GCI and identification procedures, ECM procedures, fighter combat, escort tactics and low level training. Data for this second part would be gathered as tactical trials were completed and as squadrons developed tactics individually they would be included in the SOPs as well. Some preliminary work on writing up the various aspects of the procedures had already been initiated, although some of that which John had seen left him less than impressed. Close formation flying for example had been tackled by CFE and 56 Squadron, but their 'contributions are unsatisfactory. 74 Squadron are best placed to write this section'.

Reading the minutes, it becomes apparent that these day-long 'think tanks' with experienced aviators were exhausting but at the same time stimulating sessions for all participants, not least John who played a central role. They considered all the pros and cons of operating procedures ranging from dive circles to the best ways of braking on landing (apply brakes before deploying the 'chute or after?), from let downs to practice interceptions, from whether taxi lights should be used for taxiing or signals during night ops to deciding under which section of the SOPs emergency procedures should be placed or whether or not cine use in training was really of value.

Many reports were written by John during his two years at Bentley Priory and no doubt his JC&SS training contributed in some measure to how those reports were compiled. John's next posting onto No. 54 Staff Course at the RAF Staff College Bracknell in January 1964 enhanced those skills, being taught there how to apply them specifically to meet the demands of more senior officers in their administrative roles. It was a first-rate course with a very diverse series of lectures from those outside as well as within the RAF (see Appendix H). One lecture in particular stands out in John's memory, that by Dennis Healey when he was Secretary of State for Defence. The Staff Colleges of the Royal Navy and RAF were invited to meet at the Army Staff College at Camberley for this lecture, a review of the government's defence policy, which was to be included in the next White Paper. At the end of it Healey received a standing ovation for the 1964 Defence Review was evidently going to be a very positive one. From the RAF's perspective all major programmes were being carried forward. Instead, the week after the lecture all were cancelled, including TSR2, which meant that whilst the military were being told of the government's commitment to these programmes, Dennis Healey knew that there was no such commitment. John comments, 'I was certainly not alone in being amazed and angry. How can you ever trust a politician when they do such dishonourable things?'

The Staff College course remit of covering a wide range of subjects was designed to get the student thinking and then to express those thoughts on paper in such a way as to make himself understood. A very high standard was offered and demanded. What it essentially taught was how to be an effective staff officer with increasing degrees of responsibility as promotion came. Sadly the Staff College at Bracknell no longer exists. Its buildings and grounds were sold off for private development in 2000 when it became surplus to the RAF's needs after the creation of the Joint Services Command and Staff College, which has been based at Shrivenham since August of that year.

From Bracknell John was posted on 4 January 1965 to the Offensive Support Section of the Joint Warfare Establishment at RAF Old Sarum, a holding appointment prior to an impending exchange with the USAF. If he felt an all-pervading sense of history at Bentley Priory he should have felt at least a semblance of one here too for Old Sarum was – indeed is – the second oldest continuously operational aerodrome in the UK. In 1917 four hangars were built and the first squadrons of the Royal Flying Corps moved in towards the end of that year for training prior to moving to France and from the end of the First World War flying was almost exclusively for pilot training. In 1920 Old Sarum became the home of the School of Army Co-operation, which metamorphosed over the years into the School of Land/Air Warfare. When this school amalgamated with the Amphibious Warfare School it was retitled the Joint Warfare Establishment. During John's time Ansons, Dominies and Chipmunks were flown there and it was the place where John, after a long abstinence, got back into a cockpit again.

I started off at Old Sarum by taking soldiers up in a Chippie as the best means of explaining to them how things look different from the air, the reason being that they were training to be Forward Air Controllers. Consequently they needed to be able to describe things from an airborne perspective or understand when told by reporting pilots how things looked from an airborne perspective. I'd quickly familiarised myself and converted to the aircraft and the following day took off with my first soldier in the second seat. 'What we are going to do,' I said to him, 'is assume the enemy is on that hill in the woods at the end of the ridge.' And at this point I pulled up for the simulated attack. That Chipmunk was never going to make it to the top of the hill let alone simulate anything by diving onto a target. I had to pull away! I suppose I was totally unprepared for the complete lack of power to enable me to do such things.

Working with these prospective FACs was incidental to John's prime purpose at Old Sarum. It was only because it was known that he was a former FAC himself and was an aviator to boot that he was asked to help out from time to time. His main brief was to lecture on NATO Air Defence but before he did so he reasoned that he needed to talk to NATO directly so that he could gather up to date information for presentation in his lectures. He took himself off to Versailles for four days where SHAPE – Supreme Headquarters Allied Powers Europe – the central command of NATO military forces was then based. He was directed to the office of a US Navy officer who gave John exactly what he wanted but verbally only. He was not authorised to release any written information for reasons of security. John was determined not to accept this without speaking to someone at senior level so requested an interview with the officer's boss and this was granted. To his amazement when he presented himself he found himself talking to Colonel Capers Holmes, one of Annabelle's father's old friends from the Rackheath Aggies days. John got what he wanted.

John was at Old Sarum for just six months. In June 1965 he was sent to RAF Leconfield for a week for a flying refresher because the posting he was about to take up in the States required him to fly and it had been a couple of years since he had flown anything other than the Chipmunk. So 19 and 92 Squadrons hosted him and flew him in their Hunter T.7s. It didn't take John long to feel totally at home doing so again. He was now ready to embark on a crossing of the Atlantic for an exciting couple of years with the USAF, getting to know some of the heavyweights of their Century Series fighters in the process.

CHAPTER EIGHTEEN

Voodoos, Delta Darts, Delta Daggers and the T-33

John quickly found that the way things were done in the USAF
was often very different from the RAF. If he tried to implement RAF
methods he was quietly told 'We don't do that here!' The culture of
the USAF was different too. It was an enormous, big, brash and
bold organisation with big, brash and bold aeroplanes to fly.

John knew that his appointment at Old Sarum had been a holding posting but it wasn't until he received a signal promoting him to Wing Commander that it was confirmed that he would be going to the US. Even then neither he nor Annabelle were supposed to tell anybody – which, given they had a garage full of packing cases stencilled 'Wing Commander JFG Howe, HQ US Air Defense Command Colorado Springs, USA' was a bit of a tall order! On the family front the timing wasn't exactly ideal either as Annabelle was due to give birth to their third child at any time. A frantic period of packing coupled with the need to keep the cases hidden away in the garage proved to be a not particularly easy time for her. In fact it wasn't long before they were on the move, although thankfully it was long enough for baby Jane to have arrived to join her sisters Tiggy and Caroline.

The family sailed to New York from Southampton on the *Queen Elizabeth*. Because they had three young daughters John and Annabelle were allowed to take a nanny, Carolyn, who became so close to them that in all but name she became their fourth daughter. Once they had disembarked the family took a train to Washington DC. They stayed for a few days at the British Embassy for entry formalities to be completed and were then briefed by embassy staff before flying down to Colorado Springs. No sooner had they settled into their new home there than a crisis manifested itself when young Tiggy developed a serious attack of asthma. John and Annabelle will for ever be grateful to David Disbrow, the American officer who with his family had been detailed to look after them. The advice and support they gave through this very difficult time was extraordinary. Tiggy recovered and the subsequent two years proved to be memorable. The US was an eye opener and the impetus for development in the cities in particular phenomenal, with the pace of life far faster than back home. At Colorado Springs the Howes lived in a rented house on Leeds Lane at the foot of the 14,000-foot Pikes Peak. The view was a great one to wake up to each morning!

United States Air Force Air Defense Command Headquarters (US ADC HQ) at Colorado Springs was the Command to which John had been posted. Air Defense Command first came into being in 1946 at Mitchel Field, New York. In December 1948 it was placed under the control of Continental Air Command and oversaw the build up of the United States' air defence system. On 1 January 1951 it was established as a major air command in its own right at Ent AFB, Colorado Springs, and its subsequent growth and development was spectacular. From four day fighter squadrons in 1946 the interceptor force grew to sixty all-weather squadrons in 1959.

By 1953 the US was covered by medium and high-altitude radar. But with the threat of Soviet long-range strategic bombers armed with nuclear weapons attacking the North American continent the decision was made to extend radar coverage as far beyond the American borders as possible. This brought Canada and the US into close cooperation, initially demonstrated by the construction of three radar defence lines to detect Soviet aircraft approaching over the North Pole. The first was the Pinetree Line, completed in 1954, the second the McGill Fence, completed in 1957 and the third the Distant Early Warning Line (DEW Line), also completed in 1957. Any attack across the Pacific or Atlantic would have been detected by Airborne Early Warning aircraft (Lockheed RC-121 Warning Stars), US Navy ships or offshore radar platforms (Texas Towers). The real challenge was the command and control of this complex series of electronic defences and the deployment of the necessary response were a threat to be detected. North American Air Defense Command (NORAD), a component of US Air Defense Command, was established to do that very thing on 1 August 1957. By the early 1960s a quarter of a million personnel were involved in the operation of NORAD and its main technical facility from 1963 was located at or, more accurately, in Cheyenne Mountain. Meanwhile, the emergence of the Intercontinental Ballistic Missile (ICBM) and Submarine Launched Ballistic Missile (SLBM) threat had led to the construction of a space surveillance and missile warning system in addition to those dedicated to detecting approaching enemy aircraft. With the space element factored in, North American Air Defense Command became North American *Aerospace* Defense Command, a subtle but telling name change that happened after John's departure. Similarly, United States Air Defense Command became United States *Aerospace* Defense Command.

John had the opportunity to visit the NORAD complex several times in 1966 and 1967. It is certainly impressive. The website www.cheyennemountain.af.mil has the following description of the complex.

The main entrance is approximately one-third of a mile from the North Portal via a tunnel which leads to a pair of steel blast doors each weighing

25 tons. Behind the 25 ton blast doors is a steel building complex built within a 4.5 acre grid of excavated chambers and tunnels and surrounded by 2,000 feet of granite. The main excavation consists of three chambers 45 feet wide, 60 feet high and 588 feet long, intersected by four chambers 32 feet wide, 56 feet high and 335 feet long. Fifteen buildings, freestanding without contact with the rock walls or roofs and joined by flexible vestibule connections, make up the inner complex. Twelve of these buildings are three storeys tall; the others are one and two storeys. The outer shell of the buildings is made of three-eighths inch continuously welded low carbon steel plates which are supported by structural steel frames. Metal walls and tunnels serve to attenuate electro-magnetic pulses (EMP). Metal doors at each building entrance serve as fire doors to help contain fire and smoke. Emphasis on the design of the structure is predicated on the effects of nuclear weapons; however, building design also makes it possible for the complex to absorb the shock of earthquakes. Blast valves, installed in reinforced concrete bulkheads, have been placed in the exhaust and air intake supply, as well as water, fuel, and sewer lines. Sensors at the North and South Portal entrances will detect overpressure waves from a nuclear explosion, causing the valves to close and protect the complex. All of the buildings in the complex are mounted on 1,319 steel springs, each weighing approximately 1,000 pounds. The springs allow the complex to move 12 inches in any one direction. To make the complex self-sufficient, adequate space is devoted to support functions. A dining facility, medical facility with dental office, pharmacy and a two-bed ward; two physical fitness centres with exercise equipment and sauna; a small base exchange, chapel and barber shop are all located within the complex.

Also within the complex are all the utility systems necessary to make the facility functional. The primary supply of electrical power is supplied by the City of Colorado Springs. The secondary source or back-up power supply is provided by six 1,750 kilowatt, 2,800 horse-powered diesel generators. Water for the complex comes from an underground water supply inside Cheyenne Mountain. 30,000 to 120,000 gallons of water is deposited into four excavated reservoirs. Three of these reservoirs serve as industrial reservoirs and the remaining reservoir serves as the complex's primary domestic water source. Each of the four reservoirs has the capacity to store 1.5 million gallons of water. Incoming air may be filtered through a system of chemical/biological/radiological filters to remove harmful germs and/or radioactive and chemical particles. The fresh air intake is mainly from the South Portal access which is 17½ feet high and 15 feet wide and linked to the North Portal access which is 22½ feet high and 29 feet wide. The entire tunnel from North to South Portals is nine-tenths of a mile long.

As this is written in 2008 intercontinental nuclear attack is no longer considered to be a threat and consequently the facility has been demoted to standby status, ready to be reactivated if necessary.

NORAD wasn't the only component of the US defence strategy. In 1953 development of the Semi Automatic Ground Environment (SAGE) system began, a system that was destined to become its nerve centre. The first of the SAGE sectors was put into operation in July 1958 and was rapidly joined by others during 1959 and 1960. Its purpose was to provide instantaneous information to interceptor aircraft in flight as well as trigger other defensive measures, which included missiles. On 1 September 1959 the first surface-to-air missile squadron became operational, the start of a programme echoing to a degree Sandys' doctrine, which would replace a part of the manned interceptor force with unmanned interceptor missiles. A year earlier, to provide early warning of missile attacks the Ballistic Missile Early Warning System (BMEWS) was begun with radar in Alaska, Greenland and England (Fylingdales) capable of detecting missiles in flight, deep in the Soviet Union or in other similarly distant territory.

As the 1960s transitioned to the 1970s, however, as far as ADC operating as a Command in its own right was concerned changes were afoot. In the 1970s, with the Air National Guard and Air Force Reserve assuming more of the air defence mission, the Command's role was redefined. In March 1980 it was inactivated, its resources being divided between Tactical Air Command and Strategic Air Command.

John was assigned to the Directorate of Aerospace Tactics and Training (ADOTT) within Air Defense Command and was based at Peterson AFB. Specifically he was assigned to ADOTT-D Interceptor Division, which in turn had four branches – Interceptor Branch, Life Support Branch, Tactics Branch and Training Branch and it was with the latter that John spent the ensuing two years. The Commander of ADOTT overall was Colonel Philip Loring. He had been in England during the war as a fighter pilot but had the misfortune to be shot down on his second sortie and to spend the remainder of his war as a POW. John and he became good friends and their families used to do a lot together socially. John's immediate CO at the Interceptor Division was Lt Col Carl Weaver. On his second day on the job John underwent mandatory Refresher Physiological Training and Decompression Chamber Training so that the USAF could be assured of his fitness to fly and coincidentally operate from an airfield 6,187 feet above sea level. Peterson Field, as it was initially known and from which ADOTT operated, was so named to honour an airman who lost his life in an aircraft crash on the base when it was activated as a USAAF facility in 1942. Peterson Field shared runways with Colorado Springs Municipal Airport, which had been established in 1926. During the Second World War Peterson Field began heavy bomber combat crew training with the B-24 Liberator but from June 1944 the mission changed to fighter pilot training with the P-40 Warhawk. At the end of the war the Army deactivated the base, which reverted back to the City of Colorado Springs except for the north end of the property, which became Peterson Air Force Base (as opposed to Peterson Field as it was previously known) in 1948. Over the next six years it was deactivated and reactivated several times until it was finally permanently reactivated in 1951. In 1966, after sharing facilities with the military for a quarter century, the City of Colorado Springs built a new terminal on the west side of the runways.

John's role at HQ ADC was again as a staff officer but the dearth of flying he had experienced latterly with the RAF was about to be rectified. His responsibility was to oversee the conversion and training of F-101 Voodoo, F-102 Delta Dagger and F-106 Delta Dart pilots on Tactical Fighter Training Squadrons. John's particular brief was the Lockheed T-33 element of this training – small, versatile aircraft that were used as targets for the fighters on practice intercepts. Each ADC base had T-33s assigned to it. There was a large complement at Tyndall AFB for example, which was 'the mover and shaker of the F-106 fleet' as one commentator described it. Tyndall operated eighty Delta Daggers over a twenty-five year period, the units involved including the Air Defense Weapons Centre; the 4576th Air Defense Squadron (Weapons); the 4756th Combat Crew Training Squadron; the USAF Interceptor Weapons School; the 2nd, 39th and 62nd Fighter Interceptor Training Squadrons; the 475th and 4750th Test Squadrons; and the Southern Air Defense Alert Scramble, the 'Dixie Darts'. There were thus a commensurate number of T-33s assigned to the base.

Furthermore, T-33s were used as communications and liaison aircraft. To facilitate his being able to visit the units for which he was responsible John was able to get back into the air again (with his personal call sign LEDO 12, which was registered to the appointment he held at Air Defense Command), converting to the T-33 in the process. On one day a week and one weekend a month he also had the use of an aircraft to fly to places he had never been to before, exploring the length and breadth of the US from the air. And whilst he never got to Hawaii or Alaska he did get to just about everywhere else (see Appendix I). Visiting so many bases and airfields enabled him to catch up with many an old colleague from the Korean War days and it was through their influence that some of John's Century Series fighter sorties became possible. RAF exchange officers were also found from time to time and they too facilitated flights in ADC aircraft. As he was specifically responsible for the F-101, F-102 and F-106 training squadrons it was almost inevitable that he would fly in the types himself. But he was also able to fly the F-104 Starfighter and the F-4 Phantom. Two old RAF colleagues, Jock Heron and Ted Nance, were in the US at the same time as John and it was through them that he was able to add the F-105 Thunderchief and T-38 Talon to the list. John converted onto the F-101 Voodoo but the remainder were back-seat flights in twin stickers, which enabled him to take control once airborne.

As for the T-33, it didn't have a great deal of power taking off at the elevation of Peterson AFB (not only was it high, it also had a short runway) but it did possess a tremendous range of over 1,300 miles, ideal for John's flying around the USA. He took his initial Instrument Rating with the 4756th Air Defense Wing at Peterson on 20 August 1965 (and renewed it with the 4600th Air Base Wing on 9 March 1966 and 22 March 1967). Being a two-seater, the USAF didn't really like the T-33 to be used other than with two persons on board and thus each sortie was planned for maximum efficiency. If, for example, John and a colleague had different jobs to do on a base to be visited they would team up on the one aircraft and swap seats on each leg so that each pilot could benefit from flying as targets for the big interceptors or simply hone their navigation and flying skills.

John was also involved in TACEVALS (Tactical Evaluations) from time to time and he recalls on one occasion going with the TACEVAL team to a base on the east coast. Once completed there was the almost obligatory big party, the morning after which the Commander of the squadron they had been evaluating asked John whether or not he would like to take a T-33 up to have a look at the surrounding countryside. Such offers John of course never refused. Looking at his maps the name Keystone leapt out at him so he decided to see where the Keystone Cops originated. Back at base he shot a couple of GCAs, landed and taxied in only to be greeted by a decidedly upset CO who had come roaring up in his car shouting 'What about the APCs then?' John couldn't quite understand what he meant. APCs after all were a form of medication sold by British pharmacies for headaches and were pills that contained aspirin, phenacetin and caffeine – hence their name. So he responded by saying 'No, I won't have any thanks, my headache has gone.' However, the Americans didn't use APCs for headaches. To them an APC was an Area of Positive Control and John, flying visually, had unbeknownst to him been breaking all the rules, flying straight through them without reference to Air Traffic Control!

A few months later John was flying over northern Colorado when ATC called up saying something that John didn't catch and so he asked ATC to repeat it. He didn't understand a second time so requested another repeat. The voice came back with 'Is that Commander Howe?' On being told it was, the voice returned with 'Forget it!' It seems that ATC at Colorado Springs, in the light of John's exploration of the airspace over Keystone, had put out the word regarding a renegade RAF Wing Commander in a T-33, enjoining controllers to keep an eye on him whenever he was airborne! In all seriousness there were many occasions when local dialects prevented John from understanding what he was being told on the radio (the Florida panhandle was a particular area where this was the case) but equally controllers often had great trouble understanding John too. Consequently, ATC were virtually creating purple airspace around him, keeping him out of everyone's way and everyone out of his way, much as happens with the Royal Family in the UK.

What was the state of the USAF overall when John was seconded to it in 1965?

Its strategy was of course determined by the fact that those were the days of the Cold War and the doctrine of nuclear deterrence ruled. Each side possessed nuclear weapons but the consequences of a nuclear war were too awful to contemplate and so, it was hypothesised, neither side would initiate it for fear of the mass destruction it would bring upon itself as well as inflict upon the enemy. There could thus be no winner. History shows us that mutual deterrence works but for it to do so weapons have to be scrapped in their totality or both sides have to possess similar nuclear capabilities, whereby neither has the advantage. Scrapping was a very remote option in the 1960s so East and West went to the other extreme and developed strategic long-range bomber forces and initiated the use of ICBMs, whilst at the same time deploying the means of detecting and intercepting such bombers and missiles. In time of course the policy softened from the strategic use of nuclear weapons to their tactical use. Now, in a very different world to that of the Cold War, it has softened further still to one of the use of conventional weapons and forces.

The aircraft that John encountered in the US in 1965 were a direct product of the nuclear stance of the age. On the bomber front the Boeing B-47 was the mainstay of Strategic Air Command (SAC) in the early days, an attractive swept wing aircraft designed to operate at high speed and at high altitude. But advances in radar and missiles forced the type down to low level, the most punishing of regimes in which to operate, and a completely new set of tactics were developed. The B-47 was followed by the Boeing B-52, capable of carrying a huge bomb load over very long distances but once again having to hug the earth to stand any chance of survival and giving its crews the rides of their lives in the process. The Convair B-58 Hustler, which John and the Tigers had seen at the Paris Air Show, was another aircraft that fell foul of the change in tactics. It was the world's first supersonic bomber designed to penetrate enemy territory at high altitude at twice the speed of sound. As soon as the Russians developed anti-aircraft missiles that could reach high altitude at three times the speed of sound the Hustler's *raison d'être* was obsolete. Even the SAC commander General Curtis LeMay stated in a January 1955 memo that SAC neither wanted nor needed the B-58 since its range was only half that of the B-52. Subsonic bombers could do the conventional bombing job much more cheaply and the future of strategic nuclear strike clearly seemed to belong with the ICBM then in development by both the USA and the USSR. LeMay's logic was hard to argue with.

On the fighter front this was the age of the famous Century Series of American aircraft, so called because their designations fell within the 100s, and it was these which John had first-hand experience of. The Second World War had set the pattern for the first generation of jet fighter aircraft. Korea inspired these, the second generation.

- The North American F-100 Super Sabre was the world's first fighter capable of sustaining supersonic speed. Conceived as an air superiority fighter, it was based on North American's Korean War F-86 Sabre with 45-degree swept wings. The A model of the F-100 entered service in 1954 and followed by the more capable C and D models and a two-seat combat trainer version, the F-100F, which first flew in July 1957. John's verdict on the Super Sabre was that it was not too manoeuvrable but had great range, range being a prerequisite for the huge distances that constituted the Continental United States (CONUS). He found it to be a good, solid aircraft, which he flew with the 4758th Defense Systems Evaluation Squadron at Holloman AFB on 16 December 1966.

• The McDonnell F-101 Voodoo was heavy, large, powerful and fast, also with an impressive range. It was initially designed as a penetration fighter to escort SAC bombers but that role disappeared and it instead served as a nuclear attack fighter, all-weather interceptor and reconnaissance aircraft. Even then it never was a major type in the USAF inventory because of long standing control problems, which limited its effectiveness. John remembers it as having a lot of power, not being particularly manoeuvrable but it did have a good weapons system. He qualified to fly the two-seat version, the F-101B, on 1 March 1966 with the 444th Fighter Interceptor Squadron at Charleston AFB.

• The Convair F-102 Delta Dagger, known to all in the USAF as The Deuce, was an interceptor that suffered many development problems. It finally arrived on the front line in April 1956, two years late. It was the world's first supersonic all-weather jet interceptor and the USAF's first operational delta wing aircraft. Convair built 1,000 F-102s, 875 of which were F-102As. The USAF also bought 111 TF-102s as combat trainers with side-by-side seating and these were delivered to all the Fighter Interceptor Squadrons that flew the F-102. Until the arrival of the Delta Dagger, interceptors such as the F-86, F-89 and F-101 had only been built in single control versions but neither ADC nor ATC (Air Training Command) believed a pilot could safely transition to the delta-winged fighter directly from conventional jet trainers. The side-by-side seating arrangement had been chosen to simplify radar training and in doing so likely performance loss was accepted. In contrast to the F-100 and F-101, John found the F-102 to be manoeuvrable but it was no match for the later, derivative F-106, which was essentially a hot rod version of the F-102. He flew the TF-102 (which quickly gained the epithet of The Tub) as second pilot on three occasions at Tyndall, Perrin and Nellis AFBs.

• The Lockheed F-104 Starfighter was a lightweight air superiority fighter designed to replace the F-100 Super Sabre, although it actually never did so. The initial F-104A served only briefly with Air Defense Command as an interceptor because neither its range nor armament were well suited for that role. The subsequent F-104C entered service with Tactical Air

Command as a multi-role fighter and fighter-bomber and saw service in the Vietnam War, both in the air superiority role (although it saw little aerial combat and scored no air-to-air kills) and in the air support mission. The USAF procured only 296 Starfighters in total in single- and two-seat versions, mainly because USAF doctrine at the time placed little importance on air superiority (the 'pure' fighter mission) and the Starfighter was deemed inadequate for either the interceptor or tactical fighter-bomber role, lacking both payload and endurance compared with other USAF aircraft. After 1965 it disappeared from the USAF's inventory completely, although it served for many years with European air arms. John's verdict on the aircraft was, quite simply, that it went like a rocket, fully deserving the title 'a missile with a man in it' with which the Lockheed publicity machine had christened it, but with its tiny wing its turn radius was predictably poor. He first flew in a two-seat F-104B (of which only twenty-six were built) in October 1965 at Webb AFB, with two further sorties, again at Webb, in June 1967.

• The Republic F-105 Thunderchief was a fighter-bomber that went through an extended development to enter service in August 1958 as the largest single-seat combat aircraft ever produced. It was capable of flight faster than twice the speed of sound and could drop its bombs at supersonic speeds. The F-105 was used extensively during the Vietnam conflict as a bomb carrier and as a Wild Weasel, jamming and attacking enemy radars. It was never exported. Sqn Ldr Jock Heron, John's old 43 Squadron colleague who was with the 4526th CCTS (Combat Crew Training Squadron) of the 4520th CCTW (Combat Crew Training Wing) at Nellis AFB at the time, flew him in the two-seat version of The Thud, the F-105F, in October 1966. John was particularly impressed with the weaponry the aircraft could carry. Incidentally, whilst at Nellis he and Jock shared a 43 Squadron Fiftieth Anniversary mini-reunion in the Thunderbird Hotel on the Las Vegas strip.

• The Convair F-106 Delta Dart, known to all in the USAF as The Six, began development as an improved version of the F-102 Delta Dagger. Originally known as the F-102B, extensive structural and system changes resulted in the aircraft being redesignated as an F-106A. Its first flight was on 26 December 1956 and delivery began to Air Defense Command units in July 1959. It remained the mainstay of US air defence until 1988. The F-106 was fitted with a sophisticated fire control system, which, in simplistic terms, guided the aircraft to the optimum altitude and attack position, locked on and fired the aircraft's weapons at intruder aircraft and returned the F-106 to the vicinity of its home air base, where the pilot took over control for landing. The two-seat version of The Six did not have a side-by-side cockpit like the TF-102. Instead, it was designed to be as close in configuration to the F-106A as possible and so it was designated F-106B rather than TF-106. Sixty-three were produced in total. John regarded the Delta Dart as the best of the interceptors he flew because it was very fast, possessed high performance and had very good, innovative systems. He flew four sorties in F-106Bs at Tyndall (with the Air Defense Weapons Centre) and Minot Air Force Bases (with the 5th Fighter Interceptor Squadron).

John recounts:

I remember one sortie in particular over the Rockies in an F-106B with Bob Klingensmith. We were *en route* from Minot to Peterson in October 1965, which took us through Denver airspace, when I suggested that a supersonic run in this Mach 2 aircraft at that point might be allowed. Bob agreed so I called up Denver – 'LEDO 12. Clearance requested for a supersonic run.' 'No problem,' came the response. So we did one and went on to land at Peterson. The following morning I got an early call from an irate American. 'Did you do a supersonic run yesterday dropping booms all over Colorado Springs?' I confirmed we had. 'What the hell do you think you were doing?' 'But we were cleared by Denver.' Which silenced him straight away.

Incidentally, the F-106 could cope with take-offs from and landings on Peterson Field's short runway because of its immense power in reheat in the former case and its delta wing and drag 'chute in the latter.

The USAF undoubtedly had exciting aeroplanes to fly. The RAF on the other hand, although it now had the Lightning and was acquiring the Phantom, had largely flown a far different type of offensive aircraft, which on the face of it stood no comparison. But Britain is an island and if the Soviets were to have attacked, the RAF had to get them before they approached too closely. Its role was to take off, intercept, fire, land, turn round, take off, intercept, fire and so on, for which aircraft such as the Lightning were well suited. You only have to consider the vast distances involved in the States to realise straightway that you need a different type of aeroplane. Range was of paramount importance and with that range came the ability to carry more weaponry.

The other combat aircraft that John first experienced in the States was the ubiquitous McDonnell F-4 Phantom, recognised as the most potent and versatile combat aircraft of its era. John flew the C and D models of the F-4, the C being the initial USAF version of the Navy F-4B and the D, basically a C with improved systems specifically for the Air Force. John considers the Phantom to be the best combat aircraft of all because of its versatility, its great range and an excellent weapons system that could deliver a variety of ordnance with great accuracy. He qualified as co-pilot on a twin sticker with the Fighter Weapons School at Nellis in August 1966. We will discuss the F-4's design and development a little later in our story in the context of John heading the OCU that brought the aircraft into service with the RAF.

John also flew the Northrop T-38 Talon. In the mid 1950s Northrop began design work on a new high performance, lightweight fighter, which eventually led to the F-5 and an accompanying supersonic trainer, the T-38. The first T-38A entered service at Randolph AFB Texas on 17 March 1961. Production ended in early 1972 after 1,187 had been built and the type is still in service as the USAF's advanced training aircraft for student pilots selected to fly fighters. It was at Randolph that John flew in the Talon as Ted Nance recalls.

John Howe flew with me in T-38 tail number 569 on 25th January 1967. His reputation went before him because I had no difficulty in persuading the Boss to let John occupy the front seat. This was normally restricted to pilots who had first completed the ground school on type. As I recall we did a burner climb to altitude that was just about as quick as the Lightning. My job at Randolph AFB was as a Flight Commander on the 3510th Flying Training Squadron. As instructors we were responsible for the training of pilots who were themselves to become instructors on the T-38. This was very interesting because at the time we were receiving for training many Vietnam War veterans after they had completed 100 missions over North Vietnam.

The war was inevitably on everyone's lips, but to what extent depended on where you were. At ADC HQ not so much but at Nellis, where the weapons' training was conducted, it was virtually the *only* topic of conversation. John clearly recalls Curtis LeMay's controversial dictum, with which he strongly disagreed, that 'nobody goes to Vietnam twice until everybody has been once'. This was a flawed doctrine as it meant inexperienced men were being asked to fight a war for which they were not adequately trained. For example, transport aircraft pilots were being put into the front seat of a Phantom, given some weapons training and sent off to Asia. What they lacked in experience they went some way to making up for in sheer courage but too often that was not enough. In one sense John understands the reasoning behind LeMay's directive but the practicality of it was very suspect.

John had the chance to meet (socially) some of the Vietnam aces, Robin Olds amongst them.

What particularly interested me was the opportunity to compare my experiences in Korea with Olds' in Vietnam, for they were totally different. The basis on which the Vietnam War was fought meant the Americans could never win it, the philosophy being that they weren't there to win but to keep the enemy out. But if you don't fight to win you are going to lose. Control was taken out of the planners' hands by President Johnson and Robert Macnamara, the Secretary for Defense, picking and authorising the targets to be attacked.

Annabelle adapted as readily to the American way of life and to the American people as John did. She had after all flown with Pan Am and had worked with the Americans at RAF Sculthorpe so in some respects she was better prepared for the posting. She became part of the local community very quickly in the same way that John became part of the air force, helped of course by the American propensity for welcoming people from the old country.

The family were keen to expand their horizons by exploring what they could of America from ground level, John having seen much of it from altitude. The first holiday they took was in the south-east. Maxwell AFB Alabama, where the USAF Staff College is based, has its own holiday resort at Lake Pippin on Choctawhatchee Bay on the northern coast of the Gulf of Mexico, twelve miles from Eglin AFB and within driving distance of Pensacola and Panama City. Having spent some time here in a spacious caravan they then took to the road, heading west towards New Orleans and beyond. But distressingly a few days later daughter Tiggy again had an asthma attack and there was no option but to get her back to the hospital at Colorado Springs, which necessitated a twenty-four hour, 1,200-mile drive, made all the more fraught by a breakdown. Once in hospital and receiving the necessary treatment she recovered. Asthma in the 1960s wasn't as well understood as it is today and the options for somebody suffering an attack then were far fewer than now. Hospital was the best one. With two attacks since arriving in the USA, John and Annabelle decided not to take Tiggy on their next holiday to the south-west of the country, leaving her in Colorado Springs with nanny Carolyn.

Apart from holidaying there were many other social pleasures too. One that John discovered, and that Annabelle had long since discovered, was skiing. If ever John was going to start it would be here with the proximity of good pistes and the nearest ski-lift just twenty minutes away. Hitherto he had resisted for the simple reason that he didn't want to break a leg and be off flying. But with the posting to a staff job he decided that at thirty-five this was the time to have lessons and that was the beginning of a passion for the sport. Whilst in the States he and Annabelle skied all over Colorado with the US Army. His involvement grew steadily thereafter, not just in skiing but all forms of winter sports, to such an extent that he first became Chairman and then, in the mid 1980s, President of the RAF Winter Sports Association, remaining so until January 1985. Whilst in these posts John spearheaded the expansion of the Inter Service Championships into the International Inter Service Championships involving other European services and even the Australians. John also took on the Chairmanship of the Combined Services Sports Association. He finally gave up skiing in 2003.

The day after the Falklands War started the British were invited Down Under to compete and John found that if he wrote duty orders for the selected team they were entitled to take advantage of USAF transport. Orders were duly written and the sportsmen flew out from Mildenhall to the States, then across the States and finally across the Pacific to Australia. But that option was only available to him once. Once the war had finished sponsorship was sought to enable competing teams to fly by commercial airline.

Another distinct pleasure revolved around American Football. The US Air Force Academy was located across the other side of Colorado Springs to which John went from time to time in a social capacity. There were a few RAF officers on exchange there with whom they made contact and John and Annabelle attended services in the recently built, innovatively designed and beautiful chapel. They also supported The Falcons, the Academy's football team, invariably going with the Lorings and making a day of it with a few convivial drinks before, during and after the game, all designed to aid the cheering on of the home team!

But this socially gratifying and career enhancing tour had to come to an end and it did so two years almost to the day after their arrival. It had been a very busy, eye opening, extremely interesting two years with the time passing by very quickly. The family returned to England on the *Queen Mary* on one of her very last eastbound transatlantic crossings before she was withdrawn from service.

John left the US with 3,671 hours in his log book on seventeen aircraft types. The pace of flying would lessen as his career progressed but that wouldn't be just yet. For now a brand-new challenge awaited him.

CHAPTER NINETEEN

Phantoms

*I was clear in my own mind as to what I wanted to do once the
American exchange was finished. Having brought the Lightning
into RAF service with 74 I was very keen to do the same with the Phantom.
In particular I wanted to work up a nine ship Phantom display team and
take it across to the USA to show them how to do it properly! In the
event I never got to do that but I did get the Phantom OCU.*

John Howe

In July 1966 C in C Fighter Command, Air Vice Marshal Sir Frederick Rosier, flew to the States to visit Lieutenant General Herbert B Thatcher, C in C Air Defense Command. John and Annabelle always asked, if such senior RAF officers were visiting, whether they could entertain them for an evening. They would also invite others from the RAF on exchange tours as well as those from Commonwealth air forces to join them. On this particular occasion Sir Fred stayed in the VIP quarters at Ent AFB and he was driven to John and Annabelle's house. A very good evening ensued. Shortly before midnight Sir Fred decided he wished to be taken back to his accommodation as he was flying early the next morning but was persuaded to stay a further half hour to toast Annabelle's impending birthday.

The Howe's guests were then treated to Sir Fred holding court as he regaled them with stories. And he did have some stories to tell, for he had been a member of one of John's old squadrons, 43, just prior to the outbreak of the Second World War when he led the squadron's display team of six Hawker Furies. Once hostilities started and during operations over Dunkirk with his next squadron, 229, he was shot down and badly burned whilst attempting to bale out of his Hurricane. Making a remarkable recovery, but against the advice of the doctors, he was sent to the Western Desert where he commanded 263 Wing with which he won the DSO. This was as the result of a mission in late 1941 to support another unit under attack from a force of Me-109s. Engagement over, Sir Fred saw that one of the aircraft from his Wing, an Australian Tomahawk, had been forced to crash-land behind enemy lines. Bringing down his own aircraft alongside he recovered the pilot, squeezed him into his own single cockpit, sat on his lap and tried to take off again. Overloaded, his aircraft refused to leave the ground and burst a tyre. So Sir Fred and the Australian set off to trek through enemy territory to safety, navigating their way by the stars. It took four days to cross the desert, eventually stumbling into a British Guards unit.

The story telling had been accompanied by further drinks and when in the early hours Sir Fred insisted he really had to go, he and his driver were sent on their way in the hope that they would make happy landings in their quarters. They didn't and it seems much of the rest of the night was spent looking for Sir Fred's rooms, endlessly criss-crossing Colorado Springs and Ent AFB in the process. It transpired that the driver had had more than a few drinks along with everyone else but it simply hadn't shown and he had seemed quite capable of driving. Needless to say, if John had realised, an alternative plan would have been adopted with due deference to his future career prospects! Sir Fred, who finally arrived at his quarters at seven in the morning more by luck than design, just had time to change before he had to set off again. He was not best pleased. John, who had watched him being driven away from the party, knew nothing of what happened. In fact, that was the last time John saw him until September 1967 at RAF Chivenor.

> In my flying kit and having just grabbed a quick lunch in the mess, I was about to leave when up drew a staff car and out stepped the Station CO George Mason and Sir Frederick Rosier. I stood to attention and saluted as they passed but Sir Fred saw me, walked across and pointed his finger. 'I remember you John Howe,' he said and smiled, his anger at his involuntary night out in Colorado Springs having long since turned to humour. But it was thanks to him that I got my new posting for during the course of the party in the States he had asked me what I wanted to do once the exchange was finished. So I told him it was to bring the Phantom into RAF service.

Having arrived back at Southampton after their Atlantic crossing the family had just a few days at Home Farm before moving across to their new house at RAF Coningsby. Coningsby had been chosen as the base that would host 228 Operational Conversion Unit, tasked with training crews for the new to the RAF McDonnell Douglas Phantom. 228 OCU's previous incarnation had been training night fighter crews on the Javelin but it was now reactivated with the advent of the Phantom at Coningsby, taking up residence at the eastern end of the airfield, which, John was told as he arrived, was twenty miles from the sea and eighteen inches above sea level!

Coningsby had plenty of history attached to it. At the outbreak of war it was still being built and did not become an active bomber airfield – albeit a grass airfield – until February 1941 when 106 Squadron arrived with its Hampdens. These were followed by 97 Squadron equipped with the Manchester and both squadrons participated in bombing and mining operations (including the Thousand Bomber Raid). But from September 1942 to August 1943, whilst hard runways were laid, all operational activity at Coningsby ceased. 617 Squadron under the command of Guy Gibson flew Lancasters from the station when it reopened. A special Marker Force was formed within No. 5 Group, which operated from Coningsby and its satellite airfields at Woodhall Spa and Metheringham, achieving outstanding results in the process and contributing greatly to the night bombing successes of the last fifteen months of the war. Post war, Lincolns were based there for a short period and then the Mosquito from 1946 until March 1950. After six months' inactivity B29 Washingtons arrived, remaining until 1953 when they were replaced with Canberras. In 1954 contractors moved in and over the next two years the runways were extended and new hangars and administrative buildings built. This was in anticipation of the arrival of Vulcans. After the Canberras left in 1961 Nos 9, 12 and 35 Squadrons arrived. They were there for three years until Coningsby was selected as the prospective base for the TSR2 but, at the end of 1964, the station was placed under Care and Maintenance following the cancellation of that project. Revival came in 1966 when it was selected as the first base for the RAF fighter-bomber version of the Phantom and it accordingly transferred from Bomber Command to Fighter Command. Another period of tremendous building activity got underway. In December 1967, because of the initial roles the Phantom was to perform, Coningsby was transferred again, this time from Fighter Command to 38 (Air Support) Group within Transport Command, Fighter Command itself by then having ceased to exist. At the same time the first ground training course for airmen on the Phantom's systems was started at No. 5 School of Technical Training, which, in August 1968, became No. 3 Squadron of John's OCU. But that, as far as our story is concerned, was a year in the future.

After settling into his new Lincolnshire home during July and August 1967 John set off for the School of Refresher Flying, an element of the College of Air Warfare based at nearby RAF Manby, where he had a place on Refresher Course 17 flying the Jet Provost T.4. The purpose of the course was to refamiliarise himself with flying in England, a very different experience after the wide open spaces of America, but one to which John quickly reacclimatised. Manby provided John with his first experience of the Jet Provost, which was comparable in terms of size at least with the T-33 he had flown so much in the States. But there any comparison ends for the Lockheed aircraft was developed from the F-80 Shooting Star fighter and as such it was heavier and faster than the JP (as the Jet Provost was universally known), which was conceived and built as a light trainer and consequently handled very differently.

From Manby John went down to Chivenor and flew with 63 and 79 Squadrons of 229 OCU. Chivenor and much of the surrounding area was recovering from a prolonged and very wet winter with much flooding. The station's SAR Flight had undertaken several rescues but none more potentially tragic than when a

Whirlwind made a chance sighting of a bus stranded in rising floodwater. The helicopter was returning from a call to assist a farmer cut off by the River Taw when it was seen, with handkerchiefs being waved from the windows. Master Signaller Gibson was lowered to investigate. It was difficult for him to get him onto the top of the bus because telephone wires ran directly across it. But he did see it was full of children who were, it later transpired, totally unaware of the seriousness of the situation. Not so the driver! It was considered too dangerous to winch the youngsters out so the Whirlwind returned the short distance to Chivenor to fetch a multi-seater dinghy. Back at the scene Gibson was lowered into the water together with the dinghy and a coil of rope, which was attached to the bus and a telegraph pole some way away and along which the dinghy was pulled by the Master Signaller. The children were ferried in this way in groups of five or six to high ground. By the time the last person, the bus driver, was rescued the water had risen above seat level. While the winchman was ferrying the children to safety the helicopter orbited overhead, relaying radio reports to Chivenor. The rescue was still being talked about when John arrived.

Whilst with the OCU John got to know Wales, Chivenor's main training area, very well at low level. He did a lot of flying, up to three sorties a day, the prime reason being that the Phantom was going to undertake both the fighter and the reconnaissance role in service and John was intent on becoming more than just proficient doing both on the Hunter. He was introduced to a new mark of the aircraft in the process, the Hunter FR.10, which was flown by the fighter-recce specialists of 79 Squadron. John enjoyed flying the FR.10, which was designed specifically for its purpose, with a forward-looking camera fitted in the nose. Only thirty-three were built and these were conversions of F.6s. John hadn't done any reconnaissance work since Korea. Once again he found himself being given a target, a bridge for example, and he would plan his route through Wales, taking advantage of the terrain to minimise detection. Having located it he would fly past the target at 250 feet at 420 knots, taking pictures and remembering what he saw at the same time so that when he returned to base and was debriefed he could describe it in some detail. 79 Squadron taught John the techniques of visual observation, so important because in many ways the photography was a back-up to the visual report, not the other way round.

Once he had completed his courses at Chivenor, at the end of January John returned to Lincolnshire. But with his Phantom conversion not scheduled until May, he took the opportunity to make a dozen flights in Jet Provost T.3s and T.4s at RAF Cranwell before flying off to the States again. This time he flew to Davis Monthan AFB (known simply as DM) in Arizona and RAF Course 682B being run by the 4453rd CCTW (Combat Crew Training Wing). Conversion of the pilots and navigators of 228 OCU was scheduled as two courses. John was down to go on the second of the two but a few hours before personnel of the first were due to make a Sunday departure by VC10 from Brize Norton one of the party was taken ill. John had to find a replacement immediately but, at such short notice, he decided he couldn't reasonably ask any of his staff so elected to go himself. Coningsby's CO, John Rogers, had just come back from the States, having been on a staff appointment in Washington DC, and he lent John $50 he had not yet reconverted to British currency. A staff car was provided, John was driven down to Brize Norton and within a few hours he was airborne and on his way, leaving a very understanding wife behind him. Given they'd had no notice prior to John being away for two months it was just as well she was.

Incidentally, John Rogers and John Howe had known each other since the early 1960s. The former would contest the idea that 74 Squadron introduced the Lightning into operational service for whilst the Tigers were at Coltishall doing all the 'pretty stuff' like aerobatics and formations so that the British public could see what their tax money was buying, John Rogers was Boss of 56 Squadron (The Firebirds) at Wattisham and with the Lightning F.1 and then the F.1A they were doing all the important operational work! Their relationship at Coningsby was to be a harmonious one for John Rogers knew very well what John Howe was capable of and was happy to leave the intricacies of setting up the OCU to him without interference.

The course at Davis Monthan was just over two months' long and was conducted on the Phantom F-4C, the type in which John had flown two sorties as second pilot at Nellis when he was with Air Defense Command. The 4453rd CCTW was the USAF's main training unit for this variant of the F-4. The mighty Phantom, of which over 5,000 were built, has become a legend the world over amongst aircrew and is iconic in its appeal in the same way the Lightning has become. But the two were very different aeroplanes, conceived for different roles for different services in different countries with different requirements. For John, from an operational point of view, the Phantom would be the best aircraft he ever flew. In its RAF version it was totally effective in the three roles assigned to it. To fly, it was not altogether docile and had a few vices. Making new pilots aware of what they were and how to deal with them would be at the forefront of OCU training. For example, at a certain angle of attack one of the wings would drop and the aircraft would enter a flick roll, which at the proper airspeed could be immediately rectified by pushing the stick forward. If, however, the airspeed was low this remedy was not effective and the pilot would be in trouble. In other words you had to watch your airspeed and angle of attack. On the conversion course the situation would be induced and the correction demonstrated so that the student pilot would know not to get into such a situation in the first place.

The Phantom II first flew in prototype form on 27 May 1958. It was called Phantom II because McDonnell had already produced a Phantom, the FH-1, the first American jet aircraft designed to fly from carriers. The new Phantom originated in a 1954 request for an advanced naval fighter, which resulted in the

F4H-1F, later designated the F-4A. The F-4B followed with improved General Electric J79 engines. Deliveries to naval squadrons were followed by deliveries to the Marine Corps in 1962, the same year that twenty-nine F-4Bs were loaned to the USAF for evaluation. They were duly impressed and ordered their own variant, initially designated F-110A (to follow Century Series numbering) but later changed to F-4C. Deliveries to the air force began in 1963. The RF-4C was a reconnaissance variant whilst F-4Ds were optimised for ground attack. The definitive USAF version though was the F-4E, which had an additional fuselage fuel tank, leading-edge slats for increased manoeuvrability and an improved engine. It also had an internally mounted 20-mm multi-barrel gun thereby optimising it for air-to-air work. A tactical recce RF-4E was developed from it. The F-4F was produced for the *Luftwaffe* whilst the F-4G was equipped for the SEAD (Suppression of Enemy Air Defences) role. The F-4J was the navy version with greater ground attack capabilities, which succeeded the F-4B (and which John's old squadron, 74, later flew in RAF service). The F-4K was the McDonnell Douglas designation for the Royal Navy's Phantom, Britain being the first foreign air arm to order the type. The RAF designated their F-4Ms as FGR.2s When they took on charge the Navy aircraft when the Fleet Air Arm were running down their fixed wing fleet, they designated them FG.1.

It was the FGR.2 that 228 OCU was to operate. The decision to buy Phantoms was a politically inspired necessity following the cancellation of many of the ongoing programmes by British manufacturers in the wake of Labour government mismanagement and Duncan Sandys' edict. When the latter's hypothesising proved to be based on a false premise Britain had too far to go to catch up in development terms, although the indigenous Harrier and international Jaguar (in collaboration with the French) were coming at some stage in the future. To fill the gap the Phantom was chosen but even then it was not a straightforward buy from McDonnell Douglas for the government insisted that a high proportion of its systems and equipment should be of British origin. This created no need for compromise as far as the performance of the avionics was concerned but it did lead to a reshaping of the aircraft's profile because the Rolls-Royce Spey engines that were replacing the General Electric J79 wouldn't fit into the fuselage, which consequently had to be redesigned. The intakes also had to be enlarged as the British engine needed a greater flow of air than the J79. This meant that the prospect of more thrust and better fuel economy, which the Spey promised, was negated by the higher drag the new fuselage shape created. Acceleration at low level was actually improved but at high altitude the American engines performed better. One advantage the Spey did have was that it was less smoky.

In truth, the RAF would probably have preferred an off-the-shelf Phantom and with the money saved would have bought additional aircraft. Nevertheless, in RAF and Royal Navy service it ultimately proved to be very successful and it was an aircraft that was very well liked and well respected by its crews.

Every aspect of flying and operating the Phantom was taught at Davis Monthan as a precursor to what would be taught at the OCU, the only differences revolving around the different content of British as opposed to American aircraft. (Once back in the UK, manufacturers' courses and representatives on hand at Coningsby would introduce all air and ground crew to these differences.) Davis Monthan was a very busy place because, with the requirements of the Vietnam War for a constant supply of pilots and navigators, there was an unceasing series of courses underway. At the same time there was a high turnover of instructors as some were posted out to Asia and others came in from Asia. This led to some anomalies as far as the British were concerned who knew that the quality of instruction they were receiving was not always of the best. By the end of the course the RAF contingent had become almost autonomous. In effect, the men were teaching themselves. John's log book shows a gradual disappearance of USAF personnel in the cockpit and all British crews taking to the air.

After one battle formation sortie John couldn't believe what he was seeing.

It was awful. After landing the American leader debriefed the crews and then I stood up to say to my group of very experienced pilots 'If I ever see you fly battle formation like that again you'll be in trouble, serious trouble,' and then left. We used to meet in the Officers' Club and later in the day I took a jug of beer across to the table where my pilots sat. One of them said to me 'What you should know Boss is that that battle formation was being demonstrated to us and we weren't flying the aircraft.'

What the Americans may have lacked in expertise and teaching ability they made up for, as might have been expected, in their social skills. The Brits were very well looked after. Opportunities were also taken to get away from Davis Monthan from time to time. John, for example, flew a T-33 to Colorado Springs to say hello to everyone. But the highlight of visits away from Arizona came at the end of the course when the VC10 that was to take them back home flew first to the McDonnell Douglas facility at St Louis where Phantoms were being built. John remembers the honour of meeting James McDonnell himself at the original corrugated tin hangar where he started his business manufacturing aircraft parts. By now the hangar was completely dominated by the huge sprawl of factory buildings, which from the air as John and his colleagues came in to land appeared to be 'absolutely gigantic'. Mr McDonnell was still feeling pretty pleased with himself after the recent merger with Douglas to make the huge corporation that McDonnell Douglas now undoubtedly was. This particular visit lasted for several days and they were shown around the huge complex in which they finally found in one corner of one of the buildings the British Phantoms that were under construction. From St Louis they flew to Washington DC where the radar manufacturer, Westinghouse, was hosting an event. They then headed back across the Atlantic, very conscious of what now lay ahead of them in terms of passing on all they had learned about flying the Phantom.

All the initial work of setting up and manning the OCU and determining the nature and content of the training and the courses was undertaken by Fighter Command over the course of several years prior to the arrival of the first aircraft at RAF Coningsby. This was XT891, which had taken off from No. 23 MU (Maintenance Unit) at RAF Aldergrove on 23 August 1968, piloted by John with Sqn Ldr Freeman in the back seat. It was at British manufacturer Short's works in Northern Ireland that the integration of the Rolls-Royce Spey engines took place.

228 OCU, which also carried the 64 (Reserve) Squadron number plate, was tasked with training both aircrew and ground crew on the Phantom FGR.2. To do this, it was itself organised into three squadrons with Nos 1 and 2 undertaking the conversion of pilot and navigator aircrew and as we have seen No. 5 School of Technical Training (SOTT) being absorbed into the OCU as 3 Squadron. Its brief was to train all ground crew managers and fitter tradesmen and it started doing this in November 1967. Fifteen different courses varying from twenty to twenty-two weeks in duration were available for airmen fitters of all trades from Junior Technician to Chief Technician rank. Familiarisation courses of three or five weeks were given to managers of Flight Sergeant or Squadron Leader rank.

No. 1 Squadron was tasked with the actual conversion to the Phantom and a series of lectures was prepared, including topics such as formation flying, supersonic flight, night flying, crew co-operation, local Air Traffic Control procedures and the Instrument Rating Test (IRT). They were also tasked with the air defence element of the course – the characteristics and performance of Sparrow and Sidewinder missiles, visident and night intercept techniques, attacks against low-flying targets, air combat manoeuvres and Ground Control Intercepts (GCI). No. 2 Squadron, meanwhile, concentrated on strike and ground attack, covering the performance and effectiveness of all weapons carried by the Phantom. The squadron also covered reconnaissance, its purpose, the relative importance of photo and visual recce, recognition training, use of forward facing cameras and so forth. The FGR.2 didn't carry an integrated camera suite such as the purpose-built RF-4C or RF-4E of the USAF (or indeed the Hunter FR.10s at Chivenor). Its cameras were housed in pods.

Pilots selected to convert to the Phantom would have completed a minimum of one year on an operational squadron. In other words they would be classified as second tourists. The majority of student navigators would also have had the same minimum previous experience but in practice a few first tourists were included when it was found there was a shortage of navigators with the necessary qualifications. Furthermore, it was always anticipated that when flight simulator training became available for OCU student crews some first tourist pilots would also be included. Before starting operational conversion aircrews went down to 229 OCU at Chivenor for a three-week Hunter lead-in course. As time progressed first tourists or pilots without a fighter background completed a three- or four-month course, necessary because of the Phantom's air defence role as well as ground attack and reconnaissance and many of the aircrew would only have had ground attack backgrounds. Conversely, navigators without low-level ground attack experience also attended a lead-in course at 229 OCU. Otherwise a navigator's lead-in course was conducted by 228 OCU themselves over a six-week period. Aeromedical training for both pilots and navigators was undertaken at North Luffenham.

The OCU had an establishment of thirty-five officers, fifty-one airmen and one civilian. John's team – an outstanding one in his eyes – consisted of Sqn Ldr Derek Bryant (OC 1 Squadron), Sqn Ldr Ken Hayr (OC 2 Squadron), Sqn Ldr Fletcher (OC 3 Squadron), Sqn Ldr Fred Romney (Navigational Radar Leader and invariably John's navigator when he flew) and Sqn Ldr John Nunn (Chief Ground Instructor). After the completion of aircrew officer instructor training at Davis Monthan on 9 September 1968 there followed a period of instructor work up training at Coningsby on the FGR.2 to allow for the differences between it and the F-4C. The plan was to hold three main courses each year (the first began on 28 October with graduation due on 2 May 1969) plus one Senior Officer and one IRE (Instrument Rating Examiners) course in 1969. Each main course would train twelve or thirteen crews and would comprise 301 hours of ground lectures, ninety-four pilot flying hours and eighty navigator flying hours, all spread over a twenty-five week period. The Senior Officers' course was designed to give practical knowledge of the Phantom, its syllabus consisting of the same ground school as OCU students with ten hours on the aircraft itself. In 1970, after the first main courses had been successfully completed, ten-week Postgraduate Specialist Courses in air defence, ground attack and reconnaissance began. These produced the next tranche of skilled squadron instructors.

So just how do you go about setting up something as complex and involved as an OCU syllabus? John recalls it very well.

> You have to take an overview of what has to be taught and this encompasses an almost bewildering array of subjects ranging from the aircraft itself and all its systems, its armament, handling, tactics and so on. My method was to get my chief ground instructor to create a chart to cover one wall of the ops room and on this were listed the subjects to be taught by each squadron together with dates by which each had to be completed. Each instructor was also listed as were his target dates for his specialism. I had to explain this system to C in C 38 Group, AVM Sir Harold Martin, describing it as my very own analogue computer!

As staff arrived at Coningsby John greeted and briefed them, thereby ensuring they knew exactly what was required. Regular meetings were held thereafter as the aircraft arrived, the first course began, problems were encountered and solutions found. Almost inevitably there were delays caused by random technical defects, poor weather and delayed aircraft delivery, which restricted progress during that initial month. One aircraft was deployed to Farnborough for the public to see and the first of a long line of senior officers arrived at Coningsby to see it as well – Air Marshal Sir Lewis Hodges AOC in C Air Support Command, for example, who flew in XT894 with Derek Bryant at the controls.

On 23 October a staff meeting was chaired by John to discuss the syllabus that had evolved and to satisfy themselves that what the unit was to be teaching and how it was to be taught was correct. Five days later the first aircrew course assembled. On the first conversion sortie with Derek Bryant piloting and Flt Lt Douglas Barr in the back seat, they suffered a system hydraulic failure and had to engage the barrier on landing. A few days later Douglas Barr must have wondered what he had let himself in for. In the front seat this time with Flt Lt Dave Hodges behind him (constituting the first converting pilot crew sortie on the aircraft) the very same thing happened. Incidentally the Phantoms on 228 OCU were twin stickers, whereby the rear cockpit had a (removable) control column, which offered instructors monitoring converting pilots in the front seat the opportunity to take control if anything went wrong. Converting pilots had to have completed a set period of time in the simulator before being allowed into the real thing and then only in the front seat after being taken aloft by an instructor. Aircraft on operational squadrons rarely used this twin stick capability, as a navigator wouldn't want its encumbrance in an already tightly spaced rear cockpit.

At the end of November the first Senior Officers' course started with Coningsby's Station Commander John Rogers and OC Strike/Ops Wing John Robertson included. By this time the thirteen pilots of No. 1 Course had begun Conversion Ground School and the thirteen navigators had completed their lead-in course. Things were now well and truly rolling! In January 1969 seven officers of Nos 1 and 2 Squadrons were promoted to Squadron Leader rank in the New Year's promotions list. A quick trawl through the Operations Record Book for the OCU for 1969 reveals the usual mixed bag of experience. Underlying it all of course was the increasing momentum of the crew conversion itself, but there were always other factors at play as well to complement, or more usually disrupt, the programme. So it is that the ORB records a Press and TV Day held in mid January with a Diamond Nine led by John the main event. Six USAF Phantom F-4Ds from Germany visited and were hosted by the OCU during February. The RAF crews were always very keen to tap into American experience on the type and they welcomed any opportunity to do so, such as when a few months later the United States Marine Corps gave a thought-provoking presentation on their recent combat experience in Vietnam.

A potentially nasty incident was averted when Flt Lt Ken Simpson and Sqn Ldr Roy Humphreys lost their canopy when flying low level over Scotland but they successfully completed a very cold diversion into Lossiemouth. Having suffered the usual vagaries of an English winter since operations had started, March 1969 finally saw an improvement in weather but with the increased

XN778/A, seen here taxiing in August 1974, was a 92 Squadron machine in which John regularly flew. The Lightning F2As which were unique to 19 and 92 Squadrons were considered to be the 'hot rods' of all Lightning marks and were well suited for their role so close to the East German border. *(Wilfried Zetsche)*

XM991/T was one of 19 Squadron's T4s. *(Wilfried Zetsche)*

It was a short step from Group Captain Ops at 11 Group to Commandant of the Royal Observer Corps with attendant promotion to Air Commodore. Later, in 1984 and by now an Air Vice Marshal, John was the Reviewing Officer for one of the ROC Summer Camps at RAF Scampton. By the look on John's face he had seen this chap somewhere before – but where? *(George Black)*

To Air Vice Marshal John Howe
with many thanks from:
The British Combined Services Ski Team
Australia 1982

Having taken to the slopes in the USA, skiing became as much a passion for John as it had done for Annabelle – both were very accomplished skiers. John was long involved with the RAF Winter Sports Association of which he became President in the mid 1980s. Prior to that he was Chairman, as he was when the British Combined Services Ski Team visited Australia in 1982. (*The John Howe Collection*)

On the slopes with eldest daughter Caroline and Annabelle. (*The John Howe Collection*)

As COMSOUMAR at RAF Mount Batten, John's role was not only an operational one but ceremonial too. Here he is reviewing Royal Marines at their training base at Lympstone in March 1981. John felt a real affinity with the Marines having fought with them at Suez. (*The John Howe Collection*)

The RAF Nimrods worked in conjunction with the French Aeronavale's Breguet Atlantiques which operated from de Lann-Bihoué. John toured the base in June 1981. (*The John Howe Collection*)

John's final posting again took him in another new direction, this time to the RAF Regiment where he became Director General of Security. This gave him plenty of opportunity to get into the field, an opportunity that he relished. *Peacekeeper Challenge* was an exercise organised by the USAF Security Police at Kirtland AFB New Mexico in which the RAF Regiment were invited to participate. John visited with the British team in November 1983. (*USAF*)

Whilst John didn't actually compete at Kirtland he was keen to handle some of the weaponry used by the Americans. (*USAF*)

His busy programme of visits took him back to Germany and the RAF stations there – including Gutersloh. Here he is put through his paces on the small arms range. (*The John Howe Collection*)

You know that you have made a success of your career when you have a road named after you! Such tributes are in fact a very tangible way in which success is reflected. John was a popular RAF Regiment Director General and was respected for his very hands-on approach. (*The John Howe Collection*)

In 1946 the RAF Regiment moved from Grantham to Catterick and from that time until 1991, when it relocated to Honington, the station functioned as a training establishment where all ranks gained their professional skills. At Catterick John experienced at first hand the hard, gruelling tasks Regiment gunners would face, including weapons handling, 1991.

At Catterick again and listening attentively. John always took the time to talk with the men under his command and consequently learned a lot from them. (*The John Howe Collection*)

A fine study of Air Vice Marshal John Howe at the end of his career showing his many medal ribbons. (*The John Howe Collection*)

opportunity for flying and thus demand for aircraft. Engineering Wing was initially unable to produce enough aircraft to support the full programme requirements of both squadrons. However, by April things in that respect had improved and it turned out to be the best month of flying to date with the landmark completion of the first course and the beginning of training for the second course by No. 1 Squadron. This was despite an overlap caused by the weather and unserviceabilities, which meant a very hectic time for instructors and students alike for a while. Meanwhile, students on Ken Hayr's squadron were able to fire the gun for the first time, which was understandably a very popular exercise with most students gaining above average results. Around the same time the BBC filmed a weapons sortie flown by Ken Hayr for a documentary with the aircraft carrying a full pod of unguided rockets and Ken demonstrating strafing and low-level retard bombing.

Meanwhile, Bill Wratten was in the process of finalising and practising his solo aerobatic display for the coming air show season and he was certainly very keen to show off this potent and noisy new aeroplane. It is not recorded whether the Chief of the Air Staff Air Chief Marshal Sir John Grandy who visited on 21 May (and flew with Derek Bryant) was given a sneak preview. (Derek did all the flying of senior officers rather than John as the latter had the protocol of such visits to attend to and thus had no time to take visitors aloft as well.) Bill later gave his first solo air display at RAF Wildenrath, which was predictably very well received, but then displays were suspended in the wake of the crash on 9 July of a 6 Squadron aircraft five miles from Coningsby at Miningsby whilst on a GCA approach. The aircraft involved was XV395 and was the first RAF Phantom loss. The crew baled out, navigator Flt Pearson at 1,800 feet and pilot Flt Lt Rooum at 1,200 feet, suffering only scratches and bruises in the process. John led the subsequent Accident Investigation Board (AIB) inquiry but the team couldn't understand why the control column had frozen thus precipitating the crash. The only way such a thing could happen was if the two hydraulic control systems (primary and secondary) were not totally independent as McDonnell Douglas insisted they were. All the crashed aircraft parts were recovered and laid out in a Coningsby hangar and the control systems examined in detail. It was found that between the hydraulic tank and the two hydraulic systems there was a short common pipe, which had a cylinder piston in it to regulate the flow of fluid. On this particular aeroplane the cylinder was aluminium and the piston was steel and a groove was gradually worn in the cylinder. On the day of the crash the pilot had moved the control column to correct his approach and fate played its part by decreeing that that was the moment the piston would seize in the groove and the control system froze. McDonnell Douglas accepted the AIB's finding and modifications were made to all Phantoms.

June 1969 proved to be a frustrating month and for John it was a repeat to a lesser degree of the restrictions caused by display demands that he had previously encountered with 74 Squadron. In truth, however, the OCU were pleased to take part as a counter to the intensity of work of the training programmes. This time it was the need to rehearse for a flypast for the Investiture of the Prince of Wales in July. The Phantom element of this comprised eight aircraft from 6 Squadron, which had recently moved to Coningsby, and four from the OCU. Also scheduled to take part were twelve Lightnings from Leuchars and Binbrook, temporarily based at RAF Valley, but poor weather meant only four aircraft could participate as the rest found they had insufficient fuel to complete the flypast *and* reach their designated diversions. Talking of which, there was a further diversion from the main task a few weeks later because of Exercise *Unity*, the annual firepower demonstration for NATO Chiefs of Staff on Salisbury Plain, when 2 Squadron of the OCU were required to show the firepower capacity of the Phantom. Much to the enjoyment of the crews involved four aircraft strafed, two rocketed and two dropped 1,000-lb bombs on their designated targets.

John kept a very close eye on each of the students in the OCU's care and if he felt they were not performing as they ought he would tell them personally. A lot of time was spent with the instructors, talking to them about individual students, reading the plethora of reports produced, making adjustments to the course content when necessary. John himself did little instructing for he simply didn't have the time, his energies being directed towards the successful running of the fledgling OCU. His flying was largely restricted to keeping current on the Phantom. He had by now almost 3,500 hours in his log book but this was tempered by the fact that he would shortly be flying a proverbial desk for three years. This gave every airborne minute he could grab now an added significance.

On 13 October Wing Commander Dave Goodwin arrived to begin the take over from John as OC, formally taking the reins on 24 October. John had known Dave for years from DFCS, AFDS and Fighter Command days, so he knew the OCU was going to be in the safe hands of a man who had been involved in fighter weapons training for a long time. A party was held to say goodbye to John and another much appreciated inscribed tankard was added to his collection. 228 OCU had been a tremendous challenge for him, a challenge of a type he had not had before, so the success of bringing the Phantom into RAF service by setting up the unit tasked with doing so was particularly satisfying.

CHAPTER TWENTY

CTTO, MoD and RAF Germany

I was upstairs in Air Plans when John was in Operational Requirements. He disliked it intensely. It was a constant paper chase and you were forever trying to pull the civil service and industry together. This was not John's style nor his scene. In truth he was probably the last person you would think of as being MoD material so whoever made the decision he should go there – and why?

George Black

John was now posted to the Central Trials and Tactics Organisation at HQ Air Support Command at Upavon, once again a historically significant airfield as it had been the home of the first Royal Flying Corps flying school. This was a short-term appointment, which lasted barely five months, but during the course of it his promotion to Group Captain came through. Each Command or Group in the RAF was represented at CTTO and John commanded the 38 Group section. Essentially, the organisation was a think tank whereby new operational tactics and procedures were initiated and discussed and when ideas had suitably matured, committed to a written paper. If the written paper was accepted by senior officers at Strike Command then a series of trials were organised to prove the thinking behind the paper. For example, 6 Squadron were required to carry out Phase One of an Operational Capability Trial to determine the practical radius of action of the Phantom FGR.2 for essential operational configurations and weapon loads and to establish the overall line and range errors and mean points of impact of SNEB rockets. Nine trials' sorties were scheduled for each flying day. The results from those trials were collated by CTTO and a final report prepared. Strike Command then decided how, or indeed whether or not, they would take the results forward. John in fact wasn't at Upavon long enough to generate any new thinking and his time was spent carrying on with projects that had already been initiated by his predecessors, projects involving the Harrier, Phantom and the Anglo-French anti-radiation Martel missile.

When John left Coningsby he and Annabelle had decided that, with an eye to the future, it was high time they placed their feet upon the first rung of the property ladder so they moved into a brand-new bungalow in East Grafton, not far from Upavon. Scarcely had this happened when in the wake of his promotion John's next posting to the Ministry of Defence in Whitehall came through and he immediately found himself in the world of weekend commuting, staying with friends in Surbiton during the week. What made this enforced partial separation from his young family harder to take was the fact that John didn't like his new job as Deputy Director of Operational Requirements (4), responsible for writing the specifications for the next generation of aircraft for the RAF. His aversion to it was not that it wasn't a potentially interesting posting but because it involved nothing but paperwork and, more to the point, the people at MoD weren't his type of people.

Amongst the projects John was involved with was the writing of a paper on the future of air transport within the RAF. As a result he produced something that was in essence a handbook on the existing Hercules, VC10 and other fixed and rotary winged transport types then in the inventory. This didn't go down at all well and the newly promoted Group Captain was reprimanded for not displaying the necessary forward thinking. But of course John *had* been forward thinking because the Hercules and VC10 that were used then are still in the inventory and the Hercules in particular will be for many years to come. What John had foreseen was the fact that the requirement would essentially stay the same. There would always be a need for short-range STOL tactical transports, long-range strategic transports and helicopters for transport in the battlefield. Another operational requirement that he was involved in writing (and this was far closer to John's experience) was that for a Jaguar and Harrier replacement. Included in this was his recommendation that this future hypothetical aircraft should be able to fly at 620 knots at low level away from a target. In the Cold War environment the RAF had to compete with the introduction of new aircraft types and weapons systems by other air forces with ever enhanced capability and the reality of the Cold War scenario demanded that the RAF be flexible enough to adapt quickly to new operational thinking such as, for example, the ability to exit a target area at high speed and low level. This operational requirement eventually metamorphosed into an Air Staff Target that came to be called MRCA (Multi Role Combat Aircraft), then Tornado.

John's office in Whitehall, which housed not only him but his few staff as well, was one in which a lot of time was spent sitting, thinking and kicking ideas about, ideas that would be written on a blackboard and then added to as they were developed. Symptomatic of the feelings of many of those who worked at MoD at the time was a comment scrawled across the board one morning: 'There will be no further leave until morale has improved'.

The attitude of the other Services in this particular section of MoD appeared to be very different. The Navy, for example, had just had a new Chief of Naval Staff (CNS) named and he was walking down a corridor when he came face to face with one of John's colleagues. They sidestepped, as you often do in such situations, not once but twice, whereupon the CNS said 'Group Captain. Just one more time and I really must go!' Little things perhaps, but important when it comes to working relationships, particularly when it comes to working in an environment of senior personnel. John did have one escape route though for when he became particularly disillusioned with what he was doing he could go to a different part of the MoD building and talk with his old SAAF colleague Phil Lageson, by then an Air Commodore, who had a very sympathetic ear. But it wasn't just the people. There was much unrest in the country during the two and a half years John was in London, which culminated in strikes and power cuts to the extent that hour upon hour was spent without electricity. Work had to be carried out by torchlight or even candlelight in cold, unheated offices. And this was as true for the most senior of officers who would probably be working on high priority Cold War projects under awful conditions.

John's own last project at MoD was to write a paper discussing the reorganisation of the Operational Requirements section at the Air Ministry. This he did and in it he recommended the abolishing of Deputy Director of Operational Requirements (4) amongst other changes. His paper was accepted and within months John's department was disestablished and he was posted. He had in effect written himself out of his job! When he was told where he would be going next he couldn't help but smile. He was off to command RAF Gutersloh and with that would be back to flying again. In fact, he was moving from the least liked posting of his career to his most satisfying. It was September 1972.

Because he had been so long out of the cockpit he had to be refreshed and to do this he initially spent a fortnight at RAF Manby once again on the Jet Provost T.4 with No. 1 Squadron of the School of Refresher Flying. Following this, after two weeks' leave he presented himself at RAF Coltishall to 65 Squadron (the shadow squadron number for 226 OCU) where he was to refamiliarise himself with the Lightning, necessary because RAF Gutersloh was home to two Lightning squadrons. At Coltishall he was reacquainted with the F.1 and T.4 between 30 October and 15 December, a period of pretty intensive flying. F.2As were flown in Germany and familiarisation with that particular mark would be completed once in post.

> I remember flying with JFGH when he was passing through the OCU *en-route* to Gutersloh. At that time I knew I was also bound for the same place to become a Flight Commander on 19 Squadron and I was determined not to appear in any way sycophantic so I didn't give him an easy time in an effort to establish some kind of moral superiority at least. However, I reluctantly had to admit that he was rather good. In fact he was *very* good, especially at formations, which is a skill that comes naturally and which of course John had honed with the Tigers twelve years before at Coltishall.
>
> John Spencer

Next on the agenda was four days at RAF Ternhill in Shropshire and conversion to helicopter flying, required because Gutersloh was also home to a Wessex squadron. The short course John undertook consisted of nine sorties in the Westland-built Bell 47G Sioux, designated HT.2 by the RAF and popularly known as the 'Clockwork Mouse'. This was followed by a single sortie in a Westland Whirlwind to give John experience of a larger helicopter. John had to learn the very different technique of keeping a rotor-bladed aircraft in the air, although he was only given the most rudimentary of instruction as to how to stop and start the engine. In fact, that was the case with all his subsequent helicopter flying both in Germany and later in the UK: he became an accomplished pilot but only as far as control in the air was concerned, not in getting it going in the first place!

> Obviously the more I flew the helicopter with its very different control ethos from a fixed wing aircraft the better I got. In other words when I first climbed aboard the Sioux I had absolutely no feel for it but that soon came. Helicopters are so sensitive to control and my first few hovers were interesting. However, in Germany I found that I could soon do what helicopters did there in support of the Army, letting down into holes in the forest and so forth.

On 19 January 1973, the day he officially took command of RAF Gutersloh, John was introduced to the Wessex as he was given an area familiarisation sortie with 18 Squadron, one of Gutersloh's component squadrons. And that was the day that in effect John was introduced to operations within RAF Germany and the beginning of a posting that John considers the best of his whole RAF career.

In 1979 Air Chief Marshal Sir David Lee (who was Commandant at Bracknell when John attended Staff College) wrote a paper assessing the role of RAF Germany from 1945. Much of the following is taken from that. As the RAF in Germany settled down to a relatively stable period during the late 1950s and early 1960s after the frenetic activity of the previous decade – a great expansion of resources in the late 1940s and 1950s followed by considerable contraction – a new problem began to concern NATO. Russia was not only introducing new, conventional arms into her arsenal but was also developing her nuclear capability with the inevitable result that an arms race was initiated with both sides building up their stocks of weapons and the means of delivering them. As a result a position of nuclear stalemate was approaching and NATO's policy, which centred on the maintenance of a light screen of forces well forward to identify aggression positively before calling on massive nuclear force and which hitherto had been considered appropriate, was clearly no longer adequate. This so-called trip wire policy transmuted into one of flexible response, which required a well-balanced mixture of conventional, tactical nuclear and strategic nuclear weapons. Such a range of weaponry permitted a wide range of responses able to meet any aggression at a level judged appropriate. If the level initially deployed proved not to be effective it could be escalated stage by stage with moves towards all-out nuclear warfare constantly monitored and controlled. At least the immense danger of the old strategy of massive nuclear retaliation would be greatly reduced. However, for the West, flexible response brought its own particular problems. If NATO was to contain aggression by the vast Warsaw Pact forces ranged against it, many more conventional forces would need to be deployed to Germany, backed by immediately available reinforcements. This would be an expensive business and with all Western nations feeling an economic and financial pinch at the time they were actively reducing their expenditure on defence. So it was that although the new threat had been identified in the early years of the decade it was not until 1967 that formal adoption of the new strategy by the NATO allies happened.

British defence policy was heavily committed to the V bomber force and in the early 1960s it was building up to its planned strength. To fund this expensive aircraft and its support, economies elsewhere within the RAF were sought. The choice for these economies fell on RAF Germany and accordingly the number of RAF squadrons based there had been reduced from thirty-five in 1955 to twelve in 1962. At the same time a succession of bases were handed back to the Germans. Gutersloh remained as the only RAF station east of the Rhine whilst west of the river were Wildenrath, Laarbruch, Bruggen and Geilenkirchen. Even with this much reduced force the RAF was providing a balanced contribution to each element of a flexible response strategy in spite of the fact that in 1962 it was still five years away from being formally adopted. There were day fighter/ground attack (Hunters) and reconnaissance aircraft (Canberras) towards the 'front line' and conventional and tactical nuclear weapons immediately behind the forward units (Canberras and Javelins) with the strategic response (V bombers) back in the UK at a high state of readiness.

Somewhat ironically, in spite of the strategic thinking that was going on within NATO, the mid 1960s proved to be a time of some relaxation of tension in Europe. Because her nuclear capabilities were that much stronger, Russia felt more secure and so for a short while her actions became less provocative. West Germany's contribution to NATO was rapidly increasing in value. And balance of power, albeit an uneasy one, existed between East and West with both sides content to remain watchful behind their defences. Accordingly as the 1960s unfolded there were no great changes in aircraft equipment within the RAF. The Canberra remained the mainstay of the strike force and the Javelin and Hunter filled the various fighter roles. One thing that did change was the arrival of the helicopter in the shape of the Whirlwind at Gutersloh, later replaced by the much improved Wessex. By 1966, however, the Javelin could no longer be regarded as truly competitive with Warsaw Pact all-weather fighters. The Lightning had become standard equipment in Fighter Command and in due course it arrived in Germany to replace the Gloster aircraft with 19 and 92 Squadrons at Gutersloh taking the

F.2A on strength. 92 Squadron had initially been based at Geilenkirchen but this was too far to the west for the short-ranged Lightning. In fact, Geilenkirchen closed in 1968, not because of its geographical position but because of continuing pressure on the defence budget. All twelve RAF squadrons were now concentrated on four bases.

The relative calm of the mid 1960s was shattered in August 1968 when Russian-dominated Warsaw Pact troops invaded Czechoslovakia. All NATO defences were immediately placed on a state of high alert. The number of Canberras on QRA with nuclear weapons within RAF Germany was increased and 19 and 92 Squadrons upped their readiness states. Additional squadrons within Strike Command were ready to reinforce RAF Germany at short notice. It soon became clear, however, that the Soviet Union had no motives beyond the subjugation of Czechoslovakia and had no intention of more provocation. But because of its speed and ferocity the Russian invasion had given due warning that there was great potential for extended action by them elsewhere in Europe. NATO took the warning seriously. The power of Russia's conventional air, land and sea forces impressed the alliance and her support of emergent countries in Africa showed clearly her intention to spread communist ideology by all means short of nuclear attack. It thus became very clear from 1968 onwards that whilst NATO must maintain the nuclear deterrent, it must also concentrate upon the strengthening of her own conventional arms. Britain, within the constraints of defence expenditure, committed herself to doing this by making the Vulcan squadrons of Strike Command, which hitherto had only been committed in the strategic nuclear role, available in the conventional role also. This was facilitated by the transfer of responsibility for nuclear deterrence from Strike Command to Polaris submarines. Thus SACEUR (Supreme Allied Commander Europe) was afforded a considerable addition to the strike power available without the need to find accommodation for the aircraft involved on the Continent, the Vulcan's range ensuring it could operate from the UK. At the same time efforts were made to re-equip RAF Germany with three new types of aircraft about to enter service, that is the Harrier, Phantom and Buccaneer. To convert air and ground crew and to provide the necessary facilities on the four airfields for these advanced and more complex aircraft, a temporary reduction in the front-line strength of RAF Germany was accepted in 1969 and 1970. The shortfall was made good by the availability for immediate reinforcement by UK-based squadrons of 38 Group, John's old 228 OCU in its shadow squadron guise included. Bruggen closed for ten months whilst major extensions and improvements were carried out and reopened in June 1970 with the Phantoms of 14 and 17 Squadrons. Wildenrath received the Harriers of 4 and 20 Squadrons. In 1971 15 Squadron Buccaneers arrived at Laarbruch for the nuclear strike role, joined in 1972 by 16 Squadron with the same aircraft.

When John arrived at Gutersloh with its complement of Lightnings and Wessex, RAF Germany was as powerful a force in terms of capability (although not numbers) as it had ever been. It is probably true to say that without the Czechoslovakia incident such a comprehensive re-equipment programme would not have been carried out. It is also true to say that SACEUR would have liked far more than twelve RAF squadrons in the 2nd Allied Tactical Air Force's order of battle but the British defence budget precluded any increase. Thus it was doubly important that RAF Germany should remain at the highest peak of readiness and efficiency. A comprehensive method of assessing this became a priority and the TACEVAL was invented, a tactical evaluation method that came to be adopted for use throughout all NATO air forces and is still in place today. It became probably the most important station commitment that dominated everyone's life. Its published aim was 'to assess for SACEUR against prescribed criteria the operational potential of NATO Command and assigned units, to award ratings to a common standard, to indicate deficiencies and to make recommendations where necessary.'

Once a unit was declared fully combat capable it was eligible for initial evaluation. From that point on it was re-evaluated annually on a no notice basis. Teams of up to seventy-five personnel drawn from any of the NATO air forces would arrive without warning, often in the middle of the night, and then proceed to investigate that station's alert posture, its mission effectiveness, support functions and its ability to survive. All RAF Germany stations performed extremely well in TACEVALs, Gutersloh in particular.

John had done a considerable amount of preparation prior to moving to Germany in terms of familiarising himself with much of the above and in particular with Gutersloh and the units of which he was now taking command. RAF Gutersloh had quite a history. It was the *Luftwaffe* who first built the airfield and an adjacent signals facility, beginning in 1935 and cutting down a huge swathe of Westphalian forest in the process. The first *Luftwaffe* units to move in in April 1937 were three squadrons of Junkers Ju86s. During the Second World War both bombers and night fighters were based there once the runway had been extended, the labour being provided by Soviet prisoners of war. Amongst its famous incumbents was the *Luftwaffe* ace Werner Molders. American Army units captured Gutersloh in April 1945 and a couple of months later it was handed over to the British. The buildings of the signals unit became RAF Sundern, hosting HQ 2 Group, and the *Luftwaffe* airfield became RAF Gutersloh, which went on to play an important part in the Berlin Airlift of 1948. As the Iron Curtain descended and east and west polarised into communist and non communist blocs most of the immediate post-war RAF bases moved back to the Dutch border with the exception of Gutersloh, which became the base closest to the Iron Curtain. It often used to be quoted that the NATO aircraft furthest east was the Spitfire on display by the main gate! It became home to the Lightnings of 19 and 92 Squadrons and the Wessex of 18 Squadron and then, after John's departure, 3 and 4 Squadrons flying successive variants of the Harrier. After they in turn left the RAF continued to operate

201

helicopters with 18 Squadron, by now equipped with the twin-rotored Chinook, and 230 Squadron with the Puma. In 1993, following the end of the Cold War and the reunification of Germany, the RAF vacated Gutersloh completely. Some Army units remained and Gutersloh was renamed Princess Royal Barracks.

The squadrons under John's command were themselves interesting units, in 18 Squadron's case if only for the number of disbandments it has endured over the years! It was initially formed in 1915 with the motto *Animo et Fide* (With Courage and Faith), operating in a fighter-reconnaissance role in France until it changed to that of day bombing in May 1917. 18 Squadron joined the Army of Occupation in November 1918 and remained until September 1919 when it returned to the UK where it disbanded for the first time. Reformed in 1931, again in the day bomber role, it was equipped with Hawker Harts but in May 1939 the squadron received Blenheims. It moved to the Mediterranean in October 1941, operating from Malta until January 1942 when its remaining aircraft were flown to Egypt and it was again disbanded. A new 18 Squadron went into action in April 1942, still equipped with the Blenheim, but by now Mark IVs. In the autumn it flew out to Algeria following the *Torch* landings where it remained, accompanying the armies through Sicily and into Italy with Bostons replacing the Blenheims. From September 1946, after a further brief disbandment, it operated in the maritime reconnaissance role equipped with Lancasters but fourteen days later it disbanded once again. In March 1947 it resurfaced in Malaysia with the Mosquito but again disbandment followed soon afterwards in November. Less than a month later yet another new 18 Squadron was formed, this time at Waterbeach in Cambridgeshire, equipped with Dakotas, and it was immediately involved with operations in the Berlin Airlift. Further disbandment followed the lifting of the blockade on 20 February 1950 and this time it was three years before, in August 1953, it was reformed yet again, this time at Scampton and equipped with Canberra B.2s in the light bomber role. Nobody was surprised when news came through it was to disband once more in February 1957 with its next incarnation coming in December 1958 when it found itself flying Valiants in the ECM role, which it continued to do until March 1963. The next reformation heralded a further re-roling of the squadron to that of a Battlefield Support Helicopter unit, which it has remained to this day. It moved to Gutersloh in Germany in August 1970 with the Wessex HC.2 and this was the type on strength when John arrived.

No. 19 Squadron, with the motto *Possunt Quia Posse Videntur* (They Can Because They Think They Can), formed at Castle Bromwich on 1 September 1915. By the time it arrived in France in 1916 it had been designated a fighter squadron and over the next couple of years it flew BE.2s, SPADs and Sopwith Dolphins, the latter type being commemorated in the squadron badge. Like so many squadrons, in 1919 it was disbanded but reformed at Duxford on 1 April 1923 where it stayed until 1940, successively equipped with Grebes, Siskins IIIs, Bulldogs and Gauntlets. In August 1938 it was the first squadron to receive the

Spitfire I. It operated throughout 1940 on defensive duties in No. 12 Group, alternating between Duxford and its satellite at Fowlmere, continuing to operate in Fighter Command with successive models of Spitfires until it joined 2 TAF in June 1943. February 1944 saw the arrival of Mustangs, which it continued to use for daylight escort missions during the run up to D-Day and for Army support missions after the invasion. From September it began long-range escort missions for daylight raids, which continued until February 1945 when the squadron moved to Scotland, returning south again with the end of the war. In October 1946 the de Havilland Hornet arrived, which was replaced in turn by Meteors in 1951 and Hunters in 1956. Based at Church Fenton from 1947 the squadron subsequently moved to Leconfield where it received Lightning F.2s in 1962. In September 1965 the squadron left the UK with co-located No. 92 Squadron for Geilenkirchen and then, in 1968, to Gutersloh.

Aut Pugna Aut Morere (Either Fight or Die) is the motto of 92 Squadron. Formed at London Colney as a fighter unit on 1 September 1917, it operated a variety of types for training until receiving SE.5As in January 1918. It took these to France and until the end of the war it flew both fighter and ground-attack missions. Becoming part of the Army of Occupation, it disbanded in August 1919. It reformed in October 1939 at Tangmere, and was intended to become a Blenheim fighter unit. But in March 1940 these aircraft were replaced by Spitfires. It spent the early part of the Battle of Britain on defensive duties in South Wales, operating from Pembrey. It eventually arrived in No. 11 Group on 8 September as part of the Biggin Hill Sector. It remained in the south, going over to the offensive in 1941 until September of that year when it moved to Digby in Lincolnshire. However, in February 1942 the squadron embarked for Egypt, arriving in April. On arrival it found there were no aircraft available to equip it and so its crews had to undertake maintenance duties. Spitfires finally arrived in August and with these it carried out escort and fighter sweeps in defence of the El Alamein area. Following the break out 92 Squadron followed the Eighth Army until the Axis forces capitulated. In June 1943 it relocated to Malta from where it covered the Allied landings in Sicily. It continued to act in the fighter role until becoming a fighter-bomber unit in Italy. The squadron disbanded in Austria where it had become part of the occupation force in December 1946. Then, equipped with Meteor F.3s, it reformed and moved to Duxford in February 1947 and then in October 1949 to Linton-on-Ouse in Yorkshire. After moves to Middleton St George, Thornaby then back to Middleton St George, 92 Squadron arrived at Leconfield in May 1961. During this period it was successively equipped with Meteor F.8s, Sabre F.4s and Hunters F.4s and F.6s. Having moved to Leconfield the squadron took over the role of the RAF's aerobatic display team as the Blue Diamonds with all-blue Hunters. These were replaced by Lightning F.2s in 1963 and for at least one season the Blue Diamonds operated these aircraft. However, in December 1965 it reallocated to RAF Germany with 19 Squadron.

The other two squadrons at Gutersloh during John's time were those of the RAF Regiment. 26 Squadron was formed at Yatesbury in 1951 and served at Abu Sueir, Habbaniya, Amman, Tymbou, Nicosia, Changi and Bicester prior to moving to Gutersloh. 63 Squadron, which succeeded it, came into being in August 1947 at Gatow and was also a much travelled squadron serving in Fassberg, Upavon, Middleton St George, Pembrey, Ouston, Felixstowe, Malta, Cyprus, Tengah, North Luffenham and then Gutersloh.

Such were the histories of the flying and airfield defence units with which John would work. Now, having arrived at Gutersloh, it was time to see for himself what the calibre of his new command was. He wouldn't be disappointed.

CHAPTER TWENTY-ONE

Gutersloh

Gutersloh was a tailor made posting for John. You need people like him in places like that at times like that – good operational commanders who, when the need called for it, were totally uncompromising, which in all fairness makes a very positive contribution to what the air force was and indeed is.

George Black

L ooking back at a career full of significant moments, John considers his posting to RAF Gutersloh as Station Commander as the best. Indeed, when he left two years later his feeling was such that even were he to become Chief of the Air Staff it could not match the time he spent in Germany. It was both exciting and demanding. There were many reasons for this, which can be grouped under three broad headings: the people he worked with; the relationship he fostered with the German people; and the flying. Operationally, the performance of everyone at Gutersloh was as good as it could get. The Lightning F.2As that equipped 19 Squadron (whose CO during John's time was Peter Vangucci) and 92 Squadron (led by John Mitchell) were the hot rods of the Lightning genre and were very suited to the interception role in the theatre in which they served. With more fuel (the ventral tank was given over entirely to extra fuel as the guns were in the nose and not the belly pack as with other marks of the aircraft) and more efficient engines, they could fly a reasonable sortie time at low level. Indeed, it was said that with luck you could get two hours out of an F.2A on certain mission profiles, which for a Lightning was quite a claim to make! The F.2A was developed from the F.2, the latter being externally similar to the F.1, but incorporating several internal changes, which included improved navigation equipment, a steerable nosewheel, liquid oxygen breathing and variable nozzle reheat. From 1968 thirty-one F.2s were rebuilt as Gutersloh's F.2As to incorporate various F.6 features. The engines were upgraded to Avon RA211Rs but the F.2 armament fit was retained, whilst externally the cambered wing, square-cut fin and a much enlarged ventral tank were the very noticeable differences. 19 and 92 were the only squadrons to fly this mark. John flew on Tuesdays with 19 Squadron and on Thursdays with 92 Squadron. Friday afternoons were reserved for the Wessex of 18 Squadron (their CO was Trevor Jones). Whilst a very different kettle of fish, helicopter work had its own special challenges, which John met head on, as always, and mastered. 18 Squadron's role was primarily that of army support and co-operation and as such it was very heavily tasked in ferrying troops and equipment to the battlefield and airlifting injured soldiers (and marines who also participated in the constant round of exercises) out.

It was John's choice to fly as much as he did. There was no pre-requisite for a Station Commander to do so but given he had been away from flying for so long and given the prospect of not much more operational flying in future postings, it was not a difficult decision for him to make.

John Spencer recalls:

> JFGH did indeed do a fair amount of flying as CO of RAF Gutersloh but while this was no doubt very enjoyable it also served a deeper purpose. It set the tone and demonstrated to all on the station that the front line was the *raison d'être* and that everything else was subordinate. It was a lesson I took to heart and applied when I became OC RAF Binbrook.

Apart from the flying, Gutersloh was special to John in other ways too. It was an isolated base in the sense that Bruggen, Wildenrath and Laarbruch (the other three RAF Germany bases) were on the Dutch border whereas Gutersloh was close to the East German border. There were 1,500 RAF personnel working there (and some Army too) and adding in wives and children that made for a large complement for which John was responsible. Consequently he and Annabelle were involved with many social activities with children and families. Annabelle presented medals and prizes at sports days. She ran wives' groups. She helped in nurseries. John formed The Grasshoppers, a station football club for youngsters. With dads keen to help with training at weekends and mums always wanting to support their offspring as well as providing the orange juice for half time it became a family thing. Indeed, much that happened at Gutersloh became a family thing because the base overall was akin to one large family.

Operationally, it was a similar story with men and women in all units pulling together. For all new arrivals at Gutersloh John would hold an introductory briefing, which started with a simulated radio broadcast portraying what would happen if war broke out. This gave each person an insight as to why he or she was at Gutersloh and why they would be doing the job they did. As a consequence their absolute determination that they were going to be the best was unswerving and they became the most capable operational people John had ever met and worked with, whatever their rank. This attitude was reflected in the fact that Gutersloh became known to the 2nd Allied Tactical Air Force (2ATAF) TACEVAL team as the best station in Germany. John was undoubtedly a tough commander who quickly gained the loyalty and respect of his men. Nevertheless, if they broke the rules he would come down on them very quickly.

John had no preconceived ideas about what awaited him prior to his arrival in

Germany on 15 January 1973. He had, of course, some idea of the operational aspects of the job but not the social ones and the initiatives he put in place once he had been in post for a while were actioned because he saw for himself what was needed. It was only when he was given a guided tour of the base by his predecessor, Group Captain Dusty Miller, that he began to appreciate the enormity of the task. Dusty Miller showed him everything and briefed him on the essentials. In other words, he told him everything he thought John *should* know but from 19 January when command was formally handed over he was on his own. Immediately he began a programme of virtual non-stop visiting and inspecting. He quickly got to know every section, every building, every hangar, indeed every nook and cranny. He also got to know everyone on camp by sight and every officer by name.

John was very keen that any lingering prejudice between the British and German communities be addressed. Westphalia had had strong Nazi sympathies during the war and this still lingered. In some quarters there was resentment at the British presence, especially among the older people, and so it was important to help build bridges. John invited the first Commanding Officer of Flughafen Gutersloh to his old base and showed him round. The German was delighted with the chance to compare what it had been like in his day almost thirty years before with how it was now. He would have recognised it instantly for the *Luftwaffe*'s buildings were still in use, although some inevitably had been altered and added to. Station HQ was still called the House of Richthofen. The Officers' Mess, as 19 Squadron's Graham Clarke recalls:

> …had a tower and at the top was Goering's Room where he apparently used to hold court with his fighter pilots during the war. There was a picture of Goering on the wall. The room had a low beamed ceiling and one of the beams (over a table) was hinged in the middle. Some distance away there was a small flap in the floor underneath which was a handle. The standard trick was to get a newcomer to sit at the table with a beer in his hand. Someone would then pull the handle and the centre of the beam would drop about a foot towards the unsuspecting victim's head. Result? Some consternation and then realisation that he had been 'had'.

One of the characters of Gutersloh was to be found in the Officers' Mess. His name was Willi, an absolutely pro-Nazi barman (or at least he pretended to be) who on Hitler's birthday each year would put on a barrel to celebrate and place a bust of the man on a table in the corner. He obviously had a sense of humour and was ready to disparage Germany's wartime allies if he felt it enhanced the status of the Nazi regime in British eyes. During Exercise *Field Fox* in 1974, which saw the gathering at Gutersloh of airmen of several NATO air forces, John organised a dinner in the mess to which senior NATO officers were invited. On the night of the dinner an Italian colonel was not to be found. John was hesitant to start without him and made all efforts to track him down. Willi had been aware of the problem and as John walked through to the Dining Room he called across. '*Herr* Group Captain,' he said. 'We had the same trouble!'

There was a darker side to Gutersloh post war, which has only recently come to light. It seems that during the early days of the Cold War suspected German communists were arrested because they were thought to support the Soviet Union. Believing that war with the Soviet Union was inevitable the British War Office was seeking information about Russian military and intelligence methods. Dozens of men and women were detained as were a number of genuine Soviet agents, scores of suspected Nazis and former members of the SS. They were initially housed in a prison at Bad Nenndorf but following allegations of torture and mistreatment of those arrested and the convening of courts martial to try those suspected as the instigators of such treatment, Bad Nenndorf was replaced with a purpose-built interrogation centre at Gutersloh. It is unclear when this centre closed but John recalls hearing stories of the arrival in the late 1940s of a team of engineers to work at Gutersloh, engineers who transpired to be Soviet undercover agents who engineered the escape of those held by the British.

John formed an Anglo-German friendship society and instigated a programme of openness between the base and the local population. At official functions he insisted on making his speeches in German even though he couldn't read or write or speak the language, resorting to phonetic pronunciation that often left the Germans helpless with laughter as unintended *double entendres* and puns emerged. But it drew the press and gradually relations warmed. Briefings were held two or three times a year to which all local Germans were invited. At these briefings they were told what was happening within RAF Germany, why it was happening and what Gutersloh's role was. The usual public relations issues cropped up regularly, such as engine noise at night when testing was underway and low flying by Harriers on exercise. But these issues were discussed and solved on a largely informal basis with members of the local town council invited to come on base, where John would give a presentation on noise abatement to explain the reasons for the station's flying effort and highlight the steps taken to minimise the noise level in local areas. Such facts of RAF operational life weren't automatically imposed on the local populace though. The noise resulting from engine test running around midnight was an early issue that John had to deal with and he solved that particular problem by asking what an acceptable time for such running would be. As a result such testing finished at 2230 but it also meant that when more difficult problems had to be confronted a greater spirit of compromise was in the air. As an aside there was an irony in some of this as John Spencer recalls.

Many of the locals actually enjoyed watching the aircraft in operation. On German Bank Holidays flying continued and we tried to make it as quiet as possible by adopting different profiles but ironically despite our best efforts this led to complaints. 'When we are working you make all this noise,' we were told. 'But when we are on holiday and want to watch you, you change everything!'

Harsewinkel Town Council, quite unused to this different John Howe style of approach but keen to help foster further this new spirit of co-operation, began to invite John to functions themselves. He was asked, for example, to present medals to winners at the local Schützenfest, a fair featuring a shooting match. To complement this John had medals struck featuring the RAF Gutersloh crest for presentation to locals nominated by the town council. On another occasion he visited Haus Brockenblick Ski Lodge to present Station Crests to the German civilians there. At Gutersloh itself the Annual Station Cocktail Party, at which local dignitaries and celebrities were entertained by the Officers' Mess and which was usually brought to a successful close by a Highland piper, could only reinforce the station's position with the local populace.

The local newspapers soon picked up on this new spirit of co-operation and understanding. In November 1973 *Neue Westfaelische* carried the story of a dance held in Marienfeld where many of the British who served at Gutersloh lived. Translated for the benefit of non German speakers it described 'the joyous atmosphere' in which 'people came close to each other with a glass of beer or wine and animated conversation. The language barrier was no problem, the sign language won against the difficulties.' John spoke (in German) and described how 'When I speak with my officers and airmen who live in Marienfeld I hear nothing but praise. A close relationship should develop from living side by side where everybody gets to know one another better.' The Burgermeister concluded by regretting that 'English and Germans have been living far too long side by side to each other without taking notice of each other' and expressed his hope that these 'first contacts should grow and help to a better understanding between the nations.'

It hadn't always been a case of immediate harmonious co-existence. Families posted to Gutersloh still found that some local people were difficult to get on with. They were certainly sometimes difficult to get to know. But instances of German wariness of the British reduced significantly over the time John was there. This was helped by a deliberate policy of preventing the British from descending on the town for their entertainment, the reasoning simply being that there would be no toleration for those who got drunk and caused trouble and offence. As an alternative John instituted the formation of a range of clubs on base for socialising. Set up by the different units that made up the station and run and organised by the troops themselves they proved to be very successful. John knew that to be so as he and Annabelle enjoyed many a good night in them!

John's philosophy as far as his command of Gutersloh was concerned was one of firmness and this is echoed by the recollections of those who served under him.

John Spencer was ordered to John Howe's office shortly after he arrived.

> The first thing he did was to give me a rollicking! I had had to eject from a Lightning into the sea and the Board of Enquiry found that I had been wearing insufficient flight clothing and JFGH was ordered to deliver the reprimand. But I have to say that I was at Gutersloh for eighteen months of his tenure as OC and we always got on well when contact was made and that was usually when he flew with 19 Squadron. For some reason he had something of a soft spot for me, which I could never quite understand, but perhaps had something to do with my uncompromising attitude to him when I checked him out at Coltishall!

By now an Air Vice Marshal, Phil Lageson was the Deputy Commander of 2ATAF. Although he and John were good friends, professionally Phil Lageson would treat John no differently to any other officer, regularly catching him on the hop – or trying to. When visiting a station he would invariably tear up the written brief prepared by the Station Commander and say 'Now tell me about your station'. On one of John's AOC's inspections (the one big day in any Station Commander's calendar) with John not long out of bed and still dressing he had a phone call from the AVM. 'I'm in your Airmen's Mess,' he said. 'And the place is a bloody tip, a disgrace. You get down here.' But John immediately saw through the ruse. 'No Sir. You are not on my station.' 'What do you mean I am not on your station?' 'Well, Dulcie [Phil Lageson's wife] promised to ring me when you left. And she hasn't rung!' One up to John.

George Black understands why John adopted the approach he did at Gutersloh.

> RAF Germany had had a terrible safety record for a long time and, like me, John had come from UK Fighter Command where a very professional approach to the job was evident. Germany had a reputation for a good party life and was lacking in that professional touch. John came to Germany and Gutersloh at the same time as I did to Wildenrath and we both wondered what we had come into.

Gutersloh was just three minutes' flying time from the East German border and the reality of the situation in which the base operated was always brought home very forcibly when VIPs visited. As part of their briefing John would take them to the border twenty miles away and show them the wire, patrols, dogs, watchtowers and other trappings of a communist regime. This was a border that often dissected villages. Nevertheless, on the West German side at least, the villages remained busy places, although on the East German they were deserted.

To put the comments recounted above by those who were at Gutersloh with John into perspective and to appreciate the reason for John's approach and attitude to the job he had been entrusted to do, Peter Vangucci (OC 19 Squadron at the time) provides the following insight.

I joined 74 Squadron at Coltishall a short while after John had handed over the squadron and moved to HQ Fighter Command as a staff officer. His reputation as a hard task master who brooked no nonsense lingered on but when I met him during his regular staff visits to Coltishall I found him very genial.

John arrived as the Station Commander at Gutersloh towards the end of my first year as OC 19(F) Squadron. Suffice to say that the squadron had not been the favourite of his predecessor and found it very difficult ever to appear to do anything right. The ground crew were particularly sensitive to this apparent hostility. John greeted me when we first met but I sensed a mixture of surprise and concern in his manner. I assumed he had been briefed on the perceived shortcomings of the squadron and of me. There was nothing I could say, we just had to wait for our performance to set the record straight. Nevertheless John treated the squadron fairly and this was appreciated, especially by the ground crew.

Shortly after his arrival, the NATO TACEVAL team arrived and put the station through a gruelling series of tests over a number of days. At the subsequent debrief our marks showed 19 Sqn to be number one, which we had known all along. John made a very gracious comment to this effect and the squadron celebrated with the usual party. I asked John if he would like to join us for the celebrations and he came to the squadron, leaving his hat on the entrance table as was the custom – especially in the Officers' Mess – to warn everyone that the Station Commander was present. When he came to leave the hat had disappeared. This was most embarrassing as John had not yet had his formal, arrival interview with the C-in-C and needed his No. 1 hat. There were no loud words, he simply gave me an instruction to get him another one, fast. I telephoned the hatters in London and ordered a new one but knew it would not arrive in time. So I contacted HQ RAF Germany and finally tracked down a spare Group Captain's hat of the right size and borrowed it. About three months later we had another party when the original hat mysteriously reappeared, but that's another story.

From my previous experience and his reaction to the loss of the hat I knew that John would say what he wanted in no uncertain terms. The one thing you did not reply was that it couldn't be done. So, as a squadron, we dropped everything when he asked and gave him what he wanted. The result was that we were then left for days and often weeks to run the squadron just how we wanted to without any interference until his next demand. It was a clear-cut, simple arrangement that we all – me, the pilots, engineering officers and the ground crew – liked.

Notwithstanding this very hard, but very fair, way of operating John could bend if he thought the occasion was right and was extremely loyal to those who were loyal to him. An example of the latter involved me and a

VIP visitor to the station. When these visits occurred he demanded maximum effort and very high standards to show the station in the best light possible. The programme invariably included a demonstration of Battle Flight and its speedy response to any threat from the Warsaw Pact. For one visit the programme was changed a number of times. 19 Squadron was holding Battle Flight but its participation was on, then off and finally on again. I forgot or was not aware of the latter change until too late. I raced round to Battle Flight to find John happily going through my routine and introducing me as a very busy squadron commander as if my late arrival was perfectly normal, even planned. Naturally, I apologised for my absence but he graciously put it down to the numerous programme changes.

Flexibility and sympathy with squadron imperatives were demonstrated in a different way. A very highly respected squadron Chief Technician was posted on promotion and asked the officers to attend his farewell party in the Sergeants' Mess. Unfortunately it coincided with a guest night where the station was hosting a number of important visitors. I told John the situation and asked if it would be possible for the officers to put in an appearance at the farewell party, not expecting to be able to go. However he immediately agreed we could be away for one hour, which we were, to the minute. Needless to say he went up again in our estimation and the Chief Technician was delighted when all the officers arrived in their evening mess uniform.

There was never any doubt in anyone's mind who commanded and ran Gutersloh: John Howe. But it was not an unthinking person who had an iron grip on the station. Here are two examples, one of his more flexible side and one of his sense of humour.

For many, many years there had been a tradition at Gutersloh that at Christmas the corporals and airmen could build a bar in the attic of their block for them to use over the holiday period. The bars would all be judged in a competition and the winner awarded the Station Commander's prize. As soon as the holiday season was over the bars had to be dismantled. That was an absolute condition of the concession to build. One year the squadron corporals came to me and asked if they could retain the club that they had built. I approached John and, when he reminded me of the rules on dismantling, pointed out that the corporals had no mess and no place that they could look upon as their own. He gave an approval conditional on the place being run by the standards of a mess not as an excuse for drinking, carousing and generally causing trouble. I had clear ideas on how I wanted the place to operate but asked the corporals for their suggestion for rules of operation. The list they came up with was far stricter than mine so I immediately agreed to theirs. The Dolphin Club turned into a wonderful squadron facility. There was never a moment's trouble, the place was impeccably policed by the squadron members themselves and we all used it for a quiet drink with our fellow squadron members, whatever the rank. It was still running when I finally left Gutersloh.

My second example is one of John's overriding sense of humour. One guest night in the Officers' Mess the 19 Squadron pilots and engineers decided they would see how quickly they could burn down their napkins, the table and anything else to hand. This was 19 Squadron, the so-called 'quiet ones' or 'faceless ones'. The next morning I was briefing all of the pilots about some operational matter when the phone rang and a voice said 'The Station Commander wishes to speak to you'. Oh, oh! The room was silent as the pilots heard a series of 'yes sirs' and 'no sirs' as I was the recipient of a one-sided conversation and got a real telling off for the unruly behaviour of my mob. I passed on John's unembellished message to them all of 'No more fire in the mess'. [This was a sensible restriction given there had recently been a serious fire on camp and there must be no risk of a repeat.]

My last week on the squadron turned out to be my second NATO TACEVAL. Again we came out number one on the station in absolutely clear terms, even as one of the best in NATO. The Friday of that week, my last day at Gutersloh, I was dined out in the Officers' Mess. Suddenly, at a signal, the squadron's officers rose, produced enormous water pistols with huge reservoirs and proceeded to soak those surrounding them and then turned on the top table including me, John, and all of the guests. When I tried to remonstrate with them, back came the response: 'Boss, you said no more fire, you said nothing about water.' I did not quite know what to say. There was a collective intake of breath but John thought it a huge joke and took it in great part.

Serving under John at Gutersloh was hard work but a very happy and most rewarding time. Many of the ways I ran my station when the time came were derived from my experiences with him.

It is interesting to note the number of times that final comment has been made in the course of the preparation of this biography. John's methods certainly served as template for those who found themselves in similar postings and positions in later stages of their careers. There can be no more positive testimony to their validity and effectiveness than that.

To counter John's tough stance there were many off duty moments when the mischievous, very social, very approachable man shone through as Gareth Cunningham recalls.

John and Annabelle were due to have a dinner party one evening with some fairly senior RAF officers and some local dignitaries. We were due for a

MINEVAL but we were pretty certain that John would not blow the hooter that day. Wrong! At 0500 the siren went and we spent the day running round in our NBC kit with gas masks on and off. At teatime the exercise finished and we retired to the bar in the usual fashion. As the evening wore on Ali McKay suggested that it would be a good idea to TACEVAL the Howes' house. The idea was eagerly adopted and the assembled drunks went out of the back gate and made their way there where they found the dinner party in full swing. Without blinking an eye John Howe invited us in, rang the Guardroom and ordered them to send round Joseph's Bratty Wagon to his quarter immediately so that he could feed us. And a great party we continued to have!

Joseph had been a German POW in England where he had learned to make fish and chips. His mobile wagon was parked outside the main gates every evening and bratwurst and chips was part of the local staple diet!

Tim Miller recalls that incident as well.

Another type of TACEVAL that occurred frequently was the habit of livers-in to go visit their more domesticated brethren on the married patch at the most inconvenient time, usually inspired by the closing of the mess bar. After one real TACEVAL the evening was rounded out by an impromptu visit to the Station Commander's residence. The protocol of course was to assess how quickly beer was presented and whether the household was able to maintain good humour and provide something to eat. John's solution showed initiative and a typically pragmatic resolution of the tactical situation by inviting the local Bratty Wagon to move from its site of dubious title outside the camp gates directly to the CO's house on the patch and serve until the 'guests' called uncle.

Disciplinary matters apart and the expectation that all who served under him should behave and act in the professional way that he did himself, John had a very clear view of his specific role at Gutersloh within the wider political context. During his second year in post a Russian engineer defected to the West by flying a MiG across the border then ejecting, the aircraft going on to crash. John was ordered by HQ RAF Germany to take a Wessex with Military Police aboard and go and pick the engineer up and take him back to Gutersloh. John refused, arguing that this was a Russian defecting to Germany and thus it was strictly within the West German government's jurisdiction, not his or the RAF's. His argument was accepted and it underlines John's understanding of his responsibilities as he needed to be very aware of the political situation but that did not involve him in direct political dealings. That must always be the province of governments and it was *their* political directives that were passed down to station level via the usual chains of command that he followed, not political decisions taken by the military. Even if it was HQ RAF Germany!

CHAPTER TWENTY-TWO

Front Line Ops

Overall TACEVALs succeeded because everyone was focussed on the job they had to do with the right attitude of mind. The way thinking went was 'We don't want to screw this up because if we do we'll have to do it all again. If we've got to do it, let's bloody well do it well.'

John Spencer

Gutersloh was always a busy, vibrant place. Just prior to John's arrival a Force Ten storm damaged eight Wessex of 18 Squadron and visiting aircraft of 72 Squadron. Furthermore, a large portion of the roof of the Operations Wing HQ was blown off and extensive minor damage was caused to many other buildings, installations and trees. Loose debris scattered across the airfield necessitated a declaration of Condition Black, meaning that, until cleared, parts of Gutersloh could be unsafe to operate from.' Repairs were still underway when John took command.

Regular features of Gutersloh life were MINEVALS (organised at station level), small-scale practice for the TACEVALS (overseen by 2ATAF) that RAF Germany was subject to on an annual basis. MINEVALS were held on a monthly basis except during the period immediately after a TACEVAL when everyone took a well earned rest after the rigours of that assessment. But they were soon underway again for it wasn't known exactly when the next TACEVAL team would descend. It could be less than a year from the previous visit or it could be more. A typical MINEVAL could include the flying by Lightnings of low-level search and airfield defence patterns; or the practice of the station facilities' denial procedures and a simulated evacuation of ground personnel; or exercising the Rapid Runway Repair Team in full NBC equipment. Just occasionally MINEVALS were upgraded to HQ RAF Germany-generated MAXEVALs – the term speaks for itself! Aircraft from other bases were often involved, Harriers increasingly so when they were deployed from their Wildenrath home into the field to operate from amongst the German forests. As it happened, no sooner had John taken up his posting than a TACEVAL team arrived on 29 January at 1440 hours. The point was, of course, that these were no-notice events. Inevitably, as the year came around and there had been no visit so rumours would start to fly and several false alarms were set in motion. So it had been this time – and then suddenly the 2ATAF team were there!

Despite fog, 19 and 92 Squadrons flew eighty sorties on the morning of 30 January. Troops had been drafted in to 'attack' Gutersloh (thereby testing the airfield defence regime) but 18 Squadron's Wessex proved to be invaluable during this phase of the assessment by capturing five intruders before they reached the airfield boundary. Over the following two days the team put the aircrew through a range of scenarios, which all went pretty well. The visitation concluded with a review of the whole exercise, the outcome being that for the second time running the highest rating of 'one' was awarded. Gradings were from one to four, with four necessitating a re-evaluation within three months. No danger of that at Gutersloh.

The second TACEVAL of John's tenure took place on 20 May 1974 with the 2ATAF team materialising at 1640 hours. This was considered as being 'awkward' by the station diarist as a full day's duty had just been completed by station personnel: but then again any enemy attack was not necessarily going to materialise at a 'convenient' time! Despite this, reactions were very quick and the station was fully operational again within two hours of winding down and a full programme was flown before the TACEVAL team called an administrative break at 0200 hours the next morning. The exercise then continued until another break was called at 1700 hours before the TACEVAL team finally called a halt at 1120 hours on the third day. A total of 111 sorties were flown by the Lightnings with 112 'kills' claimed and 110 'confirmed'. The gunners of 26 Squadron RAF Regiment maintained a high standard and no aircraft penetrated the airfield defence ring unnoticed. The team were very impressed and could find few faults but because facilities at the station in 1974 were not yet up to the new 2ATAF standard – a programme of updates had been initiated throughout RAF Germany – they could only award a 'two'. This was disappointing, especially as the team admitted that Gutersloh was worthy of its now to be expected grade 'one' because once again such an exceptional performance had been achieved.

Tim Miller recalls the TACEVALs and the constant rehearsal for them very well.

The atmosphere was very professional in those days in the sense of being close to the front line and relatively far from officialdom. TACEVALs were a NATO device with many artificialities as I experienced eight years later at Binbrook, but in Germany in those days they were played hard and real. The RAF Regiment men were often let loose to simulate known Spetznatz tactics. One practice MINEVAL was spiced up when the invaders kidnapped John Howe and 'interrogated' him!

There was another vital point as John Spencer recalls:

A very important factor in Gutersloh's success in TACEVALs was the catering section! Keeping the TACEVAL team well fed, especially at breakfast time, was a prerequisite and the non-Brits in particular appreciated this!

As Station Commander, John has nothing but praise for the commitment of the men under his command during TACEVALs and thus by implication how they would have performed were the 'real thing' ever to happen.

> Within two hours of the team arriving and the warning hooter sounding everyone was fully briefed, armed and in position. Twenty-four Lightnings were pulled out on to the line, armed and dispersed before flying a hundred plus sorties in a very short space of time. This necessitated the very quickest of operational turn round times and these were consistently achieved by ground crews in heavy, uncomfortable NBC kit. If there was a (simulated) threat of nuclear attack the two squadrons would taxi to either end of the runway and one would get airborne in one direction followed by the second in the other direction – a system designed to get them off the ground as quickly as possible.

Everyone contributed. Those who were not directly involved in the flying – secretaries, accountants, clerks and so forth – donned their NBC kits, collected their arms and they would be based all over the station on ground defence duties. All messes would be ready to feed hot meals twenty-four hours a day. All medical facilities were put on high alert with all staff in place. Everybody on camp was involved in this quite remarkable achievement, which was repeated consistently during MINEVALs, MAXEVALs and TACEVALs. Indeed, the same professional approach to the job was very evident during normal operational days.

TACEVALs weren't the only assessments to which personnel were subjected. At a more specific level teams from various RAF organisations would arrive to look at a squadron's and then individual pilot's performances. 18 Squadron underwent its own regular assessment procedures courtesy of No. 38 Group's Standardisation Unit, which regularly examined all pilots and crewmen. 65 Squadron from Coltishall, the Lightning Examination Unit, periodically spent several days with 19 and 92 Squadrons checking the professional ability of the aircrew. Training was a constant and very necessary factor, which alternated with operations, so much so that the one often blurred with the other. Pilots could therefore anticipate the attainment of a good annual flying hours total, although in early 1974, with the prevailing world fuel crisis in mind, training sorties were curtailed in the interests of fuel economy and pilots restricted to eighteen hours a month. Even this total was under threat for a while because of a shortage of parts and stores thanks to the imposition of a three-day working week and the consequent industrial disputes in the UK.

Instructors from the School of Refresher Flying paid an annual visit to 19 and 92 Squadrons as well with Jet Provost T.5s. These were used to provide pilots with spinning recovery practice, a manoeuvre that was never cleared for the Lightning as Peter Caygill in his book *Lightning from the Cockpit* explains.

> One of the greatest criticisms of the Lightning's stall/spin characteristics was that it had virtually no stall warning and therefore no spin warning....the only real warning was the 'yaw off' just before the flick or spin but this was likely to be too late. Once the aircraft had flicked it would most probably end up in a spin and it was thought that the average squadron pilot would be ill equipped to recover in terms of both experience and lack of cockpit indication.

Pilots were thus given ongoing experience of spin and recovery modes, which may have been of use if ever they got into that situation with the Lightning. John was included in the programme with the JPs on 4 October 1973, which he immediately followed with a sortie in an F.2A. That was the last single-seat sortie in a Lightning he made at Gutersloh: in fact it was the last single-seat sortie he made in any RAF aircraft. The immediate reason was that he broke his ankle when skiing in the Hartz Mountains with 'Straw' Hall, OC Admin Wing. Because of the location where it happened there were no medical facilities nearby, so he had to walk down on the fractured ankle to reach help, which did it little good at all. The result was a lengthy time in plaster and a restriction as to which aircraft he could fly, although the Lightning T.4 was still judged to be permissible and helicopters too. The longer-term reason for the cessation of single-seat flying was that his postings subsequent to Gutersloh took John to non-flying posts or to multi-engined flying posts. The latter brought him into contact with a whole new range of aircraft.

In between TACEVALs there were exercises designed to keep every unit of the station on top of their game. A selection of those that primarily involved the squadrons included:

- Exercise *Pegout* (August 1973 and May 1974): in which 18 Squadron deployed into the countryside around Gutersloh and sometimes beyond, complete with ground support and on which John would regularly participate himself, spending nights under canvas with the troops.
- Exercise *Wintex* (March 1973): over the course of ten days personnel from other sections reinforced the Ops Room staff. A detachment from 33 Wing, RAF Regiment, was based at Gutersloh to control its squadrons in the field and a Harrier Flying Wing Ops Centre operated from tented facilities on the airfield.
- *Reno Roulette* (April, July and October 1973) and Exercise *Playboy* (April, May, June and October 1973): low-level exercises for the Lightnings.
- Exercise *Snake Eyes* (May 1973): involving aircraft from other NATO air forces. In 1973 American and French units participated. Mirage IIIs of the latter detached to Gutersloh for the duration of the exercise and shared 19 Squadron's facilities.

- Exercise *Co-op* (June 1973): during which day and night sorties were flown by the Lightning squadrons at high and low level. Some 141 sorties were generated over a twenty-four-hour period. Whilst the exercise was underway the Wessex acted as low-level intruder spotters for the Lightnings by flying airfield search patterns, which for its time was a novel use of helicopters.
- Exercise *Active Edge* (June '73 and December '73): an aircraft generation exercise for 19 and 92 Squadrons and the station's engineering staff.
- Exercise *Heartsease* (August 1973): five 92 Squadron Lightnings deployed to USAF Ramstein.
- Exercise *Sky Blue* (September 1973): low-level sorties flown by the Lightnings in support of Army operations.
- Exercise *Autumn Leaves* (October 1973): a ground defence training exercise that involved Harriers deploying into the field. 26 Squadron RAF Regiment was tasked with the defence and security of its sites.
- Exercise *Field Fox* (May 1974): a tripartite exercise to evaluate and practise transport support operations as part of the Berlin Contingency Plan (BERCON). Six French Mirages and six USAF Phantoms took part as well as Gutersloh's Lightnings, the latter being based at Fassburg, twelve miles from the border, to protect the northern Berlin air corridor. BERCON was established as a response to any attempt by Russia to blockade Berlin. The planning to counteract any such blockade was divided into four phases. The first envisaged a scenario where the Soviet Union or East Germany interfered with access but fell short of significant blockage of access to Berlin. The second envisaged an actual blockage such as prevention of civilian ground access to Berlin, which would be characterised primarily by intense diplomatic activity, NATO military mobilisation and economic and naval countermeasures. The dominant event of the third phase, during which denial of access continued, would be the use of force. This could include non nuclear ground and/or air action in East Germany and/or in Eastern Europe and could be supplemented by world wide naval measures by the West, the purpose of this strategy being to induce the Soviet Union to restore access. The final phase would be the ultimate use of force in the form of nuclear weapons and would of course only be instigated if non nuclear action failed to restore access. As far as *Field Fox* was concerned, the fighters' role was to patrol and protect the air corridors into Berlin, not that they flew there when exercising but rather hypothetical airways were created into a West German city along which they practised the strategy.
- Exercise *Cold Fire* (June 1974): an AFCENT (Allied Forces Central Europe) sponsored exercise in which Gutersloh's participation consisted of

219

maintaining low-level search patterns continuously for ten hours a day.

• Exercise *Casino Cash* (October 1974): a 2ATAF air defence exercise during which two 19 Squadron aircraft deployed to USAF Bitburg and two of 92 Squadron to Beauvechain in Belgium. Two Danish F-104 Starfighters were attached to 92 Squadron at Gutersloh for the exercise. Low-level flying was curtailed on this occasion because of heavy bird activity at Gutersloh and a bird strike on a 19 Squadron Lightning. Gutersloh lay on intensive bird migration routes and at certain times of a year operations had to be restricted because of this.

• Exercise *Red Rat* and Exercise *Shellfish* (October 1974): two Army co-operation exercises principally involving 18 Squadron, although the Lightnings flew sorties to threaten Harriers flying in designated low-level areas.

The whole *raison d'être* for 19 and 92 Squadrons' presence at Gutersloh, indeed for Gutersloh's existence itself, was to police the border between East and West. Battle Flight was part of this and was a constant factor in the lives of the Lightning pilots. Later known as QRA (Quick Reaction Alert), it necessitated aircraft and crew being ready at five minutes' notice to get airborne in response to a perceived threat from the air by approaching Soviet bloc aircraft. Two aircraft were kept on five minutes' readiness twenty-four hours a day, seven days a week. In reality many hours were spent sitting on Battle Flight with nothing happening but patience was rewarded occasionally with an interesting scramble to intercept a western civil or military aircraft that was getting too close to the Air Defence Identification Zone (ADIZ). Scrambles were also initiated to react to East German or Russian aircraft being scrambled on the other side of the border. On occasion hot air balloons were found drifting within the ADIZ. Live scrambles were interspersed with training scrambles on a regular basis.

In the air there was absolutely no flying over East Germany but 'games' were played by the Russians who would taunt NATO by flying at medium or high altitude at speed towards the border. This would trigger a Battle Flight scramble but by the time a Lightning was airborne and *en route* the Russians would do a 180-degree turn and disappear. Scramble response time was two minutes or less.

Operationally Gutersloh's task was the defence of a portion of low-level airspace 120 miles long and sixty miles wide between the base and the border, a task shared with the Belgian Air Force. This airspace was constantly patrolled during daylight hours. (A posting to 19 or 92 Squadrons to do this was the most operationally satisfying and professional job many pilots in the air force at the time ever did because something was being done that they could really see the point of doing.) Gutersloh's allotted sector of airspace was divided into a series of ten-mile long boxes patrolled by two aircraft on low-level Combat Air Patrols (CAPs) on a racetrack pattern, their positioning such that at specific times they were at specific known points on the racetrack. Thus when they got to a certain fuel state, replacement Lightnings could launch and come straight in to take over. Low-level CAPs meant flying down to 250 feet because the Soviet 16th Tactical Air Army that faced NATO over the border at this point was equipped with low-level attack aircraft such as Su-7 Fishbeds and MiG-21 Fitters and these were the immediate threat. There were also medium bombers such as Tu-16 Badgers to counter, which was why a Hawk missile zone was in place. These bombers would not be used to bomb Germany but targets further afield such as cities and installations in the UK.

The low-level CAP system had been developed by the Belgian 350 Squadron at Beauvechain during an air defence competition. It had not been imposed on Gutersloh but had been adapted and developed purely for reasons of best practice. Prior to this the RAF had flown its sector as a 120-mile long racetrack trail, aircraft following each other around at intervals. This was not particularly satisfactory because it was complicated in terms of knowing exactly where aircraft fitted in. Furthermore it didn't give individuals the responsibility that the low-level CAP system did. If a Fishbed penetrated your sector it was nobody's fault but yours. Interestingly the Americans, who patrolled the southern sector, didn't adopt the system. The Dutch and Germans to the north did. It was a good system because it worked, so much so that the Russian and East German Air Forces across the border were often seen emulating it.

The system was used for both the real thing and for training. Training within the squadron and with other NATO air forces constituted a considerable portion of a pilot's flying hours. Deployments were regularly made to other air forces within Europe and they came to Gutersloh as did other RAF squadrons. Particularly anticipated were sister Lightning squadrons, primarily because 19 and 92 Squadrons liked to show exactly what their 'hot rod' F.2As could do when pitted against F.3s and F.6s. In fact, they could hold their own with any Allied aircraft they worked with – F-104 Starfighters, Saab Drakens, USAF and British Phantoms, Northrop F-5s, Dassault Mirage 111s, Vs and F1s and occasionally Convair F-102s and F-106s, which deployed from the States. When there were friendly aircraft around Gutersloh's squadrons operated a 'Dial a Lightning' scheme, which was an open invitation to NATO squadrons to call up the Lightnings if they wanted low-level interceptions. But care had to be exercised. Initial enthusiasm for attracting trade had to be tempered and better organised after one occasion when 19 Squadron found itself to be the focus of attention of four Phantoms, six Harriers and eight other Lightnings in an area of confined airspace within minutes of each other!

Training wise, Missile Practice Camps (MPCs) at RAF Valley were an annual feature in any squadron's programme and this was no exception for 19 and 92 Squadrons who deployed to Anglesey to enjoy the opportunity of firing a live Fireflash missile. Air-to-air refuelling was practised on such deployments. Occasionally there was the chance to enjoy the warmth of the Mediterranean sun at Decimommanu (Sardinia) for an Armament Practice Camp (APC), coded Exercise *Lightshade*. Preparation for this usually involved flying against banner-towing Canberras of 100 and 85 Squadrons. On another occasion a mini APC was held at St Mawgan in Cornwall to which 19 and 92 Squadrons sent aircraft, spending a few days at the Aeroplane and Armament Experimental Establishment (A&AEE) at Boscombe Down for gun harmonisation tests on the gun butts there *en route*.

The vital role of the RAF Regiment at Gutersloh, sitting so close to the border as it did, cannot be underestimated. In his book *Through Adversity* Kingsley Oliver explains the rationale behind their presence.

> As the Defence Planning Staffs once more focussed their attention on the case for reinstating conventional defence in Europe to replace the nuclear strategy which was becoming to look less credible as a means of dealing with the smaller scale situations which seemed more likely to arise between NATO and the Warsaw Pact countries, SACEUR formally approved the change to one of flexible response [see Chapter 20] and with it the Regiment's return to 2ATAF in Germany. The introduction of Harrier and the consequent development of close air support from field locations in the Army's area of operations made it obvious that such deployments would depend on effective local defence for the Harriers. 26 Squadron were accordingly deployed to Gutersloh to provide Light Anti Aircraft gun defence there.

John had 26 and later 63 Squadron of the Regiment under his charge. This was his first direct contact with the Rock Apes as they were (usually) affectionately known. Group Captain Kingsley Oliver was the senior Regiment Staff Officer at Rheindahlen and it was to him that John would refer if he needed to discuss the squadrons under his control but the truth was that that rarely happened. That was the case too as far as contact with other senior officers at Headquarters RAF Germany was concerned because with Gutersloh being so far removed in terms of distance from the clutch of RAF bases close to the Dutch border, John and his predecessors and successors were able to exercise a certain independence, which they took full advantage of! The first of the few occasions at which John and the Group Captain did meet was at a dinner party at Gutersloh, during which Annabelle received the distressing news that her father Cecil had died.

Not long after John arrived a detachment of 26 Squadron under its CO, Sqn Ldr Alan Collinge, was sent to Northern Ireland for three months. In 1973 the British Army of the Rhine was tasked to provide a Battalion strength unit from Germany for duty in Londonderry and 22 Light Air Defence Regiment Royal Artillery was selected for the task. However, to bring it up to the required strength 26 Squadron RAF Regiment at Gutersloh was attached to the Army to assist in the task.

Kingsley Oliver recalls:

When the squadron commander broke the news to his officers and men that they were to be detached to Londonderry for four months there was a stunned silence broken only by a question 'where is the airfield in Londonderry sir?' Sqn Ldr Alan Collinge's quick response 'on the streets' had a salutary effect on his audience.

On the day that the squadron assumed responsibility for its tactical area in Londonderry a bomb exploded without warning in a city baker's shop and while picking through the debris caused by the first bomb a second bomb detonated hurling Flt Lt France and Flt Sgt Abbott into the street. They survived, were hospitalised and then withdrawn from duty. A further two were hurt in an explosion in a bar they were attempting to evacuate. Towards the end of their stay it was anticipated that the situation could have deteriorated still further with a build up in the country towards the election of new political representatives and John's concern was such that he flew to Northern Ireland to visit the squadron. As it happened things passed off peacefully. Both John and Annabelle became very involved with the families of the Regiment who remained at Gutersloh at the time of the Northern Ireland deployment. Because the latter was considered a home posting the overseas daily allowance was stopped and this caused considerable hardship. They sought to rectify the situation through a formal approach to HQ RAF Germany and whilst the situation didn't immediately change there was some hope that as a result of their efforts it wouldn't arise again in the future

Terrorists of a different kind were the threat in Germany – the Black September Group. So whilst low-level airfield defence and security continued to be the prime concern, tactics and small arms training also reflected this rather more insidious threat to counter the possibility of which the Regiment was on constant alert. Training for the bigger job involved deployments in the same way as the airborne squadrons deployed, although in the Regiment's case it was invariably to gunnery ranges such as Den Helder in Holland for live shoots against banner targets with their Bofors anti-aircraft guns.

In June 1974 63 Light Anti-Aircraft Squadron arrived from North Luffenham to take over from 26 Squadron. 63 Squadron was in fact one half of the Joint Service Rapier Pilot Battery along with the 9th Light Air Defence Battery of the Royal Artillery, being the first RAF Regiment Squadron to be armed with the new Rapier missile, which would replace the Bofors. Rapier had begun development in the 1960s as a system to combat low-level, very manoeuvrable, supersonic targets. Entering service in 1971, Rapier, dubbed a 'hittile' because it (originally at least) relied on direct impact with the target rather than the large proximity fused warheads used by other missiles, provided a far more effective defence than had been possible thus far. At Gutersloh it was another very significant piece of kit in the defensive armoury.

Before leaving Gutersloh we must also pay some attention, as John did, to the achievements of the Air Movements Squadron. Operating from the grandiosely named Air Terminal, which was in truth a totally inadequate building, they handled increasing numbers of flights, passengers and freight during John's tenure. He soon found himself taking his hat off to the staff that operated the facility. Its inadequacies led to inevitable conflicts and disagreements, especially as the majority of passenger movements involved the Army. John recalls the day he received a call from a Flight Sergeant in the terminal who told him that he thought he was going to be in rather big trouble. In the frantic situation the terminal had been in that morning he had heard an Army Lieutenant shouting 'Staff Sergeant!'

> I didn't take any notice and he came over to me and caught me by the shoulder and said: 'Staff Sergeant, answer me when I talk to you.' 'But sir,' I said. 'I'm not a Staff Sergeant, I'm a Flight Sergeant.' So he said to me: 'In the Army you would be a Staff Sergeant.' And I said 'No sir! In the Army I would be a Major!'

The statistics for the Air Movements Squadron speak for themselves. As John arrived in January 1973 they handled 108 aircraft, 11,876 passengers and 232,403 lb of freight. By May this had risen to 302 aircraft, 14,577 passengers and 397,377 lb of freight. A new extension was opened at the terminal to help relieve congestion but this was quickly offset as numbers continued to rise inexorably. In September Air Movements reported the handling of 440 aircraft, 15,440 passengers and 331,620 lb of freight, whilst the following month the number of aircraft climbed to 458. The majority of these movements involved troops to and from Northern Ireland, although some were to take soldiers to army training grounds in Canada. By July 1974 626 aircraft, 21,736 passengers and 617,926 lb of freight were handled and although primarily a fighter base, Gutersloh was confirmed as handling more passengers and freight than any other RAF station in the world and that in spite of its very limited facilities. Many of the movements were conducted by charter aircraft as well as the VC10s, Hercules and Belfasts of the RAF. Britannia Airways were the major civilian players. The 19 Squadron Commander's house was the former *Luftwaffe* Station Commander's house and it was situated immediately adjacent to the perimeter track. At times of intense activity little sleep could be expected with the constant movement of transport aircraft. The same applied to exercises with the jets, although in those cases the CO was usually involved himself and thus he played his own part in disturbing his family.

John was dined out of RAF Gutersloh on 29 November 1974, a formal event with no shenanigans of the type previously experienced at Coltishall for example. The German people were sorry to see him leave. *Die Glocke* expressed the thoughts of many when it reported in English for the benefit of the British community.

> ...at the end of 1974 Group Captain John Howe leaves Gutersloh. With him a Station Commander goes who has been very popular with the German population. Beside the military task of commanding a station he cultivated content among the English soldiers and their families and good neighbourhood relations with the German population in Gutersloh and the surrounding communities. No doubt John Howe was the one among all previous English Commanders...who understood it best to cultivate relations, to eliminate misunderstandings and to discuss problems. The Germans don't like to see Howe go. The Commander used to have several discussions with German councillors and officials, invited numerous guests from all social ranks among the German population to the aerodrome or to his private residence 'Parceval House' and he informed the press with a pleasant frankness. Howe was an excellent representative of Great Britain and his attitude took effect on his men in a remarkable way. His wife Annabelle...was an ideal hostess at the Anglo-German parties at Parceval House.

Just before he left Gutersloh the Town Council of Harsenwinkel invited John to a gathering at which the Council Chairman bade him farewell and invited him to sign what they called their Doomsday Book. As he picked up the pen to do so John saw that he would be in very distinguished company for his signature would join those of Chancellor Konrad Adenauer, General Dwight D Eisenhower and Field Marshal Montgomery of Alamein. He felt very honoured.

John was handing Gutersloh over to Group Captain Peter Collins and was himself bound for a very different environment, the nine-month 1975 course at the Royal College of Defence Studies (RCDS). In overall concept this was Staff College at Bracknell all over again but at a much higher level and involving much more extensive travel. John would thoroughly enjoy the experience.

CHAPTER TWENTY-THREE

Diversity

*The Royal Observer Corps were in a pretty unique situation.
As Commandant you travelled up and down the country and regularly
met all sorts of people from all walks of life and received a warm
welcome wherever you went for they were all basically very nice people.
But at that stage of the game their role had to be questioned. Reporting
on nuclear fallout? With the inadequate facilities they had? In truth
when they were wound up it was because there was little justification in
their continuing. Having said all of that they were well trained,
committed and enthusiastic people belonging to an organisation with a
great spirit and I for one felt that you could turn round to any of them and
in time of war send them to do many jobs other than the nuclear one.*

George Black

John had a pretty good idea as he made his way to the Royal College of Defence Studies (RCDS) that twenty-seven years after entering the Military College in South Africa and having flown 3,500 hours on many types of aircraft his fast jet opportunities had come to an end. His current posting and the two that followed bore that out. He was now back to a desk but with his usual optimism he still saw plenty of opportunities ahead for expanding his knowledge and experience and thus his career.

The RCDS (housed in a magnificent London building that fully lived up to its prestigious Belgravia address) was, and is, home year by year to members of the RAF, Army and Royal Navy of Group Captain or equivalent rank as well as members of the armed forces, police, civil service and diplomatic corps home and abroad, who gather at Seaford House to study every aspect of defence and related subjects. Nineteen different nationalities were represented on the course of 1975 over which the Commandant, Air Marshal Sir John Barraclough, presided. The syllabus consisted of lectures in London and elsewhere from a wide range of eminent people, together with opportunities for visits overseas. John, with eleven others, selected Australia, New Zealand, Indonesia and Singapore. As recounted in Appendix J they visited Ministries of Defence and military bases, received political as well as military briefings, looked at major industries and experienced the culture of the countries visited. In short, John and his colleagues received an introduction as to how each country 'worked' and how it was run with the information imparted being at Defence Attaché level. He also visited Northern Ireland.

At the end of the course each member completed a dissertation. John chose as his title 'How Far Are the Lessons of Air Power in the Vietnam War Applicable to the Central Front of NATO', a choice prompted in part by his recent tour at Gutersloh. He did, of course, also have first-hand knowledge of the early days of the Vietnam conflict thanks to the people he met who had served in that theatre whilst on his exchange tour in the US. There had been full-blooded discussions about the war's progress both with them and with others in the USAF who had strong opinions about the politics, strategy and tactics employed. Thus began the formulation of the thoughts now encapsulated in his dissertation, which can be found under Appendix K.

Once John had returned from the Far East, and having completed his dissertation, he moved back to Bentley Priory. His second tour here was as Group Captain Operations, HQ 11 Group, with AVM Paddy Harbison as his AOC. He was thus close to the front line again and as such all those who worked under him, including Dennis Caldwell (who had been the Tigers' last Boss before their disbandment at Tengah in 1972 and so had much to share with John as regards 74 Squadron and Lightnings), were operationally minded. They therefore all talked the same language. Every aspect of 11 Group's bases and squadrons came under John's jurisdiction – operational flying, OCUs, training, flight safety, air to air refuelling, deployments overseas – and he visited all 11 Group's stations in the UK and abroad in the process. It was a busy posting. His contact was not only at senior level. As ever he made a point of speaking to non-commissioned airmen of all trades, something they appreciated and that John found very useful as the response he got gave a very good indication as to morale on stations.

Amongst the many other items on his agenda he was involved in trials regarding the application of disruptive camouflage to 11 Group's Lightnings; he monitored investigations into the loss of aircraft; he was part of a team reassessing the minimum standards of flying skill acceptable on squadrons; he and his staff were instrumental in drawing up plans for Hardened Aircraft Shelter (HAS) sites on airfields; and he was responsible for the authorisation of 11 Group squadrons to participate in Air Combat Training against USAFE F-5Es from 1977 onwards. Furthermore he managed three sorties in Lightning T.5s during his travels and these proved to be his last ever on the type. What he didn't realise at the time was that his RAF flying career was actually far from over, for new challenges and experiences in that respect lay ahead. But not immediately ahead, for next came promotion to Air Commodore and in April 1977 he became Commandant of the Royal Observer Corps.

In the years after the First World War the Air Ministry, as it was then, became aware that it needed a system to locate and intercept incoming enemy aircraft. This requirement led directly to the formation in 1925 of the Observer Corps, initially under Army control but by the end of the decade that of the RAF. This system of volunteers, posts and control centres, linked closely to fighter and anti-aircraft artillery, was destined to play a vital role from 1939, on duty as the Observer Corps was day and night, watching and listening in all weathers to identify and report the location of aircraft. So much was the Corps valued as part of the nation's defences that in 1941 it became the Royal Observer Corps (ROC), remarkable recognition indeed for a voluntary organisation. It showed its worth during the Battle of Britain with observers supplementing the developing radar network. The clear skies of 1940 made it possible for them to keep a close watch on the aerial battles and report back to Fighter Command. The radar of the day was largely ineffective inland and so the ROC was vital in facilitating successful interceptions before the enemy deeply penetrated Britain's defences, a role the ROC played until 1945. Then came the Cold War. Britain's radar system had been neglected after 1945 and when the need for it to be working to full capacity in the face of the new threat from the Soviet Union was realised it took until 1952 to repair it. Whilst that was happening the ROC was charged with continuing to be the eyes and ears of the RAF. Then, even when radar was fully functioning again and it could track and estimate aircraft locations and numbers, positive identification still called for human observation. With advancing aviation technology, however, this would not always remain the case. Second World War aircraft had ultimately flown at little more than 400 miles an hour at heights up to 30,000 feet. By 1965 front-line aircraft routinely flew at twice that height and three times the speed, which made their visual identification a far more impractical task. To counter this dramatically increased aircraft performance radar had become a rather more sophisticated tool and this, together with the development of airborne early warning aircraft such as the Shackleton, meant that the one outstanding problem of finding fast low-flying aircraft hidden from ground-based radar by hills, buildings and other obstructions had been largely overcome. So it was that the last ROC old-style surface observation posts were closed down in the mid 1960s.

That the ROC survived was by dint of it developing a new role. Since 1957 the Corps had been training to measure and report the onset, location and after effects of a nuclear attack by the Soviet Union. The ROC had always hitherto reported to the RAF but now it reported to Group and Sector Controls run by the officials and scientists of UKWMO, the United Kingdom Warning and Monitoring Organisation, which was under the control of the Home Office. This was a real culture change and one that was at first not fully accepted by many of the 10,000 volunteers manning the 867 monitoring posts in the UK when John arrived in 1977, volunteers who considered themselves still to be a RAF Command but were in fact now civil servants. At least in their Commandant they still had a senior

RAF officer based at Bentley Priory. He had a team of a dozen service and non-service personnel working with him there, with perhaps eighty Home Office staff elsewhere.

ROC observers in their new role in the field couldn't monitor the effects of nuclear explosions from flimsy surface buildings so between 1957 and 1964 they moved from surface posts to underground posts buried twenty feet beneath the surface – small reinforced concrete boxes the size of a caravan. These had simple instruments to measure explosive blast, the height and angle of flash from nuclear explosions and the lethal radiation from weapons fallout. Based on the information thus generated from this and other sources, UKWMO's responsibilities were five fold: warning of an air attack; confirmation of nuclear strike; warning of the approach of radioactive fallout; supplying government headquarters and home defence forces in the UK and neighbouring countries with details of nuclear bursts and with a scientific assessment of the path and intensity of fallout; and providing a post-attack meteorological service. Public information films of the time explained what the public were to do if nuclear attack became reality in terms of finding shelter wherever they could and remaining there until told it was safe to leave.

Former ROC volunteer Richard Edkins puts this into context.

First came the threat of an attack which would be identified by the RAF Fylingdales Ballistic Missile Early Warning System or by ground or airborne radars of NATO or the RAF. The potential attack would be assessed by the United Kingdom Regional Air Operations Centre (UKRAOC) and a decision made whether to alert the warning network. If it was so decided simultaneous TV and radio broadcasts through the BBC and commercial stations would be initiated. Two hundred and fifty control points in major police stations would in turn trigger up to seven thousand power sirens and up to eleven thousand other warning points would be triggered in key establishments and in rural areas. Some of these (including many ROC posts) would use hand sirens to re-broadcast the warning.

Nuclear detonations would be monitored by ROC underground posts. Pinhole cameras would record the altitude, size and bearing of the nuclear detonation. Blast sensors would record peak blast pressure levels of nearby explosions and fallout radiation sensors would record levels of fallout gamma radiation, which would give the time of the onset of peak radiation values and subsequently measurements of fallout decay rate. Readings from clusters of ROC posts would be plotted to triangulate detonation points, give an assessment of damage and to display and forecast movements of airborne fallout. This information would be transmitted by data line and radio link to the armed services, local authorities, the emergency services, service and transport concerns and the BBC for relay onwards to their staff and to the public.

In 1968 the air-launched nuclear deterrent gave way to submarine-launched Polaris. The ROC again survived this change in posture because there was no real substitute for its monitoring network whatever way the weapon might be delivered. Then the number of its underground posts was virtually halved as the government instituted swingeing budget cuts. Ultimately it was the vulnerability of the landline reporting system that sounded the death knell for the ROC. Nuclear detonations release a powerful electro-magnetic pulse, which causes surges down landlines of communication, something that could be overcome but only expensively. The Home Office commissioned studies for an early form of email and the internet but this was almost inevitably hindered by lack of funding.

Beyond that it was the new order of world politics, symbolised by the bringing down of the Berlin Wall, that finally led to the ROC being stood down in 1991. For a time it had seemed as if the Chernobyl disaster had given it a possible new role but it was not to be. It was ripe for closure and the collapse of Soviet Russia was enough to persuade the government to sanction its demise.

John's posting to the ROC took him by surprise. From being in the front line of RAF service he suddenly found himself in command of a poorly funded, sizeable force of uniformed volunteers and civil servants. Such postings followed a traditional pathway because ROC HQ was at Bentley Priory. Those who had served there in the role of Group Captain (Ops) as John had just done became quite involved with the Corps, particularly when exercises were underway. The rapport that existed between the RAF and the ROC meant that it was a natural step from one post to the other. But it must be said that for those who took that step there could be many frustrations and these were centred on the fact that the ROC was run by the Home Office.

John describes the scenario that confronted him on his arrival as Commandant.

The ROC had effectively been part of Fighter Command during the Second World War, then during the Cold War the Home Office became responsible for the safety of the population and the ROC was transferred to its control, at which juncture it became an organisation run by civil servants who had had little or no military training. Consequently the ROC rapidly became an extension of the Civil Service and to all intents and purposes was run like the Civil Service. The volunteers were simply civilians in uniform. So when I arrived and saw the way things had gone I realised that given its responsibilities I had to get some sort of military order and organisation going again. In my first year my driver Corporal Nick Hodges and I drove 65,000 miles (and almost as many in my second year) inspecting, visiting, meeting, talking, briefing and explaining what the ROC's role was.

In Norwich, David Hastings and his crew remember John's inspections and their anticipation of his arrival.

I have to say we really appreciated it when John was Commandant. In Norwich we had a reputation for playing it for real because we felt that was the only way to do it and as John was very much a 'play it for real' Commandant, I suppose he and we felt we were on the same wavelength. He thought highly of his volunteers and quickly got to know what they were capable of. On his regular inspections you knew that he was going to do a thorough job. He was totally supportive of everyone in the Corps provided they did things by the book, which was the only way he did things.

There was anticipation of John's arrival at Oxford too, albeit rather uneasy anticipation. John recalls:

When I arrived on my first visit I could see that everyone was on edge so I said to the CO 'Relax! I'm not a dragon you know.' To which, quick as a flash, he responded 'So what's that fire coming out of your nostrils sir!'

John again:

Britain, being so limited in landscape area, didn't have the advantages of the Soviet Union or United States who could disperse their populations. We simply couldn't so the only way we could minimise the effect of a nuclear strike was to have local observation of them and constant observation of fall out. This was the new job of the ROC. They had become the field force for the Home Office.

In my travels the length and breadth of the land I got to know virtually all of my staff and volunteers, not by name of course but by sight. But I also found there were no routine orders, no duty rosters, no emergency drills, no equipment inspections, in fact all the things that constituted good sound military practice. Through my briefings and inspections they all began to accept that they were the Home Office's troops on the ground and their objections to working for civil servants, only a few of whom were in uniform or had any military background, slowly began to evaporate.

In effect what John did was to re-establish for the volunteers of the ROC a new sense of purpose and also during his three years in post he helped to create an air of understanding and co-operation. This meant that senior officials of UKWMO began to see that the ROC was actually serving them as it was intended they should and doing it very well. Vernon Barry was UKWMO's boss. John reported to him and during the years of John's posting they came to work very closely and successfully together and consequently became good friends.

John recalls:

In my view we had the best Civil Service in the world. They were all very bright, intelligent people but they did not understand basic military procedure. They didn't have to. Neither was it the fault of the ROC who gradually distanced themselves from them. I immediately recognised this and set about putting things to rights.

When he left the ROC John was gratified to see things had come together and he admits to being very impressed by the dedication of the volunteers who manned the posts. Given the often anachronistic systems and procedures that were still in place, their performance on the ground during exercises was impressive. The Home Office fully recognised this achievement, which resulted in John being awarded the CBE.

Ten years later the ROC was disbanded. Many people in the Corps saw it as a purely political decision without regard to the requirements of the RAF who they strongly felt they could still support despite inadequate resources. It marked the end of an era, the end of a peculiarly British initiative.

CHAPTER TWENTY-FOUR

Maritime Operations

When you look back over a long career all the people you remember best
are people like John Howe, people who you knew were always around.
John was there 24/7 and so you remember him and remember him well.

Min Larkin

ecause of their appreciation of the way in which John succeeded in
reconciling the ROC's and Home Office's misunderstandings of each
other, the latter helped as much as they were able to steer his subsequent
career in his desired direction. John had initially been offered a senior post in
Training Command to follow his time at Bentley Priory but he preferred an
operational posting so senior Home Office officials approached MoD on his
behalf to see what may otherwise be available. As a consequence John was
promoted to Air Vice Marshal and succeeded AVM Sir John Severne as
Commander Southern Maritime Region (COMSOUMAR) at Plymouth and there
followed a very rewarding three-year posting during which he and Annabelle
made many lifelong friends from all three services.

John's administrative HQ was at RAF Mount Batten but the Joint Operational
HQ was at Mount Wise in Devonport. This was the focus for the joint operation
with the Royal Navy (which constituted the largest component), the Royal
Marines and the Army (the smallest component). In overall command was a full
Admiral to whom John reported, as did a Major General of the Royal Marines and
a Colonel of the Army. It was a busy HQ. Morning briefings were held on a daily
basis and these were primarily conducted by a mix of Royal Navy and RAF
officers. John appreciated these as they were operational in nature and working
with them brought immediately to mind the time he had served with the Royal
Marines at Suez. Senior Navy officers, the Admiral included, were all very shrewd
and totally on the ball, even as regards the maritime air role.

John's remit as COMSOUMAR was supplemented by the associated NATO
roles of COMAIREASTLANT (Commander Air Eastern Atlantic) and
COMAIRCHAN (Commander Air Channel). To the young in his family he was
also known as COMCHINLAUN (Commander Chinese Laundry)! His brief
encompassed maritime air operations, special operations and search and rescue
(SAR), including aid to the civil powers. The area of responsibility for SAR was

south of a line 54 degrees 30 minutes north. This meant a lot of high visibility work at times, both onshore and offshore, in the latter case a classic example being great involvement in the Fastnet race disaster of 1979 shortly before John's arrival. On average 500 rescues were controlled by his staff each year and the bravery and skill of the crews who carried these out often bordered on the legendary. SAR also involved the RAF Marine Branch whose launches were used for target towing and sea survival training for the RAF and for NATO air forces too.

For maritime air and special operations the Command was responsible for the Channel and the Atlantic out to a line where American and Canadian P-3 Orions took over and down to the Azores. The only exception to this was a small area of the Channel controlled by the French and their Breguet Atlantiques. Working with NATO allies meant visiting their operational bases and this John did on both sides of the Atlantic.

Mount Batten itself is a tall outcrop of rock on a peninsula in Plymouth Sound. For centuries it was an important defensive point for the old port of Plymouth and its harbour. For much of the period 1917 to 1945 the land and sea around it was a flying boat base for the RAF. Initially it was known as RAF Cattewater, the name changing to RAF Mount Batten in 1922. Supermarine Southamptons, Fairey IIIDs and Blackburn Irises were three of the types flown there. In 1935 Mount Batten became the Fleet Air Arm's floatplane base too but it became so crowded with the variety of aircraft and numbers of squadrons that used it that the FAA transferred to Lee on Solent, leaving the RAF and its Sunderlands in sole occupancy. Post Second World War a Maintenance Unit joined the Sunderlands then the RAF School of Combat Survival moved in. The formal end of flying came on 15 May 1959 but Mount Batten remained as a main base for the Air Sea Rescue Service, which had arrived at the beginning of that decade, and the RAF's launches became a familiar sight. At the same time HQ Southern Maritime Air Region was established here, coordinating and controlling the squadrons operating from RAF St Mawgan in Cornwall. But when 19 Group RAF Coastal Command left in 1968 that really marked the beginning of the run down of the station in terms of incumbent units. RAF Marine Branch disbanded in 1986 and Mount Batten closed in 1992. The peninsula is now a marina and centre for sea sports. There is no doubt that geographically it was in both a commanding and a picturesque position. On arrival John found that his office was fitted with a wide window that overlooked Plymouth Sound, which enabled him to survey the fine view unhindered. However, he turned the office round so that he sat with his back to it to prevent any chance of distraction.

To be candid, there were those at Mount Batten who may have been surprised at John's appointment, as he came to four-engined heavies in the maritime role from a fighter background. But his approach was simple as far as personnel on camp were concerned: he stayed in the background, his reasoning being that having been a Station Commander himself he appreciated that they wouldn't want an Air Vice Marshal interfering with the running of their station. He played things accordingly and only became involved when invited to do so. The same applied at St Mawgan where John frequently found himself when he flew with 42 Squadron. His brief did not extend to the base itself, which came under the aegis of Strike Command, not SOUMAR.

David Barton was John's ADC for the best part of two years and thus got to know his new Boss probably better than anyone during his tour. His job was to run John's diary, the office and generally keep the wheels oiled. He also had a separate brief from SASO, Group Captain Ian Balderstone.

> He said to me: 'Now look David, the COMSOUMAR needs to be kept out of the HQ and kept as busy as possible.' So I went off and organised as many trips as I could around the country. He did all the passing out parades including, I recall, Dartmouth, Cranwell, Shawbury and HMS *Raleigh*. He attended Combined Cadet Force occasions including Eton College. He made flying visits north, south, east and west. You name it, we did it. In fact it was great fun and an added bonus for me was to be able to meet all the outer office staff and my social life at SOUMAR was very busy and very enjoyable!

David himself had to quickly adapt to working for John.

> I wasn't very attuned to the ways of the world. Working with JFGH was a whole new ball game and I had to wise up quickly! I was definitely naïve and not very experienced to have to deal with somebody like this. He scared the life out of me on those occasions when I knew I had screwed up and he had caught me out. In the early days I though I could 'blag' my way out of difficult situations but he knew the ropes and had been there and back many times and could see straight through my pathetic excuses! But I soon learned many good lessons from him and with the benefit of hindsight and experience I understood that John was spot on and a very good man.

David openly acknowledges that his time at Mount Batten was demanding. But that he learned much from John's approach to the job and the way he handled those under him and indeed like so many others used that as a benchmark for the way he acted as his own career progressed.

Somebody else who kept his eye on John but in a very different way was his driver Corporal Nick Hodges who at John's request had come with him from the ROC. John and Annabelle both fully recognised Nick's worth. They thought of him as one of the family and invariably referred to him as Corporal Nick. What still surprises John is that he was never promoted despite his efforts to have that done. Conversely, Nick was quite happy to stay with his Boss. Such was their relationship he knew very well how to handle him as John recalls.

We had been at Finningley for the RAF's tribute to mark the Queen's Silver Jubilee. Once the flypast was over Annabelle and I had to get to London for an evening function and so we set off at high speed down the A1. At one point we suddenly slowed down to 70 and I asked Corporal Nick what was happening. He had just seen a police car in his mirror. It eventually caught us and pulled us over. Out of the car got a police officer who beckoned Corporal Hodges out of ours and gave him a good talking to and then drove off without issuing any booking. When he got back in I said 'Corporal Hodges. What did he say to you?' 'Well sir, he said to me, "Is that old bastard in the back making you break the speed limit?" And I said yes! And then he said "Well don't let him lad, it's your licence!"' Didn't Annabelle and I laugh!

During his first few weeks at Mount Batten John proceeded on an inspection tour of every department in the same way he had done at Gutersloh, to meet everyone and to learn what was being done and understand how and why it was being done. At the time the mission on which he was briefed included a lot of secret 'black' work involving the tasking of British and American aircraft to plot Soviet submarines in the Atlantic and off the American seaboard. Apart from visual sighting much of this was also done by means of the top-secret SOSUS System, a chain of underwater listening posts located across the Greenland–Iceland gap in the northern Atlantic Ocean.

The work that Coastal Command (as it still liked to call itself) did was very different to that to which John had been accustomed. Its members flew a very different type of aircraft to their Fighter Command cousins and there was no Battle Flight, with the only scrambling being done by SAR crews in an emergency. Furthermore, crews possessed a different mentality, which centred around the job they did and still do. They are made up of SNCO and officer aircrew and on long and monotonous missions there is inevitably much banter and camaraderie between them. This banter is an essential part of operations and helps to bond crews together so that when a contact is made and action stations called they work as one and discipline, in Group Captain Min Larkin's words, 'is then as tight as it is in the Guards'. Theirs is a highly skilled job and there are none better than the RAF's Nimrod crews. They are universally regarded as forming the world's leading maritime air force and no other can beat it at sub hunting, anti-surface warfare intelligence gathering and long-range SAR work. As this is written in 2008, despite question marks over the integrity of the aircraft's now elderly airframe, Nimrod squadrons have become one of the mainstays of NATO's air operations in Iraq and Afghanistan.

During Cold War days the Nimrod was constantly in contact with the potential enemy and as such it formed an integral part of NATO's policy of deterrence. That was its primary and very demanding role and the crews played a vital part in those often uncertain days in keeping the peace by their dedication and vigilance. But it wasn't just the Cold War for during John's tenure the Falklands War erupted and Nimrod crews flew long and dangerous patrols within twelve miles of the Argentinean coast. They were thus potential targets for enemy air defences and that is the reason why Nimrods were armed with two Sidewinder AAMs.

There were frequent exercises at Mount Wise. These exercises often lasted for days at a time, covering the wide expanses of the Atlantic, tracking submarines and surface vessels and working alongside NATO partners. But these weren't exercises in the manner of Fighter Command. By contrast, in the maritime scenario it was a deliberate, calculating process that involved, for example, constant analysis of signals from aircraft tracking vessels by overt and covert means. It was certainly not something that could be watched with the expectation that events would unfold quickly!

COMSOUMAR was undeniably a Staff appointment but that didn't stop John from pursuing the chance to fly at every opportunity. He converted to the Nimrod with 236 OCU at St Mawgan over ten days at the end of April 1980. Despite the aircraft being so very different from the fighters he was used to, under the tutelage of Squadron Leader Hynds he adapted to it quickly and was soon flying the aircraft as skilfully and with as much pride and enjoyment. He flew mainly with 42 Squadron. 42 Squadron had reformed post war in June 1952 at St Eval with Shackletons for maritime reconnaissance duties. Nimrods replaced these venerable aircraft in April 1971. During John's time the unit despatched two aircraft to Ascension Island as part of the first phase of Operation *Corporate*, the recovery of the Falkland Islands, gaining its sixteenth Battle Honour in the process. More recently the squadron has provided crews as part of the Nimrod detachment involved in Operation *Granby* and in January 1991 it set up a major detachment in Cyprus to provide additional further support to the Allied forces operating in the Middle East. Disbanded as a front-line unit on 1 October 1992, the numberplate was assigned to 236 OCU, which was by then at Kinloss.

Whilst John was at Mount Batten the CO of 42 Squadron was Wing Commander David Baugh with whom he often flew. His log books show his participation in long patrols over the Atlantic to find Soviet submarines, patrols that typically involved flying up to 1,200 miles to a designated area then six hours on patrol at 200 feet in all weathers and all of that after pre-flight preparation and briefing beforehand. With intelligence and engineering debriefing afterwards this could make for extremely demanding fifteen-hour days. There were times when such patrols became very exciting. Hunting Russian ballistic missile submarines during top secret missions over the cold, inhospitable waters of the Atlantic called for a special breed of men trained to do a highly specialised job. If as a result of that training a contact was made, that gave everyone on board a buzz of satisfaction. Flying skills at such times were tested to the full as very often the weather would be foul. Running over a target and then hauling the big aircraft round for a return run, banking steeply over the wave tops at 200 feet in the process, in an aircraft with a wingspan of 127 feet, was a very demanding operation.

42 Squadron also flew Operation *Tapestry* sorties. These had commenced on 1 January 1977 and involved fishery protection work and the monitoring of offshore oil rig and pipe installations. On average three such sorties per week were flown and the commitment continued unabated until it was finally undertaken by dedicated fishery protection aircraft in 1986. Other exercise involvement included *Ocean Safari*, which was designed to test NATO's capability to form and protect convoys for the resupply of Europe in the event of war.

If SOUMAR had been involved in the Falklands campaign John's job would have been frantic, but it was not and his Command continued to exercise its responsibilities in terms of monitoring the Soviet threat, patrolling the rigs and sea lanes as part of Operation *Tapestry* and being called upon when SAR work was required. John was of course very aware of Falkland operations and was fully briefed on developments. He was also perfectly placed to see a very busy Plymouth as the fleet got underway as it headed south. Shortly after it had all blown up (the war was triggered by the occupation of South Georgia by Argentina on 19 March 1982) John was in Gibraltar. He had flown down in a 42 Squadron Nimrod to participate in the joint services Exercise *Springtrain* in the Atlantic to the west of Portugal. All participating ships' and aircraft's crews spent an enjoyable time in Gibraltar after the exercise, taking part in a sports Olympiad as well as sampling the delights of various hostelries, whilst in the evening the Navy and Marines put on a splendid concert. Then the news broke of the invasion and the following morning the Navy vessels that had assembled in the harbour headed for the South Atlantic.

The Nimrod was the first ever jet-powered maritime patrol aircraft of any significance, earlier designs such as the Shackleton or the American Neptune and Orion using piston or turboprop engines. The Nimrod was based on the de Havilland Comet 4 and is powered by Rolls-Royce Spey turbofans. On patrol, when the overall weight of the aircraft is still high, all four engines are used but as fuel is used and weight falls the engines used are progressively reduced to two. For transit back to base the closed-down engines are restarted. Fuselage changes from the airliner included an internal weapons bay, an extended nose for radar, a new tail with electronic warfare equipment mounted in a bulky fairing on the fin and a magnetic anomaly detector (MAD) boom. From 1975 thirty-two of the original MR.1s were upgraded to MR.2 standard with a modernised electronics suite and provision for in-flight refuelling. The in-flight refuelling capability was introduced during the Falklands War as well as hardpoints to allow the Nimrod to carry the AIM-9 Sidewinder missile, which gave rise to the aircraft being called 'the largest fighter in the world'. The Nimrod, which at the time of writing is still operational in MR.2 guise, although shortly to be replaced after lengthy and expensive delays by the MR.4, has three main roles: Anti-Submarine Warfare, Anti-Surface Unit Warfare and Search and Rescue. John became proficient in all three regimes. Its extended range and refuelling capability enables the crew to monitor maritime areas far to the north of Iceland and up to 2,500 miles out into the Western Atlantic. It is a submarine hunter carrying up-to-date sensors and data-processing equipment linked to weapon systems with which to attack any hostile submarines found. For SAR operations a searchlight can be mounted in the starboard wing pod. The crew consists of two pilots (John always flew as second pilot), a flight engineer, a tactical navigator and a routine navigator, an Air Electronics Officer and two teams each of three operators. The 'dry' team operated radar, ECM, MAD and the HF radios, whilst the 'wet' team principally operated the sonar equipment but also the radios. Both teams loaded markers and sonobuoys when required, provided lookouts (there is often no substitute for the Mark One Eyeball) and operated hand-held cameras.

Whilst not so frequently as Nimrods, John flew other aircraft whilst at Mount Batten. He had been to RAF Finningley, home of the RAF SAR Wing, in February 1980 whilst still Commandant of the ROC in anticipation of his next posting. Mount Batten was, as we have seen, responsible for SAR in the southern UK and surrounding sea areas and John felt it was incumbent upon himself to be familiarised with the associated techniques and this the SAR Wing did.

22 Squadron was initially equipped with bright yellow Westland Whirlwind HAR.10 and Wessex HAR.2 helicopters before converting to Sea King HAR.3s and these were flown in John's area of responsibility from Chivenor and Brawdy. 202 Squadron covered the north of the country. The Fleet Air Arm had a large SAR presence around the coast as well and each service complemented the other in the area they covered. John participated in all aspects of helicopter work undertaken by the squadrons within SOUMAR and regularly flew Wessex and Sea Kings from RNAS Yeovilton and trained with the crews as they winched and occasionally dunked sonar, but as with the Wessex of 18 Squadron in Germany he never knew how to start and stop the engines! Whilst at Finningley John also flew the Dominie and Jetstream. All RAF navigators passed through the Air Navigation School of 6 FTS and it was in a Dominie T.1 of this unit that John flew a navigation exercise and underwent a handling check on 21 February. On the following day he was in a Jetstream of the Multi Engine Training Squadron, also a component of 6 FTS, which was responsible for training all the RAF multi-engine pilots. The Jetstream sortie was flown with the Nimrod in mind.

To complete the account of aircraft flown whilst at Mount Batten, John was aloft in a Canberra T.4 on 20 April 1980, towing a target for Surface to Air Missile firing. On 12 February 1981 he was in a Hawk from Brawdy with Sqn Ldr Cope on a familiarisation sortie, further sorties taking place later that year on 22 October and 2 November. He was reacquainted with the venerable Devon at Exeter on 19 February whilst a flight in a Jaguar T.2 followed a week later, probably from Coltishall, although this is not recorded. A Lockheed P-3 Orion, either American or Canadian, was flown on 7 October. Orions regularly exercised with the RAF's Nimrods from St Mawgan. A second sortie on 22 February 1983 in an Orion belonging to the US Navy's VP16 'War Eagles' patrol squadron completed his experience of the type.

The biggest aircraft John flew throughout his career was a McDonnell Douglas KC-10 Extender. John was on the eastern seaboard of the US with a Nimrod deployment when there was an opportunity to take a KC-10 to Dover AFB. Flying as second pilot he took the controls for much of the flight under the watchful eye of Major Detwiler. Apart from three sorties in Wessex helicopters whilst on his final posting to the RAF Regiment, this marked the end of a highly varied and challenging flying career. There could be no starker contrast between the aircraft with which he ended that career and that with which he started it, the Tiger Moth. John had come a long way in all respects. By the end of his flying career he had amassed 4,550 hours in the air.

Whilst in Plymouth John and the family lived in a splendid house called Monckswood, named after General Monck who billeted his troops in the vicinity during the English Civil War. The house, which was on the edge of the city and featured beautiful grounds and walks leading down to the sea, was rented by the MoD from Lord and Lady Studholme. After Gutersloh Annabelle and the girls initially had moved back into the bungalow they had bought near Upavon but in the wake of Annabelle's father's death and when John was at Bentley Priory the decision was made to make Norfolk their permanent home. They have been on the farm at Rackheath ever since. It was from that point on that John helped Annabelle's mother run Home Farm whenever he was on leave, employing contractors to do so at other times. He never allowed this to impact on his RAF service.

Annabelle and John jointly made many new and lasting friendships across the services when they were at Mount Batten. Another side of the posting to Plymouth was the opportunity it gave John and Annabelle of learning to sail (at HMS *Drake*) and they bought a Wayfarer in which to indulge their new-found passion. Business and pleasure could be mingled at times in this respect too when one of the single- or double-handed transatlantic races originated or terminated in Plymouth. Mount Batten was always involved in the marshalling of these races by virtue of the use of RAF Marine Branch launches. As COMSOUMAR John was made an Honorary Member of the Royal Western Yacht Club, which organised many of these races, and in the process he got to know famous yachtsmen of the day such as Robin Knox-Johnston. Another extramural post John held was that of vice president of Devonport Services Rugby Club. David Barton, who was an accomplished all round sportsman, was tasked with being John's eyes and ears on the ground whenever he played there!

Annabelle played a not inconsiderable part in Mount Batten life too: she entertained regularly, worked on various committees such as SSAFA and participated both by herself and with John in various station functions. Annabelle recalls:

I made more friends by serving on various committees when we were at Plymouth than I did anywhere else and that wasn't just with the RAF of course but with the Army, Navy and Royal Marines too. It was a multi service posting and I was certainly busy!

Annabelle felt particularly honoured when asked to launch a new marine vessel, HMAFV *Hurricane*, in June 1981. The 75-foot long *Hurricane* was a Rescue Target Towing Launch, the role of which encompassed SAR, high-speed target towing, weapons recovery, range duties and helicopter and fixed wing aircrew training and support. Annabelle still has the neck of the champagne bottle used to christen the vessel, suitably mounted.

For a short while John's time at Mount Batten had coincided with Phil Lageson (now an Air Marshal), being the AOC at Northwood. Another colleague and friend from way back on 43 Squadron was Peter Bairsto who was COMNORMAR, the northern equivalent to John's role. Shortly after, however, Phil Lageson retired and Peter Bairsto was promoted to Air Marshal and he too moved away from the maritime role. Both were replaced by others whom John did not know so well. Then after what seemed all too brief a time it was time for John to move on as his very different but thoroughly enjoyable tour came to an end as well. During the course of a conversation with AVM Les Davies in Cyprus, who John had known for years, he was told that he was taking early retirement because of family commitments and that his next appointment was to have been Commandant General RAF Regiment. John called AMP (Air Member Personnel) and told him that he had been speaking to Les, that he knew he wouldn't be taking up his next posting and that he would be glad to do it. Within a couple of days John had been given the posting.

Meanwhile, Phil Lageson was returning to South Africa. He had a friend who owned a shipping line, with whom he took a berth. John got to hear that this was on a container ship sailing to Cape Town. Whilst on patrol he was able to find the ship and fly-by, photographing it in the process. Before doing so he flew behind the vessel and as he pulled round he called the Captain to inform him that one of his containers had broken loose and had broken up as it hit the water, leaving a grey Mercedes floating on the surface! This brought its owner, Phil, quickly up on deck and some of the photos taken as John flew the length of the ship clearly depict a fist being shaken at the aircraft!

CHAPTER TWENTY-FIVE

Finals

*To me the finest testimony to the forty years and more I spent in the
Royal Air Force and South African Air Force was the fact that I had
indulged my love of flying to the limit, that I had met and served
with so many fine people many of whom had become lifelong friends
and that I had experienced things that as a youngster in a South Africa
of growing apartheid I had never thought to experience. Not least of
these were the thrill of service in Korea, the honour of introducing two
major types of aeroplane to the RAF's operational inventory, the
opportunity to live and work in the very different, very exciting world
of the United States Air Force and the privilege of commanding the
most front line of all RAF bases during the Cold War.*

John Howe

Between Plymouth and his final posting John found himself in South
America. Government Minister Michael Heseltine had been invited to
attend celebrations in Caracas, Venezuela, to mark the 200th anniversary
of the birth of Simon Bolivar on 24 July 1983 but couldn't go. In his place John
was offered the opportunity to attend, with Annabelle, in an official capacity as
representative of Her Majesty's Government. It was to be only a short visit but a
fascinating one. There were some problems logistically: for example John had to
take all his regalia including his ceremonial swords and airlines didn't at all
appreciate such things on their aircraft. They flew from London to Miami to San
Juan (Costa Rica) to Caracas with a Spanish-speaking ADC for company and to
ease their way through airport security with the paraphernalia. In Caracas John
was assigned an officer he still considers to be one of the finest he has ever met.

He was born and raised in Trinidad, had moved to Venezuela, joined the
army, rose in the ranks to Lieutenant Colonel, was detailed to look after
Annabelle and myself, was impeccably turned out, spoke perfect English
and introduced himself as Glenn Braithwaite. He was an absolutely superb
host and aide.

In typical South American style the celebrations constituted parades, march pasts, speeches and displays. King Carlos of Spain was there as were many prime ministers, presidents and senior figures, both civilian and military, from the world over. The Korean delegation saw John's Korean War medals and made a real fuss of him, indeed were very attentive. He had experienced nothing like that before. Before he left John was awarded a further medal by the Venezuelan government to add to his growing collection. This time it was the splendid Order of Francisco de Miranda, an appropriate choice by the Venezuelan government as de Miranda was a Venezuelan revolutionary whose own plan for the independence of the Spanish American colonies failed but who is widely regarded as a forerunner of Bolívar, the man the world had come to honour. Simón José Antonio de la Santísima Trinidad Bolívar y Palacios had been born in Caracas and became leader of several independence movements throughout South America in what are now the countries of Venezuela, Colombia, Ecuador, Peru, Panama and Bolivia where he is revered as a hero.

Annabelle, incidentally, was presented with an engraved gold necklace.

The highlight of the celebrations was an impressive review of the fleet, which included many visiting warships. Annabelle remembers those few hours for a particular reason.

I sat next to the wife of one of the French delegation and it didn't take long for us to get into conversation. She was particularly interested in butterflies and birds and they were there in great numbers, even around our grandstand. We both had our binoculars but instead of watching the ships we had a great time watching the birds!

In August 1983 John returned home to take up his final posting as Commandant General RAF Regiment and Director General of Security RAF, a recently created joint command. The RAF Regiment came into being during the Second World War when it was decided that a new unit specialising in defensive operations to secure airfields from attack was necessary. The RAF Regiment was officially formed on 1 February 1942. Since then its weapons and equipment may have changed but its role has changed little. This is defined nowadays as advising and planning for the defence of RAF airfields and installations against conventional ground and low-level air attack, for measures to mitigate the effects of nuclear, chemical and biological weapons and for training all combatant RAF personnel in these skills. It is in effect the Army in Blue, the RAF's Army.

However, whilst the role has remained constant, command structure has not. As Kingsley Oliver explains in his book *Through Adversity*, throughout the 1970s the Regiment had been steadily reduced in size until in the middle of that decade studies were initiated into a more economical structure for what was left of it. These studies concentrated on the possibilities of a merger of the Regiment and RAF Police. They had always worked well together in emergency situations but there were fundamental differences in their training, organisation and roles. For example, RAF policemen were trained to operate independently in law enforcement and crime prevention whilst RAF Regiment gunners were trained to work in teams. Previous studies had concluded that there was insufficient common ground between the two to justify integration but despite this in 1976 it was decided that a single Security Branch combining both the RAF Regiment and the Provost Branch should be formed. This proposal was outlined in a memo from Air Marshal DG Evans to Air Chief Marshal Sir Denis Smallwood, AOC in C HQ Strike Command at RAF High Wycombe, part of which read:

> From 1st May 1976 a new organisation will be formed encompassing the existing RAF Regiment, Provost Branch and RAF Police Trade Group and will be responsible for all the duties now undertaken by those branches and trades. The Commandant General of this new organisation will have responsibility for all aspects of security policy. This will require the Commandant General to assume an appropriate primary title to reflect his widened responsibilities. His new title will be Director General of Security (RAF). He will retain the secondary title of Commandant General in relation to his specific Regiment responsibilities. A Security Branch will be formed by a merger of the RAF Regiment and the Provost Branch but retaining Regiment and Provost specialisations up to and including the rank of Wing Commander. A Security Trade Group will be formed including all the separate trades now in the Regiment and Police Trade Groups. Each trade will retain its identity. RAF Firemen will be included in this new trade group but will no longer form part of the RAF Regiment and will discard the RAF Regiment shoulder flash.
>
> These changes will not involve any transfer of tasks or posts between the RAF Police and RAF Regiment. For practical purposes there will be no major consequential alterations to the broad current and planned strength of these two elements of what we must henceforth regard as the security arm of the service. I am sure you will now agree that we should take steps to quieten down the speculation and concern that has arisen during the recent months about the future of the Regiment and the Provost/Police. You may therefore wish to arrange for all concerned to be told of the general intentions in regard to the future security organisation ... and that there is no intention of transferring tasks or posts from the RAF Police to the RAF Regiment.

The marriage was predictably not always a happy one. Nobody in the MoD realistically believed that NCOs and airmen of the Regiment and the RAF Police would be interchangeable but, as Air Marshal Evans suggested, it was hoped that there would be opportunities for the cross posting of officers above the rank of Wing Commander. To facilitate this it was decided that in the Regiment ranks of Group Captains and above should remove their shoulder titles to avoid indicating any particular branch allegiance. This proved to be a mistake because not only was it unpopular with the officers concerned, it was hugely resented by the gunners who saw it as a blow to the Regiment in which they were proud to serve. Indeed, such was the dissatisfaction that the Regiment's badge was quickly restored to all the Regiment's officers. However, other aspects of the reorganisation were more welcome. For example, a new trade group was created to contain the separate trades of gunners, firemen and policemen, which were not interchangeable, a move welcomed by the gunners and firemen who would always be suspicious of the police.

Three years later the Royal Auxiliary Air Force Regiment (RAAFR) was resuscitated. Such had been the cutbacks in the 1970s that there were insufficient Regiment squadrons to defend RAF bases in the UK against the same threats that faced RAF bases in Germany. The RAAFR had first been formed immediately post war to resolve a deficiency in UK-based RAF Regiment squadrons but because of training issues their airfield defence role was abandoned in 1955 and the auxiliaries with it. Now they reformed and by 1982 six squadrons had been positioned on stations from St Mawgan to Lossiemouth. In 1985 a seventh was raised at Waddington to man 35-mm Oerlikon anti-aircraft guns, which had been captured on the Falklands.

This then was the Regiment that John came to. As Director General of Security RAF he was responsible to the Vice Chief of the Air Staff. Two Air Commodores were responsible to John. The first was the Director of Security (Ground Defence and Fire Services) whose particular brief was the formulation and implementation of policy for the RAF Regiment in respect of ground and nuclear, biological and chemical defences and low-level air defence other than Bloodhound Surface to Air Missiles. The RAF's fire services, crash and rescue crews, special safety training, psychological operations and the RAF Regiment Training Wing were also under his control. The second was the Provost Marshal who was responsible for the RAF Police and thus for the formulation and implementation of a policy for the prevention and detection of crime, for the security of personnel, for the gathering of information and material against subversion and espionage, sabotage and terrorism and for the maintenance of discipline outside RAF stations.

This is a convenient point at which to define what is often perceived as the disparaging term by which all those in the RAF Regiment are known – Rock Ape. It is commonly assumed that this derives from the Barbary apes on the Rock of Gibraltar but that is not the case. It is the case, however, that when the name was first coined in the 1950s it was meant disparagingly but those in the Regiment saw it differently and they neatly turned the tables by adopting it as a title of distinction. Its origin comes from an incident in the Aden Protectorate when two Regiment officers decided to amuse themselves by going out one evening to shoot some baboons that regularly came to their camp to forage for food and which were locally referred to as Rock Apes. Unwisely heading off in different directions in the gathering darkness, one officer was shot by the other when he saw movement on a rocky outcrop some distance away. A subsequent Board of Inquiry cross examined the firer of the almost fatal shot who told them that his target had 'just looked like a Rock Ape' in the half light. As Kingsley Oliver explains, this statement reverberated through the messes on RAF stations wherever members of the Regiment were serving and it was not long before the term was in general use.

John's main preoccupation during his tenure of the Director General's office was Northern Ireland when the troubles were at their height. Amongst many incidents during the two years he was involved the most significant were the IRA bomb exploding at the Grand Hotel in Brighton during the 1984 Conservative Party conference and the signing of the Anglo-Irish Agreement by Margaret Thatcher and Garret FitzGerald. The Regiment and RAF Police were involved in many aspects of security in Northern Ireland itself and on the mainland in their traditional roles as they were abroad. Their presence in Germany continued whilst the RAF Police assisted in the evacuation of refugees from Lebanon in February 1984 and in January 1985 were involved in famine relief operations in Ethiopia by providing flight line security at Addis Ababa airport. In April 1986 the Regiment and Police were on high alert after the USAF was given permission to use British bases to launch air raids against Libya in retaliation for Colonel Gadaffi's complicity in terrorist activities.

But this was also the time when the previously remote possibility of an ending of the Cold War suddenly became less remote. Mikhail Gorbachev became General Secretary of the Communist Party on 11 March 1985 and immediately set about its reform and that of the economy of the Soviet Union by introducing policies of glasnost (openness), perestroika (restructuring), and uskoreniye (acceleration of economic development). His approach to foreign policy was also very different and for those such as John who had been so directly involved with the realities of the stand off between East and West these were fast becoming very different times as Gorbachev immediately sought to improve relations and trade with the West by reducing Cold War tensions. He established close relationships with Western leaders, including Margaret Thatcher who famously remarked 'I like Mr Gorbachev, we can do business together!' On 8 April 1985 he announced the suspension of the deployment of SS-20 missiles in Europe and later that year he proposed that the Soviets and Americans both cut their nuclear arsenals in half. In January 1986 he announced his proposal for the elimination of intermediate range nuclear weapons in Europe and his strategy for eliminating all nuclear weapons by the year 2000. In fact, on 11 October 1986 Gorbachev and Reagan met in Reykjavík to discuss this and agreed in principle to eliminate all nuclear weapons by 1996, not 2000, which led to the signing of the Intermediate-Range Nuclear Forces Treaty in 1987. It was all happening so very quickly. But by 1987 John had retired and the consequences of rewriting the political and military maps of the mid 1980s he could leave to others to work out.

Whilst the main thrust of the Regiment and RAF Police during these momentous times remained the security and policing of Northern Ireland and other dwindling areas in the world where the United Kingdom maintained a presence, there was a major irritant in England as well. This was the presence at RAF · Greenham Common of the Women's Peace Camp, which had been established in September 1982 to protest at the siting of USAF Tomahawk cruise missiles there. In April 1983 thousands of protestors formed a fourteen-mile human chain from Greenham Common to the Aldermaston nuclear power station and the ordnance factory at Burghfield. A year later the women were evicted by Newbury District Council but within twenty-four hours they had all returned and the camp was re-established. Greenham Common was a continual thorn in the side of John and his successors right through to 2000 when it finally disbanded. The missiles had gone in 1991 but the women were demanding the right to house a memorial on the site. They may have been making a point and living in a democracy they had every right to do so. But all those who were sent down to deal with them and to guard the camp were absolutely shocked by the women's behaviour and the filthy conditions in which they chose to live. In some cases their lack of attention to personal hygiene left even the most hardened of Rock Apes incredulous.

The truth was that John had taken over a Regiment that was in first class condition thanks to the excellent command and direction of his immediate predecessor, AVM Henry Reed-Purvis, who had always had a brilliant reputation within the organisation and whose legacy was a standard of excellence that would be difficult to improve upon. John initially thought that this would be a very hard act to follow but in fact it wasn't because everything ran so very well. As would be expected he was keen to ensure its continued efficient working by instituting a programme of visits and inspections so that he could quickly learn how it operated. Catterick, the home of the Regiment, was central to this (John is remembered there to this day by the fact that a road on camp was named after him on his retirement) but there were other places in the UK and abroad in which John took a keen interest as well. At home he was, for example, at RAF Leeming and RAF Rudloe Manor (which housed the headquarters of the RAF Provost and Security Service) whilst abroad he returned to his former base at Gutersloh. Also abroad he went to the US in November 1983 and the 1606th Air Base Wing at Kirtland Air Force Base. This was for *Peacekeeper Challenge*, a security police competition as the Wing history confirms:

The Air Force Office of Security Police whose headquarters were at Kirtland from 1978–1991 sponsored this event for the third year in a row from 12th to 19th November 1983. The competition was considered worldwide because it included fifteen teams not only from USAF major commands all over the world but also the US Army Military Police School and the British Royal Air Force Regiment. There were eleven different events in the competition with winners for each event but no overall winner. The Military Airlift Command (MAC) team placed first in three events, more than any other team. It won the M60 machine gun and defender challenge events plus the physical fitness competition. MAC also won the Air Force Sergeants Association award for 'the major command team best exemplifying leadership, teamwork and the Air Force warrior spirit.'

Some thirty-seven dignitaries attended the competition and award banquet held at Kirtland's enlisted club on 19 November. Among them were Lt Gen Robert W. Bazley, the Air Force Inspector General, Air Vice Marshal J. F. G. Howe, Commandant General of the Royal Air Force Regiment from the United Kingdom and Brig Gen P. Neal Scheidel, the Air Force Chief of Security Police.

John fully appreciated the fact that the standards of the Regiment and RAF Police were extremely high and within their ranks there were many fine officers, NCOs and men. This was all down to the military training they received and which was to say the least uncompromising, something John approved of thoroughly and which equipped them admirably to deal with Northern Ireland and Greenham Common. These were the sorts of issues that John was very happy to deal with. He was in effect on the front line again and he saw it as a fitting way to end his career. It was full circle for him because these were the regimes he had become used to at the very beginning over forty years before at military college in South Africa.

Air Vice Marshal John Howe retired from the RAF on 30 November 1985 after almost thirty-eight years' service with the RAF and SAAF and after having attended a mandatory resettlement course at Aldershot where he was instructed in the practical matters of DIY, plumbing and welding! He smiles at the recollection of this and reflects that he would far rather have gone to Agricultural College. Since Cecil Gowing's death nine years earlier the farm at Rackheath had increasingly been taking more of his off-duty time at weekends and when on leave. What John particularly enjoyed was the contrast between life on the farm and the services, two very different regimes, which for him complemented each other very nicely.

Her Majesty the Queen is Air-Commodore-in-Chief of the Regiment and when a new Director General takes up his post he traditionally has an audience with her as he does when he leaves that post. On John's retirement he was driven to Buckingham Palace to meet her and during the course of the conversation Her Majesty asked him what his retirement plans were.

I replied by saying 'We have a farm in *the* most beautiful part of Norfolk' but then suddenly remembered Sandringham! So I quickly rectified my mistake with 'Actually Ma'am, it's the *second* most beautiful part of Norfolk' – which amused her!

John's post-nominals tell the story of his career very eloquently. He is entitled to wear the medals of a Companion of the Most Honourable Order of the Bath (CB), awarded when he retired; a Commander of the British Empire (CBE), awarded for the work he did with the Royal Observer Corps; the Air Force Cross (AFC), awarded for his work with 74 Squadron; and the American Distinguished Flying Cross (DFC) and three Air Medals, awarded for his exploits in Korea. In addition he received a Queen's Commendation for Valuable Service in the Air for his work in the Middle East with 43 Squadron. Nor must we forget the Order of Francisco de Miranda.

Actually John didn't completely retire for in November 1988 he joined the Army by being appointed an Honorary Colonel of Airfield Damage Repair (ADR) Squadrons, a component of the 77th Engineer Regiment Royal Engineers. John held the post until November 1993, the Queen having signed his appointment, which was traditionally held by a retired senior RAF officer because of the interface between the Army and RAF it afforded. The *raison d'être* of ADR was, as its name suggests, the repair of cratered runways were RAF bases ever to be attacked. John's duties were not onerous but included visits and inspections both in the UK and RAF Germany when the squadrons were on exercise.

John also took on other responsibilities on retirement, including the vice-presidency of the Norfolk branch of the SSAFA and the presidency of the RAF Association, Eastern Area. He also became for a while the RAF Benevolent Fund representative in Norfolk. But ultimately he had to relinquish all these because of the farm and he found himself unable to give them the time they deserved. Shortly before his retirement from the RAF he was asked if his name could be put forward as the RAF nomination for the Governorship of the Isle of Man. John had never refused anything requested of him throughout his career and once again he was pleased to acknowledge his agreement. As it happened the job went to a Major General who had been born there, which in retrospect was a great relief as all retirement energies were required for Home Farm as Annabelle recalls.

> Another career loomed. We put the farm down to grass, with very little help fenced it and bought a flock of two hundred breeding ewes after both John and I had completed sheep management courses and a sheepdog training course as well. We had up to five hundred sheep on the farm after lambing. Grass management, haymaking and marketing the lambs kept us very busy. We have also had horses at livery. But in 2003, after almost twenty years of hard working but very fulfilling farming, the sheep were sold and the farm handed on to our daughters. Now we are in real retirement and enjoy living in the same farmhouse and watching the farm evolve under new management whilst I keep my hand in the garden.

Home Farm, which John and Annabelle have known for so long, has proved to be the perfect place for relaxing, for welcoming friends and family and for watching aircraft on approach to Norwich Airport and, until recently, to Coltishall. The phone rings regularly as old service friends make contact. Lunches are taken with them, which give both husbands and wives the perfect opportunity to reflect and reminisce, and just occasionally the scrapbooks are brought out and seminal moments in a long and exciting career are reflected upon.

John reflects:

> I suppose I may have made Air Marshal if I had been able to resist the urge to speak my mind and thereby occasionally irritate my seniors. In most respects it did me no harm when I did so and I got the things I wanted doing, done. But the higher up the ladder you climb the more likely you are to ruffle the feathers of those around you – and above you. In short I would have progressed further if it hadn't been for me! But I could turn that round by saying the reason I did get as far as I did was due to the support of Annabelle! She was always the perfect Royal Air Force wife – I knew I was right that day at Sculthorpe when I vowed to marry her!

Looking back over the years it has become very apparent that *Upward and Onward*, 2 Squadron SAAF's motto, has been so appropriate to the career of Air Vice Marshal John Howe.

APPENDIX A

RAF Rank and the Equivalent in the SAAF

RAF	SAAF
Pilot Officer	2nd Lieutenant
Flying Officer	Lieutenant
Flight Lieutenant	Captain
Squadron Leader	Major
Wing Commander	Lieutenant Colonel
Group Captain	Colonel
Air Commodore	Brigadier
Air Vice Marshal	Major General
Air Marshal	General
Marshal	Field Marshal

APPENDIX B

Report by the *Impi Queen*

3MBF/~~201/1/51~~ *So/1/AIR.*   6

3 Motor Boat Flight
P.O. Box 12
Langebaan

7th. May 1951

Officer Commanding
Air Operational School
Langebaanweg.

REPORT ON ACCIDENT TO SPITFIRE NO. 5625.

No. P.8063, WO.11, HUTTON, Ronald Dennis, Coxswain
Duly sworn states:-

1.   On 3rd. ~~April~~ *May* 1951 I was the coxswain aboard A.S.R.L.
(H.S.) R15, carrying out Range Duties off Tooth Rock.

2.   At approximately 1039 hours it was reported to me
by Cpl. Luyt that the pilot of Spitfire 5625 said over the
R.T. " I'm Baling".

3.   As the Spitfire was in sight it was noted that the
engine had stalled, and that the pilot was attempting to
re-start same. His efforts proved to be fruitless and on
descending to an altitude I should estimate to be about 2,000
feet, the pilot headed the aircraft out to sea and bal'ed out.
The time was then 1040 hrs.

4.   The Rescue Launch was started up immediately the
pilot was heard to say " I'm baling". By 1040 hrs the launch
making way towards the then descinding pilot.

5.   A/Cpl. Luyt handed the headphones to me and he
proceeded to fix the Rescue Net in position and get the
necessary gear ready. I requested Aircraft "Spot" (Harvard
Aircraft) to keep me in touch with the pilot who was then
out of sight as he was by that time in the water and not
always visible from the Rescue Launch. Aircraft "Spot"
co-operated and directed me to the pilot. R. 15 arrived on
the scene and the pilot was rescued at 1047 hrs.

6.   A message was sent to "Impi Control" by R.T.
requesting that they arrange to have a doctor standing by
as it was not possible for me to ascertain what internal
injuries had been sustained. It was evident that there were
no external injuries.

7.   The Rescue Launch arrived at Langebaan Jetty at 1120 hrs
and the pilot was put ashore.

8.   A/Cpl Luyt, 2nd. Coxswain, acting Wireless Operator
on this exercise as there is only one Wireless Operator on
strength at this station, and he was aboard the other craft
doing duty on South Range at this time.

2nd Lt J.F.C. Howe.

.... P.8063.
COXSWAIN: A.S.R.L.(H.S.)R15.

The deponent declares and acknowledges that he has

/read

APPENDIX C

F-51D Mustangs Operated by 2 Squadron in Korea

American serial	SAAF serial	Date lost	Cause	Pilot
45-11370	301	2/3/51	Enemy action	Ruiter
45-11390	302	5/9/51	Enemy action	Biden
45-11360	303	7/10/51	Lost on ops	Lombard
45-11399	304	15/2/51	Enemy action	Doveton
45-11429	305	4/3/51	Enemy action	Swemmer
45-11563	306	30/8/51	Enemy action	Blaauw
45-11632	307	7/2/51	Enemy action	Leah
45-11648	308	24/2/52	Enemy action	Taylor
44-63400	309	11/5/51	Enemy action	Kruger
44-73191	310	2/10/51	Enemy action	Muller
44-74168	311	5/12/50	Lost in action	Davis
44-74432	312	22/7/51	Enemy action	Staats
44-74489	313	30/4/51	Enemy action	Gillers
44-74788	314	2/6/51	Lost – cause unknown	Sherwood
44-74814	315	20/3/51	Enemy action	Armstrong
44-74984	316	9/7/51	Enemy action	Pearce
44-73338	317	2/3/51	Enemy action	Badenhorst
45-11419	318 *Shy Talk*	20/4/52	Enemy action	Baransky
45-11475	319	2/2/51	Enemy action	Wilson
45-11704	320	20/3/52	Enemy action	Taylor
45-11541	321	10/3/51	Enemy action	Davis
44-11477	322	11/5/51	Lost on ops	Blaauw
44-15091	323	12/8/51	Enemy action	Muller
44-73084	324	3/12/51	Enemy action	Whitehead
45-11456	325 *Patsy Dawn*		Crashed on delivery to SAAF	
44-74344	326		Returned to USAF	

American serial	SAAF serial	Date lost	Cause	Pilot
44-74174	327	13/11/51	Enemy action	Collins
44-74718	328	1/7/51	Enemy action	Verster
44-73068	329	29/8/51	Enemy action	Green
44-73892	330	15/5/51	Enemy action	Rorke
44-72134	331	23/7/52	Enemy action	Hallet
44-14390	332	1/6/51	Enemy action	McDonald
44-74503	333	9/6/51	Enemy action	Liebenberg
44-84903	334 *Buggs*		Returned to USAF	
44-74511	335	23/7/51	Enemy action	Bekker
44-72983	336	26/7/51	Enemy action	Howe
44-73049	337	22/6/51	Enemy action	Frisby
44-74461	338	23/7/51	Enemy action	duPlooy
44-73688.	339	24/7/51	Enemy action	Snyman
44-74757	340	29/10/51	Enemy action	Joyce
44-74759	341	2/3/51	Enemy action	Norman-Smith
44-74632	342	9/1/51	Enemy action	Grunder
44-74748	343 *Hazel*		Returned to USAF	
44-74750	344	9/8/51	Enemy action	Van den Bos
44-84867	345	24/11/51	Enemy action	Krohn
44-63515	346	29/11/51	Enemy action	Rensburg
44-63822	347	16/8/51	Crashed on landing	
44-84862	348 *Lilian/Sandra*	5/5/52	Lost on ops	Moir
44-72271	349	14/8/51	Enemy action	de Jongh
44-14449	350	1/1/52	Enemy action	Rautenbach
44-64101	351	9/12/51	Enemy action	Montanari
44-74565	352	9/9/51	Enemy action	Barlow
44-84863	353	1/6/52	Lost – cause unknown	Parsonson
44-84553	354	10/3/51	Enemy action	Meiring
44-84771	355	27/9/51	Lost on ops	Earp
44-14297	356	28/11/51	Enemy action	Whitehead
44-74745	357	20/9/51	Enemy action	Severtson
44-84750	358	31/1/52	Enemy action	Earp-Jones
44-74992	359	29/10/51	Lost – cause unknown	Shawe
44-72656	360	14/10/52	Enemy action	Maxiwell

American serial	SAAF serial	Date lost	Cause	Pilot
44-74863	361 *Miss Marinouchi*	22/10/52	Enemy action	Pearson
44-73903	362	29/2/52	Enemy action	Lellyet
44-63853	363	4/11/51	Enemy action	Pappas
44-84887	364		Returned to USAF	
44-84649	365	13/11/51	Enemy action	Grobler
44-84882	366		Returned to USAF?	
44-84902	367		Returned to USAF	
44-84872	368	1/3/52	Enemy action	Newton
44-84761	369 *My Boy*		Returned to USAF	
44-73073	370	20/2/52	Lost on ops	Newton
44-74617	371	15/1/52	Enemy action	Montgomery
45-11707	372	15/1/52	Lost on ops	Casson
44-74021	373	3/6/52	?	Van der Spuy
44-13851	374	17/1/52	Flying Accident	Staats
44-11417	375	2/11/52	Lost on ops	Haburn
44-74619	376	14/1/51	Lost – cause unknown	Vinzyl
44-11551	377		Returned to USAF	
44-73092	378		Returned to USAF	
44-74046	379 *Jean*		Returned to USAF	
44-74165	380	22/8/52	Enemy action	Kotzenberg
45-11411	381		Returned to USAF	
45-11470	382		Returned to USAF	
44-73960	383	25/11/52	Shot down by USMC Skyraider	Moir
45-11607	384		Returned to USAF	
44-73065	385		Returned to USAF	
44-73582	386		Returned to USAF	
44-74786	387		Returned to USAF	
44-73227	388 *Anne*		Returned to USAF	
44-73409	389		Returned to USAF	
45-11646	390		Returned to USAF	
44-72806	391	9/7/52	Enemy action	Scott
44-84890	393		Returned to USAF	
44-74189	393		Returned to USAF	
44-84929	394		Returned to USAF	
45-11738	395		Returned to USAF	

APPENDIX D

Korean Airfield Identification Codes

K1	Pusan West		K29	Sinanju
K2	Taegu		K30	Sinuiju
K3	Pohang		K31	Kilchu
K4	Sachon		K32	Oesichon-dong
K5	Taejon		K33	Hoemun
K6	Pyongtaek		K34	Ch'ongjin
K7	Kwangju		K35	Hoeryong
K8	Kunsan		K36	Kanggye
K9	Pusan East		K37	Taegu West
K10	Chinhae		K38	Wonju
K11	Ulsan		K39	Cheju-Do No 1
K12	Mangun		K40	Cheju-Do No 2
K13	Suwon		K41	Ch'ungju
K14	Kimpo		K42	Andong
K15	Mokp'o		K43	Kyongju
K16	Seoul		K44	Changhowon-Ni
K17	Ongjin		K45	Yoju
K18	Kangnung		K46	Hoengsong
K19	Haeju		K47	Ch'unch'on
K20	Sinmak		K48	Iri
K21	Pyongyang		K49	Seoul East
K22	Onjong-ni		K50	Sokcho-ri
K23	Pyongyang		K51	Inje
K24	Pyongyang East		K52	Yanggu
K25	Wonsan		K53	Paengyong-do
K26	Sondok		K54	Cho-do
K27	Yonpo		K55	Osan-Ni
K28	Hamhung West		K56	not built

APPENDIX E

Rackheath Hall, Home Farm and Airfield

There are two families that dominate the story of Rackheath Hall. The Pettus family built the original hall around 400 years ago. It became the home of Sir Edward Stracey in 1780 when he bought the estate and it is the Straceys who were responsible for the current hall, built in the Italianate style in 1820, standing in what was then a deer park. Sir Edward became a baronet and his descendants inherited the title. The second baronet enlarged his father's building, a process completed by Sir George, the third baronet. At the same time improvements were made to the estate and woodland. An ornate bridge that has long since gone once spanned the lake. And the lake is known to this day as the Dry Lake because when it was excavated the underlying ground proved to be porous and the water continually drains away. The locally renowned Golden Gates, which were erected in 1851 and flanked by gatekeepers' lodges, have also gone (they are in store with a view to perhaps having them restored in the future). The lodges are still there.

Around 1900 a fire broke out at Rackheath Hall. The office of the Chief Constable was contacted (at the time he was also responsible for the fire service) and he inexplicably decided against sending any assistance. The building was saved by the estate workers' own efforts. In 1917 it was occupied by the Army, the 64th Highland Division to be precise, who ran an Officer's School of Instruction there.

In 1919 2,400 acres of the Stracey Estate was sold for £60,000 leaving the Sir Edward of the time with just 600 acres. Home Farm, which lies immediately adjacent to the Rackheath Hall, remained in his possession.

The hall was put up for sale in 1949 after the death of Sir Edward. It was bought by a local manufacturer of potato crisps who carried on that business there as well as dealing in antiques. Once he decided to sell in 1979 it passed through several hands until finally, and thankfully given the vandalism that was by the 1990s being inflicted on the fine old building, it was converted into luxury apartments.

The 467th Bomb Group at Rackheath

The 467th Bomb Group was one of the last to arrive in Norfolk, flying in to Rackheath from 12 March 1944 when the first B-24 Liberator arrived. The Group very quickly made its mark and developed into one of the most efficient and effective units within the Eighth Air Force. The Commanding Officer of the Rackheath Aggies, as they were known, was Colonel Albert J Shower and he remained so throughout the Group's stay in England. Colonel Shower was a stern disciplinarian and a hard taskmaster but he also recognised that recreation was important for morale. To that end the base had a busy social and sports programme, everything from film shows and dances in the Red Cross Club with music provided by Rackheath's own band, The Airliners, to tennis tournaments played on Sir Edmund Stracey's courts at Rackheath Hall.

The 467th was a component of the 96th Combat Bomb Wing along with the 458th at Horsham St Faith and the 466th at Attlebridge. It was ready for operations within a month of its arrival. It continued to fly missions until 25 April 1945 and by then it had flown 212. Some 5,538 sorties had been flown by the 467th's constituent bomb squadrons for the loss of only twenty-nine aircraft in combat. On 13 May they were selected to lead the Victory Flypast over the Eighth Air Force headquarters at High Wycombe. By the middle of June most of the B-24s had left Rackheath and returned home.

Today the old control tower still stands and indeed has been recently restored (as offices) but much of the rest of Rackheath's airfield buildings have been demolished or absorbed into the industrial estate that covers much of the site. The concrete road leading to Rackheath Hall from the Golden Gates was built when the Americans moved in and there are traces of other roads and buildings in woodland and on estate farmland. Some of these were occupied by families who had been bombed out of their homes in Norwich during the war and were only abandoned when housing in Norwich had been rebuilt.

In the village of Rackheath itself a fine memorial to the 467th Bomb Group was erected and was unveiled by Colonel Shower when he was aged eighty.

APPENDIX F

Cecil Gowing

John Howe's father-in-law Cecil Gowing was himself an aviator flying early, fragile bombers in France during the First World War. Then in the inter-war years he became a founder member of the Norfolk and Norwich Aero Club. He and John spent many hours discussing aviation matters and talking about their respective careers and when John was commanding 74 Squadron at Coltishall Cecil was a frequent and well respected guest in the Officers' Mess.

98 Squadron

Before joining the Royal Flying Corps, Private Cecil Gowing served with the Colours in the Norfolk Regiment of Infantry as part of the Army Reserve, enlisting on 26 May 1916. He was discharged on 9 May 1917 on being appointed to a commission. His training with the RFC commenced two days later at Thetford in Norfolk, thirty-five miles from the family home. Flying aircraft such as the DH.6, RE.8 and DH.9, his first (five-minute) solo was flown on 5 June 1917. Disaster struck during his fifth solo on 8 June, however, when he crashed. His log book states: 'Crash caused by another machine fowling [sic] mine from rear in the air.'

Cecil was badly injured and he was hospitalised for six months in Cambridge and then Plymouth. He finally returned to flying under instruction on 20 April 1918 in a BE.2c, going solo again on 16 May. His first firing on a target was on 18 May and on the 21st he practised 'aerial fighting' as he logged it. Amongst his papers is a handwritten 'quick' guide to the use of a bombsight.

> Attain the height from which you intend to release the bomb. Register this in feet on the scale. By means of a stop watch take the time that any auxiliary object in line with your target requires to pass between the sight's lines A & B. Alter your height in feet to this new time in seconds. Immediately target appears at end of sight line A release bomb.

All training flights appear to have been conducted over East Anglia, predominantly over Norfolk and north Suffolk, and it wasn't unknown for him to make aerial visits to the family home. One log book entry reads 'a 90 minute sortie at 5,500 feet including vertical turns over Whitehall Farm, Rackheath'.

On 9 August he joined 98 (Bomber) Squadron at Blangermont in north-western France. The squadron was flying the two-seat de Havilland DH.9A, which managed a stately 114 mph on its 400-hp Liberty engine. Armament was a fixed forward-firing .303-in Vickers and a Lewis gun aft. The bomb load was 450 lb. 98 Squadron had participated in the Battle of Amiens the day before Cecil's arrival. This constituted a concerted attack on the enemy's airfields in the morning and in the evening the railway stations at Peronne and other locations. Selected extracts from his log books for the following three months include the following entries.

19 August 1918 – to bomb Roisel. Attacked by three enemy aircraft.

25 August 1918 – to bomb Valenciennes railway station. Five direct hits. Also hit a factory.

The DH.9s were by now being covered by fighter escorts because of their poor performance.

30 August 1918 – to bomb Valenciennes railway station but engine became u/s and dropped behind the formation. Attacked by eight enemy aircraft. The SE.5 escort brought one down. Tail of my aircraft damaged.

3 September 1918 – to bomb Cambrai railway station. Nine direct hits and two trains set on fire. Archie [anti aircraft fire] hot on return. Radiator damaged and again fell behind formation. Attacked by five enemy aircraft (Fokker biplanes). Sent one down but my machine badly damaged. Engine seized at 8,000 feet. Landed in our lines at Peronne.

15 September 1918 – to Orchies Junction. One direct hit. Archie hot.

16 September 1918 – to Valenciennes. Four direct hits. Attacked by ten enemy aircraft.

24 September 1918 – Water jacket shot by front gun while testing. Landed near Montreuil.

There is a story behind this incident. The exhausts of the DH.9 were so positioned that after every flight the pilot returned with one side of his face blackened by exhaust smoke. A modified exhaust such as that used by the Bristol Fighter was necessary to prevent this and Cecil's fitter duly procured one and fitted it to his DH.9. The next day the squadron got airborne as usual and climbed to the west over the Channel to obtain sufficient height before turning back over the lines. It was the usual practice to warm the front and rear guns. When Cecil fired his front gun there was a frightful noise and the engine stopped. The fitter had located the new extended exhaust so that it passed right in front of the machine-gun and this deflected the first few rounds into the engine! Having in effect shot himself down Cecil survived a forced landing.

27 September 1918 – to Bertry aerodrome. Direct hits. Formation attacked by five enemy aircraft. Archie good. Fuel pipe cut.

1 October 1918 – to Aubroy aerodrome. Hits on officers' quarters.

1 October 1918 (second sortie) – to Aubroy Junction. Direct hit on station and ammo train. 900 casualties.

9 October 1918 – to Mons. Hits on station and town.

14 October 1918 – to Audenarde. Grouping good. Archie hot. Few Huns. Snipe escort.

27 October 1918 – moved to Abscon 'drome.

As the British Army rolled eastwards the squadron moved up behind it. Abscon lay ten miles to the west of Valenciennes. The airmen were billeted in an old nunnery.

1 November 1918 – to Flenu near Mons. Attacked by twenty enemy aircraft. Archie vg.

From this point on until the end of the war only a few reconnaissance flights were flown by 98 Squadron.

11 November 1918 – to the south west of Charleroi and north east of Mons. Dawn recon. Hun still retreating with speed and destruction. Ammo trains on fire. Archie and flaming onions [the name given by allied airmen to the string of balls of light fired by a German five barrel revolving gun].

98 Squadron stayed in France until 20 March 1919, acting mainly as a holding unit for all the disbanding DH.9 squadrons. Returning to England on that date it disbanded on 24 June at Shotwick near Chester.

From OC 98 Squadron, Major PE Sherran, on Cecil Gowing's demobilisation:

2nd Lt CG Gowing joined this unit under my command on August 9th 1918 and has been with it since that date. He has proved to be an exceptionally fine pilot and has taken part in a great number of long distance bombing raids over the enemy lines in which he has always showed exceptional ability and keenness. During the time he has been under my command he has been one of my best officers and on his being demobilised I am very sorry to lose his services. As a pilot he is very steady. In fact from his record with my squadron he has proved to be very capable indeed of handling a machine under any conditions and I have every confidence in recommending him for any position connected with the handling of an aeroplane.

The General Officer Commanding in the Field, Sir John Salmond, had the following to say on Cecil Gowing's demobilisation:

On relinquishing your connection with the Royal Air Force and taking up the duties and responsibilities of civil life again, the General Officer

Commanding Royal Air Force in the Field wishes to place on record his appreciation and thanks for the services you have rendered to your King and Country. He hopes that the experience gained by you in the Great War will be of material benefit to you in your future career and enable you to look back on the years passed in the RAF with pleasure and not to feel that the time so spent has been wasted.

A Personal Account

Cecil Gowing left an incomplete personal account of his early flying days. The document is undated but references in it to the Americans at RAF Lakenheath suggest it was written post 1948 and one to Lord Iveagh suggests roughly 1967. As will be seen, the memoir finishes abruptly at an intriguing point in mid sentence, never to be completed.

When I left school in the middle of WWI I admit that it was sheer cowardice that made me join the Royal Flying Corps for I had three brothers in the infantry who were out in France and when they came home on leave I used to hear their grim tales of the horrors of trench warfare, mud over your ankles, rats and vermin to live with and not getting your clothes off for weeks at a time – not to mention the ghastly method of fighting when they went 'over the top' in an attack to face a hail of bullets and shell fire and a casualty rate of one in three.

So when at an inspection during my early training a General said to us 'my young men, your life, from an early point of view, is going to be one of extreme luxury punctuated by moments of intense fear' this certainly was an apt description of those days with the RFC out in France and when you came back to base you had a clean, dry (sometimes) tent and a camp bed and a Mess Tent to feed in which was the ops room as well in our case! As for the fighting, the man who could handle his 'plane well and use his gun properly stood a good chance of coming out on top except when you ran out of ammo. Or got a stoppage. Then you broke off and dived like hell and headed for home. The Hun invariably had had enough too and did the same (if you were lucky!) otherwise if he wanted to carry on being nasty and continue the chase you were liable to get a request such as our CO once handed out at a debrief. 'Will pilots please be more careful in their anxiety to get more revs not to bend the throttle levers. I have had several complaints from the hangars lately and the Ack Emmas [mechanics] have had to fit new ones in some cases.'

I had my first 'moments of intense fear' before I went out to France when I was training. I was flying a 'Rumpety', which was a Maurice Farman pusher with the engine behind you and the pilot sits out in a nacelle stuck out in the front and quite blind to the rear. It was a beautiful summer morning, just after dawn, and I was feeling monarch of all I surveyed when bang! None of the controls were working and down we went end over end like a leaf. Luckily I was only up about a thousand feet. I undid my belt and thought 'well this is it' but to my surprise I woke up two days later to find myself in hospital. A few days later my CO who came to see me told me that a Russian pilot on his first solo had flown into me from behind and cut my tail off! [This was on 8 June 1917]

Six months later, when the doctors and nurses had patched me up, I went back to the same aerodrome (Thetford). Incidents always followed me around during my flying career, such as my engine cutting at about twenty feet on take off and finishing up with my nose (or rather that of the 'plane) blocking the front door of the Officers' Mess: then there was the little bit of bother with Lord Iveagh who got quite upset when I dropped a live bomb (only a 25 pounder) in front of his mansion [Elvedon Hall to the west of Thetford], accidentally of course. I was on my way to our Live Bomb Target at Lakenheath when one of them came unhooked. It *would* happen over the only house that was on my course! However it was all patched up between myself and his Lordship when I met him about fifty years later! Then on another early morning occasion I was caught poaching and warned off by the Duke of Grafton's gamekeeper [on the Euston Estate to the south of Thetford]. Our base was in the middle of the best game shooting area in the UK and we found it quite easy, in the open spaces, to knock partridges down with the undercarriage, which was held together with a mass of wires, as was the whole plane, and if you flew at full throttle you could just go fast enough to overtake them and knock then down, land quickly and pick them up! This really was good fun.

Having completed thirty hours solo flying I was sent to the School of Aerial Gunnery in the North of England only to be told the very next morning to report to the Air Ministry (London). Not having unpacked I journeyed south again and on reaching the Air Ministry I was told to proceed to France and join 98 Sqdn [on 9 August 1918]: this order of course gave me reason to conclude that I must be in a category above average and in no need of further training. However, my pride was short lived for on my first attempt to fly in formation with the rest of the squadron we went into thick cloud at about 5,000 ft. and I couldn't see the 'plane in front that I had quite closely formated on up till now. That was the last I saw of them!! I should have explained that when I got into the first aeroplane with my instructor he said 'now you see those three instruments in front of you, well they are there only there to give you a rough idea but they are not to be relied on. I want you to get used to flying by instinct – listen to the whistle of the wires for speed, keep your nose on the horizon to fly level and you will feel the wind on the side of your face if you are side slipping.' So I asked him what happened in a cloud and his reply was 'practise it and you'll find out.' I recalled his words and after hearing my wires shriek to a crescendo that was really frightening and the wind blowing first on one side of my face then the other I came out below the cloud nearly upside down! Having regained control again I made another attempt to practise the art of cloud flying and after some very careful manoeuvring and steady climbing, as I thought, in the direction of Belgium where our target, an enemy aerodrome, was I eventually came out into the blazing sunshine on top of the cloudbank. What a wonderful sight, the first time I had seen it, but where are the other boys? Not a plane to be seen so I flew around in circles waiting for them to come out really enjoying the sunshine and flying above what looked like a snowfield until I suddenly remembered to look at the dial on the fuel tank and saw that I had used three quarters of it, so even if I knew how to find my target I wouldn't have enough fuel to get home! And to cut the story short and after landing to refuel at a French aerodrome, miles behind or west of the lines, I reached my base hours after the squadron had returned to find I had been reported Missing. So with trembling knees I reported to the CO. After telling him the story and showing my log book he said that if he wasn't so short of pilots he would have sent me back to finish my training but now I must do it behind the lines on German targets in the air and on the ground!

So the real fun started and I learned more about aerial combat and cloud flying in my first few weeks in France than ever I could have done in England: and not only did I learn these tactics but nearly to my undoing I discovered something called slipstream [on 3 September 1918] when I innocently climbed up from under the formation to take my place at the back, where all new boys had to start, and the machine just wallowed over out of control and went down in a spin and I needed every one of the two thousand feet we were up to to get control again before hitting the tree tops! I just overtook the formation and got into place as they reached the lines. This was nearly an hour later. We had orders to get to 10,000 feet before crossing the lines while we operated in this sector, which was around the river Somme because on the opposite side the famous 'Baron von Richtoven' had his flying circus of coloured Fokker D VIIs and one wanted all the advantage of height when they attacked and I am afraid they accounted for quite a number of our squadron. Although it may sound like a fairy tale I should have been one of their many victims if had not been for a lucky horseshoe which I had fastened to the three-ply at the back of my seat and while over Cambrai at 12,000 ft my engine was hit and very badly damaged, and stopped by Archie (very good shooting at that height!) and I had to glide for home. The Circus was high above us and, waiting for such a winged bird as me, three of them came tumbling down to finish me off and although they registered a great many hits on the poor old bus and one single round through my right foot, the might have been fatal burst which would have gone into the middle of my back was stopped by the rusty horseshoe! Which was bent double, so thanks to it and more than my share of good luck I glided back to land a few yards in front of the British front line of trenches amongst the shell holes and sheer devastation where I had to spend three days with the infantry in the trenches. They were the three most terrifying days of my whole life. I was there for two dawn attacks and the preparation for these, an hour of thunderous heavy gunfire with the counter artillery fire of the enemy, was like all Hell let loose. When zero hour came and the officers blew their whistles and led their troops up the ladders and over the top to the attack and a very thin chance of survival I was left alone with a tremendous admiration for the great courage of our infantry. When they had pushed back the Germans and a vehicle took me back to the squadron I realised how true the General's words were – 'the life of the RFC is one of extreme luxury etc. etc.'

The only distinction that I can claim during my service with the RFC and the RAF – and it was not one to be proud of! – was that I was one of the few, if not the only one, who had shot myself down. It happened like this. I asked our Flight Sergeant if he could do anything to prevent the exhaust fumes from the stub pipes drifting onto your face every time one looked over the edge to the left, not to mention the noise. Yes said the sergeant, I will get you an extension pipe from the Bristol Fighter Squadron next door. They have them fitted on their Rolls Royce engines. So the next day [24 September 1918] came when I proudly taxied out with the rest of the boys to take off on a mission at dawn with my new exhaust pipe. There was no noise. In fact, it was like flying a different aeroplane it was so pleasant! During the tedious climb to 10,000 feet we invariably went over the coast so that the dreaded Circus opposite didn't spot us. This gave us the opportunity too of testing our guns, which fired through the propeller. It was always rather comforting to find that it worked alright as they didn't always behave quite the same at 10,000 feet as they did at ground level! So I stuffed my nose down towards the English Channel and that lovely brrrrr of the Vickers gun rang out – but it was accompanied by bits of steel, clouds of steam and boiling water, which came drifting past, and in a very short time the engine seized up and once again I glided down. Luckily the coast wasn't far away and I started looking for the ideal field for a forced landing, which we were taught to look out for when the engine failed. I was lucky to find one with a road running beside it for the inevitable truck to approach by. However before that a big car came down the road and stopped. In it was a full blown General who asked me if I wanted help. Of course I said yes and he replied 'jump in'. He told me that the little walled town with only one gateway was British Army GHQ only a mile away and his driver would take me to the Officers' Club where I could contact my unit and have some breakfast. We drove on through the gateway where two sentries 'sloped arms' as we passed through, the General's flag still flying on the front of the car. I was dropped at the very smart club where the waitresses, looking very attractive in GHQ colours of red and blue, told me that breakfast was not served until 8 o'clock. So I decided that to kill time I would walk back to my plane where I always carried a hat and a pair of shoes and razor etc. in case of emergency in the locker. But when I reached the gateway guarded by the two sentries I was challenged and asked for the password of the day, which of course I hadn't got, so told them that I had driven through in the General's car. 'General who?' 'Driver's name?' 'Number of the car?' My answer to these questions was 'don't know' and their answer to that was 'consider yourself under close arrest'. I was wearing very scruffy looking flying kit, long sheepskin boots, a coat all stained with castor oil (from flying behind a rotary engine) with no badges of rank showing, so they were quite justified in taking me for a spy! I was marched up the street and duly locked up in a room at HQ where I was kept till midday. When I was taken before a Major who listened to my story and then got on the 'phone to my squadron and verified it, I was released and told to go back to my plane and wait for the truck, which eventually towed my plane back. I was threatened by the CO with a Court Martial for....

And that is where Cecil's own entertaining account of his wartime exploits sadly and abruptly ends.

The Norfolk and Norwich Aero Club

After the war Cecil became very involved with the Norfolk and Norwich Aero Club. During October 1914 the old cavalry training ground on Mousehold Heath to the east of Norwich was taken over by the Royal Flying Corps, an airfield was laid down and a Reserve Aeroplane Squadron moved in. A year later the first aircraft to be built by Boulton and Paul, an FE.2B under licence, made its maiden flight from the new airfield. Whilst they continued to build aircraft under licence, from 1917 Boulton and Paul designed and built their own as well, assembling and testing them at Mousehold. They continued to do so until 1934 when the aircraft side of the business was sold. Meanwhile on 25 February 1927, largely thanks to the vision and commitment of Norwich's Lord Mayor and the Sheriff of Norfolk, the Norfolk and Norwich Aero Club was founded. Cecil was elected to the Committee, which proceeded to raise funds through public subscription. The first aircraft was a de Havilland DH.60 Moth, the second an Avro 548 and the third an Avro Avian. Soon events for the general public started to be organised, such as a 'Great Aerial Display' over Whit weekend in 1929. Celebrities too began to appear. Amy Johnson arrived in her Puss Moth *Jason II* in March 1931 and the following year Captain Barnard's Flying Circus entertained the crowds.

In 1932 Mousehold Heath was chosen as the site for the new Norwich Airport and a year later on 21 June 1933 HRH The Prince of Wales arrived in his personal de Havilland Dragon to perform the opening ceremony. From that point on airliners, air taxis and aerial photography aircraft operated alongside those belonging to the club. In May 1938 and 1939 Empire Air Days were held with an entrance fee of 6d for adults, 3d for children and 1/- to park cars.

As war clouds gathered again the club became an official RAF Volunteer Reserve Training Centre. Its aircraft were impressed into military service and it was itself disbanded. The clubhouse was bombed in October 1940. The airfield itself never became operational during the war but was rather a storage and maintenance unit. The last fixed wing aircraft to use it left in 1946.

Cecil's own flying with the Norfolk and Norwich Aero Club was spasmodic and was subject to the amount of time he could spare from the farm. In fact, his last flight appears to have been in March 1937 and beyond that date he didn't fly again. During the Second World War he kept his feet firmly on the ground as a member of the almost clandestine 202 Battalion of the Home Guard. It was not by choice though. With the outbreak of war he had applied for service again in the RAF in a flying capacity but to his profound disappointment when he attended the necessary medical he was found to be colour blind. His wartime farming activities were of course of immense importance and the productivity of White Hall Farm reflected that. He was not altogether divorced from the RAF though. He was awarded the rank of Flight Lieutenant and commanded 232 Squadron of Sprowston Air Training Corps. Whilst she has no knowledge of her father's activities in the Home Guard (he never talked about those), Annabelle does have fond memories of young lads being paraded up and down outside the windows of the farm on warm summer evenings and undertaking other training tasks on the wide expanses of the farm estate – and indeed Rackheath estate. There is little doubt that the proximity of the Americans on the airfield there was a lure to the youngsters as well as the adults. Cecil and his family forged enduring friendships, which lasted until long after the war and their return to the USA, friendships that endure to this day.

APPENDIX G

Bentley Priory

Built in 1766 on the site of a twelfth century Augustinian priory for James Duberly, who had an evidently lucrative contract to supply the army with clothing, Bentley Priory was extended twenty years later by the architect Sir John Soane for the First Marquis of Abercorn, John Hamilton. It was during Hamilton's possession that Bentley Priory became a magnet for political and literary celebrities such as Pitt, Wellington and Wordsworth. Amongst others who also frequented its salon were Lord Nelson and Lady Hamilton with her husband Sir William and, later on, Sir Walter Scott.

Hamiltons lived at Bentley Priory until 1846 when the Dowager Queen Adelaide, widow of King William IV, leased it until her death in 1849. In 1863 the Hamilton family sold the estate to Sir John Kelk who spent great sums of money on further improvements, including the building of the famous clock tower. In 1882 the Priory was converted into a private residential hotel but this was not a success and in 1908 it became a girls' school until in 1922 the school closed and the property stood empty for four years.

In 1926 the Priory estate was split up and one lot comprising Bentley Priory itself and some forty acres of land was sold to the Air Ministry for £25,000. Flying Training Command was the first incumbent but on its departure to Shropshire in 1936 Fighter Command under its first Air Officer Commanding, Air Marshal Sir Hugh Dowding, moved from Uxbridge and established its headquarters there. Bentley Priory was pivotal to the success of the Battle of Britain. Staff working on a new command and control system that was developed to integrate radar with the tactical control of fighter aircraft were housed here and the Operations and Filter Rooms, essential for the control of air assets, were set up. Bentley Priory went on to control fifty-two operational squadrons during the Battle. Later in the war it was utilised for the planning of the D-Day landings. The huge Battle of Britain operations room was still in use during John's posting, albeit having been extensively updated and upgraded, and exercises were regularly held to test Fighter Command's proficiency. But on 30 April 1968 Fighter Command lost its individual identity when it was amalgamated with other operational commands to form Strike Command.

In 1974 the Department of the Environment completed a thorough investigation into the state of the buildings and concluded that because of the spread of dry-rot it would have to be closed. A campaign was almost immediately launched to save the Priory. A decision was made in its favour and work started on is restoration and refurbishment in 1979. In June of that year a potentially disastrous fire broke out but insurance monies enabled the restoration to continue.

In 1995 11 and 18 Groups amalgamated and Bentley Priory became Group Headquarters but from 1 April 2000 it ceased to operate as such. Latterly Bentley Priory became home to a number of independent units including the Defence Aviation Safety Centre, RAF Ceremonial, the Directorate of Communications and Information Systems and Air Historical Branch. Within the building is the Officers' Mess and the office of Air Chief Marshal Sir Hugh Dowding preserved with its original furniture. Many historic Battle of Britain artefacts are kept at Bentley Priory, which is also notable for the number of royal portraits hanging on its walls.

Sadly, as this is written in 2008 there is no future operational use for Bentley Priory with all its incumbent units imminently relocating to RAF Northolt. When this happens the buildings will be handed over to Defence Estates and the site will be redeveloped. Plans, however, include a museum in the main rooms of the house, which will be open to the public and will record and interpret the history of Bentley Priory and in particular its Battle of Britain and Cold War heritage. The site of the Cold War bunker will also be available for public access. The latest plans for the site overall include the building of luxury flats in the grade II* listed mansion.

RAF Staff College Bracknell

No. 54 Staff Course, 1965

Syllabus

January

Overview of topics and activities for the month

Opening address by the Commandant, Air Vice Marshal DJP Lee, followed by the opening phase of the course, which included basic English, service writing, researching, graphs and charts and the use of files and papers.

Lectures

The English Language (Senior Tutor of Humanities from RAF College Cranwell). Clear Thinking (Housemaster from Eton College). Public Speaking (Staff Member of the Guildhall School of Music and Drama). Defence Reorganisation (AVM CN Foxley Norris). The Uses and Misuses of Graphs and Charts (RAF Technical College Henlow). Defence Reorganisation and the Air Ministry (Assistant Under Secretary of State of the Air Ministry).

February

Overview of topics and activities for the month

The economy of Britain, strategy and principles of war, appreciation writing and operations orders.

Lectures

International Payments: The Current Situation (Bank of England). The Impact of Defence on the Nation's Resources (HM Treasury). Industry and Management (Federation of British Industries). Trades Unions and Industrial Relations (The Trades Union Congress). The Principles of War (Air Cdre Carter). Manpower in the RAF (AVM Sir John Weston).

March

Overview of topics and activities for the month
Operations orders, appreciations, the aircraft industry, communism, strategy and atomic energy. Visits to BAC Weybridge and 7 MU at Quedgeley. An address by AOC in C Flying Training Command AM Sir Augustus Walker and AOC in C Signals Command AVM TUC Shirly.

Lectures
The Theory of Communism. Modern Communist Practice and the Communist Threat to Internal Security. Economy of the USSR. Soviet Foreign Policy. Communications Security. Nuclear Weapons. Psychological Warfare. The Formulation of Defence Policy and British Strategy (Air Vice Marshal DJP Lee).

April

Overview of topics and activities for the month
Africa, deterrence, the Far East.

Lectures
An African Viewpoint (Nigerian High Commission). African Problems (Foreign Office). British Policy in Africa (Foreign Office). South Africa (South African Ambassador). The Nuclear Deterrent (Marshal of the RAF Sir Dermot Boyle). Military Support in the Far East (Group Captain Ops Far East Air Force). Ethics of the Nuclear Deterrent. An Australian View of the Far East (Head of the Australian Joint Services Staff London). US Policy in the Far East (The American Embassy). British Policy in the Far East (Foreign Office).

May

Overview of topics and activities for the month
The Middle East, the British Army, land and air warfare, air transport operations. Visits to the Joint Warfare Establishment Old Sarum and the Royal Navy Staff College Greenwich. An address by AOC in C Transport Command AM Sir Kenneth Cross.

Lectures
An Arabian View of the Middle East (Iraqi Embassy Press Attaché). Israeli View of the Middle East (Israeli Ambassador). UK Military Support in the Middle East. US Policy in the Middle East (US Embassy). British Policy in the Middle East (Foreign Office). The Army in British Strategy (Army Staff College Camberley). Helicopter Operations (HQ Transport Command). Conventional Weapons in Counter Air Operations (RAF College of Air Warfare Manby).

June

Overview of topics and activities for the month
Administrative planning, the British Army, the Royal Navy, maritime operations.

Visits to Royal Naval establishments at Portsmouth and Yeovilton; The Joint Anti Submarine School, Londonderry; RAF Ballykelly; The School of Infantry, Warminster; The Royal Armoured Corps Centre Bovingdon; The School of Artillery Larkhill. An address by AOC in C Maintenance Command AM Sir Norman Coslett.

Lectures
The Science of Logistics. Technical Problems at Air Force Department Level. Organisation of the Royal Navy. The Fleet Air Arm (Vice Admiral Sir Richard Smeeton). Submarine Command and Operations (Rear Admiral HR Law). The Army of Tomorrow (Lt Gen Sir John Hackett).

July

Overview of topics and activities for the month
Maritime operations, Western Europe.

Lectures
Coastal Command (AM Sir Anthony Selway). British Amphibious Capability. The Role of the Royal Navy (Vice Admiral Sir John Frewen). The Causes of War. The Future Relations between Britain and Europe (Foreign Editor of *The Sunday Times*). An Introduction to NATO (Lord Coleridge). The Organisation, Role and Functions of SHAPE. British Policy in Europe (Foreign Office).

August

Summer break. Visits to units of the Allied Air Forces Central Europe and French Air Force at Creil to give an insight into the organisation and administration of NATO forces and an idea of the problems facing the commanders of those forces.

September

Overview of topics and activities for the month
Air defence and offensive air operations. Presentation by the Ministry of Defence (Air). Addresses by AOC in C Fighter Command, Sir Douglas Morris and AOC in C Bomber Command AM Sir John Grandy. Visits to the SBAC Show, Farnborough; Fylingdales (to see the BMEWS Forward Radar Site); Leconfield (to see the organisation and operation of a fighter airfield): and Patrington to see a Master Radar Station

Lectures
Work Study (Air Cdr ARD MacDonnell). Fighter Command (Group Captain DCH Simmonds). Civil Defence. Air Launched Missiles (Bomber Command). The RAF Benevolent Fund. The Theory of Ballistic Missiles. Operational Aspects of Ballistic Missiles (RAF College of Air Warfare Manby).

October

Overview of topics and activities for the month
Offensive air operations, the United States Air Force, the Royal Canadian Air Force, operations orders. Teams from the USAF (Maxwell AFB Staff College) and RCAF (Staff College Toronto), USAF officers serving with the 3rd and 17th Air Forces and RCAF officers serving in Canada and Europe assembled at Bracknell to take part in joint studies. Visits to the Bomber Command stations at Coningsby, Honington, Marham, Scampton, Waddington, Wittering; to the USAF Strategic Air Command base at Brize Norton; and to the Meteorological Office at Bracknell.

Lectures
The Organisation of the USAF. The Press and Public Relations. Suez – A Study in Air Operations.

Lectures presented at the Army Staff College, Camberley
The Commonwealth (the Duke of Devonshire, Minister of State). Commonwealth Problems (Patrick Kealty, *The Guardian*).

November

Overview of topics and activities for the month
Joint service studies and research and development. Presentation on Aerospace by members of the RAF College of Air Warfare; and on the British Army by the Army Staff College, Camberley. Visits to RAE Farnborough and the Institute of Aviation Medicine

Lectures
The Organisation of Science in Support of the Services. Operational Requirements (AM Sir Christopher Hartley). Amphibious Warfare. The 1964 Trade Structures (Deputy Director of Manning (RAF)).

Addresses at the Army Staff College, Camberley
The Secretary of State for Defence, Denis Healey. Admiral of the Fleet, Earl Mountbatten of Burma, Chief of the Defence Staff. Lieutenant Colonel RN Jones, United States Marine Corps.

December

No. 54 Staff Course dispersed on 12 December with an address by the Commandant; by the Chaplain in Chief, the Venerable FW Cocks; by the Air Member for Supply and Organisation, AM Sir John Davis; by the Air Secretary, ACM Sir William MacDonald; by the Air Member for Personnel, ACM Sir Walter Cheshire; and by the Chief of the Air Staff, ACM Sir Charles Elworthy.

APPENDIX I

Airfields Visited by Air Flying Lockheed T-33s from Peterson Field

August 1965 – June 1967

AAB = Army Air Base
AFB = Air Force Base
NAS = Naval Air Station
RCAF = Royal Canadian Air Force

Amarillo AFB	Hamilton AFB	Offutt AFB
Bagotville (RCAF Station)	Hill AFB	Olathe NAS
Barksdale AFB	Holloman AFB	Olmstead AFB
Biggs AFB	Homestead AFB	Perrin AFB
Brookley AFB	Kelly AFB	Portland International Airport
Cannon AFB	K I Sawyer AFB	Randolph AFB
Carswell AFB	Kingsley Field AFB	Reese AFB
Castle AFB	Kirtland AFB	Richard Gebauer AFB
Charleston AFB	Langley AFB	Robbins AFB
Davis Monthan AFB	Little Rock AFB	Scott AFB
Des Moines Municipal Airport	Loring AFB	Selfridge AFB
Detroit Metropolitan Airport	Luke AFB	Stewart AFB
Dobbins AFB	MacDill AFB	Shaw AFB
Duluth AFB	Malmstrom AFB	Sheppard AFB
Eglin AFB	Maxwell AFB	Tinker AFB
England AFB	McChord AFB	Tucson International Airport
Fort Lauderdale International Airport	McGuire AFB	Truax Field AAB
	McLelland AFB	Tyndall AFB
Fresno Airport	Memphis NAS	Walker AFB
George AFB	Minot AFB	Webb AFB
Glasgow AFB	Mountain Home AFB	Williams AFB
Goose Bay (Canada)	Nellis AFB	Wright Patterson AFB
Grand Forks AFB	North Island NAS	

APPENDIX J

Royal College of Defence Studies

Far East Tour

D uring September and October 1975 overseas tours took place. Students had a choice of North America, Europe, the Mediterranean and the Middle East, Japan and the Far East, South East Asia and Australia, South West Asia or Africa. John chose South East Asia and Australia. The tour was led by Rear Admiral Dick Clayton. Ten course members participated, each being given a special responsibility. John's was protocol, a duty he shared with Brigadier General Kiessling. A brief synopsis of the thirty-five day tour reads as follows:

14 September 1975 – Left Brize Norton by RAF VC10. Landed at Tengah (Singapore) after refuelling stops at Akrotiri and Gan. From Singapore flew to Sydney and then on to Christchurch in New Zealand. Here the course toured local farms and were briefed on local government, tourism and the development of South Island. They visited the RNZAF base at Wigram before departing for Wellington where they were briefed at the Ministry of Defence on New Zealand's defence policy, the economy and national development. Next stop was Taupo where the Wairakei Geothermal Power Project was visited as was the Forest Research Institute at Rotorua and a thermal reserve at Whakare Warewa. Here a briefing was given on 'The Maori in an Urban Community'. Hamilton came next where they were shown a freezing works. A tour of the RNZAF base at Te Rapa was organised after which the party departed for Auckland for two briefings on the problems of industrial production for a limited market and problems associated with the policing of a multi racial city. That concluded the New Zealand sector of the tour

Arriving at Sydney the party were briefed at the High Commission before visiting the Opera House and taking a harbour tour, which included lunch on board HMAS *Watson*. Ansett then flew the visitors to Canberra and the Tidbinbilla Deep Tracking Station. The following day comprehensive briefings were given on Australian foreign policy, defence policy, defence capability, the economy and

275

trade relations followed by a seminar on 'Current Problems in Australian Defence Policy'. Moving on to Hobart (Tasmania) a state briefing was given prior to a tour of the city after which the RAAF flew the party to Scotts Peak for a tour of the hydro works and the Mount Lyell Mining and Railway Company. Adelaide was next on the itinerary with a visit to the Barossa Valley Winery before moving north to Alice Springs, Ayres Rock and the Hermansburgh Mission Aboriginal Settlement. Back in Adelaide a visit to Trades Hall included a briefing by union leaders. The party then headed west to Perth and Parliament House for state briefings before an audience with the British Consulate General followed by a visit to RAAF Pearce.

Perth marked the end of the Australian sector of the tour and take-off the next morning was for Indonesia and Bali for a couple of days' R&R at the Bali Beach Hotel. Back in Jakarta the party was briefed at the National Defence College on Indonesian domestic and foreign policy, the country's economic problems and its defence capability. This was followed by an audience with the Governor of Jakarta prior to departure for Medan in Sumatra for a day's rest prior to the long flight home on 17 October via Tengah, Gan and Akrotiri.

Royal College of Defence Studies – Dissertation

How Far are the Lessons of the Use of Air Power in the Vietnam War Applicable to the Central Front of NATO?

by Group Captain JFG Howe AFC RAF
July 1975

Introduction

Since 1945, of the NATO nations only the United States of America has had experience in the application of modern air power over an extended period. The war in Vietnam brought the USA into conflict with weapon systems extensively employed by the Warsaw Pact (WP) countries. If NATO's effectiveness in deterring or waging war against the WP is to be improved it is worth examining the conflict in Vietnam to determine what lessons can be learnt and applied, particularly concerning the use of air power. In the light of the recent British defence review which commits us predominantly to Central Europe, the applicability of the lessons will be examined with particular reference to the Central Front. The war in Vietnam saw almost all the traditional uses of air power. To highlight the lessons, I will outline the history of the American involvement and, in more detail, describe the air war in North Vietnam (NVN) which may be considered as the strategic level of operations and that in South Vietnam (SVN) which may be considered tactical.

The Gradual Involvement

The origins of the war in Vietnam can be traced back to the mid-1940s when the communist forces under Ho Chi Minh began fighting the French for the independence of Vietnam which had been restored to French rule at the end of World War II. After the defeat of the French at Dien Bien Phu in 1954 Vietnam was divided at the 17th parallel by the Treaty of Geneva. The partition was to be ended after free elections had decided on the type of government the people wanted for a unified state. The provision was so worded that the votes of the two parts of Vietnam were to be combined. This meant that the votes of the numerically superior communist North would outweigh those of the republican South by about two million. The USA backed SVN in its refusal to hold the elections on those terms and used the case of East and West Germany as a precedent for doing so. There followed a referendum in the South which clearly established a South Vietnamese desire for a separate democratic republic. At the same time it indicated to the North that they had no hope of taking over the South politically and they concluded that the use of force was the only way open to them. Thus the classic stages of insurgency warfare began with the Viet Cong (VC) guerrillas attempting to subvert the South with the active assistance of NVN. This struggle began in 1955 and culminated twenty years later in total victory for the North. It was during the last ten years of the war that the USA became actively involved in combat and it is from this period that the lessons are drawn.

From the early 1960s the USA had been increasing military and economic aid to SVN. In 1964, when the position had deteriorated enough to cause concern in Washington, the President decided, against the old American tenet never to become involved in a land war in Asia, to increase substantially the number of American military and civilian advisers. Later in 1964, after the Gulf of Tonkin incident, the President ordered the bombing of four patrol boat bases and an oil depot in NVN. The aim was to teach the leaders of NVN a lesson. It failed and the hostilities in SVN continued to escalate. After attacks by the VC on American bases early in 1965 the President authorised the air war against NVN. By summer 1965 a campaign of sustained almost daily air strikes was well under way both in North and South Vietnam and most of the important bombing policy issues had already been settled.

The Air War Against North Vietnam
The President and Secretary for Defence apparently accepted the military view that a limited, gradual programme would exert less pressure on NVN than a programme of heavy bombing attacks from the outset and that restraint was unlikely to get NVN to scale down or stop the insurgency or enter reasonable negotiations. They felt, however, that all-out bombing would pose far greater risks of widening the war and would signify intentions out of proportion to the limited objectives of the USA in Southeast Asia which were, broadly, to prevent North from conquering South Vietnam. They believed it would carry unacceptable political penalties and prevent the achievement of American goals at a relatively low level of violence. They decided, accordingly, to proceed with the bombing in a slow, steady, deliberate manner beginning with a few infiltration associated targets in southern NVN and gradually moving northward with progressively more severe attacks on a wide variety of targets. Populated areas were studiously avoided. Each group of targets and in many instances individual targets had to be

passed for approval through a chain of command which included the Defence Secretary, the Foreign Secretary and the President himself who defined the objectives of the air campaign:

- To back American combat personnel and allies by demonstrating that the aggressor could not attack SVN from the security of a sanctuary.
- To exact a penalty from NVN for her violations of the 1954 and 1962 Geneva Accords.
- To limit the flow or substantially increase the cost of infiltrating men and material from NVN.

Large important target systems, the destruction of which it was later shown could have had immediate effects on NVN's capacity and will to wage war, were not attacked. Haiphong harbour continued to be used to import the resources NVN needed. The hydro-electric industry and POL storage and distribution centres were untouched. On the other hand jungle tracks and the Ho Chi Minh trail received special attention with predictable results. The area was far too large, well covered and mountainous and the targets too fleeting for any results to be cost effective. The supplies of men and materials were not prevented from reaching SVN although the flow was undoubtedly reduced. By adopting this strategy the physical and psychological impact of the use of air power was forfeited by the USA and the people of NVN slowly became accustomed to the air war and like the British in World War II found they could take it.

In addition two other major disadvantages emerged. In order to achieve the required reductions in the flow of supplies to SVN it was calculated that a given tonnage of bombs was required to be dropped each month. Considering the targets and the vast area involved this tonnage was necessarily huge and a very large number of aircraft had to be deployed to Indo-China from the USA. There was then no satisfactory command and control system and the only way some semblance of control could be maintained at the highest level was to impose a programme for attacks similar to a railway timetable. Consequently the timings and routes into and out of NVN became established and this, coupled with the flight refuelling over the Gulf of Tonkin, deprived the aircrew of tactical surprise. The irresolute strategy also gave NVN time to build up a formidable ground-based air defence system against which only American technical ingenuity eventually enabled their aircraft to survive. The Wild Weasel flak suppression system and tactics were evolved to reduce the loss rate. In this, electronic jamming and anti-radar missiles were used by a small number of aircraft operating ahead of the main attacking force to confuse and wherever possible to destroy the radar and the Soviet surface to air missiles (SAMs) with which the NVN was equipped. In air to air combat, electronic countermeasures (ECM) and tactics were developed to exploit the latest American fire control systems and the losses were two to one in favour of the USA. (In Korea they had been twelve to one.) High speed, high manoeuvrability, integral guns, agile air-to-air missiles and an ECM fit became recognised as essential requirements for survival in air combat.

By early 1968 sufficient men and material had been infiltrated into SVN for the VC and NVN army to launch what became known as the Tet Offensive in an effort to defeat the USA and her allies in the field. The approaches and environs of nearly every provincial capital in SVN were attacked. Air power saved the day and how it did will be described in the next section. Although the Tet Offensive failed and the bombing of NVN was stopped when they agreed to negotiate, it did show that American strategy and use of air power had also failed and that new policies had to be evolved. Thus 'Vietnamisation' was born, the aim of which was the ultimate withdrawal of all allied forces once SVN had shown it could take care of itself.

Negotiations for a peaceful settlement to the war continued sporadically for about the next four years. The USA had offered the withdrawal of all American and allied forces over an agreed period, the release of prisoners of war on both sides and a ceasefire 'in place' with no time limit on it. This latter clause encouraged the NVN army to get 'in place' and could therefore be considered one of the contributory causes of the 1972 invasion which resulted in the reopening of the bombing campaign against NVN.

On 30 March 1972 14 NVN divisions invaded SVN across the demilitarised zone (DMZ) into the central highlands towards Kontum and in Binh Long province towards An Loc. The collapse of SVN seemed imminent. From the preparations made for air defence in NVN it was clear they expected the bombing to be resumed and that they thought they would be able to take it as they had in the mid-1960s. However, they did not know of the development by the USA of the new laser guided bombs with which their aircraft were now equipped. These were remarkable in their accuracy. For example, nearly 1,000 sorties had been flown against Thanh Hoa bridge south of Hanoi and it had not been hit. Even electro-optical weapons had been unsuccessful due mainly to the limitations imposed by weather and electro-magnetic interference from the ECM upon which the aircraft relied so heavily for their survival. This time it was knocked out in the first attack by four Phantoms. It was now possible for the American aircraft to attack a wide range of targets near and even in populated areas without causing widespread damage to civilian property and life. The political risk of widening the war had been drastically reduced by this technological breakthrough. Road and rail communications from China and between Hanoi and the northern front, warehouses, power stations, factories, repair facilities, radio stations, supply dumps and hydro-electric power stations were attacked with accuracy hitherto unknown and with few losses. An additional effect was to stretch to the limit the manpower resources NVN required to maintain the impetus of the invasion in the South.

In May the port of Haiphong was mined. It was clear that this would have no immediate effect on the battles which were raging in SVN but would threaten the food supplies from early 1973. However, the main purpose was to warn the USSR that if they continued to provide NVN with superior offensive weapons they must expect a response which might not exclude them. The tactic was successful: communist ships in Haiphong made no attempt to leave and those en route were diverted. By September NVN decided to return to the negotiating table and the bombing of NVN was stopped. Resolute, accurate, hard-hitting air attacks had won an important political battle for the USA.

The negotiations, however, turned out to be fruitless because they were being used by NVN only for political point scoring and to gain time to recover and regroup her forces. This became clear when mounting evidence showed that NVN was about to launch another major offensive and on 18th December the bombing of NVN was resumed. This time the full might of American air power in Southeast Asia, including B-52s for the first time, was used in an integrated, co-ordinated operation. The strategic bombers, fighter bombers, ECM and chaff dispensing aircraft, defence suppression aircraft, fighter escorts, target markers, reconnaissance and tanker aircraft were all concentrated in time and space during the attacks. As a result in 12 days of intensive operations rail traffic in the Hanoi-Haiphong area was almost totally suspended and repair crews eventually made no effort to restore even token traffic. Several hundred warehouses and storage dumps were virtually destroyed. Three major hydro-electric power plants were reduced to less than a quarter of their normal output causing a complete blackout of all but the critical functions of government and defence. The capability of NVN to wage war in the South had been seriously degraded. This was not accomplished without losses but the concentration of the integrated air forces had saturated and eventually reduced to impotency the NVN air defences. Within a very short time NVN returned to the negotiating table and a ceasefire came into effect on 28th January 1973. Since then, however, the American and allied forces have withdrawn from Indo-China and NVN, after mounting a new offensive early in 1975, has finally conquered SVN who had been deprived of the air power on which they had come to rely so heavily.

The Air War In South Vietnam

The air operations in SVN were tactical by nature and included all the traditional and some new uses of air power. Perhaps the most interesting were the various roles allotted to helicopters. They were used extensively to enable large numbers of infantry soldiers to be deployed rapidly over comparatively long distances over country which had virtually no land lines of communication. Landing troops directly into combat is a hazardous operation when there is no direct fire support and the success of seek and destroy operations depended to a great extent on tactical surprise. Thus a preparatory fire suppression programme would have been nugatory. Armed helicopters however could provide this support. At first troop-lift helicopters were equipped with machine guns to act as escorts for troop-lift formations. The first real gunship was the Huey UH-1A which was first used in 1962 to escort the CH-21 and proved an immediate success. As the war progressed, larger numbers of gunships appeared on the battlefield and were used for preparatory suppressive fire around landing zones when beyond artillery range and eventually for close support. Inevitably electronic equipment was added to increase the effectiveness of weapons and operations in poor visibility and at night. Larger guns and rockets enabled them to perform well against trucks and tanks. However, in contested air space the helicopter proved very vulnerable and in SVN many hundreds were shot down.

The traditional uses of tactical air power in the close support, interdiction and logistic support roles were probably best illustrated during two set piece battles of remarkable similarity – Khe Sanh during the Tet Offensive in 1968 and An Loc during the Easter invasion of 1972. For brevity, the battle of An Loc only is examined here.

At An Loc the enemy had surrounded the garrison and were pouring in more than 1,000 artillery, mortar and rocket rounds a day. Enemy anti-aircraft fire was intensive and accurate and included the latest Soviet SAM, SA-7. Despite these odds and the pounding of the city, the SVN army held on and in doing so compelled the NVN army to launch set piece armoured attacks to try to capture this important provincial capital. Because the defence perimeter was clearly defined it was possible for the defenders to work out the best lines for the enemy to attack and thus anticipate their likely assembly areas. In helping to break these attacks hundreds of sorties were flown and even B-52s were used effectively. They could hit assembly areas accurately from 30,000 feet by day, night and in all weather. This combination of fighter and strategic bomber fire power meant that enemy formations were caught time and again in the open and destroyed before they could attack. Once again it was shown that concentrated, conventional close air support and interdiction operations against massed target arrays can reduce an initially overwhelming threat to a level which ground forces can tolerate. However, these operations can only be really effective when air superiority is enjoyed. Even with this fire power however, it is doubtful if the An Loc defenders could have held out without intensive supply by air drop. Two new very accurate systems were used. The first relied on a prepositioned team with its radar and computer equipment to control the drop from the ground. The second required the aircrew to calculate the dropping point by using an offset aiming point. High velocity parachutes were used to improve accuracy as were new packing techniques to absorb the shock when the pallets hit the ground. These air supply operations could be carried out in the face of some ground based anti-aircraft defences because the drops were made from heights above those at which defences were effective. Had there been enemy SAM or fighter opposition the results might well have been different.

Command and Control
The effectiveness of air power in the north and south depended critically on how the air forces operated and it became clear early on that it was essential to establish some form of command and control appropriate to the operational environment. To quote General George J Eade USAF: 'the USA forces developed a lash-up system in Southeast Asia consisting of radio-relay aircraft, airborne command posts, EC-121s and offshore shipboard systems. All these elements were limited in terms of capability and we tied them together as best we could. In effect we had all the elements of an AWACS but it was in bits and pieces and quite limited. As a result we had a massive command and control problem.' However, over the years a command and control system was evolved which enabled the inherent flexibility of air power to be exploited as far as possible under the operating conditions in Vietnam. Nevertheless the routine nature of the operations and attendant lack of surprise continued to give the enemy air defences an initiative they could and should have been denied.

The Major Lessons and their Application
The factors which, historically, have most influence on the use of air power once it has been decided to use force are the national aims and strategy of the countries involved and any political constraints they impose, the existence and nature of any alliance and the combat environment.

The aims of the USA were quite clearly neither to win nor lose and that this should be seen to be so. It followed therefore that the political constraints imposed upon the American air operations were severe when one compares what they achieved with what they could have achieved. The USA had the capability to supply air power rapidly and in sufficient strength to have reduced to ineffectiveness in a very short time the ability of NVN to wage war in the south. The two major air offensives in the north in April and December 1972 demonstrate this. However, the restrictions imposed by the President and his political advisors were such that the government of NVN doubted the American resolve to support SVN and a long war became inevitable. As a result NVN was given time to study, adjust to and then counteract American strategy, tactics and weapons. They had time to deploy and put to good use a world wide propaganda machine which eventually turned American public opinion against their government's involvement in Vietnam. They saw on television the battles at first hand and saw that many thousands of casualties were being suffered for no apparent reason. They were not winning and they were not losing which made the continuous loss of life incomprehensible – there was no apparent purpose. The bombing of NVN was not helping to achieve what they thought should be the aim – win or disengage. It had by now of course become impossible for America to win or disengage under the existing leadership and the Tet Offensive, though a failure, brought this home to the President. He therefore announced his decision not to stand for re-election. From all these facts emerges, in my view, the most important lesson for NATO. If we have to fight in Central Europe we must, right from the outset, fight to win. Our determination to do so must not be suspect. The strategy of flexible response must not be allowed to degenerate into a self-defeating gradualism. This does not mean that there should be no political constraints imposed on military commanders. It does mean that the political leaders of NATO must realise that if force limitations which are implied by the very term flexible response are accompanied by extensive political constraints NATO will lose.

The Alliance in the Indo-China war was initially between SVN and the USA with Thailand as a sleeping partner. Later Australia and South Korea participated, but in all matters the USA dominated. The predominance of American equipment was obvious. American procedures were used and in general the combat operations were carried out in accordance with American doctrine. The air war against NVN was almost exclusive to the USA and as a result was controlled from Washington. Thus there was a very high level of standardisation within the air forces of the Alliance. On the other hand NATO consists of 17 nations, each claiming an equal voice and the result is very little standardisation in a situation where it is at least as, if not more, important than it was in Indo-China. This is not to say that a single standard of, say, tactical procedures, doctrines, weapons systems and electronic warfare equipment would be ideal because a multiplicity of each greatly increases the operational problems for the WP. However, there must be a balance between having on the one hand a multiplicity of options which though operationally desirable in some respects are extremely costly and reduce the flexibility of air power – and on the other having totally standardised systems which are in an alliance extremely flexible and cost effective but have operational and often national economic disadvantages. NATO leaders are currently striving to achieve this balance through collaborative research, development and procurement ventures such as MRCA, Roland, F-16 and other military projects where costs are shared.

The combat environment includes the climate and topography of a theatre as well as the enemy threat, type and level of conflict. The climate and topography of Vietnam and Central Europe differ markedly. Although cloud, light, visibility and precipitation affect air operations similarly wherever they occur, the weather in Vietnam and Europe differs markedly. In Vietnam the seasons are marked by the monsoon and almost four months of the year are wet. Under these monsoon conditions it is difficult to mount conventional air operations because the visibility is reduced by low cloud and precipitation. In the dry season when the sky is reasonably clear of cloud the visibility is often reduced to less than two miles by the smoke from burning paddy fields. The Vietnamese farmers burn their rice in much the same way as ours burn straw after harvesting the crop. Overall then the weather in Vietnam cannot be considered good and it was found that for long periods only the F-111 and A-6 aircraft could operate effectively at the lower levels – this by virtue of their extremely complex and expensive avionic equipment – and the B-52 from high. When visibility is poor, electro-optic and laser guided weapons lose their advantage because the target cannot be seen in time to launch or control them although unguided weapons can still be used effectively. Thus a mix of weapons was used in Vietnam.

The weather in Central Europe differs markedly. Many short periods of very poor weather occur in the winter and the summer, though normally dry with good visibility, does generate inversions which trap industrial smog at the lower levels thereby reducing it. Additionally, hours of daylight vary much more and seasonally in Europe than they do in Vietnam. The conclusion to be drawn, therefore, is that when the weather is good enough we must use laser guided weapons, preferably propelled, to provide the greater stand-off range which better visibility will permit to increase the effectiveness and survivability of the air forces: and when the weather will not permit the use of these guided weapons, conventional unguided weapons delivered with the accuracy modern avionics can achieve must be used. In good weather, our force requirement to achieve a certain goal will therefore be much lower but for similar reasons the enemy air defence system will be more effective. In poor weather our force requirement to achieve a certain goal will be much higher but the enemy air defence system is likely to be less effective. Our aim, therefore, should be to fly in balanced formations in most weather conditions by day and night.

The topography too is very different. Vietnam is long, narrow, mountainous, jungle covered and has very few surface lines of communication. Central Europe has large open plains, wooded hills and many surface lines of communication. Central Europe is very good country for massive armoured operations which is our main ground threat whereas the Vietnam theatre offered fewer ideal tank battle grounds.

The conflict in Vietnam, apart from a few set piece battles which could be equated with minor limited war operations, was a counterinsurgency war. In Europe the whole gamut of modern weapons and electronic warfare could be employed on a massive scale on the land, sea and in the air. NVN never presented a threat in the air and the American and allied ground forces became accustomed to operating under an umbrella of total air superiority all the time and indeed never had enemy aircraft attack them. In Europe the NATO allies can expect to be outnumbered in manpower, weapons and aircraft and the fight for air superiority will be hard. Without air superiority our land forces will face superior land forces who command and operate under the umbrella of their own substantial air forces. Our own offensive support operations, whose aim must be to reduce the enemy threat to a level which our land forces can tolerate, will not be effective unless we can establish some sort of air superiority, be it only local and temporary. Our air superiority campaign therefore must aim to destroy enemy aircraft wherever they can be engaged. Air combat engagements in Vietnam against modern Soviet fighters showed that our fighters will need high performance, integral gun systems, short to medium range highly manoeuvrable air to air guided missiles, all round vision canopies, electronic warfare equipment and enough fuel to exploit these characteristics. In the battle against the air defence system of NVN, electronic countermeasures, anti-radiation missiles, appropriate tactical formations and special air defence suppression missions all combined to overcome the formidable air defences deployed by NVN. The opposition on the Central Front will be even more extensive and formidable but the experience gained in Vietnam should be exploited. We must procure the type of equipment and develop the tactics which were successful in Vietnam if our losses are not to be prohibitive. Those aircraft not capable of fighting or evading the air defences will have to rely for survival on speed, routeing and screening – that is, flying so low that the natural screening of the surface features provides adequate cover against detection or engagement. In addition they should take advantage of the American concept of medium level penetration and thus provide the WP with the formidable problem of three dimensional air defence in depth.

Fixed wing and helicopter transport support operations in SVN were very effective. Troops and equipment were moved quickly over comparatively long distances and in great quantities. Fixed wing aircraft supply dropping, even within range of some anti-aircraft defences, was also effective, mainly because of ECM. However, operations by comparatively slow, large, unmanoeuvrable aircraft would probably not be cost effective in any environment where enemy fighters ranged and even in conditions of air superiority would be risky. Thus air transport support operations in Europe are likely to be successful only under cover of night, adverse weather, distance from the enemy, or if specially covered by an overwhelming fighter escort force. In any case, operation over enemy territory is liable to be disastrous.

The helicopter was also used in an air support role in Vietnam. One suspicion confirmed was that they do not yet have the performance to operate with a sustainable loss rate in contested air space. We should, therefore, plan to use helicopters only over friendly forces and only when the enemy does not have undisputed air superiority. The age of the armed helicopter ranging freely over the battle area in Central Europe is not yet at hand. However, the anti-tank missile-armed helicopter has been shown to be a powerful weapon. It seems to me therefore that there should be a compromise. In my view we should retain an option to fit anti-tank guided weapons to our air force and army helicopters. They could be very useful in conditions where the enemy has broken through our lines and the weather is such that offensive support aircraft cannot operate. The helicopters, controlled directly by the land forces, could then provide very mobile and flexible fire power by stemming and mopping up operations until the land forces redeploy to counter the threat.

Included in the combat environment is command and control. In SVN the operations were controlled in accordance with a well tried system, built up over the years during various wars. Basically, any unit needing support not already programmed passes its request to its headquarters which decides whether the request should be approved and if so what priority it should be given. If approved, the request is passed to the air force control centre which allocates the task to missions either on the ground or already airborne, depending on the urgency. The aircrew then contact the unit making the request and carry out the task under control of land or airborne Forward Air Controllers. This system is well established in NATO. On the other hand, the command and control of the air war over NVN presented innumerable problems. Initially control was exercised procedurally with the inevitable result that tactical surprise was forfeited – a lesson not learnt from the Korean War! When some radar control became available, the possibilities of combining airborne and ground control became clearer, particularly during the bombing of NVN in December 1972 by the integrated attack forces. Concentration of force to saturate the defences and to deliver heavy blows was the aim. The success led eventually to the development by the USA of the Tactical Air Control System (TACS). It provides a commander with the back up system of command and close radar control when the ground system breaks down. I can see that it would facilitate marshalling and redeployment and retasking of integrated attack forces if that should ever be necessary. However, the electronic warfare (EW) environment and the low intensity of operations if integrated force tactics are used, lead me to doubt its cost effectiveness. Moreover the airborne control centre would be too vulnerable or be too far back to be effective in EW conditions or would require a disproportionate air defence force to protect it: in addition its use in peace time as a matter of course could lead aircrew to become dependent on it. Its absence in war could cause chaos and in the long run reduce flexibility instead of increase it. Thus TACS should only be considered as one of many methods for controlling integrated attack forces.

On the other hand, tactical operations which seldom require deep penetration are very different. Whereas the integrated force is made more effective by virtue of its concentration, it means in practice that fewer sorties per aircraft per day are flown. The success of the shorter range tactical operations depends to a large extent on the number of effective sorties generated and recovered. The size of the tactical formations varies generally from two to eight aircraft. Many would be controlled by Forward Air Controllers but many more may be expected to fly interdiction and armed reconnaissance missions. Thus there would be a multiplicity of operations to provide with close control. In my view the electronic war envisaged in Central Europe is unlikely to permit free and discrete radar and radio control at all times even when we have local air superiority. An integrated force attack could achieve this and of course the shorter range tactical operations would benefit. In my view therefore, an attempt to provide close control for all air operations from an airborne facility would not give the commander the flexibility he and his forces require. I believe the opposite would be true. I believe that air defence operations are best when they have close control but they can still be effective when they have none and the aim should be to make this true for all other air operations. There is no doubt however that a commander must have the overall picture of the air battle available to him constantly if he is to deploy his forces to the best effect and automatic data processing is probably the best means current 'state of the art' technology can provide. But I believe detailed control should be decentralised as far as practicable.

Conclusion
The air war in Vietnam has highlighted several lessons which could apply to operations on the central front in Europe despite the differences between the two theatres. The aim of the USA in Vietnam was to stop the North from waging war on the South and thus ensure the survival of the latter as a democratic state. The strategy preferred by the USA was the slow build-up of pressure on the government of NVN by a strictly constrained bombing campaign of gradually increasing intensity spreading northwards, rather than a hard hitting offensive which could have achieved immediate results. This apparent reluctance to use the power available combined with the lack of a will to win were interpreted by the NVN as irresolution and weakness. A long drawn out war therefore became inevitable. The lack of victory coupled with rising casualties created a situation, exploited by communist propaganda, in which the American public objected to the continued commitment in Vietnam and the war then became impossible to win. The lesson for NATO is that if we do not fight to win, right from the outset of hostilities, we will lose. Our use of air power must therefore be appropriate in strength and resolute in action.

The predominance of the USA in the alliance which fought in Vietnam ensured standardisation of equipment, weapons and procedures. Without this uniformity the costs would have been even higher. NATO is not dominated by the USA although it is indisputably the most powerful ally by far. Consequently, each nation has had its own research and development, procurement and sales programmes and often these have either overlapped or conflicted and there are a multiplicity of weapons systems and procedures in use. While this creates enormous problems for the Warsaw Pact, it is possible to substantially reduce the number of different options available to NATO, thereby saving the money and increasing flexibility, without significantly reducing the problems for the enemy. Standardisation within NATO is an aim which has been embraced by all leaders within the Alliance.

The combat environment in Vietnam showed that electronic warfare has increased in significance and ECM equipment must be fitted if aircraft are not to suffer unsustainable losses. The development of laser-guided weapons increased accuracies to the extent that individual targets could be hit by far fewer aircraft than before, thus saving effort and enabling more targets to be attacked within the prescribed political constraints. The major limitation, however, was weather which for long periods reduced operations to those capable of being flown by only those aircraft with the most sophisticated avionics – the F-111 and A-6. Unguided weapons were not so affected. The lesson for NATO, therefore, is that there must be a balanced mix of laser-guided and unguided weapons as well as of sophisticated aircraft capable of operating totally blind and those which need visual acquisition of targets to operate. In addition the ECM, tactics and integrated attack forces used for the major bombing offensives over NVN could well be imitated for the deeper penetrations which will be required of NATO in the central region. Air combat against modern Russian fighters in Vietnam showed that to survive let alone fight for air superiority, NATO fighters must have high performance and be equipped with highly manoeuvrable, guided air to air missiles and integral guns. Air transport support is still required to augment land lines of communication and both fixed and rotary wing aircraft have their part to play. However, the Vietnam experience showed that these aircraft are unlikely to survive in contested airspace and therefore their operation in the central region will have to be over friendly territory only and then under cover of darkness or weather. On the other hand armed helicopters could be useful to plug any holes the enemy armour might punch in our lines, at least until our land forces can be suitably redeployed. A favourable air situation would be a prerequisite for successful helicopter operations in this role.

The command and control of air power in Vietnam was initially very primitive. Over the years the disadvantages of not having a satisfactory system led eventually to what is now known by the American forces as the Tactical Air Control System. The aim is to provide close control for every mission flown, regardless of role, using radar and radio from an airborne control centre. The concept, if applied to the Vietnam theatre and thus the threat encountered there, is unquestionably good. However, in my view, the electronic war, coupled with the number and types of enemy aircraft likely to operate on the central front in Europe are such as to reduce the effectiveness of such an option which is extremely expensive. Moreover, forces which become accustomed to close control are likely to lose some flexibility and, if deprived of all control, which is not beyond the realms of possibility in a European scenario, are likely to become disorganised and suffer the resultant loss of effectiveness. I believe therefore that NATO should regard any such system as a secondary, or bonus, facility which is not reliable but helpful if it is available.

APPENDIX L

John Howe and the Media

There were several occasions during John's career when the international press were invited to view the modern RAF at work, none more so than when 74 Squadron introduced the Lightning into operational service, when the Tigers flew at the Farnborough and Paris air shows and when John flew the first Phantom into RAF Coningsby. Below is a selection of the colourful newspaper reports that briefings often generated, full of journalistic licence and hyperbole but a joy to read! The articles have not been corrected in terms of fact or description and are reproduced as published.

RAF Coltishall Press and Media Days
A three day publicity exercise was arranged by the Air Ministry in February 1961 with the world's media being invited to Coltishall to watch the Lightning in action. And it really was the world's media. For some time afterwards John and the squadron continued to receive photographs and other items, including an embroidered Tiger's Head from Japan, from many of those who had attended in appreciation of their hospitality.

The Daily Sketch (London, UK)

Here it is. The pride of Britain. The RAF's operational squadron of Lightnings. Look at the machine. It can catch any bomber. It can outfly any fighter. It takes only 30 seconds to get airborne from its base at RAF Coltishall Norfolk where I saw it in action yesterday. It's almost fireproof. It can fly in any weather. Look at the man. In the cockpit is Squadron Leader John Howe, CO of The Tigers of 74 Squadron (motto *I Fear No Man*). No wonder he calls the Lightning the best fighter in the world! He and his pilots (in their five flying suits) have so little to do. Radar enables it to find and destroy a target automatically. Look at the missile. It's the Firestreak. Here's how it works. Electronic computers and other devices click towards a glowing blip on the radar screen. A light flickers on...The pilot presses a button. And however much the target wriggles the Firestreak follows and blasts it from the sky.

The Evening News (East London, South Africa)

Secrets of the Lightning, the wonder Flying Brain of the RAF, were disclosed here today when No 74 Squadron, the first to be equipped with the aircraft, was on show. Said the commanding officer, Squadron Leader John Howe: 'The fact that it is felt to be the best fighter in operational service in the world today gives our pilots the highest possible morale.' The pilots of the squadron (motto *I Fear No Man*) believe the Lightning can catch any bomber and outfly any fighter in service. The fighter's 1,400mph – twice the speed of sound and soon to rise to 1,500mph – is twelve times that of the SE5A used by Mick Mannock, Britain's top scorer when he fought with the squadron in World War I.

The Lightning is to supersede the Javelin day and night all weather fighter and the Hunter VI. Strange that this deadly killer should have been conceived by a team headed by WEW Petter, the genius now retired to a life of religious meditation on a Swiss mountain.

Its normal equipment is two 20mm Aden guns and two Firestreak air to air missiles. The Lightning carries wonderful electronic equipment and a computer which feeds essential information to the pilot and the weapons. Squadron Leader Howe, who is 30, is the only South African to Command No 74 (The Tiger) Squadron since the Battle of Britain days of Sailor Malan. He said his pilots could find and destroy the enemy without ever seeing him except perhaps for a flash and flame as the enemy was hit.

Pilots under training were followed by an instructor in a Hunter 'chaser'. To reach operational height together the Hunter had to be given a height start of six miles. The pilot was shown where to fire at an unseen target by a series of lights. Once the electronics had locked on to a target that target was knocked down.

I saw a pilot clothed in one of the new suits which help them to breathe when fighting at a height of twelve miles. A lining supplies streams of cool air to all parts of the body. A pressure suit has air bladders and an immersion suit gives the pilot a chance of life if he comes down in the cold sea. On return to base in bad weather a pilot can effect an automatic descent without aid from the ground.

Future Lightnings are working to complete automaticity in take off, finding and destroying an unseen target and landing without the pilot having to touch anything. But there is no likelihood I gather of the pilot being superseded. There will always be the problem of deciding whether an aircraft is friend or foe.

The Eastern Evening News and *The Eastern Daily Press* (Norwich)

Britain's fastest fighter – twice the speed of sound in level flight – was on show to the Press at Coltishall today. The English Electric Lightning is the RAF's first truly supersonic fighter. And 74 Squadron based at Coltishall, formerly of St Faith's, is the first RAF squadron to be equipped with this all weather single seater day and night fighter. 'The best fighter in operational service today,' suggests Squadron Leader John FG Howe the 31 year old South African squadron commander. 'We know we can catch the bombers and going on past experience we know we can outfight any known modern fighter in service today. The performance of the aircraft, coupled with the ease with which it is flown, gives the pilots confidence and the fact that it is felt to be the best fighter in operational service in the world today gives our Lightning pilots the highest possible morale.'

The arrow shaped Lightning – in take off flight reminiscent of some vast insect from outer space – can fly above 60,000 feet and intercept enemy aircraft flying at Mach 2, twice the speed of sound. Eventually this fighter will be capable of flying regularly at 1,500 mph. Powered by two Rolls Royce Avon turbojet engines with reheat, it is considered that it will cope with Britain's air defence requirements well into the 1970s era. At present it supplements the Javelin two seater all weather fighter which it will eventually replace. Radar, radio and electronic devices have made a navigator unnecessary in the Lightning. The pilot can hit his target without ever seeing it visually. The radar searches above and below the horizon and when the target is found automatic lock-on gear prevents contact being lost. Computers process the radar information and steering information which is provided to the pilot on his attack sight enables him to close to missile firing range of the target, many times longer than gun range. If the target takes evasive action the radar immediately gives the pilot the information needed to keep proper contact. When within range the homing heads of the de Havilland Firestreak missile automatically lock on to the target and the pilot is instructed to fire electronically. Missiles fired, guns empty, the aircraft can make base unaided by ground control thanks to its navigation system.

Farnborough, September 1961

The Cape Times (South Africa)

Squadron Leader John Howe, South African commander of the Royal Air Force's Lightning squadron, has been leading his pilots in more displays in their faster than sound aircraft. Earlier this month they thrilled the crowds at the air show at Farnborough. The displays were part of the annual Battle of Britain celebrations and were also the fourth time that the 1,500 mph Lightnings of No 74 Squadron – known as the Tiger Squadron – had taken part in an air display. But Squadron Leader Howe emphasises that his squadron is not an aerobatic squadron. Aerobatic displays are merely a secondary role. The squadron's principal role is operational flying.

Before taking part in the Farnborough display the squadron practised for three weeks. 'We wanted to put on a good show so I got permission to try to roll a big formation of nine aircraft and this takes a lot of practice,' said Squadron Leader Howe. During the display the squadron flew at a very low speed of about 450 miles an hour. The speed was held down because the planes would otherwise have gone out of sight too quickly. Squadron Leader Howe said the squadron pilots did not drink or stay out late the night before they flew. But there were no special rules about this because they were not needed. 'The chaps know what the score is and play it pretty cool.'

Squadron Leader Howe said the Lightning was a marvellous plane. It was easy to handle and had all the power in the world. 'You just open the throttles and away you go!' It was also very manoeuvrable. 'It's a very nice machine in every way.'

Last week Squadron Leader Howe appeared on British television in a programme which featured some of the greatest fighter aces in aviation history. He was shown in his Lightning fighter and spoke for about a minute saying that fighter pilots of today had to devote much hard work, hard training and discipline to their jobs. But one should not get the impression that there was no fun left in flying. There was, provided it came from knowing one was doing a job well.

Asked how he liked the RAF Squadron Leader Howe said: 'I think it is a magnificent service. It is marvellous. I plan to devote my life to it.'

On Leaving the Tigers
The Sunday Tribune (South Africa)

Squadron Leader John Howe, the former SAAF pilot who fought in Korea and later took command of the famous No 74 Fighter Squadron which has staged breathtaking aerobatics for royalty and the crowds at Farnborough, was himself honoured by the squadron recently. His parents, Mr and Mrs George Howe of Oxford Street, East London, have heard how after giving a display for the Queen Mother Squadron Leader Howe flew back to the squadron's base. It was to be his last operation before being transferred to a post at Fighter Command in Stanmore.

It is customary for the flight leader to land last but on this occasion the pilots persuaded him to land first. When he was on the ground they flew off and then returned in a grand flypast in his honour in the formation of the letter H for Howe. The No 74 Squadron is equipped with Britain's latest fighter, the 1,500mph swept wing Lightning. The Tigers – as the fliers are known – have as their motto *I Fear No Man*. The squadron was commanded during the Battle of Britain by South Africa's greatest war time pilot Group Captain A G 'Sailor' Malan.

Unidentified South African paper

An East London born Royal Air Force officer who must be regarded as one of Britain's elite fighter pilots received an added tribute to his already long record of achievement this week when he was awarded the Air Force Cross in the Queen's Honours list. He is Squadron Leader John Howe, 31 year old son of Mr and Mrs George Howe, who until recently was Officer Commanding the famous No 74 (Tiger) Squadron. He is now stationed at Fighter Command Headquarters near London. Last week John Howe sat for his Wing Commander's examination. Within a few weeks John will receive an invitation to Buckingham Palace to have the red and white decoration of the Air Force Cross pinned to his breast.

Phantoms

Boston Standard (Lincolnshire)

The RAF's first Phantom thundered down on to the main 9,000 ft east-west runway at RAF Coningsby at 1.45pm on Friday and as the orange and white striped braking 'chute burst out from the tail helping the giant all-purpose all-weather jet to a stop, a new era in the crowded history of the station had begun. After housing wartime Hampden bombers back in 1940 and playing a major war role with other later bombers in the years that followed – the famous 617 Squadron was formed at Coningsby – the station has been host to Canberras and Vulcans. It was to have had the ill-fated TSR2 but after that was cancelled it reverted to a repair and maintenance station with what was a skeleton staff compared to busier days.

In recent weeks the booming of the big Vulcans has brought the post war atmosphere back to Coningsby and its cheek by jowl neighbour Tattershall. The Vulcans were rehearsing ground staffs and operations rooms personnel for the eagerly awaited Phantom F4M, the RAF's newest strike and reconnaissance aircraft: and for RAF Coningsby's new international role. It is international because aircrews to be trained in future at Consingsby will be formed into squadrons ready to serve anywhere in the world with Phantoms.

The man who will train the first crews, South African born Wing Commander John Howe – he is the first commanding officer of the first Phantom conversion unit No 228 – piloted the first RAF Phantom to the station on Friday. He flew it from RAF Aldergrove where the new Phantoms are delivered after being ferried across the Atlantic from the St Louis factory of McDonnell Douglas, the American aircraft firm. Minor modifications are carried out at Aldergrove to fit the plane for RAF service. Coningsby expects to get one a week for the next few months then more until they have 40 to 50 Phantoms. All future Phantom pilots for the RAF will be trained at Coningsby along with ground crews. 'It will mean a lot of flying,' said Group Captain Rogers answering a query about aircraft noise and its possible effect on the area. 'But the area is used to heavy bombers and has recently had Vulcans. The Phantom is probably not quite so noisy as the Vulcan but when we are fully operational we shall invite Ministry of Defence noise level test teams here to do a check. Special suppressors have been fitted to our ground test installations and that will reduce engine noise on the ground.'

Technical chiefs from McDonnells, Rolls Royce and other firms associated with the Phantom joined off duty RAF men and their families near the runway to see the plane arrive. (It is known as the Fifty Fifty Phantom because there are so many made in England parts in this American plane.) Among the onlookers was Mrs Annabelle Howe, Norfolk born wife of the pilot, and their three daughters Caroline, Nicola and Jane.

Promotions and Postings
Unidentified South African paper

An East London man serving with the Royal Air Force in Britain, Wing Commander John Howe, has recently been promoted to Group Captain in charge of Fighter Defence. Group Captain Howe...was the first pilot to fly the RAF's new Phantom jet fighter. He served for many years as a squadron leader of Lightning aircraft and is now an Assistant Director of Operations with Buccaneers, Phantoms and Harrier fighter planes under his command. His promotion arrived in May this year when he was stationed at the Air Ministry in London. Mr and Mrs G Howe said yesterday they were delighted with the news. 'We were very pleased for John's sake. He loves the Air Force,' said Mrs Howe.

The Star (South Africa)

A virulent attack of flu yesterday nearly ruined the finest hour in the career of East London born Air Commodore John Howe when he was invested with the CBE (Commander of the British Empire) at Buckingham Palace. The investiture was carried out by Prince Charles. Air Commodore Howe, a jet fighter pilot with the South African Air Force in Korea [sic] said 'I was feeling so poorly that I hardly knew what was happening. But I decided nothing short of death would stop me going to the palace. It was worth it because it helped tremendously, absolutely marvellously, when Prince Charles put the ribbon round my neck.' His wife Annabelle and two eldest daughters Caroline16 and Tiggy 15 attended the ceremony. Air Commodore Howe had to return direct to his sick bed and a family celebration has been postponed.

The Daily Dispatch (South Africa)

An East London officer serving with the Royal Air Force, John Howe, has been promoted to the rank of Air Vice Marshal. This is possibly the highest rank attained by any South African who has served with the RAF.

APPENDIX M

Career Timeline

April 1948	Enrolled at South Africa's Military College.
April 1950	Joined the South African Air Force.
	Central Flying School at AFB Dunnottar.
March 1951	No. 4 Operational Training Unit at AFB Langebaanweg.
May 1951	Korea with 2 Squadron SAAF, component of the 18th Fighter Bomber Wing of the USAF.
October 1951	Seconded to the 19th Infantry Brigade of the 24th Infantry Division, IX Corps US Army as a Forward Air Controller.
December 1951	Returned to South Africa and 1 Squadron at Swartkop.
April 1952	QFI Course at AFB Dunnottar.
June 1952	QFI at CFS at AFB Dunnottar.
August 1954	Resigned commission with the SAAF.
October 1954	Joined the Royal Air Force as a Flying Officer. Central Flying School at RAF Little Rissington.
January 1955	No. 4 Flying Training School at RAF Middleton St George.
January 1956	Promotion to Flight Lieutenant.
	229 Operational Conversion Unit at RAF Chivenor.
April 1956	222 Squadron at RAF Leuchars.
September 1956	Seconded to 40 Commando Royal Marines as a Forward Air Controller.
November 1956	Landed on the beaches at Suez with 40 Commando.
January 1957	Returned to 222 Squadron at RAF Leuchars.
October 1957	43 Squadron at RAF Leuchars.
July 1958	Detached to Cyprus with 43 Squadron.
October 1958	Returned to RAF Leuchars with 43 Squadron.
June 1959	No. 5 Day Fighter Combat School course at RAF West Raynham.
October 1959	229 Operational Conversion Unit at RAF Chivenor (staff appointment).
January 1960	Junior Command and Staff School Course at RAF Bircham Newton.
February 1960	Promotion to Squadron Leader.
	Appointed Commanding Officer of 74(F) Squadron at RAF Coltishall.

December 1961	HQ Fighter Command at RAF Stanmore.
January 1964	RAF Staff College Bracknell.
January 1965	The Joint Warfare Establishment at Old Sarum.
July 1965	Promotion to Wing Commander. Exchange posting with the USAF to HQ Air Defense Command Colorado Springs.
August 1967	Refresher Flying Course at RAF Manby.
September 1967	No. 129 Fighter Ground Attack Course at 229 Operational Conversion Unit at RAF Chivenor.
November 1967	No. 40 Fighter Recce Course at 229 Operational Conversion Unit at RAF Chivenor.
January 1968	RAF Coningsby to form the first RAF F-4 Phantom unit.
April 1968	Davis Monthan Air Force Base Arizona for RAF Phantom Course 682B with the 4453rd CCTS.
August 1968	Appointed Commanding Officer of 228 Operational Conversion Unit RAF Coningsby.
December 1969	The Central Tactics and Trials Organisation, HQ Support Command, RAF Upavon.
May 1970.	Promotion to Group Captain. MoD as Deputy Director Operational Requirements RAF (DDOR4).
September 1972	Refresher Flying Course at RAF Manby.
October 1972	Lightning Refresher Course at 226 Operational Conversion Unit RAF Coltishall
January 1973	Senior Officers Flying Course (Helicopters) RAF Tern Hill.
January 1973	To RAF Gutersloh Germany as Station Commander.
January 1975	Royal College of Defence Studies, Seaford House, London.
October 1975	Group Captain Operations, HQ 11 Group, RAF Bentley Priory.
April 1977	Appointed Commandant of The Royal Observer Corps.
April 1980	Nimrod Conversion Course, 230 Operational Conversion Unit, RAF St Mawgan.
May 1980	Promotion to Air Vice Marshal. Appointed Commander Southern Maritime Region RAF Mount Batten.
August 1983	Appointed Director General of Security RAF
30 November 1985	Retirement from the Royal Air Force.
November 1988	Appointed Honorary Colonel, Airfield Damage Repair Squadrons (of the 77th Engineer Regiment, Royal Engineers)

APPENDIX N

Aircraft Flown

A brief description of each type flown is given and where possible a note of the individual aircraft and where they were flown over the course of John Howe's thirty-eight year military flying career. During that career with the South African Air Force and Royal Air Force he flew 3,556 hours as first pilot by day, 296 hours as second pilot by day, 337 hours dual by day, 229 hours as first pilot by night, 8 hours as second pilot by night and 28 hours dual by night. Or 4,454 hours in total.

Note: Information taken from John's log books is in italics.

Aeronca 7AC Champion
Founded in 1928 as the Aeronautical Corporation of America the company changed its name to Aeronca in 1941 and produced the Aeronca Grasshopper, a light liaison and observation monoplane, which served extensively throughout the Second World War. The company also manufactured hundreds of trainers and gliders for the war effort. The post-war era saw the release of a succession of popular aircraft such as the Champion, the Chief and Super Chief, the Defender and the Arrow. From 1945 to 1950 Aeronca built thousands of light aircraft, at one stage fifty a day emerging from the factory, but with the onset of recession the company was forced to abandon all production, which ceased in 1951. In twenty-three years Aeronca had manufactured 17,408 aircraft in fifty-five model forms. Today Aeronca is a major aerospace sub-contractor.

AOS Langebaanweg. Defence Flying Club: January 1954 – May 1954
ZS-AYK and ZS-BBW.

Aerospatiale – Westland Puma HC.1
First flown in April 1965 the Aerospatiale SA.330A was designed as a medium-weight troop transport having been developed by Sud-Aviation and Westland Helicopters to fill an RAF and French army requirement for a helicopter of this type. Production of the Puma was started in 1968 with the first UK-built aircraft joining the RAF in 1971. Powered by twin Turbomeca Turmo IVC engines the Puma can carry sixteen combat troops at 160 mph for a range of 350 miles.

RAF Gutersloh, July 17th 1974
XW204.

Avro Anson

The Anson was known to all as 'Faithful Annie' because of the length of its RAF service, from 1938 to 1968. For the majority of this time it was used as a navigation trainer and general communications aircraft. Almost 7,000 were built in Britain and many more overseas. After the war the C.19 transport version and T.21 navigation trainer were fitted with metal wings and tailplane as opposed to the original fabric-covered versions.

Royal Air Force Bovingdon: December 1961 – December 1963
Seven sorties flown but the designation and serial numbers of the aircraft
involved not recorded.

British Aerospace/Hawker Siddeley Harrier T.4

To increase the combat capabilities of the VTOL (Vertical Take Off and Landing) Harrier, in 1975 it received a laser sensor in the nose and radar warning receivers (RWR). Fifty GR.1s and GR.1As were upgraded to this new GR.3 standard and thirty-six new aircraft were ordered. With the GR.3 entering service some of the two-seat T.2 trainers received the laser nose and RWR and were redesignated the T.4.

RAF Gutersloh: June 20th 1974
XW933.

British Aircraft Corporation Jet Provost

During the genesis of the Jet Provost the company that designed it went through various redesigns of its own. Percival Aircraft had become part of the Hunting Group in 1944 but the aircraft it built still bore the Percival name. In 1954, however, it became Hunting Percival followed in 1957 by a further name change to just Hunting and finally in 1960 to the British Aircraft Corporation who purchased a controlling interest in Hunting.

Jet Provost T.4

The T.3 was developed into the T.4 with a more powerful Viper engine, giving it a much greater rate of climb, which was of advantage to student pilots who were progressing to a more advanced level. Some 198 T.4s were delivered to the RAF between 1961 and 1964. During the 1960s and 1970s aerobatic teams equipped with the T.4 became familiar sights at air shows up and down the country. They included The Macaws from the College of Air Warfare, The Poachers from RAF Cranwell and The Red Pelicans from the Central Flying School.

No 3 Squadron, College of Air Warfare School of Refresher Flying RAF
Manby: August 1967 to September 1967
Aircraft coded 10, 12, 14, 16, 19, 21, 22, 23, 24, 26, 29, 31 and 33.

RAF College Cranwell: March – April 1968
Aircraft coded 28, 81 and 88.

RAF Coningsby: August 1968 – November 1968
Aircraft coded 585 and 656.

No 1 Squadron, College of Air Warfare School of Refresher Flying RAF
Manby: September 1972 – October 1972
Aircraft coded 10, 14, 15, 16, 18, 20, 23, 27and 28.

Jet Provost T.5

The requirement for high altitude training was restricted by the fact that the Hunting Jet Provost T.4 was not pressurised and so a new pressurised version was developed as a private venture by BAC, the prototype flying in February 1967. It won the immediate approval of the RAF and entered service with the RAF's Central Flying School at Little Rissington in September 1969. Some 110 were delivered. The T.5 differed externally from earlier versions by a redesigned hood and a more bulbous shape to accommodate the pressurised cockpit. Between 1973 and 1976 ninety-three were modified with an upgrade in avionics equipment and became T.5As.

RAF Gutersloh: July 17th 1974
XS218.

Convair TF-102 Delta Dagger

The F-102 was a scaled up version of Convair's experimental XF-92A and the first prototype was flown on 24 October 1953. It was destroyed eight days later when the engine flamed out. Flight tests with a second aircraft proved the F-102 to be incapable of reaching the speed of sound, the Pratt & Whitney engine not being powerful enough to overcome transonic drag. Implementation of the area rule theory proved to be the answer. This necessitated a radical revision of the fuselage profile but so reduced transonic drag that Mach 1.2 was reached with no problem on the rebuilt YF-102A's first flight. Thereafter production to the much-delayed aircraft proceeded smoothly. Some 873 F-102As were built. The TF-102A combat proficiency trainer featured a wider front fuselage and side by side seating. Some 111 were built, the type retaining the full operational equipment and armament of the single-seater.

Tyndall AFB: 12th August 1965
Full serial number not shown – only the last three digits.
344.

Nellis AFB: 26th July 1966
Full serial number not shown – only the last three digits.
369.

Perrin AFB: 9th December 1966
Full serial number not shown – only the last three digits.
341.

300

Convair F-106B Delta Dart

The F-106 was originally known as the F-102B in acknowledgement of its evolution from the earlier aircraft but given it turned out to be a very different aeroplane with its revised area ruling, more powerful engines and new weapons system it was soon redesignated and given the name Delta Dart. Its maximum speed was Mach 2.3, twice as fast as the Dagger. The first deliveries to the USAF were in June 1959. The F-106B, a tandem two-seat version (as opposed to the side by side arrangement of the TF-102), retained the full operational capabilities of the A model. Sixty-three were built.

5th Fighter Interceptor Squadron Minot AFB. From McLelland AFB to Minot AFB. From Minot AFB to Peterson AFB: 3rd October 1965
572529.

Air Defense Weapons Centre, Tyndall AFB. 11th August 1965: 21st December 1965
572540 and 580902.

5th Fighter Interceptor Squadron Minot AFB, 23rd June 1966
580901.

De Havilland DH82A Tiger Moth

The Tiger Moth is amongst the most famous of de Havilland designs and over 8,000 were produced. The first was flown on 26 October 1931 with initial production at de Havilland's Stag Lane factory until it moved to Hatfield. Further production took place abroad and many of the world's air forces used the Tiger Moth, including the South African Air Force with whom John flew them.

South African Tiger Moths were initially received to equip the civilian flying schools under the Union Air Training Group programme. The fifty-two surviving airframes were impressed by the SAAF at the outbreak of the Second World War. A further 739 were shipped to South Africa but ninety-three of these, a mix of Morris and Australian-built examples, were lost at sea. At the end of the war a hundred were crated and shipped to India whilst many others were sold off to civilian operators. The Defence Flying Club also received a batch and around thirty are still to be found in the country.

CFS Dunottar: May – August 1950
509, 2216, 2226, 2292, 2303, 2323, 2415, 2461, 2494, 2498, 2456, 2463, 4606, 4634 and 4709.

CFS Dunnottar. Instructors' Course and Instruction: March 1952 to December 1953
592.

CFS Dunnottar. Defence Flying Club: March 1952 to December 1953
ZS-BFS, ZS-BFX, ZS-BTH, ZS-BVV and ZS-DDT.

De Havilland DH104 Devon

De Havilland's first civilian post-war production aircraft was the Dove, known as the Devon in military service. Adapted in 1947 as a communications aircraft from the Dove 4, the Devon C.Mk.1 served with a number of air forces outside the UK, including nine in South Africa. Production ended in 1967 with 542 aircraft completed.

1 Squadron at AFS Swartkop: February 1952
108.

CFS Dunnottar. Instructors' Course and Instruction: March 1952 to
December 1953
107.

HQ Southern Maritime Region RAF Mountbatten: February 19th 1981
A cross country sortie in an unspecified aircraft and from/to unspecified
locations.

De Havilland Vampire

The de Havilland Vampire was the second jet-engined aircraft commissioned by the RAF during the Second World War (the first was the Meteor) but it never saw combat. Originally named the Spidercrab, the aircraft was entirely a de Havilland project, Goblin engine included. It proved to be an exceptionally versatile aircraft, was built in several countries and equipped many of the world's air forces in its various versions.

DH100 Vampire FB.5

The fighter-bomber FB.5 became the most numerous combat variant. South Africa obtained ten Vampire FB.5s in 1950. The RAF took delivery of 930 in total, serving with nineteen frontline squadrons before being relegated to the advanced training role.

1 Squadron at AFS Swartkop: February – March 1952
202, 203, 206 and 208.

AOS Langebaanweg. Instructors' Course and Instruction: January 1954 –
May 1954
203, 204, 205, 206, 209 and 210.

No 4 Flying Training School RAF Middleton St George: January 1955 –
December 1955
Some serials shown without prefix letters.
104, 146, 187, 308, 356, 458, 627, VV628 and 690.

229 Operational Training Unit RAF Chivenor: January 1956 – March 1956
Some serials shown without prefix letters.
VZ842, 112, 174, 185, WA238, WA254, 276, WA435, 473, 545 and 606.

DH100 Vampire FB.52
The SAAF took delivery of ten FB.52s (an export version of the FB.6 that had been developed for the Swiss Air Force) in 1951 and a further six in 1952.

1 Squadron at AFS Swartkop: February – March 1952
213, 214 and 219.

AOS Langebaanweg. Instructors' Course and Instruction: January 1954 –
May 1954
213.

DH115 Vampire T.11
By June 1950 single-seat Vampires were in service with, or on order from, fourteen countries and at that date there was no two-seat trainer to go with them. De Havilland therefore decided to instigate the design of such a machine and entrusted this to their associate company, Airspeed, at Christchurch. The DH115 Vampire T.11 was the result. Some 526 were built.

Central Flying School RAF Little Rissington: October 1954 – December
1954
Some aircraft logged show codes only.
XD376/IZ, XD379/IV, IW, IX, NC, ND, NE, NG and XE893/IS.

No 4 Flying Training School RAF Middleton St George: January 1955 –
December 1955
WZ546, WZ558, WZ566, XD595, XE 827, XE 828, XE829, XE830, XE832, XE848, XE849, XE850, XE852, XE853, XE854, XE857, XE862, XE863, XE865, XE866, XE873, XE874, XE875, XE887 and XE927.

229 Operational Training Unit RAF Chivenor: January 1956 – March
1956
Some serials shown without prefix letters.
477, VZ507, 826, 873, XE877 and 923.

222 Squadron RAF Leuchars: April 1956 to September 1957
Some serials shown without prefix letters, one with code only.
XD391, 507, 591, XE857, 871, 895, XE897, XE925, E.

43 Squadron RAF Leuchars: October 1957 to June 1959
Some aircraft logged show codes only.
XD391, XE925, X and Z.

DFCS RAF West Raynham: June 1959 to September 1959
Aircraft logged shows code only.
IRS.

De Havilland DH115 Vampire T.55

Six two-seat T.55s (the export version of the T.11) were delivered to South Africa in 1952 followed by a further twenty-one later specification T.55s in 1954 and 1955. Most were later phased out at the same time with nineteen passed on to Rhodesia. Two remained in trials use into the mid-1980s.

> *AOS Langebaanweg. Instructors' Course and Instruction: January 1954 –*
> *May 1954*
> *221, 222, 223, 224, 225, 226, 228, 230, 231, 232, 234, 236, 237, 239, 243,*
> *247, 248 and 249.*

De Havilland Canada DHC-1 Chipmunk

Developed just after the Second World War, the DHC-1 Chipmunk was the first aircraft designed by de Havilland of Canada. The Chipmunk first flew on 22 May 1946. Initially 218 were built for the Royal Canadian Air Force followed, after a change to the Gipsy Major 8 engine, by 735 for the RAF's primary pilot training bases. These were designated as Chipmunk T.10s. The British version also differed from the Canadian by being fully aerobatic. Another 217 were built for export sale and sixty were built under licence in Portugal. Not fully retired until 1996, many examples are still flying in private hands world-wide.

> *Joint Warfare Establishment RAF Old Sarum: January 1965 – June 1965*
> *WB558 and WP963.*

English Electric Canberra T.4

The Canberra was a classic design, which remained in front-line service with major air forces for over fifty years in its many roles and under many designations. In the UK the aircraft remained in service as the PR.9 until July 2006 for tactical reconnaissance and photographic mapping, The Canberra T.4 was the first trainer variant of an aircraft that had its origins in 1944 as a replacement for the unarmed high speed, high altitude de Havilland Mosquito bomber.

> *236 OCU RAF St Mawgan: April 20th 1980*
> *WJ879.*

English Electric Lightning

The only all-British supersonic aircraft to enter production and the last all-British single-seat fighter, the English Electric Lightning defended UK air space for more than twenty-five years. Its genesis was a protracted one. Design studies for a manned supersonic research aircraft began at English Electric in July 1948 under Chief Designer WEW Petter. On 12 May 1949 the company was awarded a contract to proceed with detail design work on its proposal, by now designated P.1 (Project 1).

The P.1 configuration featured a highly swept-back wing and a long fuselage. The two Armstrong Siddeley Sapphire engines were housed inside the fuselage in a staggered arrangement, one above the other. A disadvantage was that most of the fuselage volume was taken up with intake ducting and jet pipes, leaving little room for fuel. As a result the wing was designed as a complete integral tank without any separate bag tanks. Two P.1s were ordered on 1 April 1950 with a third airframe constructed for static testing.

On 4 August 1954 the first P.1A prototype made its maiden flight at Boscombe Down. The new aircraft handled extremely well and exceeded Mach 1.0 in level flight on 11 August 1954. The second P.1A prototype joined the flight test programme on 18 July 1955. This aircraft featured two Aden guns in the upper nose and a bulged ventral fairing to accommodate an additional fuel tank. It was then fitted with a simple afterburner and resumed flight-testing in January 1956. It eventually reached a top speed of Mach 1.53.

The design team now turned its attention to a supersonic fighter derivative of the P.1 (the P.1B), which required a redesigned fuselage and canopy with the cockpit raised to provide a better all-round view for the pilot. A long spine fairing from the canopy to the base of the fin provided additional equipment space. Rolls-Royce Avon engines promised speeds above Mach 2 with reheat. A redesigned circular air intake with a central conical bullet managed the shock waves that appear at such high speeds. Guns and air-to-air unguided rockets were recommended as armament.

The first P1.B fighter version took to the air on 4 April 1957 and went supersonic on the same flight. Ironically it was on this day that Defence Minister Duncan Sandys announced that all fighters then in development for the RAF would be cancelled and replaced by missiles, except for the English Electric P.1, which had advanced too far to cancel. Mach 2 was first reached by the P.1B on 25 November 1958. The first of twenty pre-production aircraft made its maiden flight on 3 April 1958, the large number of test aircraft allowing development to progress rapidly. In August 1958 it was announced that the name Lightning had been chosen for the type and this was officially conferred in October. XM134 was the first full production Lightning F.1, making its first flight on 29 October 1959. Controller (Aircraft) release certifying the aircraft fit for service was achieved in December of that year with a handful of aircraft going to the AFDS (Air Fighting Development Squadron) of the Central Fighter Establishment. No.74 Squadron at Coltishall received its first Lightning F.1s on 29 June 1960.

Lightning F.1
This mark, which didn't differ greatly from the P.1B, first flew on 29 October 1959, powered by two Rolls-Royce Avon 210 engines with four stages of reheat. It carried two 30-mm Aden guns in the fuselage and two Firestreak or two 30-mm Aden guns in a removable weapons pack. It was fitted with a basic navigation system and AI 23 radar.

74 (F) Trinidad Squadron RAF Coltishall: March 1960 to November 1961
Some aircraft logged show codes only.
XM134/A, XM135/B, XM137/D, XM139/C, XM140/M, XM144/J,
XM145/Q, XM146/L, XM147/P, XM164/K, XM165/F, XM166/G,
XM167/H, R and T.

Lightning F.1A

65 Squadron (226 OCU)RAF Coltishall: October to December 1972
XM171, XM172, XM180, XM215, XM216 and XM217 [the latter is an
error in John's log book as this serial was never allocated].

Lightning F.2A

The Lightning F.2 prototype first flew on 11 July 1961 and externally resembled the F.1A, itself an improved version of the F.1, with provision for a detachable in-flight refuelling probe under the port wing, improved windscreen rain dispersal and a UHF instead of a VHF radio. The F.2 had the same radar and Avon 210 engines as the F.1 but with fully variable afterburning, an improved cockpit layout, a better flight control system and all-weather navigation aids. Thirty-one F.2s were rebuilt to F.2A standard with a new wing (cranked and cambered leading edges), a new larger and more angular vertical tail and a 610-gallon ventral tank integral to the fuselage, which therefore could not be jettisoned as the earlier non-integral 250 gallon tank could. 19 and 92 Squadrons had initially taken delivery of F.2s and these were upgraded to F2A standard.

19 and 92 Squadrons RAF Gutersloh: January 1973 – November 1974
Squadron allocation not indicated.
XN724, XN726, XN727, XN728, XN730, XN731, XN732, XN733, XN771,
XN776, XN777, XN778, XN780, XN781, XN782, XN784, XN786, XN792,
XN793 and XN794.

Lightning T.4

The Lightning T.4 entered service on 29 June 1962 with 226 OCU at Middleton St George. It was a side by side two-seater trainer for the F.1, F.1A, F.2 and F.2A marks of Lightning. Powered by a pair of Rolls-Royce Avon 210s, its forward fuselage was 11.5 inches wider than the single-seaters.

Royal Air Force Fighter Command, Bentley Priory, RAF Stanmore:
December 1961 – December 1963
XM972. A second aircraft was flown during this period but serial or location
not noted.
65 Squadron (226 OCU) RAF Coltishall: October to December 1972
XM969, XM972, XM974, XM994, XM996 and XM997.

19 and 92 Squadrons RAF Gutersloh: January 1973 – November 1974

Squadron allocation not indicated.
XM968, XM972, XM973, XM991 and XM995.

Lightning T.5

Whereas the Lightning T.4 was the trainer for the early Lightning marks, the T.5 was for the F.3 and F.6. Based on the F.3 airframe, it was fitted with Avon 301 engines and had the square-topped fin. The first two production T.4s were converted to serve as prototypes for the T.5, the first of which performed its maiden flight on 29 March 1962. As with the T.4 the T.5 was combat-capable. Twenty-two were built for the RAF with initial deliveries being made in April 1965. Both trainer versions of the Lightning were given the nickname 'Tub' because of the wide cockpit.

Royal Air Force Fighter Command, Bentley Priory, RAF Stanmore:
October 1975 – April 1977
Location of these sorties not recorded.
XS416, XS457 and XV328.

Gloster Meteor

The Gloster Meteor was the first British jet fighter, first flying in 1943 and commencing operations in July 1944. Neither aerodynamically advanced nor particularly fast it proved to be an effective fighter of which 3,900 of all marks were built.

Meteor F.8

As improved jet fighters began to emerge in the years following the war so Gloster redesigned the Meteor F.4 in an effort to match that improvement. The result was the F.8, the prototype of which flew on 12 October 1948. Initial deliveries to the RAF began in August 1949. The F.8 featured a fuselage stretch, which was intended to shift the aircraft's centre of gravity. A new vertical tailplane with straight edges was also fitted, which made the new variant distinctively different from its predecessors. Other important changes were the inclusion of Derwent 8 engines, structural strengthening, a new Martin-Baker ejection seat and a revised blown cockpit canopy that improved pilot visibility. The type became the mainstay of RAF Fighter Command between 1950 and 1955, though it was increasingly outmatched by newer swept-wing fighters developed during this period and was eventually replaced in RAF squadron service by the Hawker Hunter.

222 Squadron RAF Leuchars: April 1956 to September 1957
WK713.

43 Squadron RAF Leuchars: October 1957 to June 1959
Serials shown without prefix letters or with code only.
940, J, K, N, R, X and Y.
229 OCU RAF Chivenor: October 1959 to December 1959
VZ567 and WH286.

Meteor T.7

As the Meteor F.4 entered service the lack of a trainer with comparable performance became an increasing problem. Recognising this, Gloster Aircraft developed a two-seat, dual control version of the Meteor F.4 as a private venture. The Air Ministry ordered 650 examples for delivery between 1948 and 1954, around 500 of which served with the RAF as its first jet trainer, the balance going to the Fleet Air Arm and foreign air forces. RAF aircraft served with Flying Training Command to provide trainee pilots with initial jet aircraft experience. Although superseded in this role from the mid 1950s by the de Havilland Vampire, Meteor T.7s remained in service with operational units for refresher training and as high-speed communications aircraft.

Central Flying School RAF Little Rissington: October 1954 – December 1954
Code only shown.
05.

No 4 Flying Training School RAF Middleton St George: January 1955 – December 1955
One sortie – unknown serial or code.

222 Squadron RAF Leuchars: April 1956 – September 1957
WF861.

43 Squadron RAF Leuchars: October 1957 – June 1959
Serial shown without prefix letters or with code only.
942, C, D, J, X and Z.

DFCS RAF West Raynham: June 1959 – September 1959
Code only shown.
J.

229 OCU RAF Chivenor: October 1959 – December 1959
WH173.

74 (F) Trinidad Squadron: March 1960 – November 1961
WL341.

Hawker Hunter

The Hawker Hunter was developed in response to an Air Ministry specification issued in 1948, entering service as the Hunter F.1 in 1954. Extensive teething problems were ultimately solved and the Hunter family extended to a succession of variants culminating in the definitive F.6. The aircraft had a wing with a 35° sweep, a single Rolls-Royce Avon turbojet engine (except for the F.2 and F.5 variants, which had an Armstrong Whitworth Sapphire) with intakes in the wing roots, and a high-mounted tailplane. It was armed with four 30-mm Aden cannon in a detachable pack in the nose with underwing fittings for bombs and rockets. Later variants had improved wing design and a more powerful engine. A trainer version with side-by-side seating for instructor and pupil was produced as the T.7. The Hunter was prized for its superior handling ability and in mature versions was a versatile, robust and extremely reliable aircraft. The Hunter F.6 was retired from the fighter role in the RAF in 1963 with ground-attack versions serving until 1970. Some remained in use for training and secondary roles into the early 1990s. Export Hunters still serve with various countries in the early twenty-first century.

Hunter F.1

The first production Hunter F.1 flew on 16 May 1953 powered by the Avon Mark 113 turbojet with 3,450 kg of thrust. A total of 113 F.1s were built at Hawker's Kingston plant with another batch of twenty-six built at the Blackpool plant. In RAF service they were initially painted with a disruptive camouflage pattern of dark green and dark sea grey on top with silver on the bottom, although the silver would be quickly replaced by light grey. This scheme would be more or less standard for the rest of the Hunter's career in RAF service and was indeed adopted by a number of the many other air arms that flew the type.

229 Operational Conversion Unit RAF Chivenor January – March 1956
WT624, WT625, WT631, WT635, WT653, WT659, WT685, WT695, WT697, WW602, WW636, WW637 and WW644.

222 Squadron RAF Leuchars: April 1956 – September 1957
WT637/G.

Hunter F.4

The Hunter F.4 with increased range and more reliable engines first flew on 20 October 1954. After development 111 Squadron was the first to be equipped with the version at North Weald in June 1955 followed by 98 and 118 Squadrons in Germany. By the end of 1956 a total of twenty-two squadrons were equipped with the F.4 along with thirteen squadrons based in Germany and thus the Hunter F.4 became the main ground attack and fighter aircraft of the RAF. A total of 188 were built at the Kingston factory and another 177 at the Blackpool site.

222 Squadron RAF Leuchars: April 1956 to September 1957
Codes only shown.
304, A, B, 43B, C, D, E, F, G, GAM, H, J, K, P, Q, R, S, SC, T, U, W and X.

43 Squadron RAF Leuchars: October 1957 to June 1959
Codes only shown.
GAM, A, B, C, D, E, F, G, H, J, N, O, P, Q, S, T, U and W.

229 OCU RAF Chivenor: October 1959 to December 1959
Codes only shown.
2, 4, 5, 6, 8, 14, 15, 17, 20, 23 and 25.

Hunter F.6

The first production Hunter F.6 flew in March 1955 at a time when the F.4s were entering service and acceptance trials were satisfactorily completed by the end of the year. By the end of 1956 the mark was entering service and with its improved flying controls and more powerful Avon engine it quickly established itself as the RAF's standard fighter. By 1958 all RAF day fighter squadrons in Europe had converted to the Hunter F.6. But from 1960 onwards, with the change to an integrated defence system combining ground-to-air missiles with the medium-range missiles of the Lightning, the Hunter fighter squadrons disbanded and the role of the Hunter became exclusively that of ground attack and ground support duties such as reconnaissance.

43 Squadron RAF Leuchars: October 1957 to June 1959
Codes only shown.
A, B, C, D, E, F, G, H, K, N, O, P, Q, R, S, T and U.

DFCS RAF West Raynham: June 1959 to September 1959
Codes only shown.
A, B, C, D, E, F, G, M, P, S, T, U and 132.

74 (F) Trinidad Squadron: March 1960 to November 1961
XE559/D, XE591/G, XE610/ J, XF504B, XF419/C, XF511/P, XG164/H, XG198/Q, XK136/ A and XK142/ L.

63 Squadron, 229 OCU RAF Chivenor: September 1967 to January 1968
Codes only shown.
31, 33, 34, 35, 37, 39, 41, 46, 48, 49, 53, 54, 56 and 59.

79 Squadron, 229 OCU RAF Chivenor: September 1967 to January 1968
Codes only shown.
2, 3, 7, 8, 9 and 10.

Hunter T.7

Design work was initiated early in the Hunter programme on a two-seat trainer version. This was started as a private venture in 1953 and initial drawings encompassed both side by side and tandem versions. A RAF specification issued in 1954 called for a side by side version. This was based on the Hunter F.4 and by mid 1956 early problems with airflow problems around the new canopy and wider front fuselage had been overcome. The Hunter T.7 as it was now designated began production with XL563, the first production aircraft, flying at Kingston on 11 October 1957. 229 OCU at Chivenor was the first to receive the T.7 in 1958.

43 Squadron RAF Leuchars: October 1957 to June 1959
Codes only shown.
T and 588 (?).

DFCS RAF West Raynham: June 1959 to September 1959

Codes only shown.
M and N.

229 OCU RAF Chivenor: October 1959 to December 1959
Codes only shown.
90, 92 and 93.

74 (F) Trinidad Squadron: March 1960 to November 1961
Codes only shown.
X.

Royal Air Force Fighter Command, Bentley Priory, RAF Stanmore:
December 1961 – December 1963
Three sorties flown but serial numbers of aircraft and location not
recorded.

19 and 92 Squadrons, RAF Leconfield: June 1965
Codes only shown.
L and V.

229 OCU RAF Chivenor: September 1967 to January 1968
Codes only shown.
81, 83, 84, 85, 86, 88, 89, 91 and 97.

Hunter FR.10

Following a trial installation in a Hunter F.4 of a forward-facing camera, a version of a Hunter F.6 similarly modified was ordered for use by the RAF in Germany. The first FR.10 was flown in November 1959. The only squadrons to take delivery of a full complement of the mark were Nos 2 and 4 in Germany with ones and twos issued to various other squadrons, including a pair to 79 Squadron of 229 OCU.

79 Squadron, 229 OCU RAF Chivenor: September 1967 to January 1968
Codes only shown.
11 and 13.

Hawker Siddeley Dominie T.1

In 1961 de Havilland began working on a small business jet known as the DH125 Jet Dragon. The first of two prototypes flew on 13 August 1962 powered by the Bristol Siddeley Viper turbojet. It was renamed the HS125 when de Havilland became a part of Hawker Siddeley and has gone on to become a best selling corporate aircraft with over a thousand being built, latterly by Raytheon in the USA. The HS125 Series 2 was built for the RAF as the Dominie T.1 and T.2 navigation trainer and as the CC.1, CC.2 and CC.3 liaison aircraft.

6 Flying Training School RAF Finningley: February 21st 1980
XS727.

Hawker Siddeley Hawk T.1

In 1964 the RAF specified a requirement for a new initial jet trainer to replace the Folland Gnat. The SEPECAT Jaguar was originally intended for this role but it was soon realised that it would be too complex an aircraft for initial jet training. Accordingly, in 1968 Hawker Siddeley began the design of a much simpler strictly subsonic trainer, the HS1182. Renamed Hawk in 1973 the aircraft first flew in 1974. It entered RAF service in April 1976, replacing the Gnat and Hawker Hunter in the advanced training and weapons training roles respectively. Some 176 T.1s were delivered to the RAF.

HQ Southern Maritime Region RAF Mountbatten: May 1980 – August 1983
Location of flights not specified.
XX172, XX248 and XX317.

Hawker Siddeley Nimrod

Nimrod development began in 1964 as a project to replace the Avro Shackleton and was based on the Comet 4 airliner. The Comet's engines were replaced with Rolls-Royce Spey turbofans and major fuselage changes were made, including an internal weapons bay, an extended nose for radar, a new tail with Electronic Support Measure (ESM) sensors and a Magnetic Anomaly Detector (MAD) boom. After a first flight in May 1967 the RAF ordered forty Nimrod MR.1s. The first example entered service in October 1969 and five squadrons were eventually equipped. Starting in 1975 thirty-two aircraft were upgraded to MR.2 standard. Changes made included modernisation of the electronic suite and provision for in-flight refuelling as well as additional ESM pods on the wingtips.

Still in service in 2008, but shortly to be replaced with the much delayed but greatly enhanced MR.4, the Nimrod MR.2 carries out three main roles: Anti-Submarine Warfare (ASW), Anti-Surface Unit Warfare (ASUW) and Search and Rescue (SAR). Its extended range enables the crew to monitor maritime areas far to the north of Iceland and up to 2,500 miles out into the Western Atlantic. With air-to-air refuelling range and endurance is greatly extended. As a submarine killer the MR.2 carries sensors and data processing equipment linked to the weapon systems. In addition to weapons and sonobuoys a searchlight can be mounted in the starboard wing pod for SAR operations.

Nimrod MR.1

Serials shown in John's log book indicate that these aircraft were flown as MR.1s prior to conversion and then as MR.2s after conversion.

236 OCU RAF St Mawgan: April 20th – April 30th 1980
XV244.

HQ Southern Maritime Region RAF Mountbatten: May 1980 – August 1983

[After 236 OCU most of John's Nimrod flying was with 42 Squadron from RAF St Mawgan.]
XV246.

Nimrod MR.2

236 OCU RAF St Mawgan: April 20th – April 30th 1980
XV226, XV262, XZ282 and XZ286.

HQ Southern Maritime Region RAF Mountbatten: May 1980 – August 1983
[After 236 OCU most of John's Nimrod flying was with 42 Squadron from RAF St Mawgan.]
XV231, XV233, XV235, XV244, XV246, XV249, XV250, XV251, XV254, XV258, XV261, XV262 and XV282.

Hunting Jet Provost

Developed by Hunting Percival Aircraft from its piston-engined Percival Provost primary trainer of the late 1940s the Jet Provost was built in response to a RAF requirement for a jet-powered primary trainer so as to provide pupils with all-through jet training. A redesign led to the Alvis Leonides engine in the nose of the Provost being replaced by an Armstrong Siddeley Viper and the fitting of a nosewheel undercarriage. The first Jet Provost T.1 flew in the summer of 1954 and the type was successfully trialled by 2 FTS alongside the existing Piston Provost. No particular problems were found with the use of jet instead of piston-powered propulsion and it was also found that pilots on the Jet Provost took less time to reach their solo flying stage than on the existing Provost.

For a note on the Hunting Company see under British Aircraft Corporation.

Jet Provost T.3

The success of the Jet Provost trials led to an order for the T.3, a version that had a more powerful Viper engine, improved canopy vision, tip tanks for extra fuel, a shortened undercarriage and Martin-Baker ejection seats. The first of 201 aircraft of this mark were delivered to 2 FTS at Syerston in the summer of 1959 with the first all jet *ab initio* course being completed the following June.

RAF College Cranwell: March to April 1968
Codes only shown.
30, 35, 45, 49 and 52.

Lockheed F-104 Starfighter

The Starfighter was initially conceived as a day interceptor, hence the design was geared towards performance at the expense of range and all-weather capability. This, together with engine and other problems, served to restrict its service with Air Defense Command as a front-line aircraft to just two years from 1958 to 1960, after which they were issued to the Air National Guard, although some were later recalled and re-engined and sent to Vietnam where they were used in a support role over the demilitarised zone.

F-104B

With the performance characteristics of the Starfighter the provision of a two-seat trainer was considered a priority. Fitting the extra seat necessitated a drop in fuel capacity, although this was partially offset by the fitting of a new fuel tank in the cannon bay in place of the weapon.

Webb AFB: 21st and 22nd June 1967
571301.

F-104D

Just twenty-two F-104Ds, a two-seat variant of the F-104C fighter bomber for Tactical Air Command, were built.

Webb AFB: 26th October 1965
571331.

P-3 Orion

The P-3 Orion was based on the Lockheed L-188 Electra turboprop airliner and served as the replacement for the post-war era P-2 Neptune. The P-3 has an internal bomb bay under the front fuselage, as well as underwing stations, which can carry missiles such as Harpoon. It carries a magnetic anomaly detector (MAD) in the tail and has domed windows for observation. Sonobuoys can be dropped from externally loaded tubes or from inside the fuselage. The first production version first flew 15 April 1961and over the years many variants have been developed.

HQ Southern Maritime Region RAF Mountbatten: May 1980 – August 1983
A familiarisation sortie on 7th October 1981 in an unidentified aircraft
from St Mawgan.

A familiarisation sortie on 22nd February 1982 in an unidentified aircraft
of LF3 from St Mawgan. LF is the tailcode of US Navy Patrol Squadron
VP16 War Eagles, which flew/flies the P-3C version of the Orion.

Lockheed T-33

In May 1947 Lockheed initiated at its own expense the design of a two-seat trainer and the Air Force authorised the modification of a P-80C airframe to serve as the prototype for the then designated TP-80C. To provide room for the instructor behind the pilot the fuselage fuel tank was reduced in size and the fuselage itself was lengthened by inserting a plug forward and aft of the wing. Wingtip tanks were added to compensate for the reduction of fuel carried in the fuselage. The TP-80 first flew on 22 March 1948 and was a success. Twenty aircraft were ordered by the USAF but this was soon increased. The designation was changed from TP-80C to T-33A in May 1949. The first production model had an Allison J33-A-23 engine but there was subsequently a series of engines of increased thrust culminating in the Allison -A-35 of 5,400 lb. All T-33 aircraft were produced under USAF contract, including those for the US Navy. The type served as an instrument trainer and utility aircraft as well as a test aircraft. In support of the NATO build up in the early 1950s, Canada undertook to provide training not only for its own aircrews but also for 7,000 allied personnel. Canada began building its own T-33As powered by a 5,100-pound-thrust Rolls-Royce Nene 10 engine. It was designated the T-33A Silver Star Mk.3 and France, Greece, Portugal, Turkey and Bolivia were soon using the Canadian-built T-33s. Similarly Japan began producing the aircraft. At least 1,058 Lockheed-built T-33s were delivered to friendly and neutral nations as part of the Mutual Defense Aid Program: others were transferred directly from the USAF inventory overseas. In total around 7,000 examples were built.

Peterson Field, Colorado Springs USA: August 1965 – June 1967
Full serial numbers not shown – only the last three digits.
100, 139, 325, 340, 343, 366, 422, 478, 506, 508, 509, 510, 511, 512, 513,
514, 526, 532, 533, 534, 535, 536, 538, 553, 554, 564, 578, 586, 607, 627,
639, 702, 704, 706, 707, 757, 758, 759, 761, 766, 948 and 984.

RAF Course 682B, 4453 CCTS Davis Monthan Air Force Base: May 10th –
June 19th 1968
533 and 564.

McDonnell Douglas F-4 Phantom

Entering service in 1960, the F-4 was designed as the first modern fleet defence fighter for the US Navy. By 1963 it had been adopted by the USAF for the fighter-bomber role. When production ended in 1981 5,195 Phantom IIs had been built (McDonnell's had already used the name Phantom for an earlier aircraft). Compared with what had gone before in this class of aircraft the F-4 was big dimension wise with a maximum take-off weight of over 27,000 kg. It was capable of reaching a top speed in excess of Mach 2 and had an initial climb rate of over 41,000 feet per minute. It could carry almost 8,500 kg of weapons on nine external hardpoints. These included air-to-air and air-to-ground missiles and unguided, guided and nuclear bombs. However, it was not until the F-4E was introduced that the Phantom got a gun.

McDonnell merged with the Douglas Aircraft Company on 28 April 1967 to form the McDonnell Douglas Corporation (MDC).

F-4C Phantom

The adoption of the Phantom by the USAF (it had been designed as a Navy plane)

315

was decided by a fly off between the US Navy's F-4B and the F-106, which was at the time the air force's best fighter. The Phantom won hands down. It demonstrated better speed, altitude, range, radar range, weapons load-carrying capacity and seventy per cent better maintenance man-hours per flying hour. Compared with the F-4B the USAF aircraft, designated F-4C, possessed added ground attack capability and dual controls for a second pilot in the back seat, although certain Navy features were retained such as folding wings and an arrester hook.

4525th Fighter Weapons Wing Nellis AFB, August 15th 1966:18th April 1967
Full serial numbers not shown – only the last three digits.
942 and 949.

RAF Course 682B, 4453 CCTS Davis Monthan Air Force Base: May 10th –
June 19th 1968
?348, 637414, 637415, 637420, 637430, 637440, 637450, 637480,
637481, 637482, 637491, 637504, 637508, 637510, 637513, 637556,
637566, 637615, 637637, 637642 and 640758.

F-4D Phantom

Almost identical externally to the F-4C, under the skin the F-4D had changed. It was the first purpose-designed USAF Phantom and was optimised for air-to-ground operations and thus, whilst retaining the same basic airframe and engines of the F-4C, the avionics were very different.

479th Tactical Fighter Wing George AFB: 23rd March 1967
650591.

Phantom FGR.2

By the mid 1960s British defence procurement was in something of a mess. The Hawker P1154 and TSR2 had been cancelled and the proposed purchase of the F-111K also became a non-starter. In place of the P1154 the Harrier and Jaguar were being developed for the strike attack role but they were some way from entering service. So a stopgap was required. The FGR.2 version of the American Phantom was that stopgap and was ordered for strike, attack and reconnaissance. For the British Phantom (the RAF version was the F-4M in the McDonnell Douglas designation sequence) a number of British companies submitted bids to supply the high British equipment content the aircraft would have. BAC built the aft fuselage, fins, rudders and tailcones, stabilators and inboard leading edges. Short Brothers built the outer wing panels and leading edge flaps. Delaney Galley produced the heat exchangers and titanium insulation blankets. Goodyear UK was responsible for the brakes and Ferranti, Marconi and Cossor the majority of the avionics. Rolls-Royce supplied the Spey engines, installation of which necessitated a redesign of the rear fuselage. A proportion of the aircraft the RAF took on charge were twin stickers with controls in the rear cockpit as well as the forward.

228 OCU RAF Coningsby: August 1968 – October 1969
XT891, XT893, XT894, XT896, XT899, XT902, XT903, XT904, XT905,
XT906, XT908, XT909, XT911, XT914, XV394, XV395, XV396, XV403,
XV404, XV407, XV408, XV409, XV414, XV416, XV418, XV420, XV424,
XV425, XV429, XV436 and XV437.

McDonnell F-101 Voodoo

In 1946 the USAF had a requirement for a long-range penetration fighter that could escort the Convair B-36, which was then about to enter service, and McDonnell designed the XF-88 in response. However, a change in USAF requirements led to that particular project being cancelled but it was resurrected in 1951 as a potential replacement for the F-89 Scorpion. The original fuselage of the XF-88 was lengthened by thirteen feet, extra fuel tankage was inserted and the F-101A for Tactical Air Command was born.

F-101B

After the F-101A and the reconnaissance version, the RF-101A, came the F101B, a two-seat single control all-weather interceptor, which first flew in March 1957 and ultimately equipped sixteen squadrons of Air Defense Command. Some 359 were built.

444th Fighter Interceptor Squadron Charleston AFB, 14th – 17th February
1966: 25th February 1966: 27th February 1966: 1st March 1966
560322, 580332 and 570344.

Tyndall AFB: 11th August 1965
560267.

F-101F

The dual control version of the F-101B.

K I Sawyer AFB: 6th January 1966
570386.

McDonnell Douglas KC-10 Extender

The KC-10 Extender is an air-to-air tanker aircraft in service with the USAF, which was derived from the civilian DC-10-30 airliner. Conversion involved relatively minor modifications, the largest of which was the addition of a boom control station in the rear of the fuselage and extra fuel tanks under the main deck. First deliveries to Strategic Air Command (then in control of airborne refuelling assets) commenced in 1981.

HQ Southern Maritime Region RAF Mountbatten: November 6th 1983
As second pilot into Dover AFB from an unrecorded location.
791710.

Northrop T-38 Talon

After two years of private venture development by Northrop based on the design that became the F-5 Freedom Fighter, the USAF authorised construction of seven YT-38 prototypes of a tandem two-seat trainer, which first flew in April 1959. This led to a production run of 1,187 T-38 Talons, the first being delivered to the 3510th Flying Training Wing at Randolph AFB in March 1961.

Williams AFB: 27th December 1966
600580.

3510th Flying Training Squadron Randolph AFB: 25 January 1967
600569.

North American Harvard

After nine Harvard Mk1s were delivered to the SAAF between February 1940 and November 1942, 436 Mk IIA and 197 Mk III aircraft, renumbered from RAF serials, were delivered as part of the British Commonwealth Air Training Scheme. On settlement of the lend-lease arrangement between South Africa and the USA after the war 280 of the survivors were returned, although around 120 were retained for SAAF use. A further sixty-five ex-USAF AT-6As and AT-6Cs and USN SNJ-3s and SNJ-4s were delivered in 1952/3 and in 1953/4 thirty T-6Gs were bought. Final deliveries were in 1961 and comprised four Harvards (two Mk IIs and two Mk IIIs) of the Belgian Air Force. Conversely ex-SAAF machines were sold on to other air forces, notably the Portuguese in 1969.

In SAAF service the Harvards were designated Mk IIA (US designation AT-6C), Mk III (US designation AT-6D or SJN-4), AT-6C (those machines delivered directly post war from the USA) and T-6G (remanufactured versions of former Second World War machines). They were flown by CFS and 40 Squadron in SAAF service. The last course at CFS to use the Harvard was in 1995. John was invited to attend the closing ceremony and was able to watch a huge formation of these venerable machines make a formation flypast, land, taxi and then simultaneously cut their engines. It was very impressive and very moving. This, incidentally, had been the first time that John had been invited to attend a SAAF ceremony since his resignation in 1954.

Harvards are now regarded as National Treasures in South Africa and a notice to this effect was published in the *South Africa Government Gazette*, stating 'The National Monuments Commission hereby declares ten Harvard aircraft....to be cultural treasures on account of the historical and technical importance thereof....' The balance of the SAAF's Harvards were sold on the civilian market with many going to the USA but a further eight remained in South Africa with private owners.

Harvard Mk IIA and III

CFS Dunottar: August 1950 – March 1951
7001, 7004, 7008, 7017, 7024, 7043, 7051, 7068, 7084, 7096, 7110, 7111,

7120, 7124, 7127, 7145, 7150, 7153, 7156, 7168, 7171, 7172, 7176, 7220, 7244, 7276, 7291, 7296, 7303, 7305, 7306, 7343, 7382, 7386, 7392, 7465 and 7471.

No 4 OTU Course AOS Langebaanweg: March – May 1951
7012, 7086, 7161, 7237, 7333, 7385, 7428 and 7460.

1 Squadron at AFS Swartkop: February – March 1952
7033, 7059, 7073, 7096, 7152, 7314, 7401 and 7458.

CFS Dunnottar. Instructors' Course and Instruction: March 1952 to December 1953
7001, 7008, 7022, 7024, 7028, 7039, 7043, 7049, 7051, 7052, 7053, 7062, 7063, 7073, 7110, 7111, 7120, 7124, 7127, 7132, 7133, 7135, 7142, 7145, 7150, 7152, 7154, 7156, 7161, 7166, 7168, 7171, 7174, 7175, 7176, 7177, 7202, 7210, 7211, 7214, 7244, 7246, 7248, 7259, 7276, 7284, 7291, 7296, 7301, 7303, 7304, 7305, 7306, 7335, 7337, 7343 7357, 7377, 7382, 7386, 7406, 7407, 7414, 7455 and 7471.

AOS Langebaanweg. Instructors' Course and Instruction: January 1954 – May 1954
7020.

Harvard Mk IIC

CFS Dunnottar. Instructors' Course and Instruction: March 1952 to December 1953
7635, 7636, 7637, 7638, 7639, 7640, 7641, 7642, 7643, 7644, 7645, 7646, 7648, 7650, 7651, 7652, 7653, 7654, 7655, 7656, 7657, 7659, 7662, 7664, 7665, 7666 and 7667.

AOS Langebaanweg. Instructors' Course and Instruction: January 1954 – May 1954
7703, 7704, 7705 and 7707.

North American F-51D Mustang

The Mustang was produced initially not as a requirement for the US Army Air Force but for the RAF. Designated the P-51 (P for Pursuit) it was produced in several versions until the P-51D of 1943 when, with the insertion of an additional fuel tank behind the pilot's seat, its range was sufficient to escort USAAF bombers from England to Berlin and back, thereby giving them much needed protection all the way to their targets. Apart from a lack of range there had been other shortcomings in early models. For example, the visibility from the original standard canopy was very restricted. Often the first indication a pilot had that he was under attack was the impact of bullets on his aircraft. On the P-51D a bubble canopy was fitted. Also, the originally fitted four .50 calibre machine-guns were unreliable and gave insufficient firepower. On the D model the number of machine-guns was increased from four to six. They were mounted differently to reduce the chances of jamming and ammunition capacity was increased. In addition a K-14B gyro-computing gunsight replaced reflector sights. One problem that wasn't solved related to the cooling system, a single hit to which could bring a Mustang down. The critical components of this cooling system were in the forward and lower sections of the fuselage and so the aircraft proved to be more vulnerable to ground fire than it was to enemy aircraft.

Post war, the designation was changed from P to F-51 (F for Fighter). The 18th FBW took the Packard Merlin 1650-engined Mustang to war in Korea and the SAAF was given examples of this aircraft for 2 Squadron's use, the arrangement being that it would only pay for those aircraft written off. As it happened that was the fate of the majority. The first F-51Ds were received by 2 Squadron at Pusan East in Korea on 14 November 1950. Ninety-six are believed to have eventually been delivered with a serial range from 301 onwards. All were ex-USAF. Seventy-four were lost or written off in Korea, thirty-four of the pilots being killed or missing. The type was replaced by the F-86 Sabre and on 29 December 1952 the last serviceable twenty-two Mustangs performed a flypast over K-46 before being delivered to a USAF Maintenance Unit on 31 December. The survivors went to the Philippine Air Force and Royal Korean Air Force.

2 Squadron SAAF. Korea: June – October 1951

SAAF serial	USAF serial	SAAF serial	USAF serial
302	45-11390	303	45-11360
308	45-11648	310	44-73191
312	44-74432	316	44-74984
318	45-11419 *Shy Talk*	320	45-11704
323	44-15091	326	44-74344
327	44-74174	329	44-73068
334	44-84903 *Buggs*	336	44-72983
338	44-74461	339	44-73688
340	44-74757	341	44-74759
343	44-74748 *Hazel*	345	44-84867
347	44-63822	348	44-84862 *Lilian/Sandra*
352	44-74565	354	44-84553
356	44-14297	358	44-84750
369	44-84761 *My Boy*	371	44-74617

North American F-100F Super Sabre
In a project designed to evolve a fighter capable of sustained supersonic level flight, the F-86 Sabre was taken as a starting point but was soon unrecognisable as such as the F-100 Super Sabre emerged with a contoured low drag fuselage and wing and tail surfaces swept to 45 degrees. The first F-100A was delivered to the 479th Fighter Day Wing at George AFB in September 1954. The F100B was an all-weather fighter whilst the F-100C could carry out both the ground attack and interception mission. The D differed from the C in having an automatic pilot, jettisonable underwing pylons and modified vertical tail surfaces. The TF-100C was a two-seat trainer variant, which served as the prototype of the F-100F (essentially a two-seat version of the D model). Some 339 of this variant came off the production line.

4758th Defence Systems Evaluation Squadron, Holloman AFB: 16th December 1966
563994.

Piper J-3 Cub
The Cub first appeared late in 1930 as the Model E-2 and was built by the Taylor Aircraft Corporation. Sales increased slowly but steadily and in 1936, when five hundred of the improved Model J-2 Cubs had been sold, William T. Piper bought out his partner, CG Taylor. In total 1,200 J-2s were produced. The J-3 that followed and of which more than 5,500 were delivered to the US Army during the Second World War, became the best known Cub of all. It is claimed that more pilots learned to fly in a Piper Cub than in any other aircraft.

Germiston Flying Club: March 1953 to December 1953
ZS-AVA and ZS-AWL.

Republic F-105F Thunderchief
The complexity of the bombing and navigation system of the single-seat F-105D left the USAF in need of a two-seat training version for use in instructing new pilots. After several cancellations of proposed variants on cost grounds the F-105F ultimately became that trainer and was a minimum change derivative of the F-105D in which the two crew members were seated in tandem ejector seats underneath separate clamshell-type canopies. The cockpits were provided with dual controls. The rear cockpit was a virtual duplicate of the front cockpit so the rear pilot could fly the mission even if the front pilot were incapacitated. The maiden flight of the first F-105F was on 11 June 1963, during which it reached a speed of Mach 1.15. Service introduction was in December 1963 with the 4520th Combat Crew Training Wing based at Nellis AFB and with the 4th Tactical Fighter Wing based at Seymour-Johnson AFB where it flew alongside the F-105Ds already serving. In total 143 F-105Fs were built from 1963 to 1964.

4520th Combat Crew Training Wing Nellis Air Force Base: 26th October 1966
638285.

Scottish Aviation Jetstream T.1

The original Handley Page design dates from 1965. The first production model twelve-seater Jetstream 1 flew on 6 December 1968 and over the next year thirty-six were delivered. But late deliveries and engine problems had driven development costs sharply upwards and Handley Page went bankrupt, the production line eventually shutting down in 1970. However, there was enough interest in the design for it to be picked up by Scottish Aviation who continued production. In February 1972 twenty-six aircraft were ordered by the RAF who used them as multi-engine trainers under the name Jetstream T.1.

6 Flying Training School RAF Finningley: February 21st 1980
XX491.

SEPECAT Jaguar T.2

The Jaguar programme began in the early 1960s in response to a British requirement for an advanced supersonic jet trainer and a French need for a cheap subsonic dual role trainer and attack aircraft with good short field performance. SEPECAT (the *Société Européenne de Production de l'Avion d'Ecole de Combat et d'Appui Tactique*) was subsequently formed in 1966 as a joint venture between Bréguet (the design leader) and the British Aircraft Corporation to produce the airframe and a separate teaming of Rolls-Royce and Turboméca to develop the Adour afterburning turbofan engine. The first of eight prototypes flew on 8 September 1968 and the RAF subsequently procured thirty-five Jaguar T.2 trainers.

HQ Southern Maritime Region RAF Mountbatten: February 27th 1981
Location not recorded.
XX829.

Supermarine Spitfire IX

SAAF Spitfire service is as follows. The first examples (Mk Vs) were received by 1 Squadron in the North African desert on 4 November 1942. Further squadrons to receive Mk Vs included 2, 4, 7, 9, 10, 40 and 41. Eventually these as well as 3 and 11 Squadrons received Mk IXs. 1 Squadron was also the largest SAAF user of Mk VIIIs, these eventually being replaced by Mk IXs. 2 Squadron is known to have had two Mk VIIIs on strength. All were RAF machines and carried RAF serials and were flown back to RAF Maintenance Units as SAAF squadrons left Italy.

After the war eighty Mk IXs were presented to the SAAF and a further fifty-six purchased. Fifty-three were flown to South Africa, the first five departing

Pershore on 12 April 1947 and routeing via Fayid, Luxor, Wadi Halfa, Atbara, Khartoum, Malakal, Juba, Kisumu, Tabora, Kasama, N'dola, Heany, Salisbury and Belvedere toSwartkop (Pretoria). The last of the air deliveries arrived at Swartkop on 7 February 1948. The remaining eighty-three Spits were shipped to South Africa between April 1948 and May 1949 with the number of incidents to individual aircraft during air delivery believed to have been the deciding factor in adopting this mode of transport. Fifty of the aircraft were the F.IXe model with the 'high-back' cockpit profile. Eighty-six had tear drop canopies. They served with 1, 2, 4 and 60 Squadrons as well as the Central Flying School and Air Operations School. At the latter they suffered a high accident rate as training for Korea intensified. The type was officially retired on 7 April 1954.

Spitfire Conversion Course CFS Dunnottar: January – March 1951
5508, 5510, 5525, 5531, 5555, 5563 and 5582.

No 4 OTU Course AOS Langebaanweg: March – May 1951
5508, 5519, 5520, 5531, 5535, 5555, 5556, 5563, 5582, 5593, 5596, 5605, 5615, 5616, 5619, 5625 and 5634.

AOS Langebaanweg. Instructors' Course and Instruction: January 1954 – May 1954
5508.

Westland-Bell Sioux HT.2
When production of the Model 47 by Bell and its licensees ended over 5,000 of the type had been built. It was the first helicopter to gain an Approved Type Certificate and in March 1946 was issued the first commercial helicopter licence in the USA. The model 47G utilised all of the design improvements that had been incorporated as production progressed into the 1970s. The 47G became famous as the helicopter flown in the late 1950s television show, 'Whirlybirds', which those of an older generation all remember fondly, and then later in MASH. The Westland-built British version was named Sioux and was ordered by the Army (designated the AH.1) as a light observation helicopter and the RAF as a basic training helicopter (the HT.1 and HT.2).

Helicopter Familiarisation Course RAF Ternhill: January 1st – 4th 1973
XV318, XV319, XV323 and XV324.

Westland Sea King HAR.3
The Sea King programme in the UK began with a 1959 licence agreement with Sikorsky and initially development concentrated on a Royal Navy anti-submarine version of the helicopter. In 1975 fifteen HAR.3s were ordered for the RAF to be used on long-range Search and Rescue and they were based at several sites around the UK including Boulmer, Coltishall and Lossiemouth.

Sea King Training Flight RAF Finningley: February 20th 1980
XZ596.

HQ Southern Maritime Region RAF Mountbatten: May 1980 – August
1983
Location not recorded.
XZ585, XZ586, XZ588, XZ589, XZ594, XZ598 and ZA105.

Westland Wessex

The Wessex was a turbine-engined development of the Sikorsky S-58 and first flew in May 1957 as an HAS.1 for the Royal Navy.

Wessex HC.2

The first RAF version was the HC.2, a high performance development of the Navy aircraft with a pair of Bristol Siddeley Gnome engines. It was ordered for transport, ambulance and general-purpose duties. With a crew of two or three it could carry sixteen troops and apart from 18 Squadron served with 72 Squadron and 240 OCU as well as 22 and 84 Squadrons on SAR duties.

18 Squadron RAF Gutersloh: January 1973 – November 1974
XR501, XR502, XR504, XR505, XR507, XR509, XR516, XR518, XR519,
XR521, XR529, XS674, XT681, XV720, XV722, XV724 and XV728.

22 Squadron RAF Finningley: February 20th 1980
XT602.

HQ Southern Maritime Region RAF Mountbatten: May 1980 – August
1983
Location not recorded.
XR501, XT674, XT675, XT680 and XV729.

Commandant General of the RAF Regiment and Director General of
Security RAF: August 1983 – November 1985
Two sorties from Aldergrove in an unidentified Wessex HC.2: 20th March
1984.
XT606. With 84 Squadron in Cyprus: 4th April 1984.

Westland Wessex HU.5

A later version of the Wessex was used by the Royal Marine Commandos and designated the HU.5.

HQ Southern Maritime Region RAF Mountbatten: May 1980 – August
1983
Location not recorded.
XS497 and XS520.

Westland Whirlwind

The Whirlwind was the Westland-built version of the Sikorsky S-55 and first came into service with the Navy and RAF as the HAR.2 from 1955.

Whirlwind HAR.10

The HAR.10 first flew in 1961 and differed in that the original Pratt & Whitney 600-hp engine was replaced by a 1,060-hp Rolls-Royce Bristol Gnome, which imparted a cruising speed of 104 mph and a range with ten passengers of just 108 miles.

*Helicopter Familiarisation Course RAF Ternhill: January 1st – 4th 1973
XN127.*

HQ Southern Maritime Region RAF Mountbatten: May 1980 – August 1983

Location not recorded.
XD186, XP344, XP347, XP350 and XP403.

Whirlwind HAS.7

The HAS.7 was the first British helicopter designed specifically for anti-submarine work when it entered service in 1956. It was equipped with radar and dipping ASDIC, named after the Anti-Submarine Detection Investigation Committee and later called SONAR (SOund NAvigation and Ranging), and could also be equipped with a torpedo but could not carry both this and ASDIC simultaneously. In this version the engine was a 750-hp Alvis Leonides Major 755/1. It had a hovering ceiling of 9,400 feet and a range of 334 miles at 86 mph.

HQ Southern Maritime Region RAF Mountbatten: May 1980 – August 1983

Location not recorded.
XN299.

BIBLIOGRAPHY

Books and the written word will always be a primary and secondary source for researchers and I consulted many. Particularly useful were the following:

The History of the US Air Force by David A Anderton, Aerospace Publishing, London (1981)

Shorts Aircraft since 1900 by CH Barnes, Putnam, London (1967)

English Electric Lightning by Martin W Bowman, Crowood Press, London (1997)

Lightning from the Cockpit by Peter Caygill, Pen and Sword, Barnsley (2004)

Tigers by Bob Cossey, Arms and Armour Press, London (1992)

Century Jets, edited by David Donald, Airtime Publishing, Norwalk Connecticut (2003)

Norfolk Airfields and Airstrips by Huby Fairhead and Roy Tuffen, Norfolk and Suffolk Aviation Museum, Norwich (1986)

Suez – The Double War by Roy Fullick and Geoffrey Powell, Leo Cooper, London (2006)

The Modern Royal Air Force by Terry Gander, Patrick and Stephen, London (1984)

Suez 1956: Operation Musketeer by Robert Jackson, Ian Allan, London (1980)

World Military Aircraft since 1945 by Robert Jackson, Ian Allan, London (1979)

Defence Policy and the RAF 1956 – 1963 by TCG James, Air Historical Branch, London (1987)

McDonnell F-4 Phantom: Spirit in the Skies, edited by Jon Lake, Aerospace Publishing, London (1992)

The Royal Air Force in Germany 1945 – 1978 by ACM Sir David Lee, Air Historical Branch, London (1979)

Hawker Hunter – Biography of a Thoroughbred by Francis K Mason, Patrick and Stephen, London (1981)

'The History of No. 2 Squadron SAAF in the Korean War' by Col PMJ McGregor, *The South African Military History Society Journal*, Vol. 4, No. 3

South Africa's Flying Cheetahs in Korea by Dermot Moore and Peter Bagshawe, Ashanti Publishing, Cape Town (1991)

An Illustrated History of the RAF by Roy Conyers Nesbit, CLB, London (1992)

Through Adversity by Kingsley M Oliver, Forces and Corporate Publishing, Rushden (1997)

Aircraft of the South African Air Force by Herman Potgeiter and Willem Steenkamp, Jane's, London (1981)

Norfolk Airfields in the Second World War by Graham Smith, Countryside Books, Newbury (1994)

North American T-6 by Peter C Smith, Crowood Press, London (2000)

The Royal Marines. From Sea Soldiers to a Special Force by Julian Thompson, Sidgwick and Jackson, London (2000)

De Havilland Vampire. The Complete History by David Watkins, Sutton Publishing, London (1996)

The Parish of Rackheath 1066 – 1997 by WS Watts, Privately Published, Norwich (1997)

'Bob Rogers. His personal story as told to Roger Williams', South African Air Force Association (2000)

The Parliamentary Debates (Hansard) Fifth Series, Volume CDIX, House of Lords Official Report, London (1980)

World Air Power Journal, Vol. 22, Aerospace Publishing, London (1995)

INDEX